# BLACK PANTHER

# WORLD OF WAKANDA

The **Dora Milaje** (pronounced "DOR-ah muh-LAH-jay," and which means "Adored Ones") are the personal bodyguards of the Black Panther and the royal family, recruited from every tribe of Wakanda. An ancient tradition originally designed to help keep the peace among the rival tribes, the *Dora Milaje* used to also be potential wives-in-training for the king, but that aspect has since fallen by the wayside. And now the time has come for the *Dora Milaje* to perhaps evolve even further...

[This story takes place before the events of **BLACK PANTHER #1.**]

# BLACK PANTHER
# WORLD OF W

collection editor **JENNIFER GRÜNWALD** · assistant editor **CAITLIN O'CONNELL**
associate managing editor **KATERI WOODY** · editor, special projects **MARK D. BEAZLEY**
vp production & special projects **JEFF YOUNGQUIST** · svp print, sales & marketing **DAVID GABRIEL**
book designers **JAY BOWEN** & **MANNY MEDEROS**

editor in chief **AXEL ALONSO** · chief creative officer **JOE QUESADA**
president **DAN BUCKLEY** · executive producer **ALAN FINE**

BLACK PANTHER: WORLD OF WAKANDA #1-6. First printing 2017. ISBN# 978-1-302-90650-4. Published by MARVEL WORLDWIDE, INC.; a subsidiary of MARVEL ENTERTAINMENT, LLC. OFFICE OF PUBLICATION: 135 West 50th Street, New York, NY 10020. Copyright © 2017 MARVEL No similarity between any of the names, characters, persons, and/or institutions in this magazine with those of any living or dead person or institution is intended, and any such similarity which may exist is purely coincidental. **Printed in the U.S.A.** DAN BUCKLEY, President, Marvel Entertainment; JOE QUESADA, Chief Creative Officer; TOM BREVOORT, SVP of Publishing; DAVID BOGART, SVP of Business Affairs & Operations, Publishing & Partnership; C.B. CEBULSKI, VP of Brand Management & Development, Asia; DAVID GABRIEL, SVP of Sales & Marketing, Publishing; JEFF YOUNGQUIST, VP of Production & Special Projects; DAN CARR, Executive Director of Publishing Technology; ALEX MORALES, Director of Publishing Operations; SUSAN CRESPI, Production Manager; STAN LEE, Chairman Emeritus. For information regarding advertising in Marvel Comics or on Marvel.com, please contact Vit DeBellis, Integrated Sales Manager at vdebellis@marvel.com. For Marvel subscription inquiries, please call 888-511-5480. **Manufactured between 4/21/2017 and 5/22/2017 by QUAD/GRAPHICS WASECA, WASECA, MN, USA.**

10 9 8 7 6 5 4 3 2 1

# AKANDA

## "DAWN OF THE MIDNIGHT ANGELS"

writer **ROXANE GAY**

consultant **TA-NEHISI COATES**

penciler **ALITHA E. MARTINEZ**

inkers **ALITHA E. MARTINEZ** (#1-2)
**& ROBERTO POGGI** (#2-5)

color artist **RACHELLE ROSENBERG**

cover art **AFUA RICHARDSON**

assistant editor **CHRIS ROBINSON**

editor **WIL MOSS**

## "THE PEOPLE FOR THE PEOPLE"

writers **YONA HARVEY & TA-NEHISI COATES**

artist **AFUA RICHARDSON**

color artist **TAMRA BONVILLAIN**

## "DEATH OF THE WHITE TIGER"

writer **REMBERT BROWNE**

consultant **TA-NEHISI COATES**

penciler **JOE BENNETT**

inker **ROBERTO POGGI**

color artist **RACHELLE ROSENBERG**

cover art **RAHZZAH**

editor **CHRIS ROBINSON**

letterer **VC's JOE SABINO**

executive editor **TOM BREVOORT**

BLACK PANTHER created by **STAN LEE** & **JACK KIRBY**

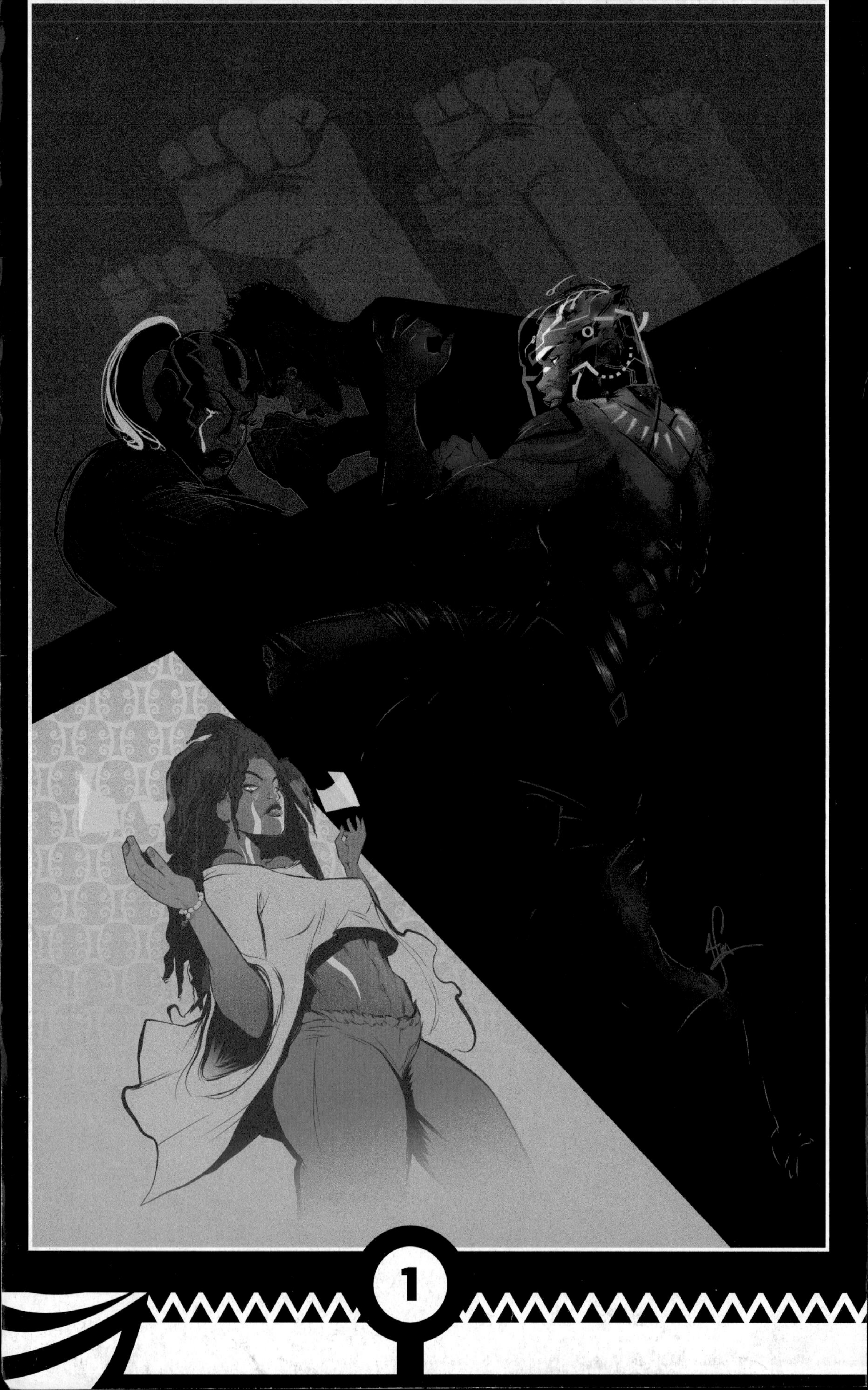
1

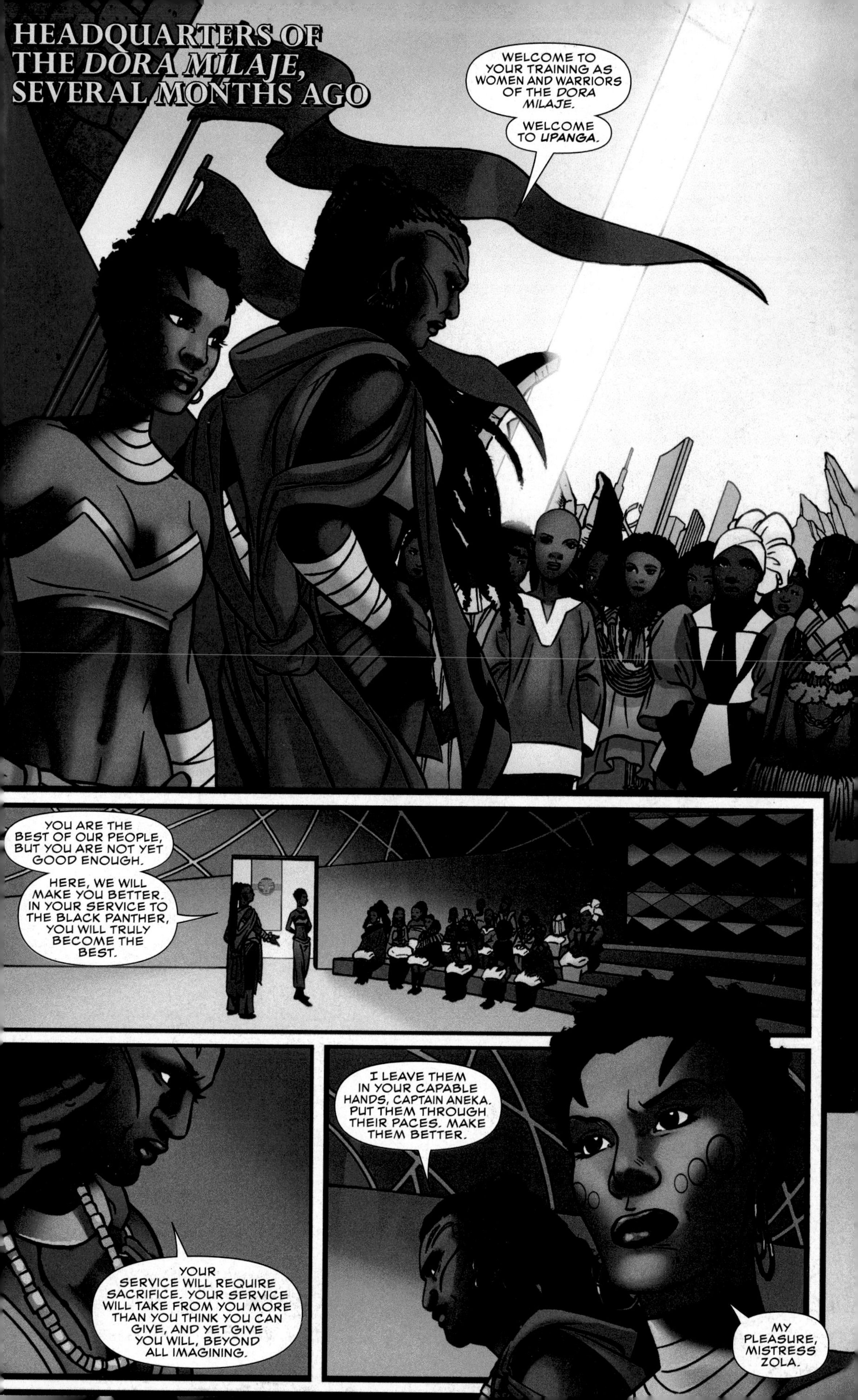
HEADQUARTERS OF THE *DORA MILAJE*, SEVERAL MONTHS AGO
WELCOME TO YOUR TRAINING AS WOMEN AND WARRIORS OF THE *DORA MILAJE*.
WELCOME TO *UPANGA*.
YOU ARE THE BEST OF OUR PEOPLE, BUT YOU ARE NOT YET GOOD ENOUGH.
HERE, WE WILL MAKE YOU BETTER. IN YOUR SERVICE TO THE BLACK PANTHER, YOU WILL TRULY BECOME THE BEST.
YOUR SERVICE WILL REQUIRE SACRIFICE. YOUR SERVICE WILL TAKE FROM YOU MORE THAN YOU THINK YOU CAN GIVE, AND YET GIVE YOU WILL, BEYOND ALL IMAGINING.
I LEAVE THEM IN YOUR CAPABLE HANDS, CAPTAIN ANEKA. PUT THEM THROUGH THEIR PACES. MAKE THEM BETTER.
MY PLEASURE, MISTRESS ZOLA.

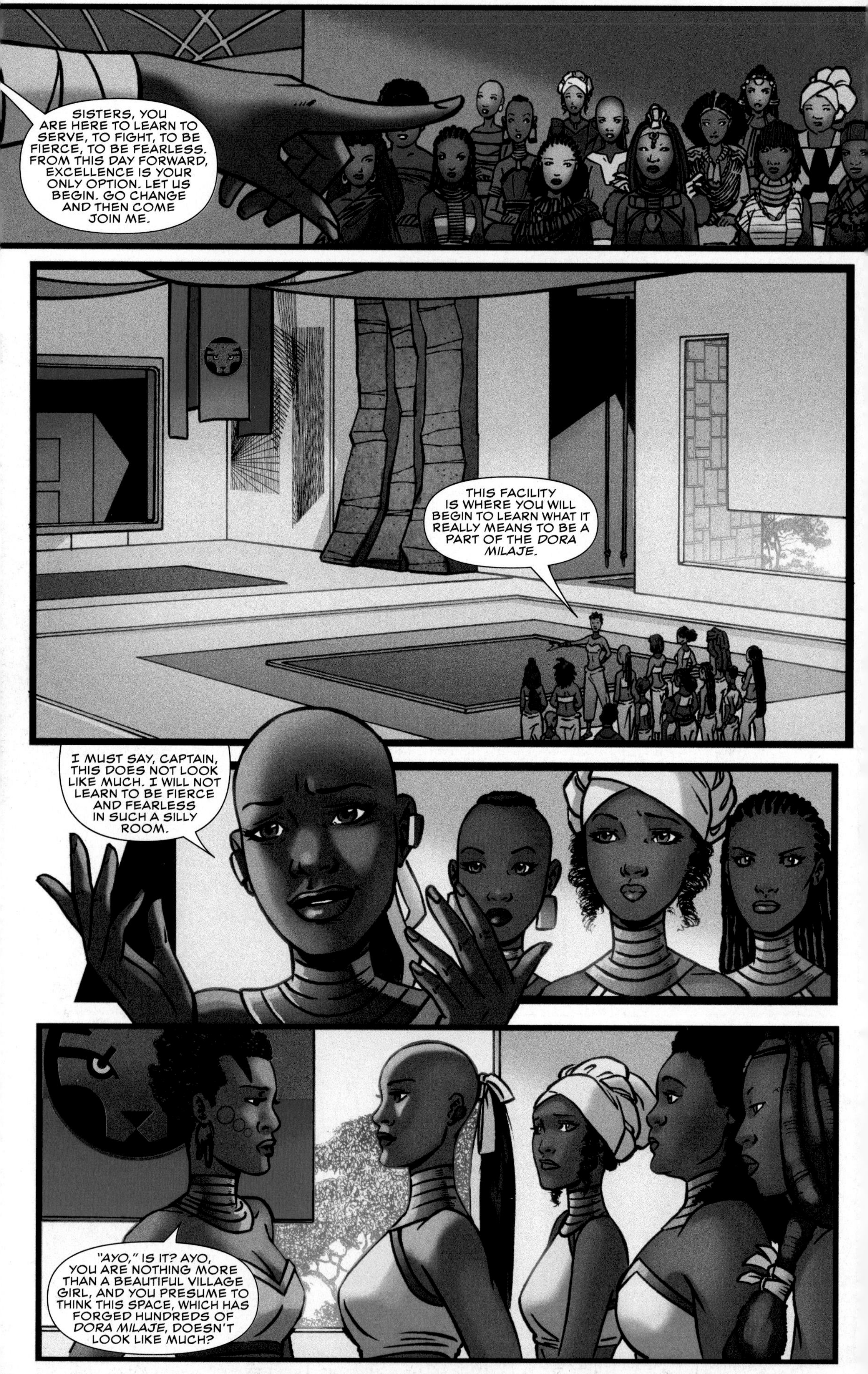
SISTERS, YOU ARE HERE TO LEARN TO SERVE, TO FIGHT, TO BE FIERCE, TO BE FEARLESS. FROM THIS DAY FORWARD, EXCELLENCE IS YOUR ONLY OPTION. LET US BEGIN. GO CHANGE AND THEN COME JOIN ME.
THIS FACILITY IS WHERE YOU WILL BEGIN TO LEARN WHAT IT REALLY MEANS TO BE A PART OF THE *DORA MILAJE*.
I MUST SAY, CAPTAIN, THIS DOES NOT LOOK LIKE MUCH. I WILL NOT LEARN TO BE FIERCE AND FEARLESS IN SUCH A SILLY ROOM.
*"AYO,"* IS IT? AYO, YOU ARE NOTHING MORE THAN A BEAUTIFUL VILLAGE GIRL, AND YOU PRESUME TO THINK THIS SPACE, WHICH HAS FORGED HUNDREDS OF *DORA MILAJE*, DOESN'T LOOK LIKE MUCH?

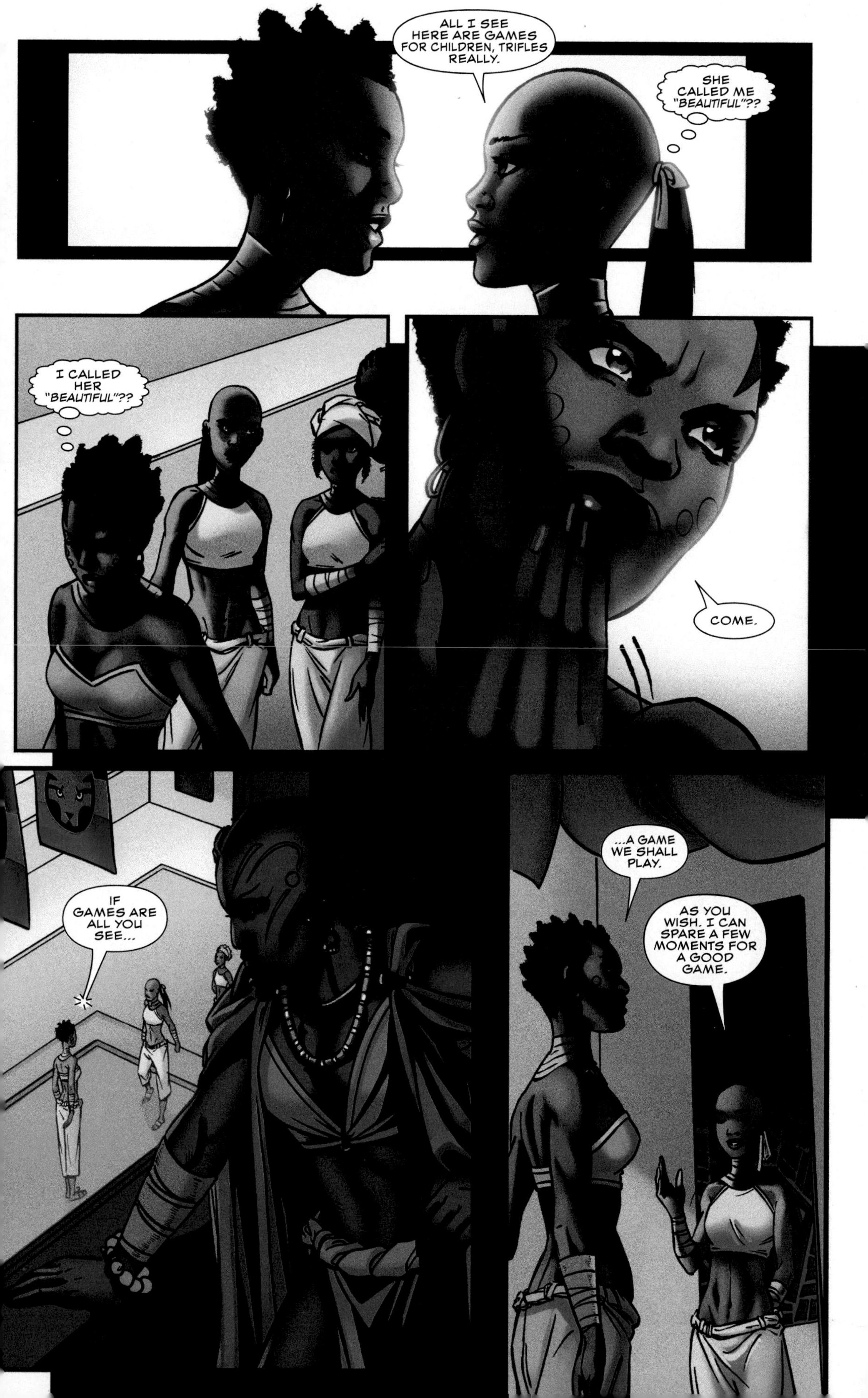
ALL I SEE HERE ARE GAMES FOR CHILDREN, TRIFLES REALLY.
SHE CALLED ME "BEAUTIFUL"??
I CALLED HER "BEAUTIFUL"??
COME.
IF GAMES ARE ALL YOU SEE...
...A GAME WE SHALL PLAY.
AS YOU WISH. I CAN SPARE A FEW MOMENTS FOR A GOOD GAME.

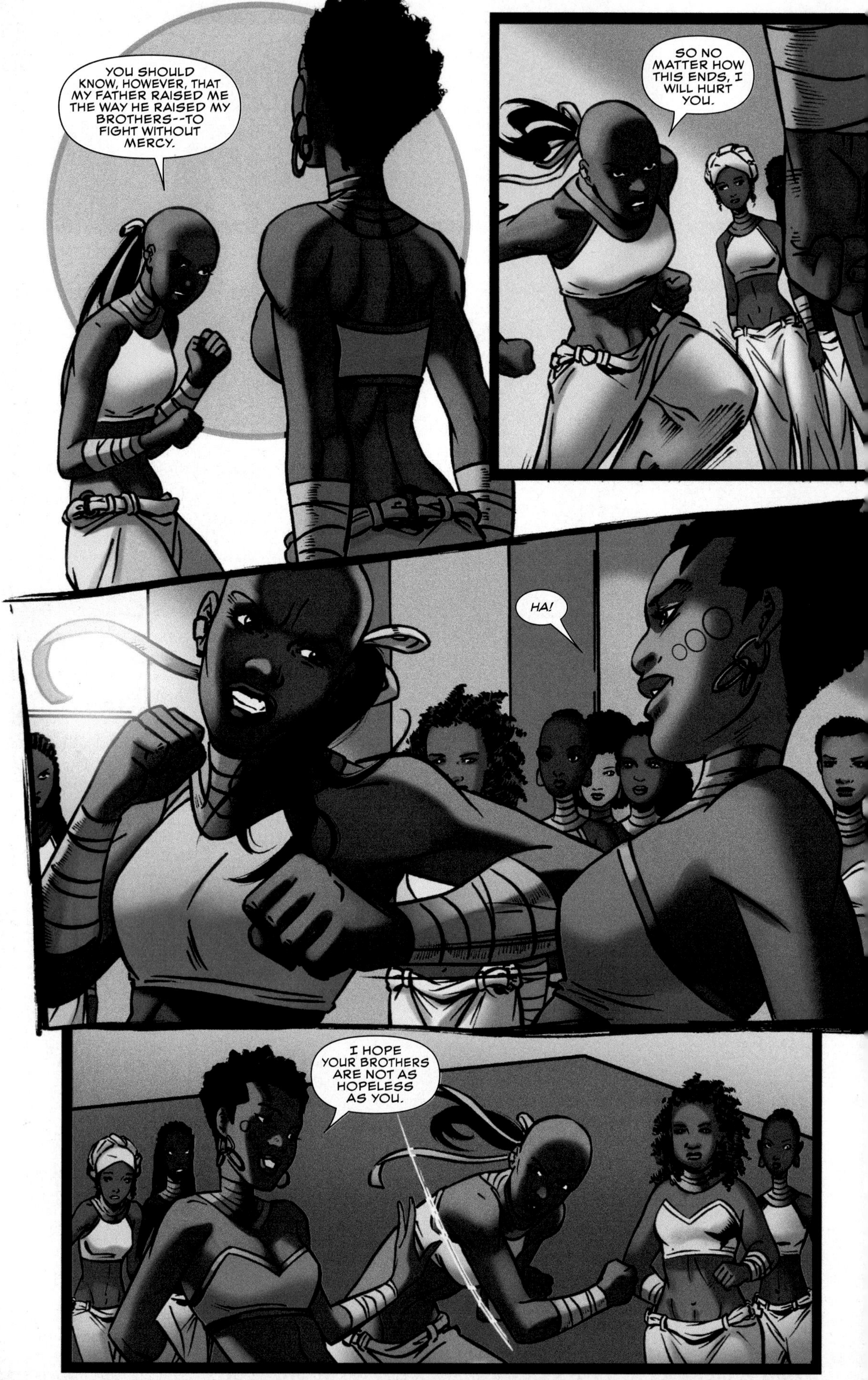
YOU SHOULD KNOW, HOWEVER, THAT MY FATHER RAISED ME THE WAY HE RAISED MY BROTHERS--TO FIGHT WITHOUT MERCY.
SO NO MATTER HOW THIS ENDS, I WILL HURT YOU.
HA!
I HOPE YOUR BROTHERS ARE NOT AS HOPELESS AS YOU.

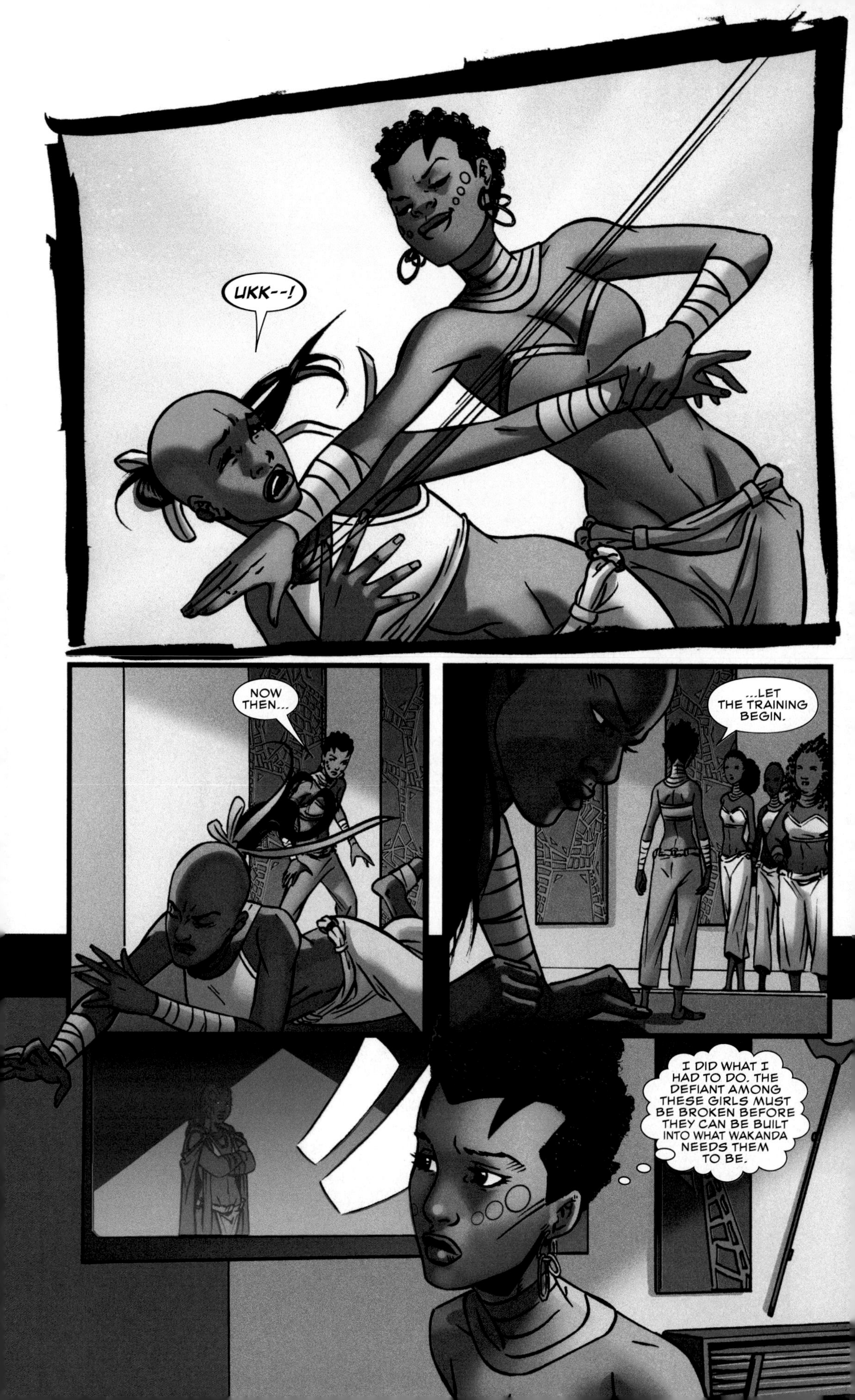
UKK--!
NOW THEN...
...LET THE TRAINING BEGIN.
I DID WHAT I HAD TO DO. THE DEFIANT AMONG THESE GIRLS MUST BE BROKEN BEFORE THEY CAN BE BUILT INTO WHAT WAKANDA NEEDS THEM TO BE.

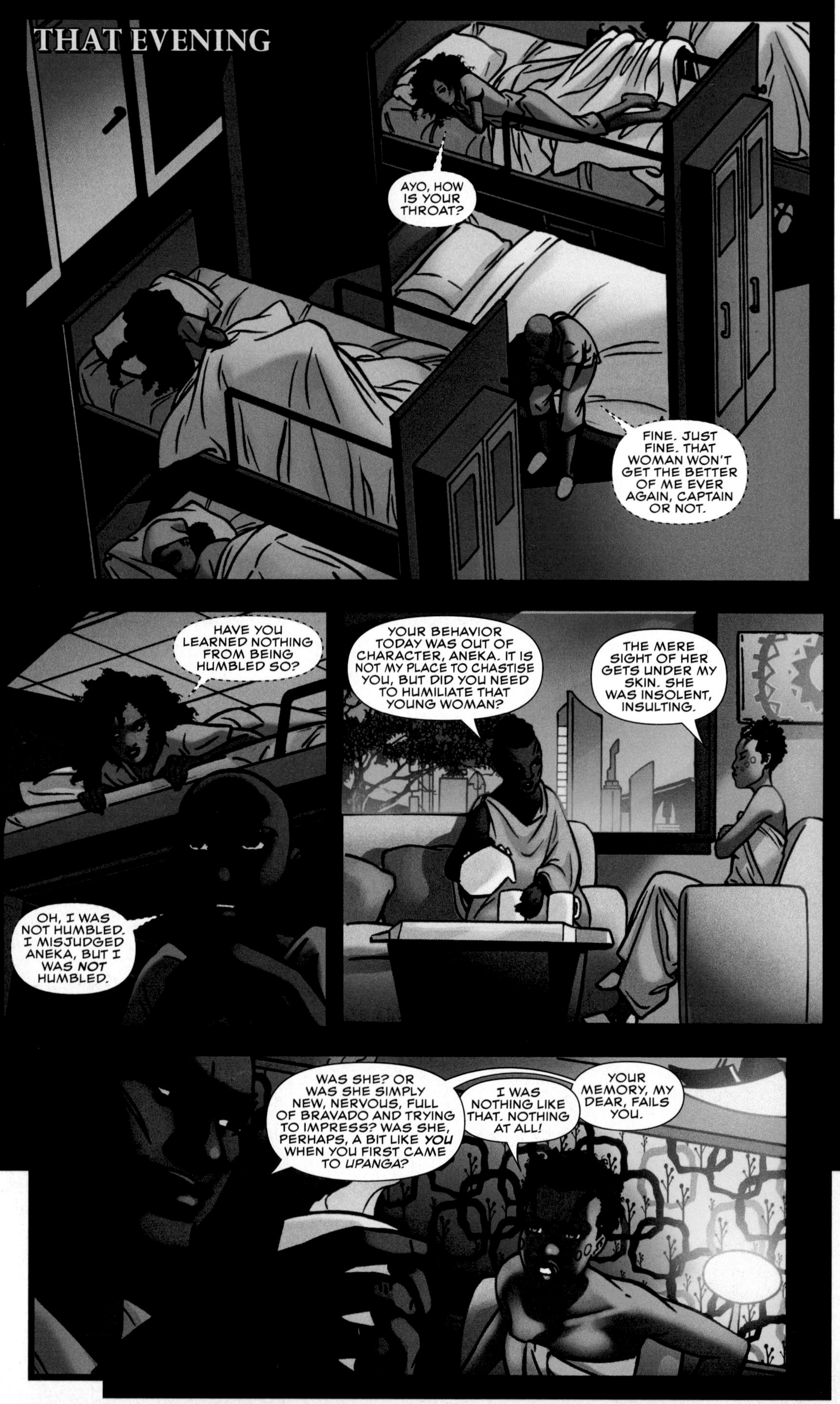
THAT EVENING
AYO, HOW IS YOUR THROAT?
FINE. JUST FINE. THAT WOMAN WON'T GET THE BETTER OF ME EVER AGAIN, CAPTAIN OR NOT.
HAVE YOU LEARNED NOTHING FROM BEING HUMBLED SO?
OH, I WAS NOT HUMBLED. I MISJUDGED ANEKA, BUT I WAS *NOT* HUMBLED.
YOUR BEHAVIOR TODAY WAS OUT OF CHARACTER, ANEKA. IT IS NOT MY PLACE TO CHASTISE YOU, BUT DID YOU NEED TO HUMILIATE THAT YOUNG WOMAN?
THE MERE SIGHT OF HER GETS UNDER MY SKIN. SHE WAS INSOLENT, INSULTING.
WAS SHE? OR WAS SHE SIMPLY NEW, NERVOUS, FULL OF BRAVADO AND TRYING TO IMPRESS? WAS SHE, PERHAPS, A BIT LIKE *YOU* WHEN YOU FIRST CAME TO *UPANGA*?
I WAS NOTHING LIKE THAT. NOTHING AT ALL!
YOUR MEMORY, MY DEAR, FAILS YOU.

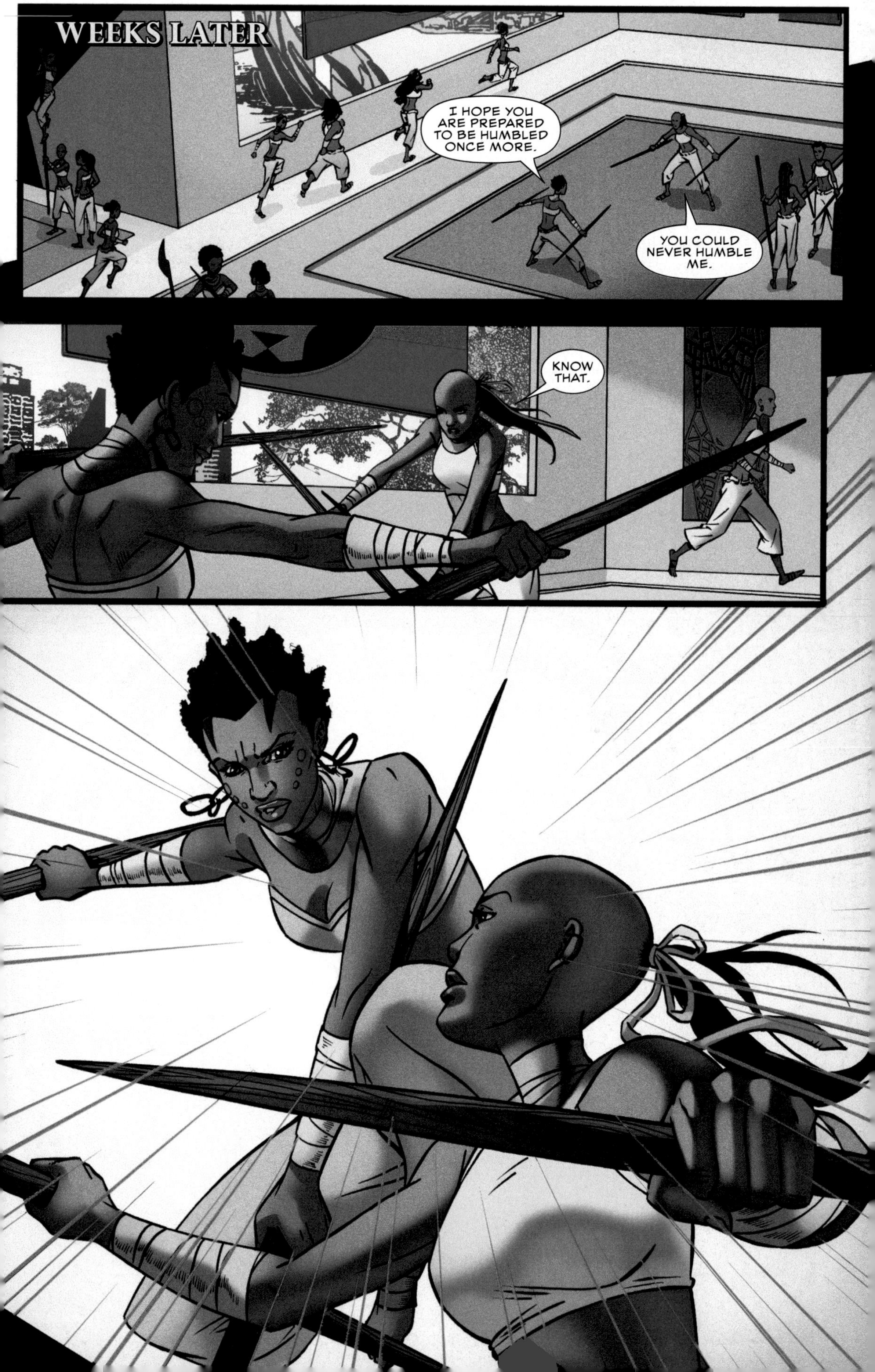
WEEKS LATER
I HOPE YOU ARE PREPARED TO BE HUMBLED ONCE MORE.
YOU COULD NEVER HUMBLE ME.
KNOW THAT.

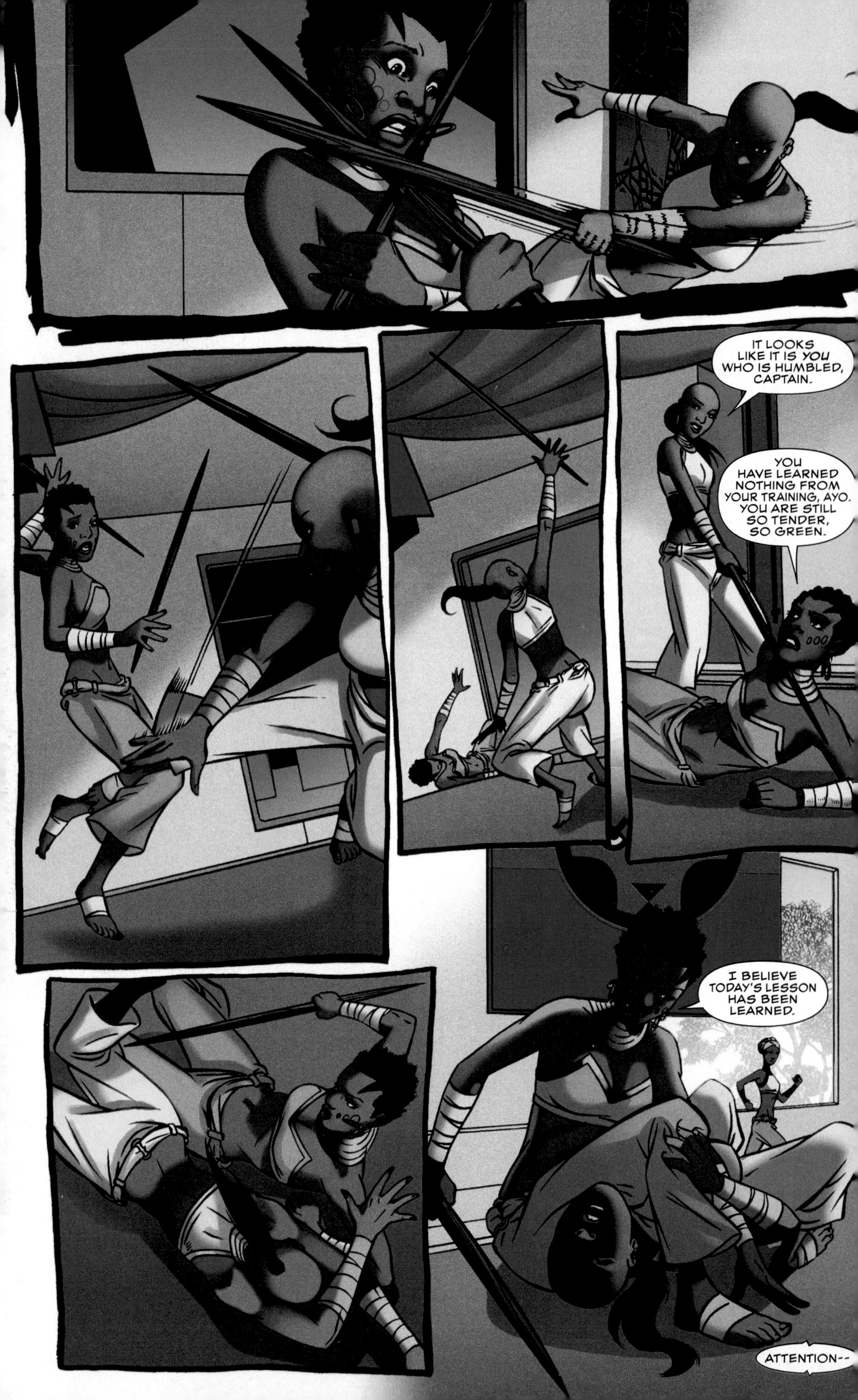
IT LOOKS LIKE IT IS YOU WHO IS HUMBLED, CAPTAIN.
YOU HAVE LEARNED NOTHING FROM YOUR TRAINING, AYO. YOU ARE STILL SO TENDER, SO GREEN.
I BELIEVE TODAY'S LESSON HAS BEEN LEARNED.
ATTENTION--

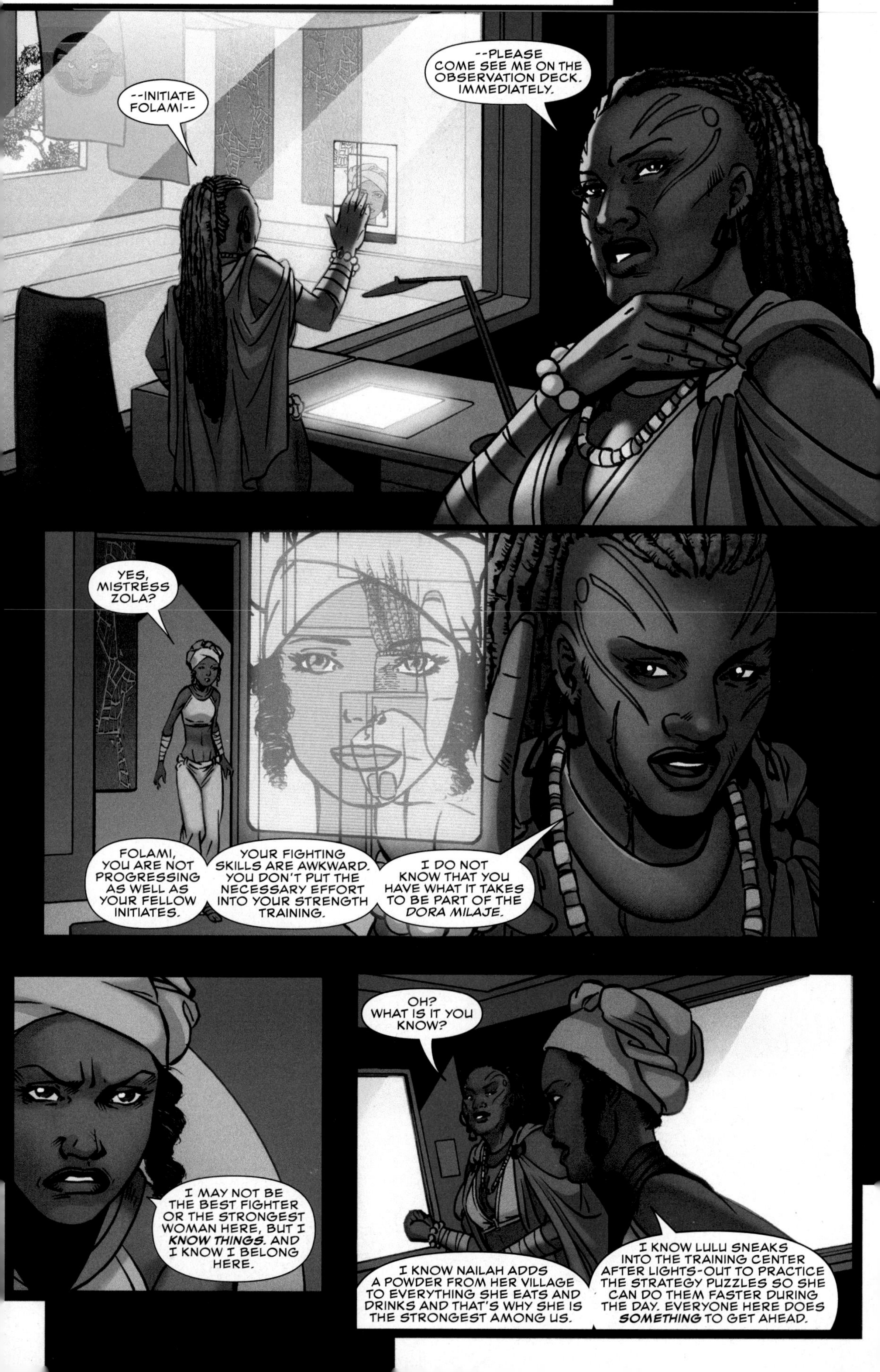
--INITIATE FOLAMI--
--PLEASE COME SEE ME ON THE OBSERVATION DECK. IMMEDIATELY.
YES, MISTRESS ZOLA?
FOLAMI, YOU ARE NOT PROGRESSING AS WELL AS YOUR FELLOW INITIATES.
YOUR FIGHTING SKILLS ARE AWKWARD. YOU DON'T PUT THE NECESSARY EFFORT INTO YOUR STRENGTH TRAINING.
I DO NOT KNOW THAT YOU HAVE WHAT IT TAKES TO BE PART OF THE *DORA MILAJE*.
I MAY NOT BE THE BEST FIGHTER OR THE STRONGEST WOMAN HERE, BUT I ***KNOW THINGS***. AND I KNOW I BELONG HERE.
OH? WHAT IS IT YOU KNOW?
I KNOW NAILAH ADDS A POWDER FROM HER VILLAGE TO EVERYTHING SHE EATS AND DRINKS AND THAT'S WHY SHE IS THE STRONGEST AMONG US.
I KNOW LULU SNEAKS INTO THE TRAINING CENTER AFTER LIGHTS-OUT TO PRACTICE THE STRATEGY PUZZLES SO SHE CAN DO THEM FASTER DURING THE DAY. EVERYONE HERE DOES ***SOMETHING*** TO GET AHEAD.

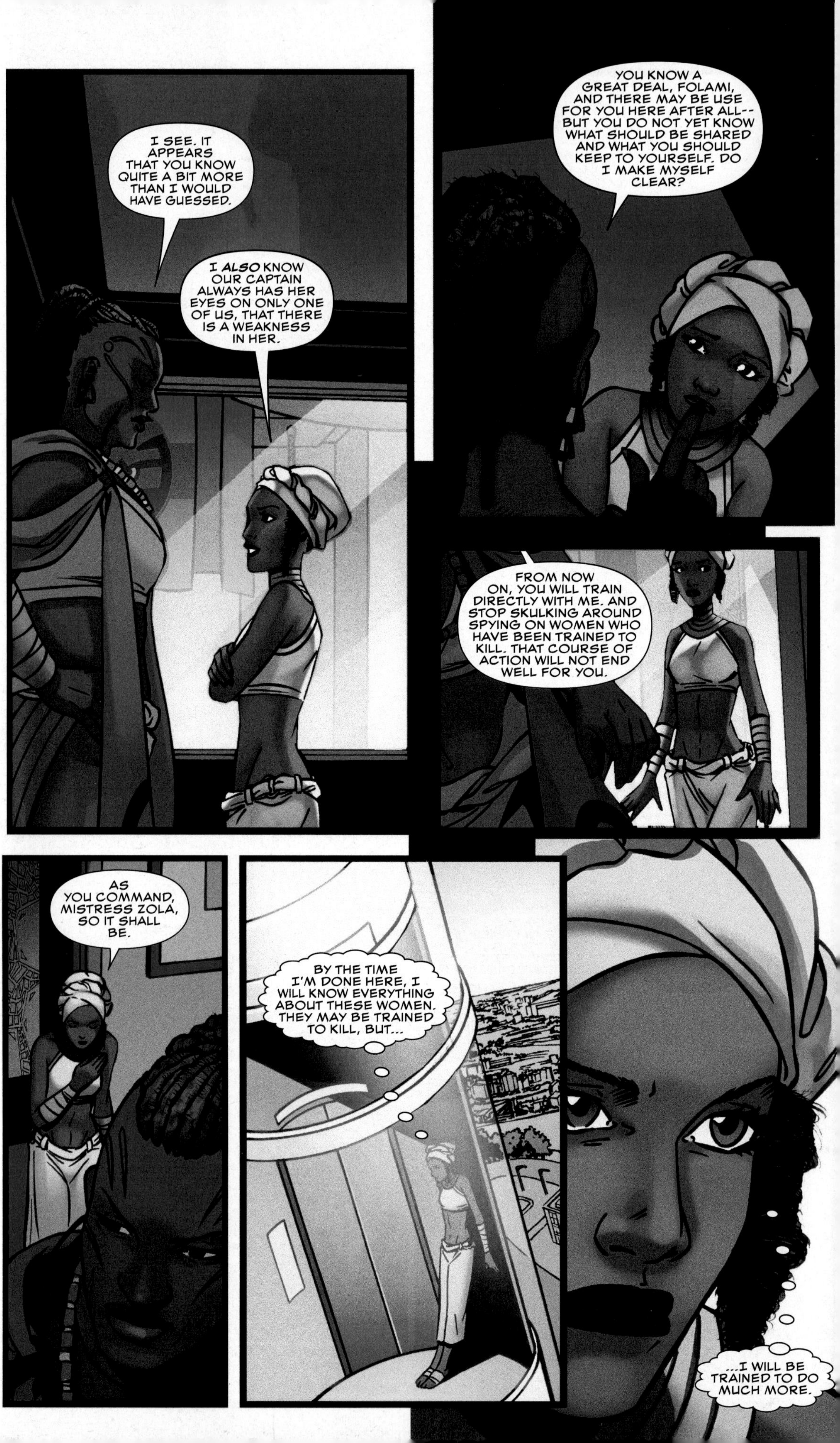
I SEE. IT APPEARS THAT YOU KNOW QUITE A BIT MORE THAN I WOULD HAVE GUESSED.
I *ALSO* KNOW OUR CAPTAIN ALWAYS HAS HER EYES ON ONLY ONE OF US, THAT THERE IS A WEAKNESS IN HER.
YOU KNOW A GREAT DEAL, FOLAMI, AND THERE MAY BE USE FOR YOU HERE AFTER ALL-- BUT YOU DO NOT YET KNOW WHAT SHOULD BE SHARED AND WHAT YOU SHOULD KEEP TO YOURSELF. DO I MAKE MYSELF CLEAR?
FROM NOW ON, YOU WILL TRAIN DIRECTLY WITH ME. AND STOP SKULKING AROUND SPYING ON WOMEN WHO HAVE BEEN TRAINED TO KILL. THAT COURSE OF ACTION WILL NOT END WELL FOR YOU.
AS YOU COMMAND, MISTRESS ZOLA, SO IT SHALL BE.
BY THE TIME I'M DONE HERE, I WILL KNOW EVERYTHING ABOUT THESE WOMEN. THEY MAY BE TRAINED TO KILL, BUT...
...I WILL BE TRAINED TO DO MUCH MORE.

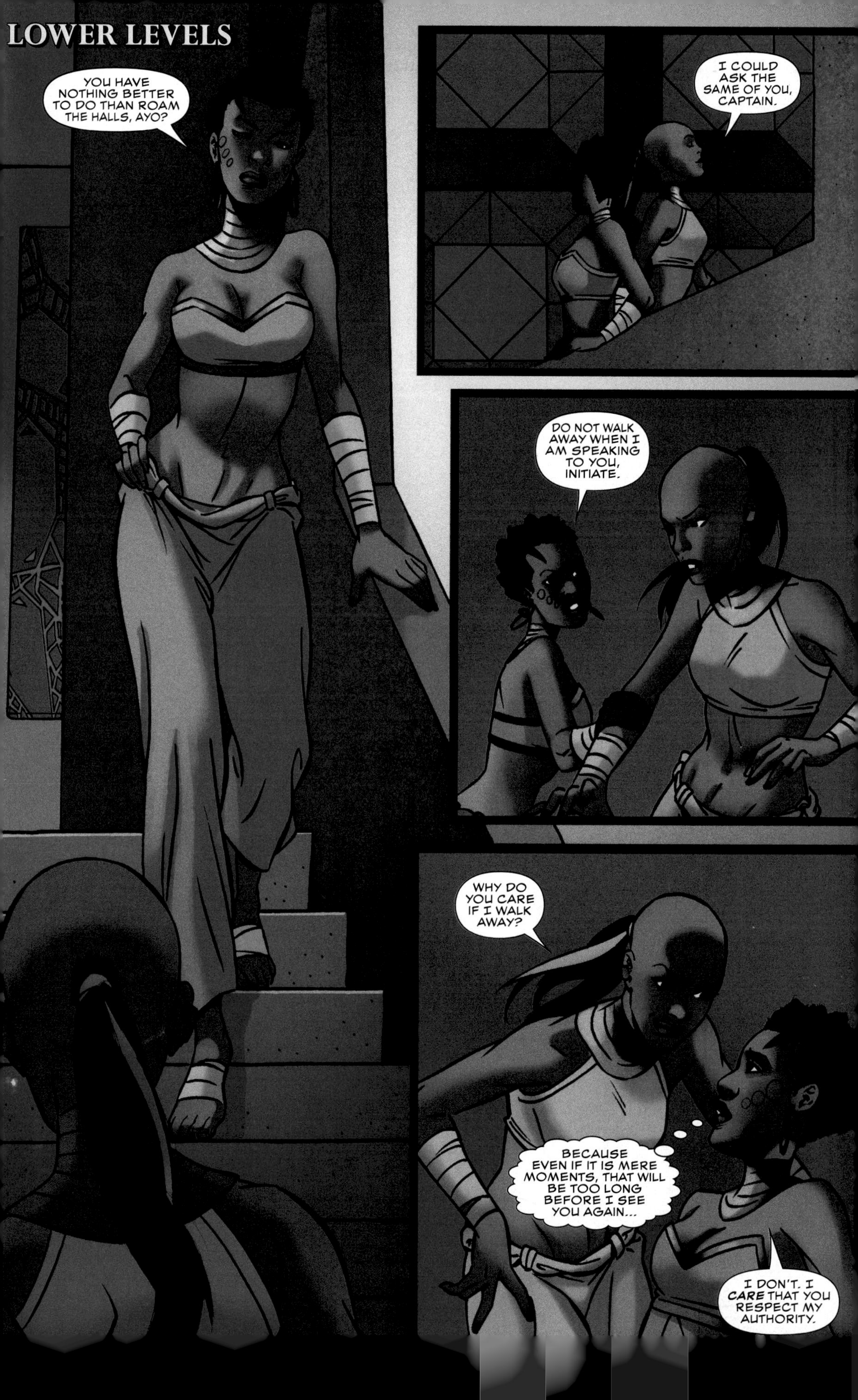

LOWER LEVELS
YOU HAVE NOTHING BETTER TO DO THAN ROAM THE HALLS, AYO?
I COULD ASK THE SAME OF YOU, CAPTAIN.
DO NOT WALK AWAY WHEN I AM SPEAKING TO YOU, INITIATE.
WHY DO YOU CARE IF I WALK AWAY?
BECAUSE EVEN IF IT IS MERE MOMENTS, THAT WILL BE TOO LONG BEFORE I SEE YOU AGAIN...
I DON'T. I CARE THAT YOU RESPECT MY AUTHORITY.

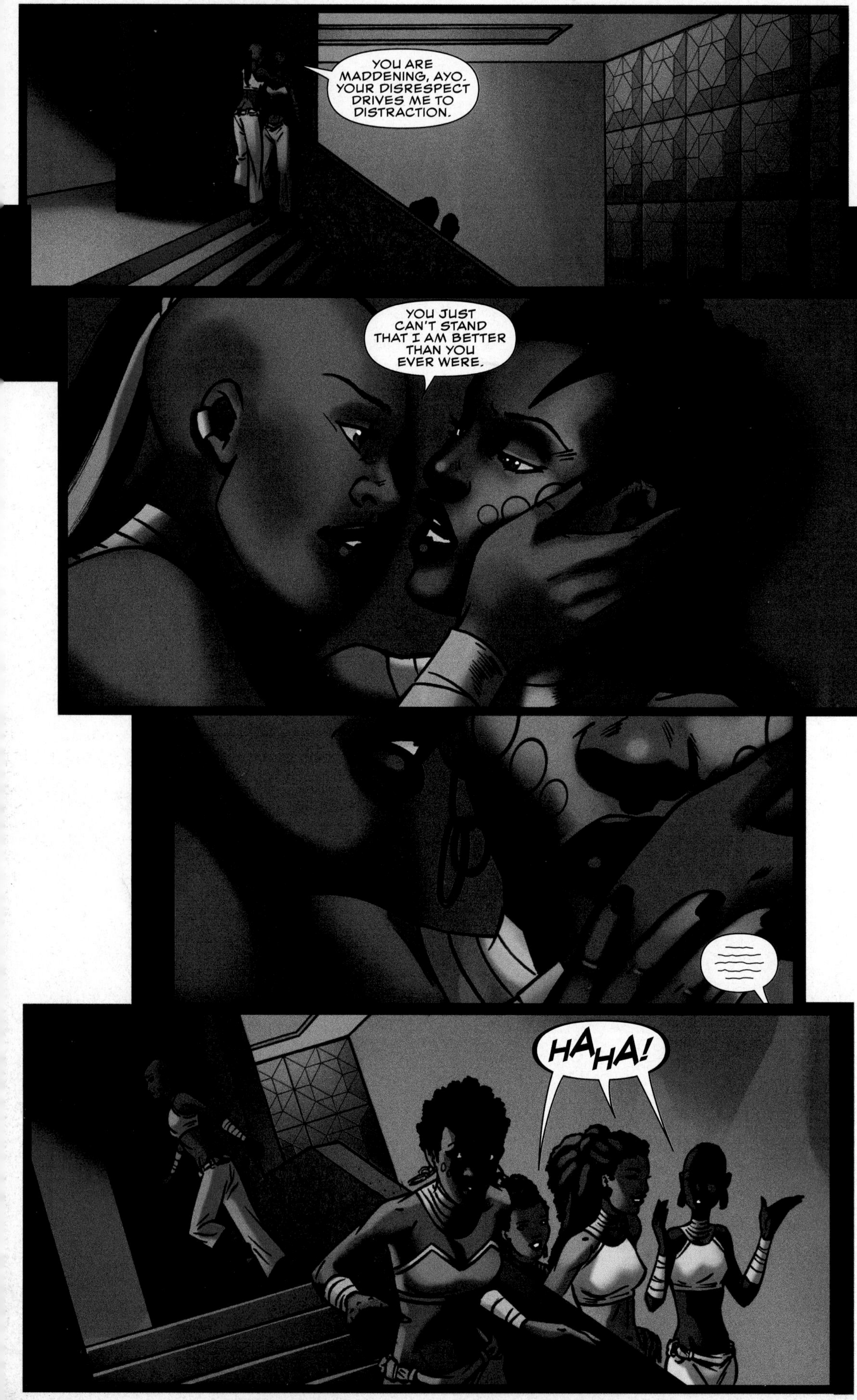
YOU ARE MADDENING, AYO. YOUR DISRESPECT DRIVES ME TO DISTRACTION.
YOU JUST CAN'T STAND THAT I AM BETTER THAN YOU EVER WERE.
HAHA!

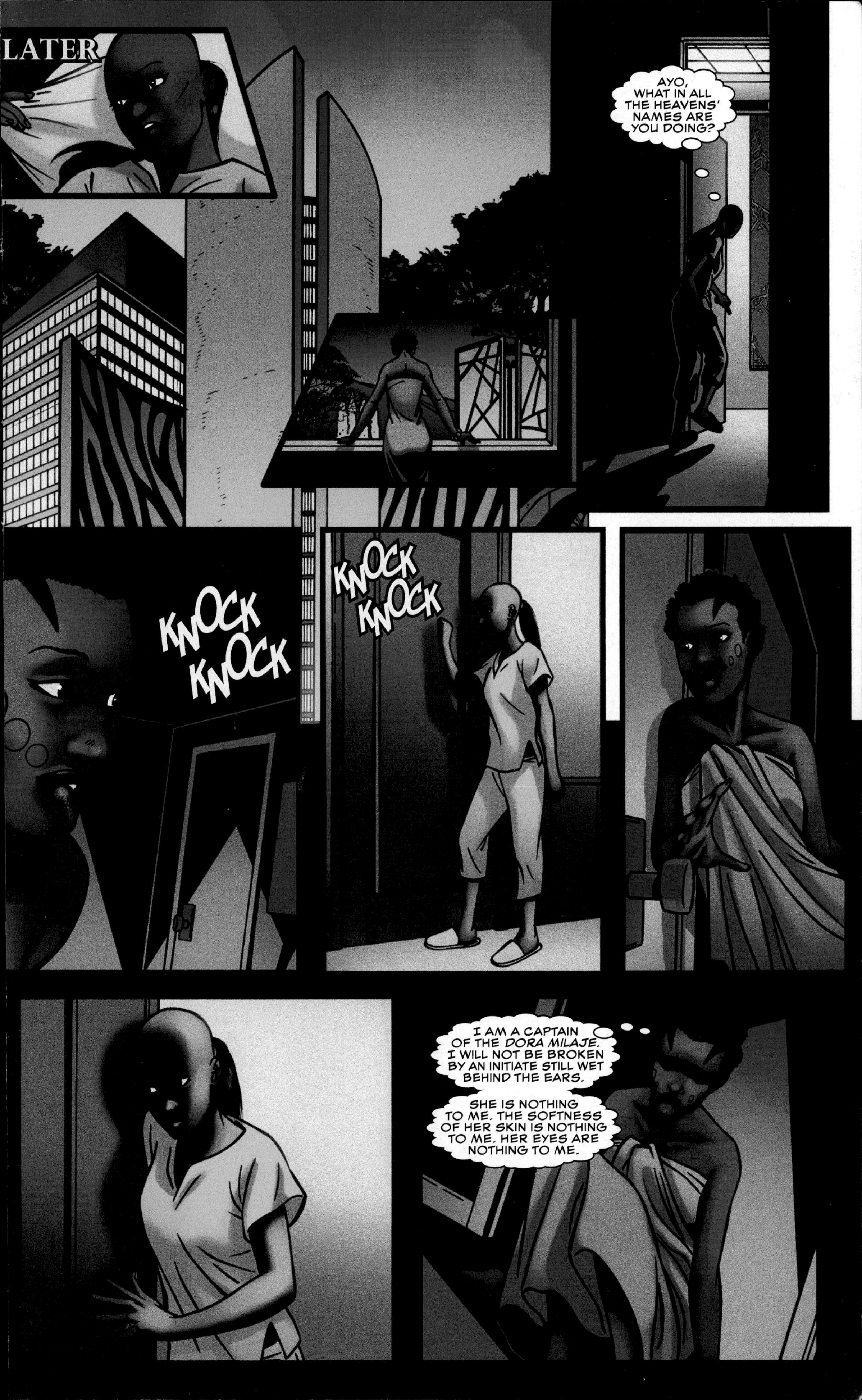
LATER
AYO, WHAT IN ALL THE HEAVENS' NAMES ARE YOU DOING?
KNOCK KNOCK
KNOCK KNOCK
I AM A CAPTAIN OF THE DORA MILAJE. I WILL NOT BE BROKEN BY AN INITIATE STILL WET BEHIND THE EARS.
SHE IS NOTHING TO ME. THE SOFTNESS OF HER SKIN IS NOTHING TO ME. HER EYES ARE NOTHING TO ME.

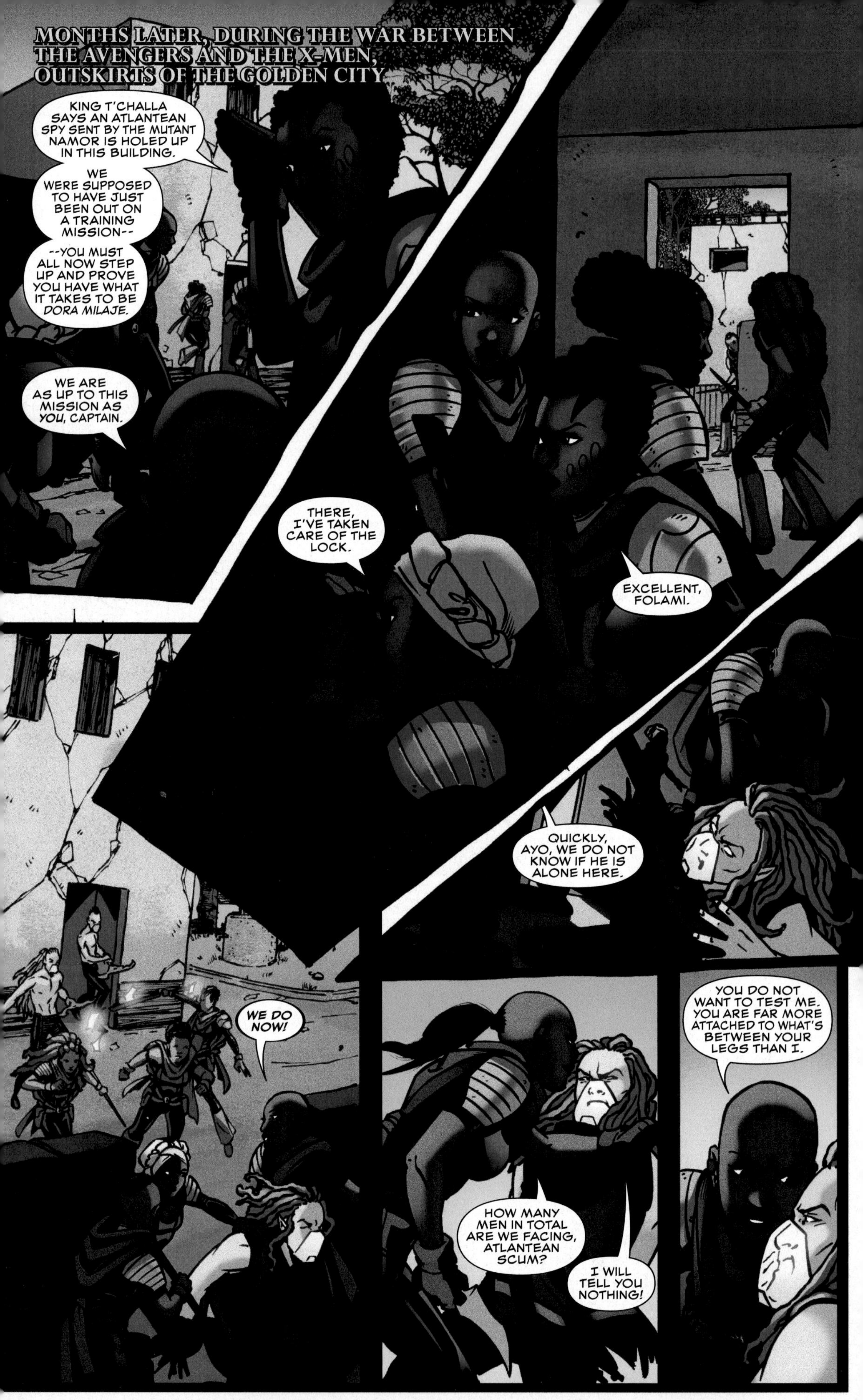
MONTHS LATER, DURING THE WAR BETWEEN THE AVENGERS AND THE X-MEN, OUTSKIRTS OF THE GOLDEN CITY
KING T'CHALLA SAYS AN ATLANTEAN SPY SENT BY THE MUTANT NAMOR IS HOLED UP IN THIS BUILDING.
WE WERE SUPPOSED TO HAVE JUST BEEN OUT ON A TRAINING MISSION--
--YOU MUST ALL NOW STEP UP AND PROVE YOU HAVE WHAT IT TAKES TO BE *DORA MILAJE.*
WE ARE AS UP TO THIS MISSION AS *YOU,* CAPTAIN.
THERE, I'VE TAKEN CARE OF THE LOCK.
EXCELLENT, FOLAMI.
QUICKLY, AYO, WE DO NOT KNOW IF HE IS ALONE HERE.
WE DO NOW!
HOW MANY MEN IN TOTAL ARE WE FACING, ATLANTEAN SCUM?
I WILL TELL YOU NOTHING!
YOU DO NOT WANT TO TEST ME. YOU ARE FAR MORE ATTACHED TO WHAT'S BETWEEN YOUR LEGS THAN I.

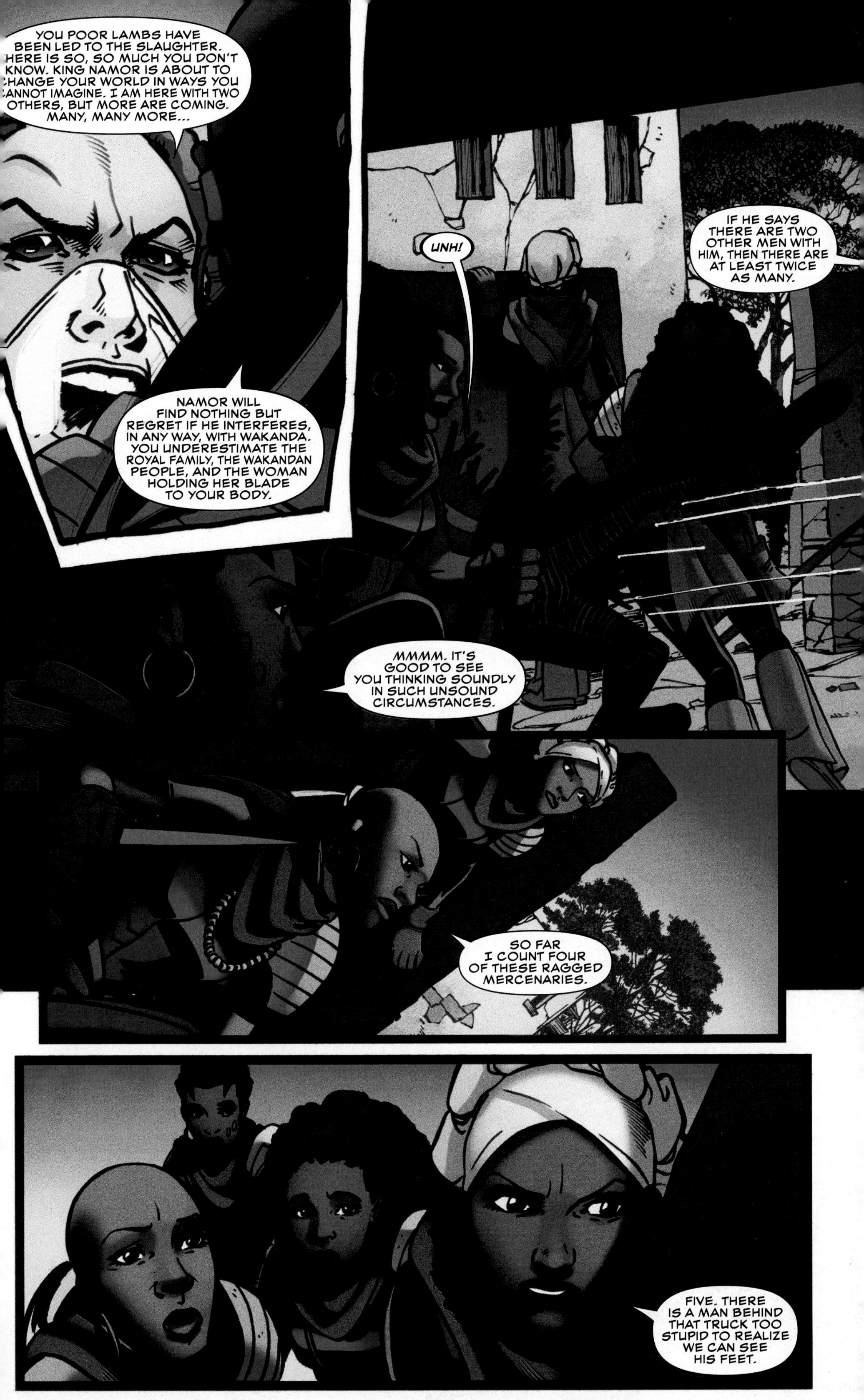
YOU POOR LAMBS HAVE BEEN LED TO THE SLAUGHTER. THERE IS SO, SO MUCH YOU DON'T KNOW. KING NAMOR IS ABOUT TO CHANGE YOUR WORLD IN WAYS YOU CANNOT IMAGINE. I AM HERE WITH TWO OTHERS, BUT MORE ARE COMING. MANY, MANY MORE...
NAMOR WILL FIND NOTHING BUT REGRET IF HE INTERFERES, IN ANY WAY, WITH WAKANDA. YOU UNDERESTIMATE THE ROYAL FAMILY, THE WAKANDAN PEOPLE, AND THE WOMAN HOLDING HER BLADE TO YOUR BODY.
UNH!
IF HE SAYS THERE ARE TWO OTHER MEN WITH HIM, THEN THERE ARE AT LEAST TWICE AS MANY.
MMMM. IT'S GOOD TO SEE YOU THINKING SOUNDLY IN SUCH UNSOUND CIRCUMSTANCES.
SO FAR I COUNT FOUR OF THESE RAGGED MERCENARIES.
FIVE. THERE IS A MAN BEHIND THAT TRUCK TOO STUPID TO REALIZE WE CAN SEE HIS FEET.

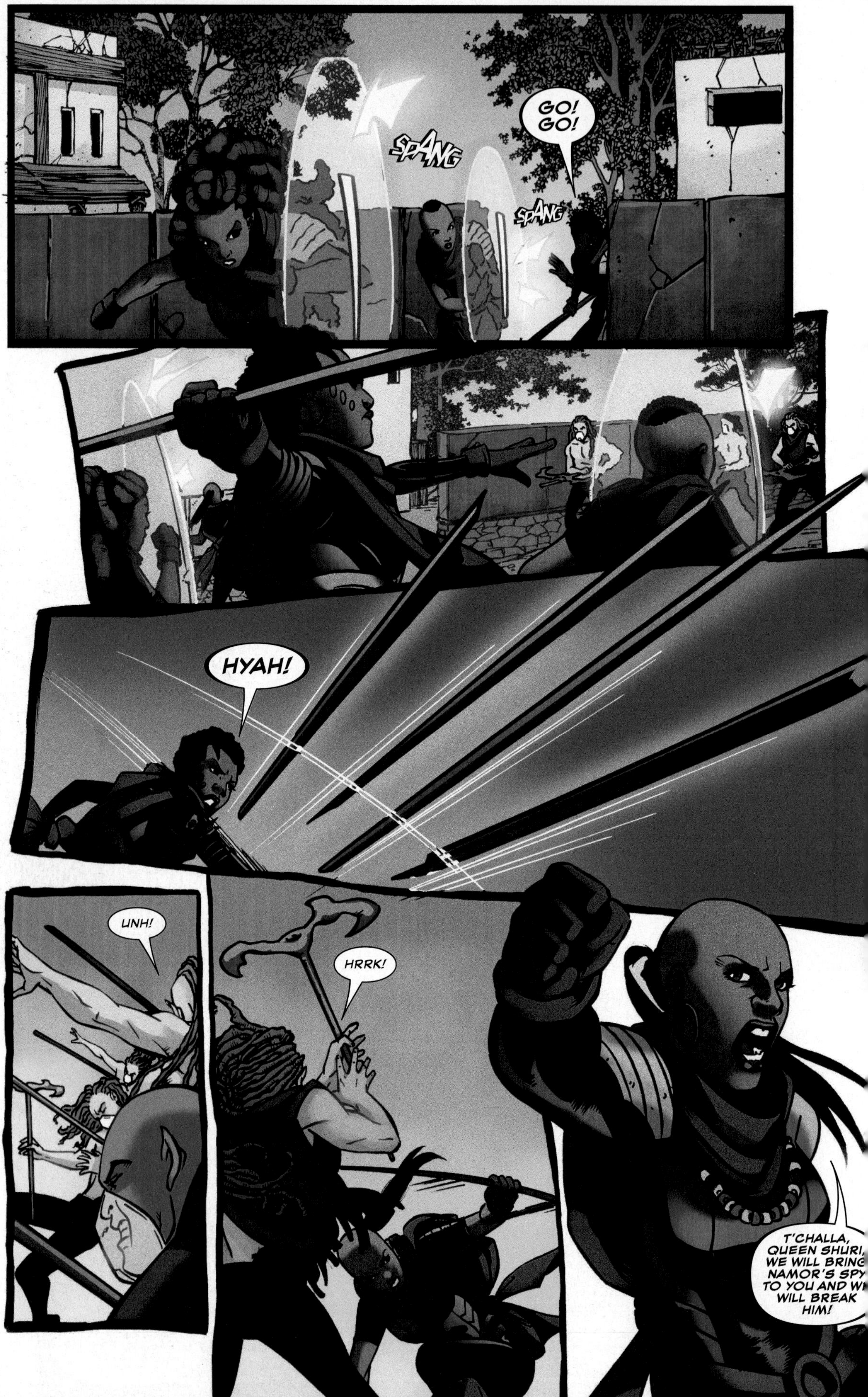
SPANG
GO! GO!
SPANG
HYAH!
UNH!
HRRK!
T'CHALLA, QUEEN SHURI, WE WILL BRING NAMOR'S SPY TO YOU AND W
WILL BREAK HIM!

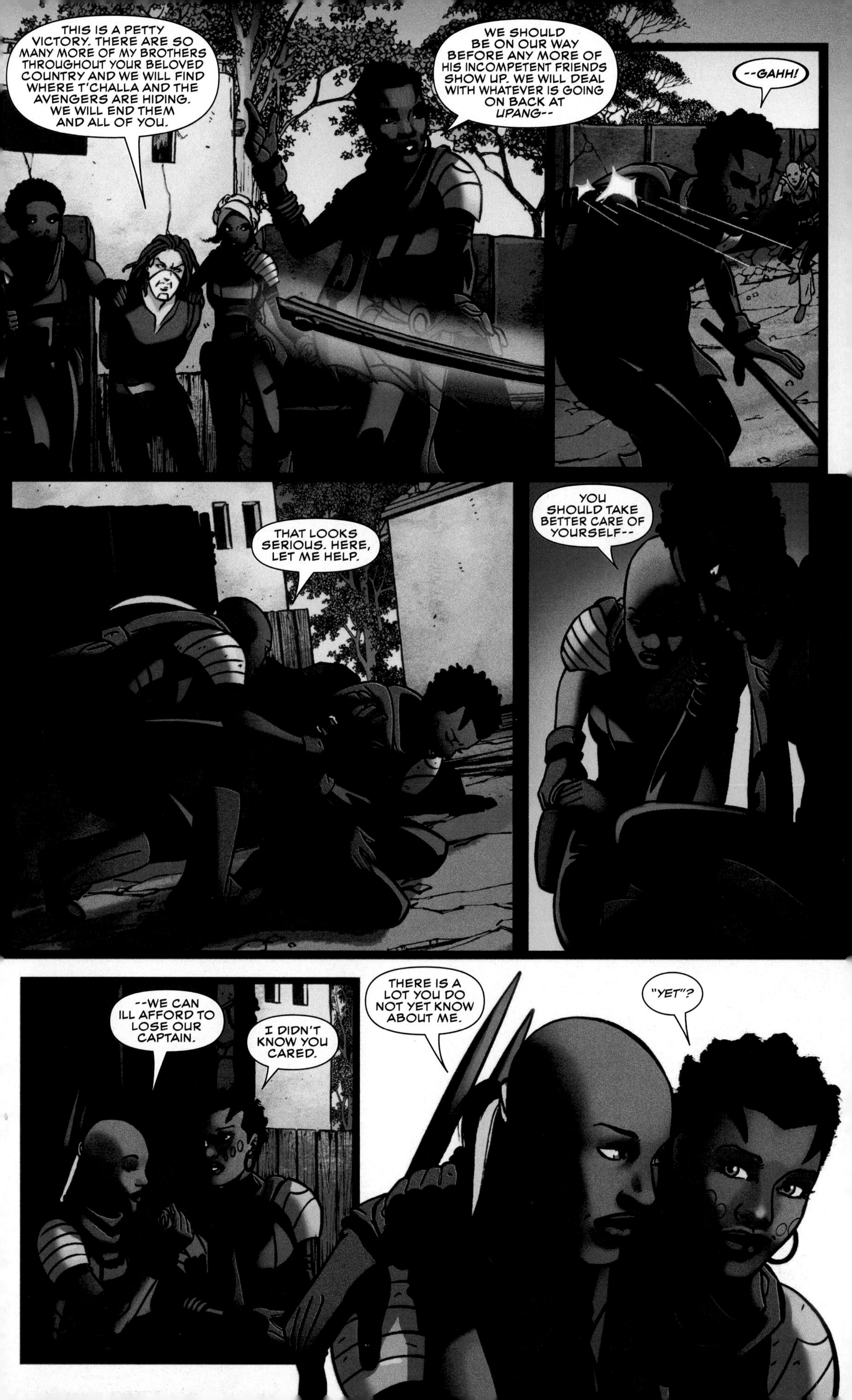
THIS IS A PETTY VICTORY. THERE ARE SO MANY MORE OF MY BROTHERS THROUGHOUT YOUR BELOVED COUNTRY AND WE WILL FIND WHERE T'CHALLA AND THE AVENGERS ARE HIDING. WE WILL END THEM AND ALL OF YOU.
WE SHOULD BE ON OUR WAY BEFORE ANY MORE OF HIS INCOMPETENT FRIENDS SHOW UP. WE WILL DEAL WITH WHATEVER IS GOING ON BACK AT *UPANG*--
--GAHH!
THAT LOOKS SERIOUS. HERE, LET ME HELP.
YOU SHOULD TAKE BETTER CARE OF YOURSELF--
--WE CAN ILL AFFORD TO LOSE OUR CAPTAIN.
I DIDN'T KNOW YOU CARED.
THERE IS A LOT YOU DO NOT YET KNOW ABOUT ME.
"YET"?

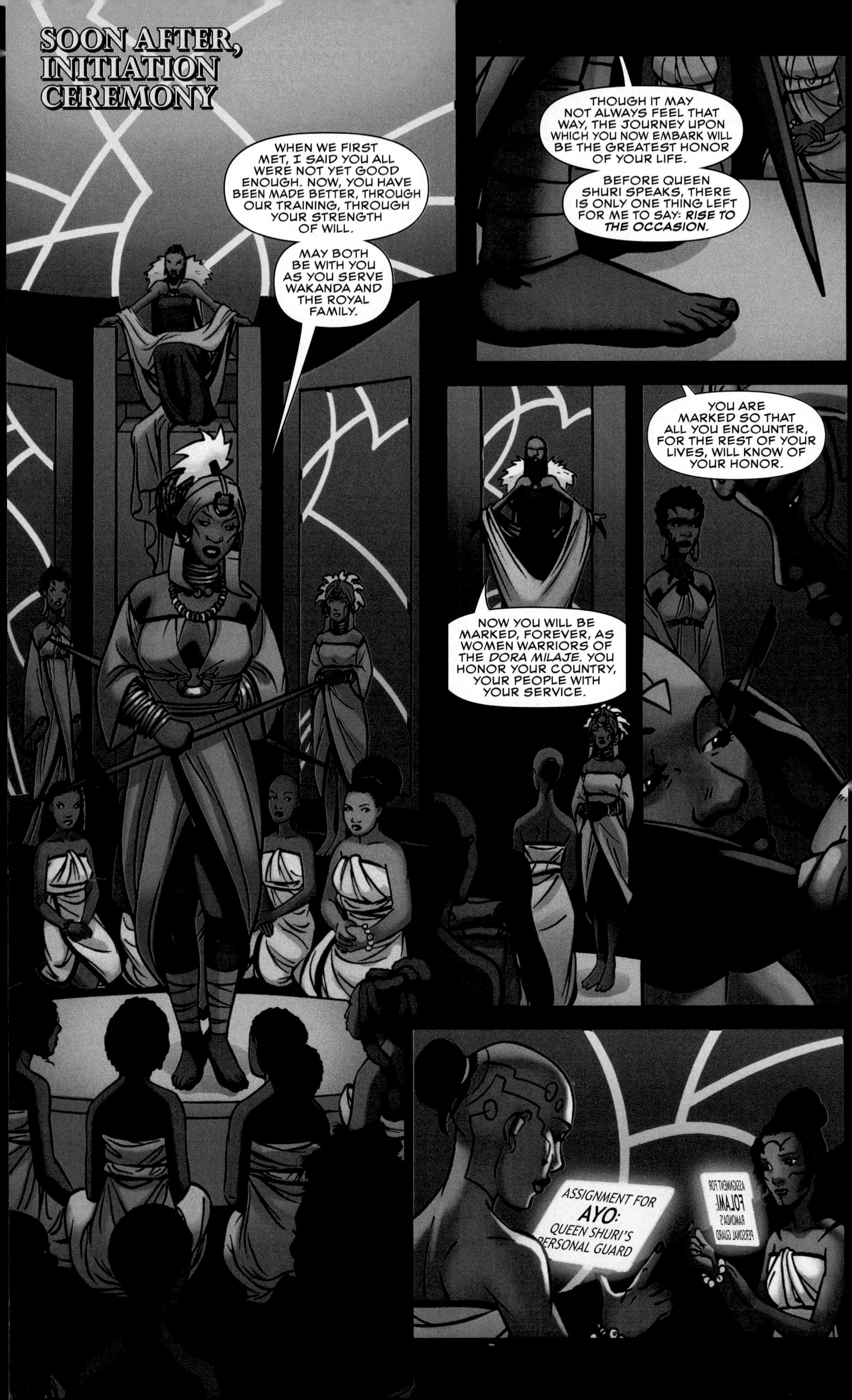
SOON AFTER, INITIATION CEREMONY
WHEN WE FIRST MET, I SAID YOU ALL WERE NOT YET GOOD ENOUGH. NOW, YOU HAVE BEEN MADE BETTER, THROUGH OUR TRAINING, THROUGH YOUR STRENGTH OF WILL.
MAY BOTH BE WITH YOU AS YOU SERVE WAKANDA AND THE ROYAL FAMILY.
THOUGH IT MAY NOT ALWAYS FEEL THAT WAY, THE JOURNEY UPON WHICH YOU NOW EMBARK WILL BE THE GREATEST HONOR OF YOUR LIFE.
BEFORE QUEEN SHURI SPEAKS, THERE IS ONLY ONE THING LEFT FOR ME TO SAY: RISE TO THE OCCASION.
NOW YOU WILL BE MARKED, FOREVER, AS WOMEN WARRIORS OF THE DORA MILAJE. YOU HONOR YOUR COUNTRY, YOUR PEOPLE WITH YOUR SERVICE.
YOU ARE MARKED SO THAT ALL YOU ENCOUNTER, FOR THE REST OF YOUR LIVES, WILL KNOW OF YOUR HONOR.
ASSIGNMENT FOR AYO: QUEEN SHURI'S PERSONAL GUARD
ASSIGNMENT FOR FOLAMI: RAMONDA'S PERSONAL GUARD

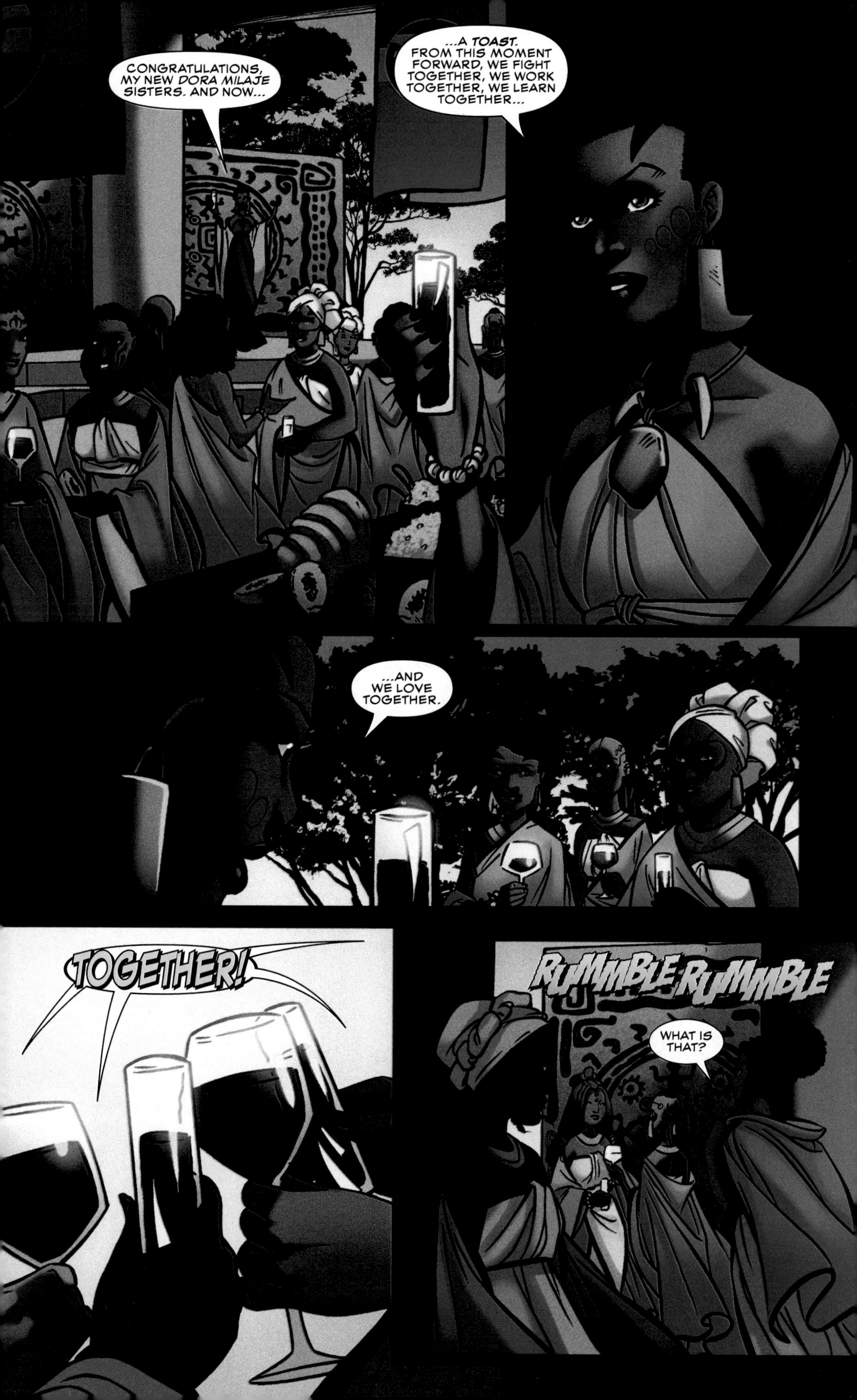
CONGRATULATIONS, MY NEW DORA MILAJE SISTERS. AND NOW...
...A TOAST. FROM THIS MOMENT FORWARD, WE FIGHT TOGETHER, WE WORK TOGETHER, WE LEARN TOGETHER...
...AND WE LOVE TOGETHER.
TOGETHER!
RUMMBLE RUMMBLE
WHAT IS THAT?

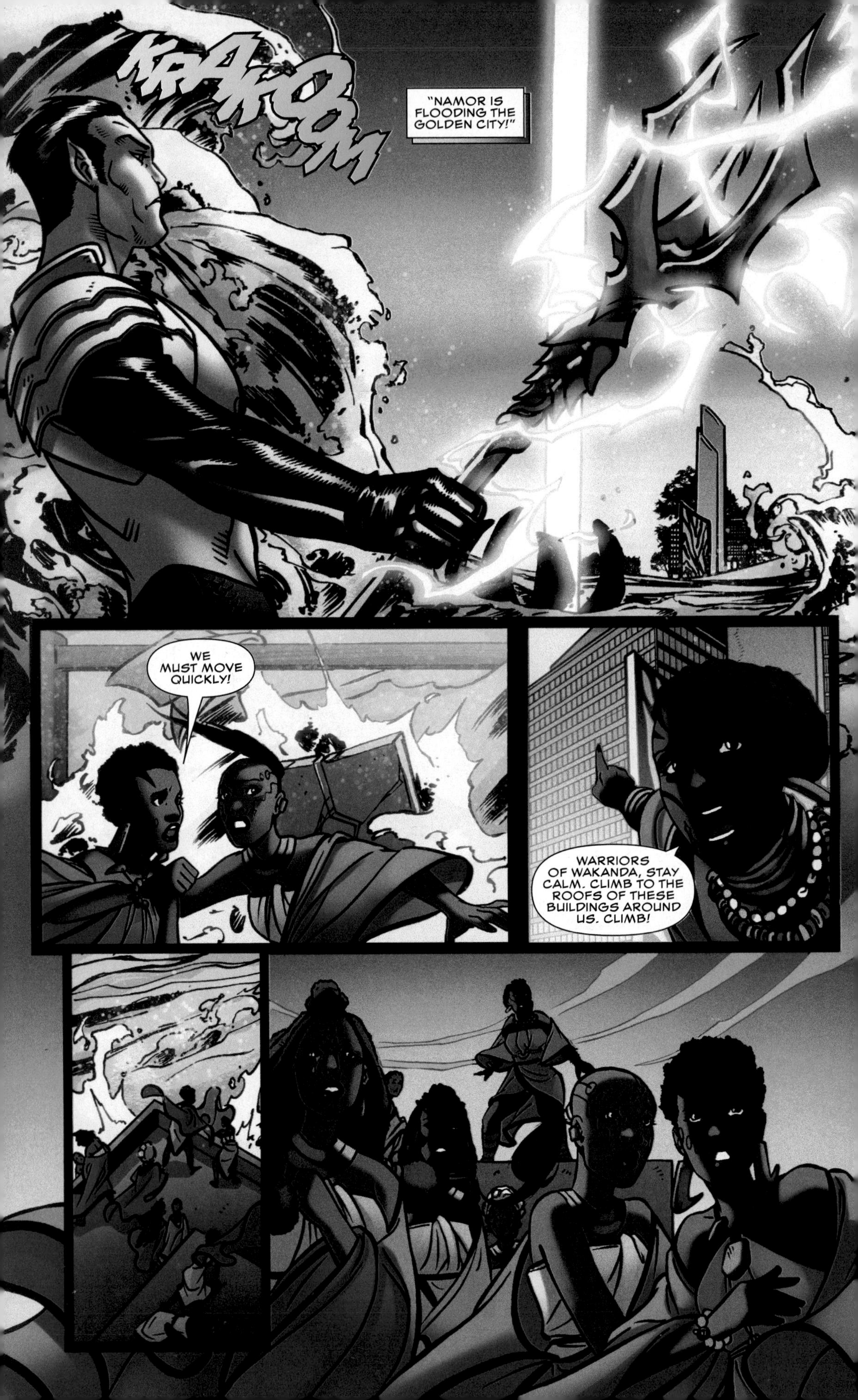
KRAKOOM
"NAMOR IS FLOODING THE GOLDEN CITY!"
WE MUST MOVE QUICKLY!
WARRIORS OF WAKANDA, STAY CALM. CLIMB TO THE ROOFS OF THESE BUILDINGS AROUND US. CLIMB!

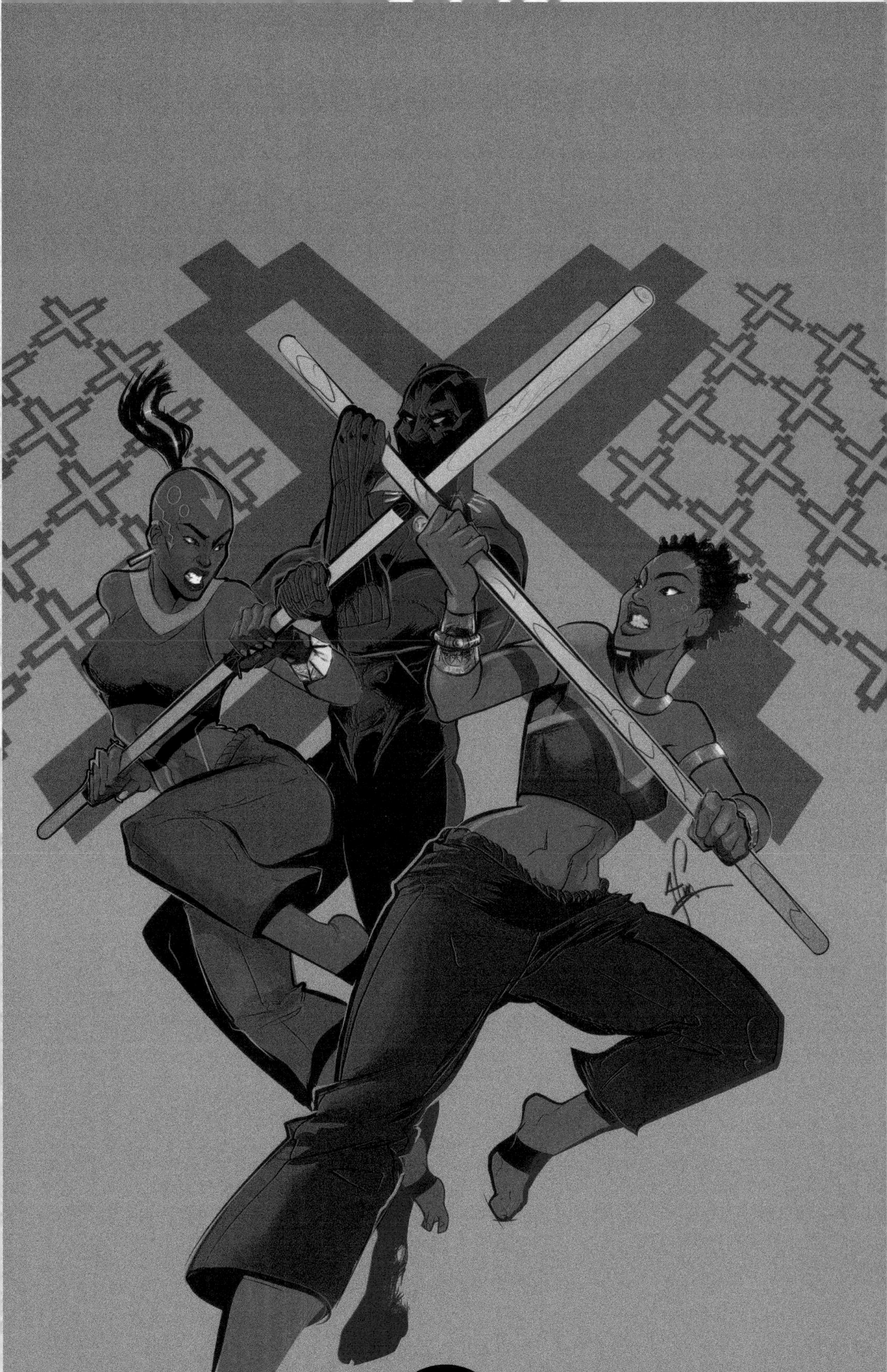

2

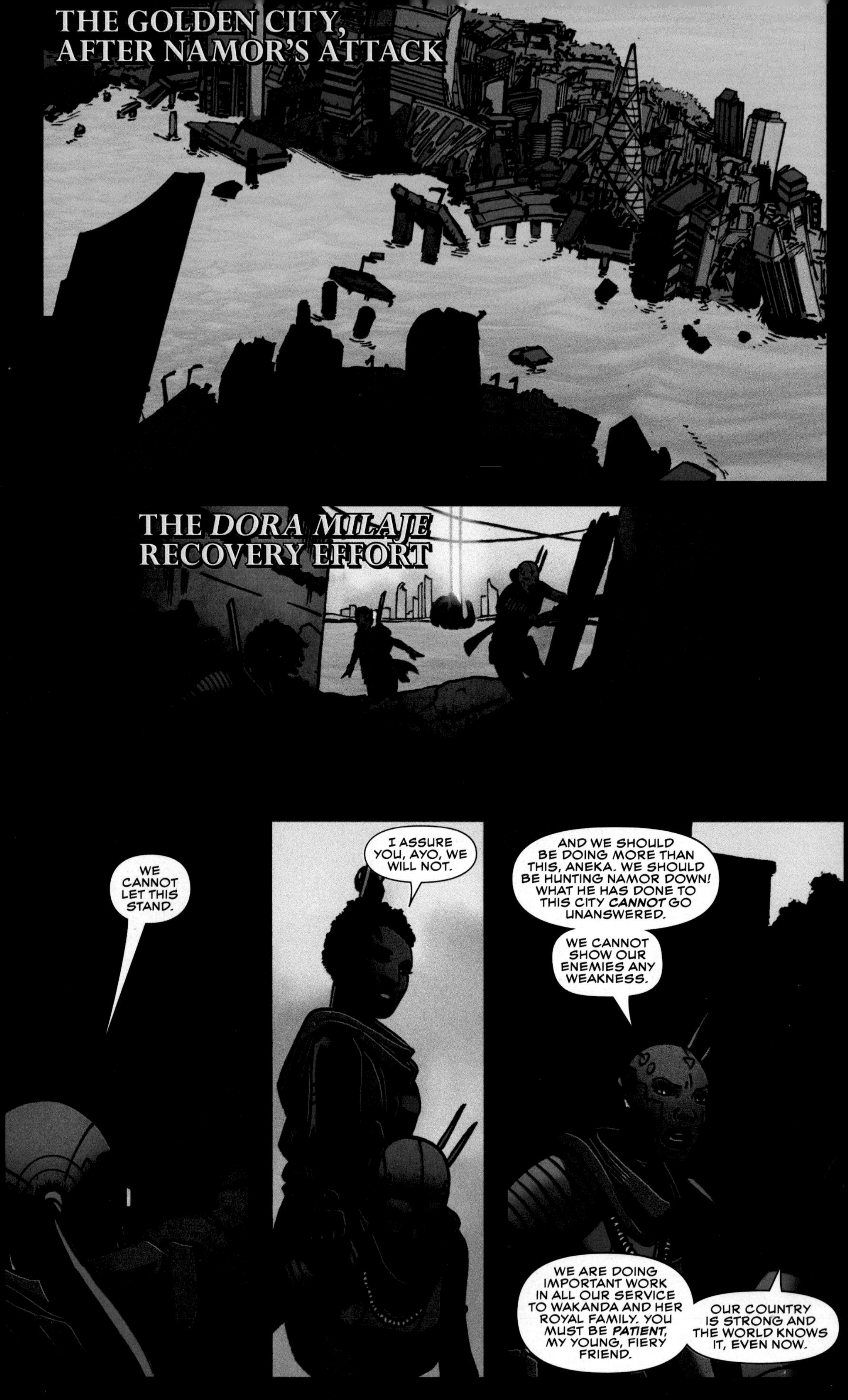
THE GOLDEN CITY, AFTER NAMOR'S ATTACK
THE DORA MILAJE RECOVERY EFFORT
WE CANNOT LET THIS STAND.
I ASSURE YOU, AYO, WE WILL NOT.
AND WE SHOULD BE DOING MORE THAN THIS, ANEKA. WE SHOULD BE HUNTING NAMOR DOWN! WHAT HE HAS DONE TO THIS CITY CANNOT GO UNANSWERED.
WE CANNOT SHOW OUR ENEMIES ANY WEAKNESS.
WE ARE DOING IMPORTANT WORK IN ALL OUR SERVICE TO WAKANDA AND HER ROYAL FAMILY. YOU MUST BE PATIENT, MY YOUNG, FIERY FRIEND.
OUR COUNTRY IS STRONG AND THE WORLD KNOWS IT, EVEN NOW.

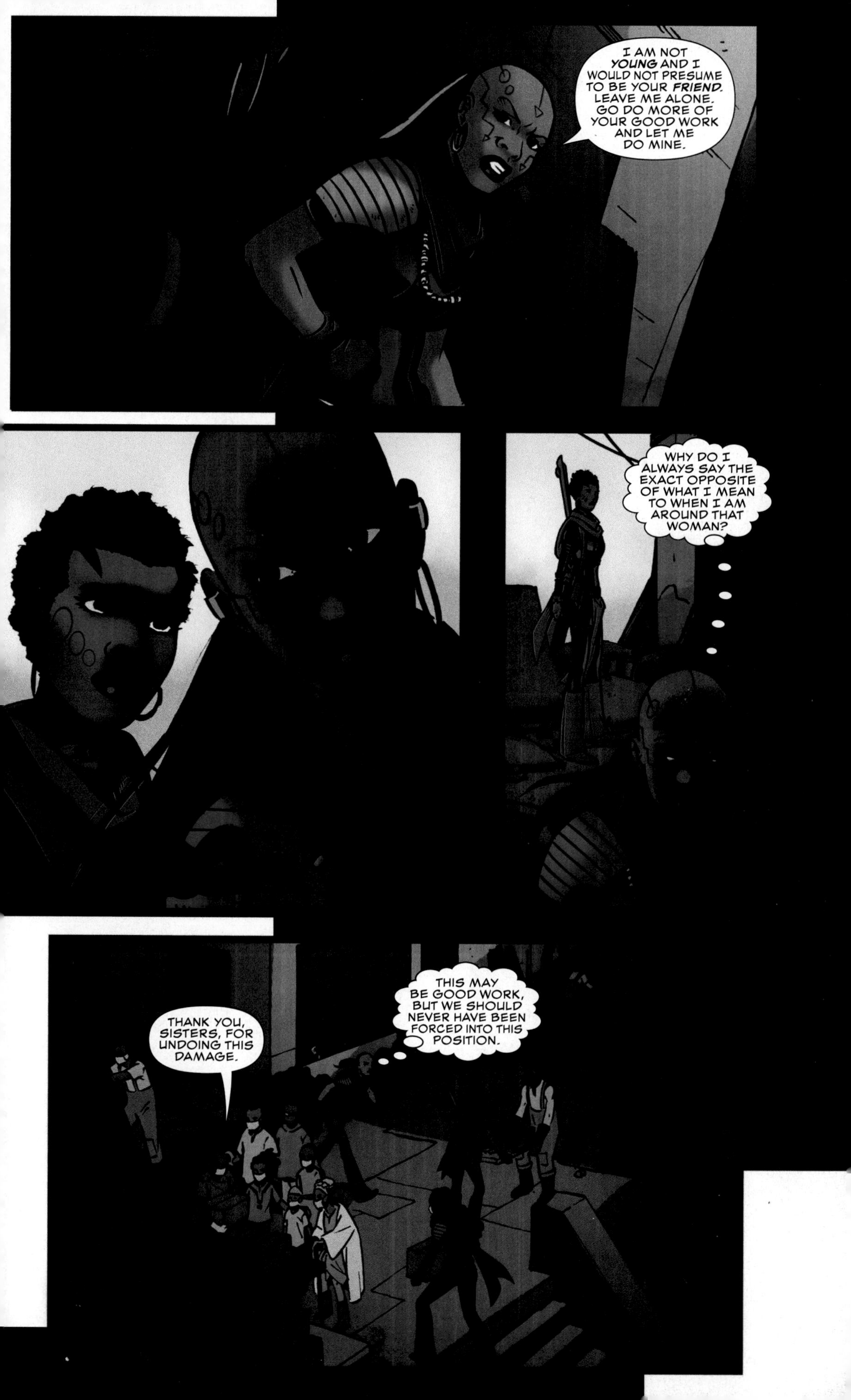
I AM NOT YOUNG AND I WOULD NOT PRESUME TO BE YOUR FRIEND. LEAVE ME ALONE. GO DO MORE OF YOUR GOOD WORK AND LET ME DO MINE.
WHY DO I ALWAYS SAY THE EXACT OPPOSITE OF WHAT I MEAN TO WHEN I AM AROUND THAT WOMAN?
THANK YOU, SISTERS, FOR UNDOING THIS DAMAGE.
THIS MAY BE GOOD WORK, BUT WE SHOULD NEVER HAVE BEEN FORCED INTO THIS POSITION.

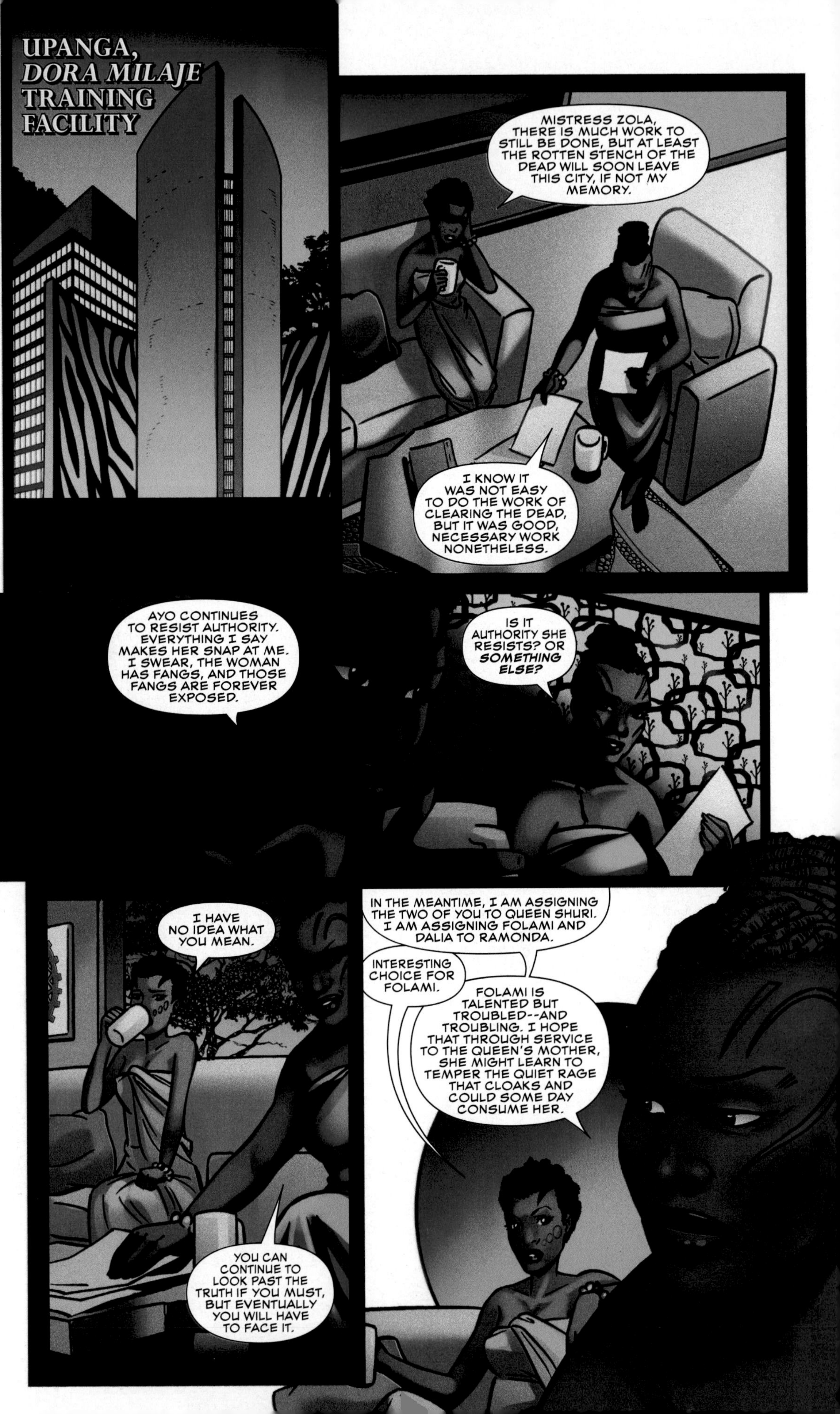
UPANGA, *DORA MILAJE* TRAINING FACILITY
MISTRESS ZOLA, THERE IS MUCH WORK TO STILL BE DONE, BUT AT LEAST THE ROTTEN STENCH OF THE DEAD WILL SOON LEAVE THIS CITY, IF NOT MY MEMORY.
I KNOW IT WAS NOT EASY TO DO THE WORK OF CLEARING THE DEAD, BUT IT WAS GOOD, NECESSARY WORK NONETHELESS.
AYO CONTINUES TO RESIST AUTHORITY. EVERYTHING I SAY MAKES HER SNAP AT ME. I SWEAR, THE WOMAN HAS FANGS, AND THOSE FANGS ARE FOREVER EXPOSED.
IS IT AUTHORITY SHE RESISTS? OR ***SOMETHING ELSE?***
I HAVE NO IDEA WHAT YOU MEAN.
YOU CAN CONTINUE TO LOOK PAST THE TRUTH IF YOU MUST, BUT EVENTUALLY YOU WILL HAVE TO FACE IT.
IN THE MEANTIME, I AM ASSIGNING THE TWO OF YOU TO QUEEN SHURI. I AM ASSIGNING FOLAMI AND DALIA TO RAMONDA.
INTERESTING CHOICE FOR FOLAMI.
FOLAMI IS TALENTED BUT TROUBLED--AND TROUBLING. I HOPE THAT THROUGH SERVICE TO THE QUEEN'S MOTHER, SHE MIGHT LEARN TO TEMPER THE QUIET RAGE THAT CLOAKS AND COULD SOME DAY CONSUME HER.

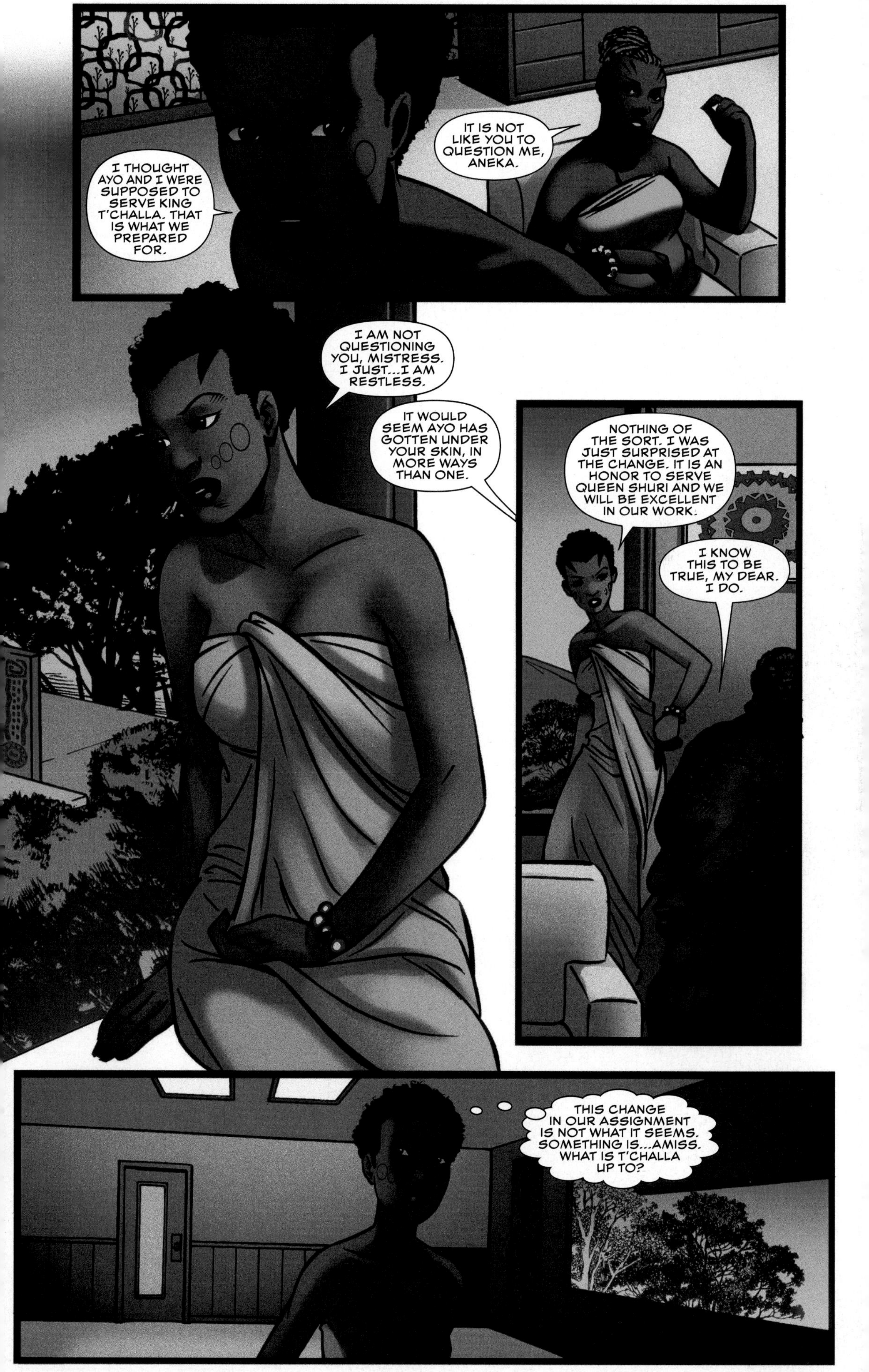
I THOUGHT AYO AND I WERE SUPPOSED TO SERVE KING T'CHALLA. THAT IS WHAT WE PREPARED FOR.
IT IS NOT LIKE YOU TO QUESTION ME, ANEKA.
I AM NOT QUESTIONING YOU, MISTRESS. I JUST...I AM RESTLESS.
IT WOULD SEEM AYO HAS GOTTEN UNDER YOUR SKIN, IN MORE WAYS THAN ONE.
NOTHING OF THE SORT. I WAS JUST SURPRISED AT THE CHANGE. IT IS AN HONOR TO SERVE QUEEN SHURI AND WE WILL BE EXCELLENT IN OUR WORK.
I KNOW THIS TO BE TRUE, MY DEAR. I DO.
THIS CHANGE IN OUR ASSIGNMENT IS NOT WHAT IT SEEMS. SOMETHING IS...AMISS. WHAT IS T'CHALLA UP TO?

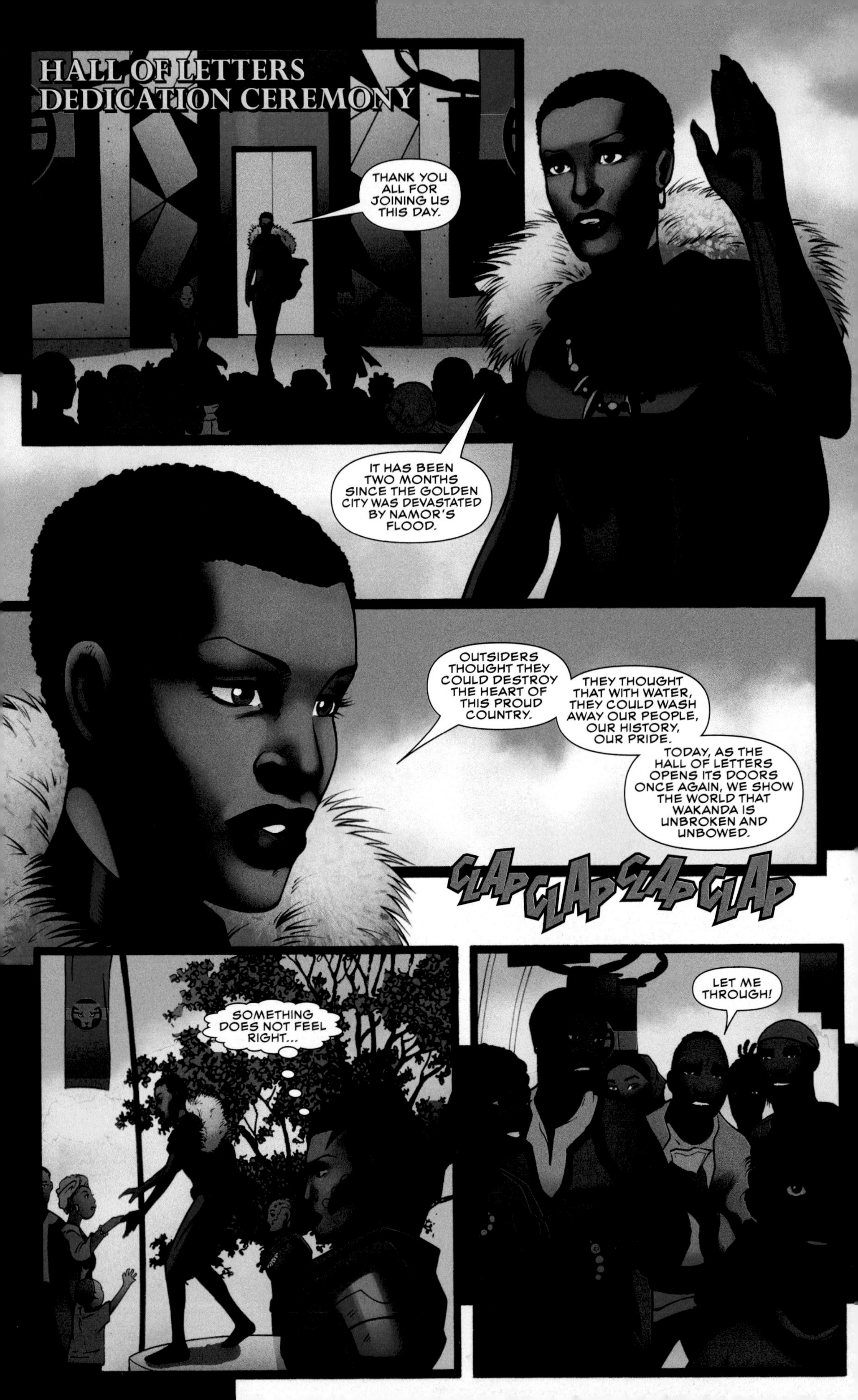
HALL OF LETTERS DEDICATION CEREMONY
THANK YOU ALL FOR JOINING US THIS DAY.
IT HAS BEEN TWO MONTHS SINCE THE GOLDEN CITY WAS DEVASTATED BY NAMOR'S FLOOD.
OUTSIDERS THOUGHT THEY COULD DESTROY THE HEART OF THIS PROUD COUNTRY.
THEY THOUGHT THAT WITH WATER, THEY COULD WASH AWAY OUR PEOPLE, OUR HISTORY, OUR PRIDE.
TODAY, AS THE HALL OF LETTERS OPENS ITS DOORS ONCE AGAIN, WE SHOW THE WORLD THAT WAKANDA IS UNBROKEN AND UNBOWED.
CLAP CLAP CLAP CLAP
SOMETHING DOES NOT FEEL RIGHT...
LET ME THROUGH!

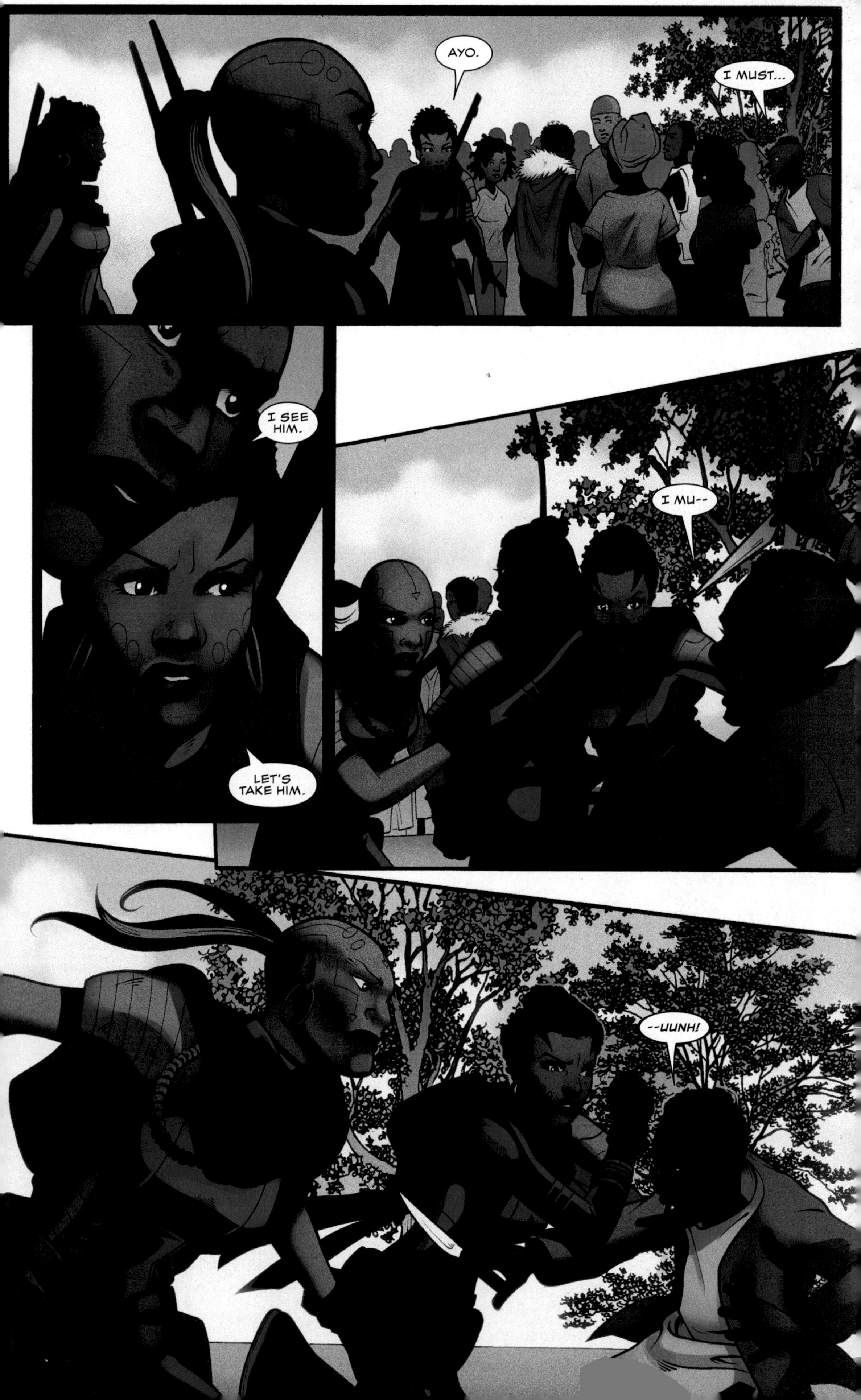
AYO.
I MUST...
I SEE HIM.
LET'S TAKE HIM.
I MU--
--UUNH!

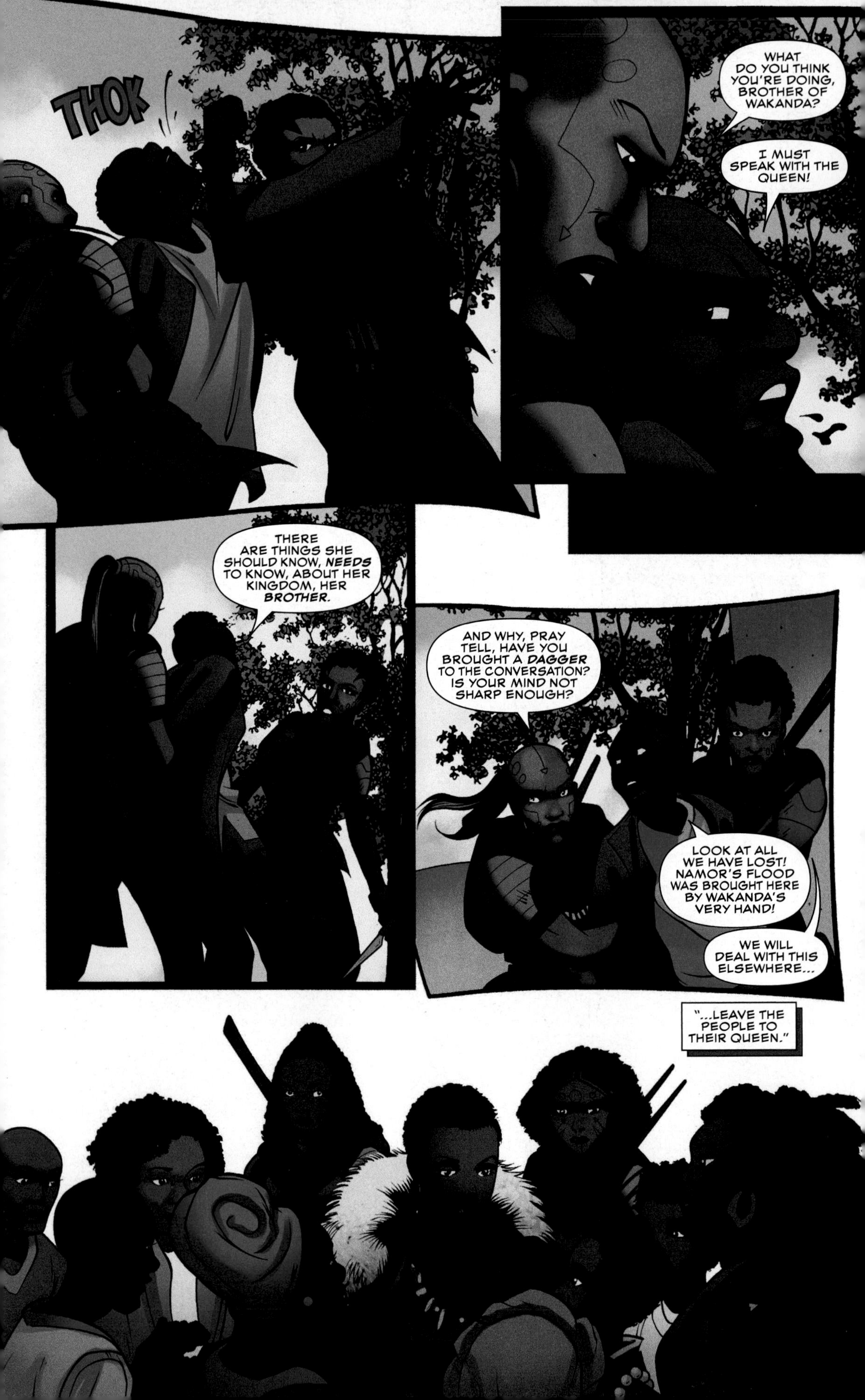
THOK
WHAT DO YOU THINK YOU'RE DOING, BROTHER OF WAKANDA?
I MUST SPEAK WITH THE QUEEN!
THERE ARE THINGS SHE SHOULD KNOW, *NEEDS* TO KNOW, ABOUT HER KINGDOM, HER *BROTHER*.
AND WHY, PRAY TELL, HAVE YOU BROUGHT A *DAGGER* TO THE CONVERSATION? IS YOUR MIND NOT SHARP ENOUGH?
LOOK AT ALL WE HAVE LOST! NAMOR'S FLOOD WAS BROUGHT HERE BY WAKANDA'S VERY HAND!
WE WILL DEAL WITH THIS ELSEWHERE...
"...LEAVE THE PEOPLE TO THEIR QUEEN."

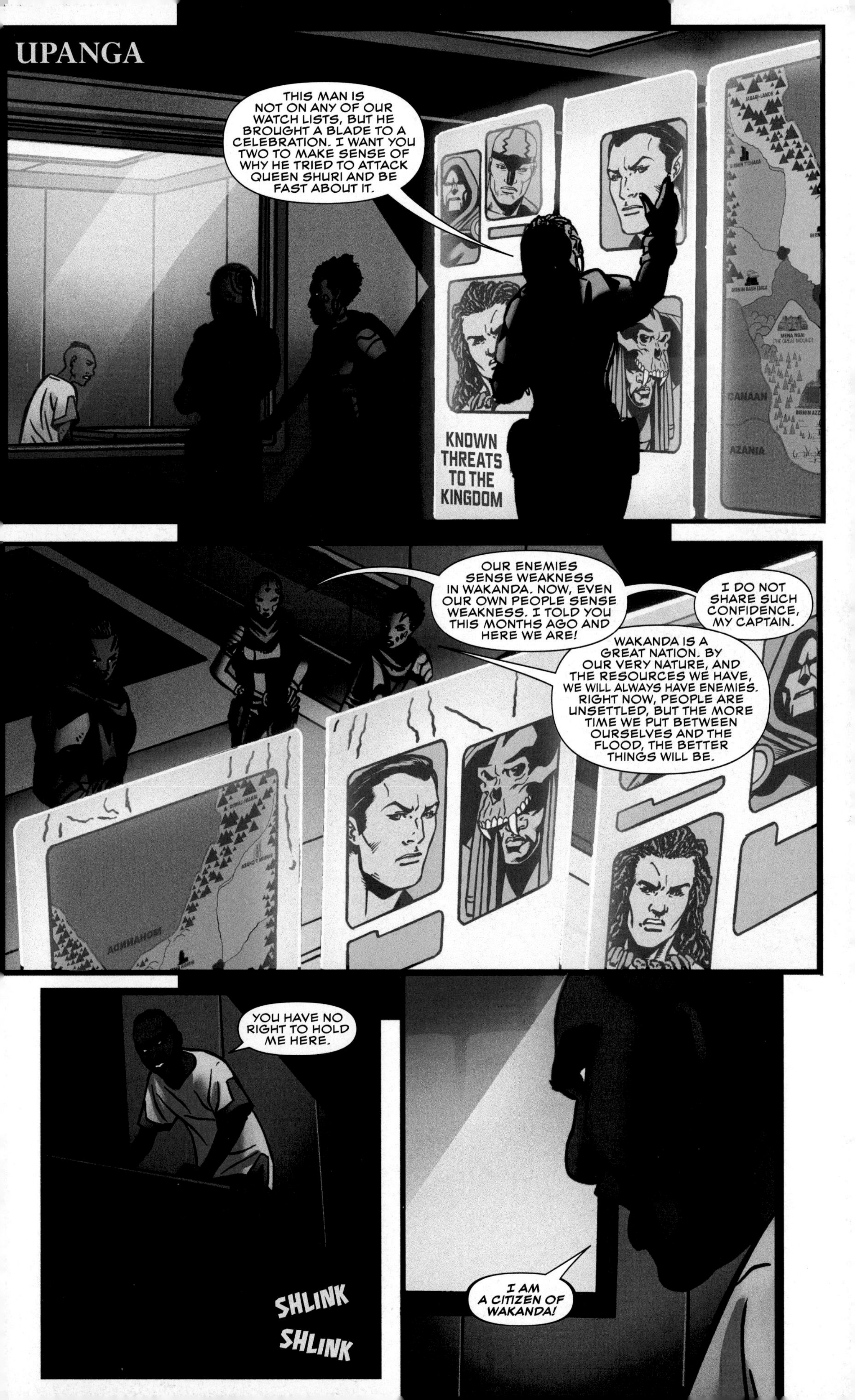

UPANGA
THIS MAN IS NOT ON ANY OF OUR WATCH LISTS, BUT HE BROUGHT A BLADE TO A CELEBRATION. I WANT YOU TWO TO MAKE SENSE OF WHY HE TRIED TO ATTACK QUEEN SHURI AND BE FAST ABOUT IT.
KNOWN THREATS TO THE KINGDOM
CANAAN
AZANIA
OUR ENEMIES SENSE WEAKNESS IN WAKANDA. NOW, EVEN OUR OWN PEOPLE SENSE WEAKNESS. I TOLD YOU THIS MONTHS AGO AND HERE WE ARE!
I DO NOT SHARE SUCH CONFIDENCE, MY CAPTAIN.
WAKANDA IS A GREAT NATION. BY OUR VERY NATURE, AND THE RESOURCES WE HAVE, WE WILL ALWAYS HAVE ENEMIES. RIGHT NOW, PEOPLE ARE UNSETTLED, BUT THE MORE TIME WE PUT BETWEEN OURSELVES AND THE FLOOD, THE BETTER THINGS WILL BE.
YOU HAVE NO RIGHT TO HOLD ME HERE.
SHLINK
SHLINK
I AM A CITIZEN OF WAKANDA!

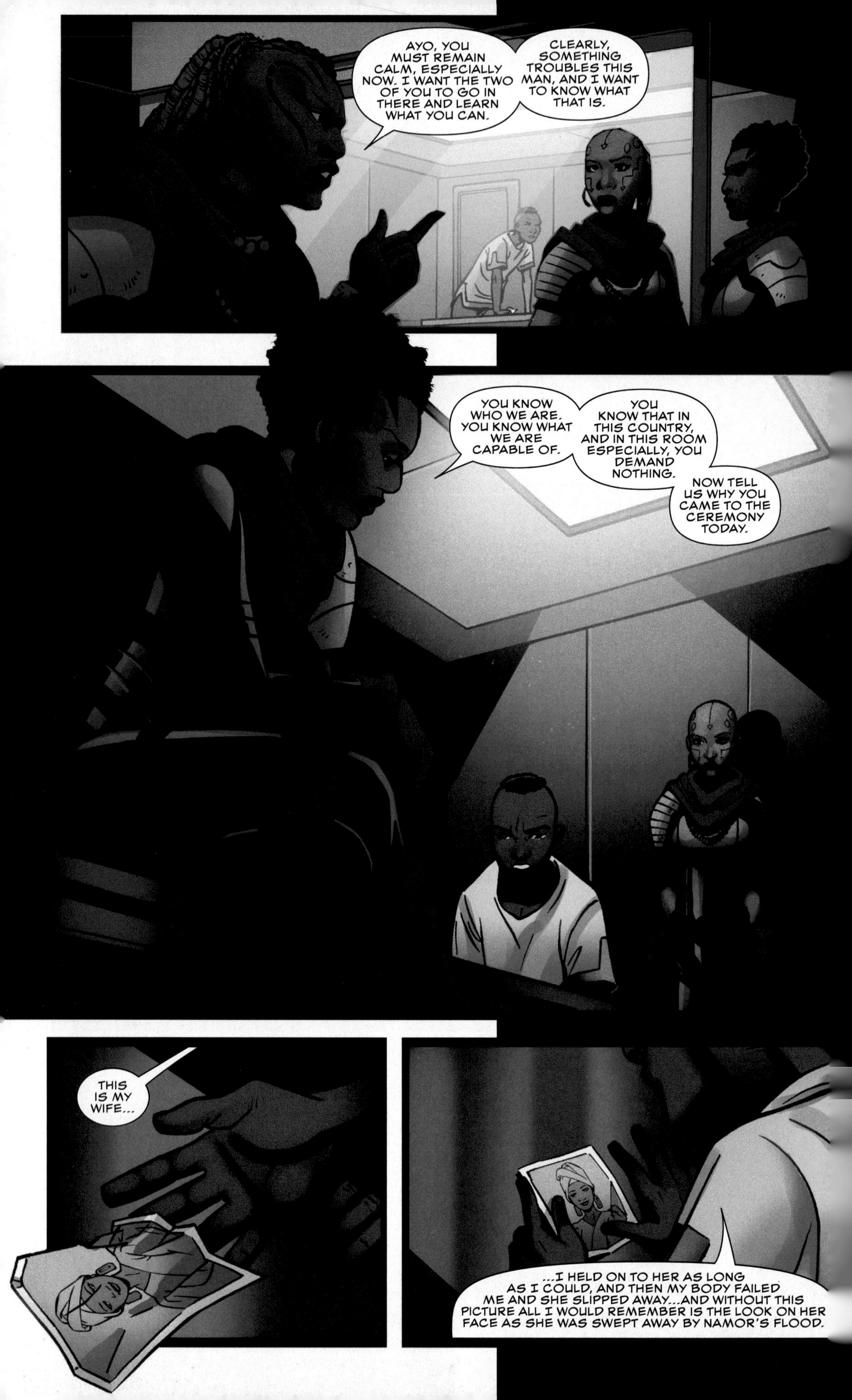
AYO, YOU MUST REMAIN CALM, ESPECIALLY NOW. I WANT THE TWO OF YOU TO GO IN THERE AND LEARN WHAT YOU CAN.
CLEARLY, SOMETHING TROUBLES THIS MAN, AND I WANT TO KNOW WHAT THAT IS.
YOU KNOW WHO WE ARE. YOU KNOW WHAT WE ARE CAPABLE OF.
YOU KNOW THAT IN THIS COUNTRY, AND IN THIS ROOM ESPECIALLY, YOU DEMAND NOTHING.
NOW TELL US WHY YOU CAME TO THE CEREMONY TODAY.
THIS IS MY WIFE...
...I HELD ON TO HER AS LONG AS I COULD, AND THEN MY BODY FAILED ME AND SHE SLIPPED AWAY...AND WITHOUT THIS PICTURE ALL I WOULD REMEMBER IS THE LOOK ON HER FACE AS SHE WAS SWEPT AWAY BY NAMOR'S FLOOD.

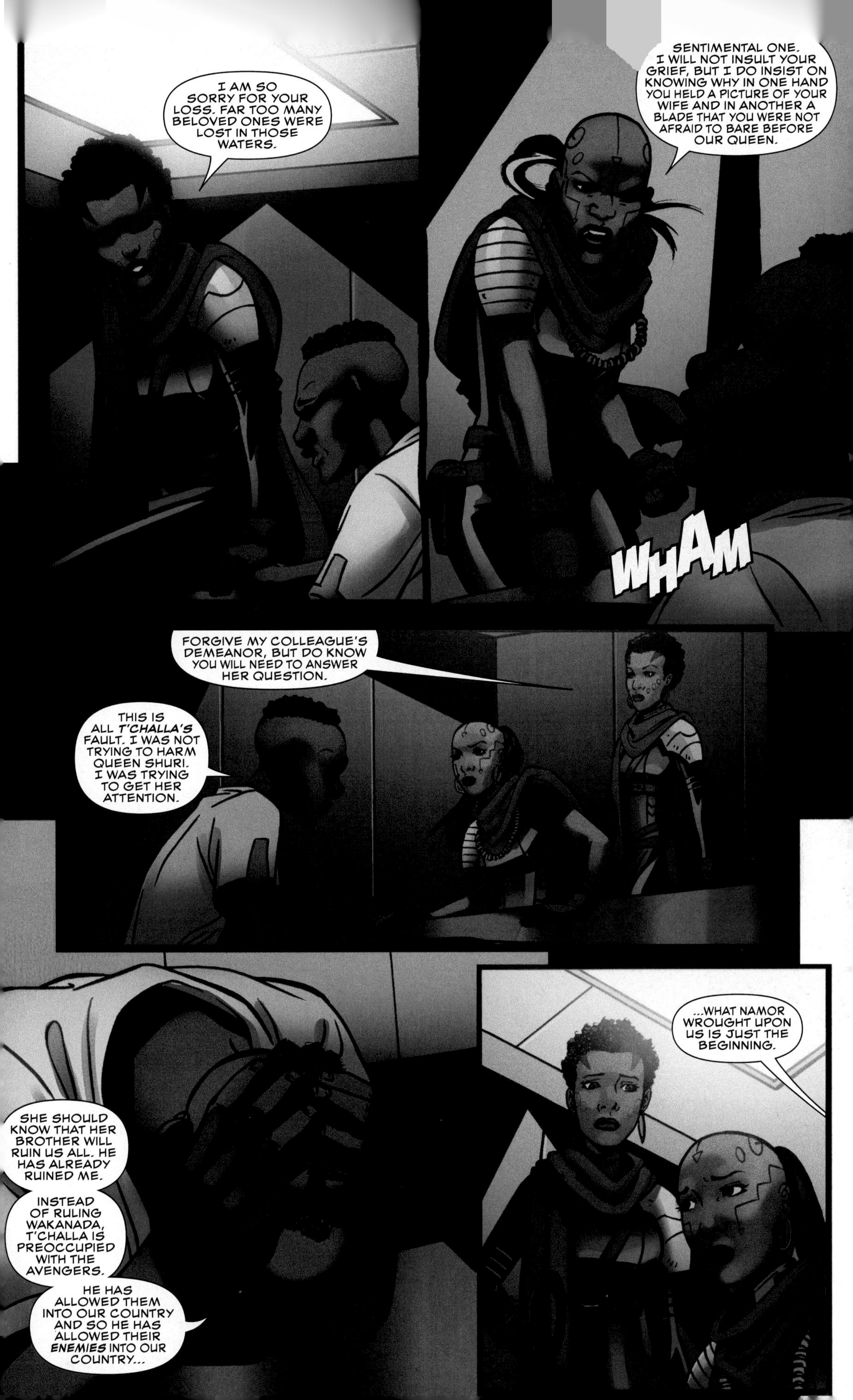
I AM SO SORRY FOR YOUR LOSS. FAR TOO MANY BELOVED ONES WERE LOST IN THOSE WATERS.
SENTIMENTAL ONE. I WILL NOT INSULT YOUR GRIEF, BUT I DO INSIST ON KNOWING WHY IN ONE HAND YOU HELD A PICTURE OF YOUR WIFE AND IN ANOTHER A BLADE THAT YOU WERE NOT AFRAID TO BARE BEFORE OUR QUEEN.
WHAM
FORGIVE MY COLLEAGUE'S DEMEANOR, BUT DO KNOW YOU WILL NEED TO ANSWER HER QUESTION.
THIS IS ALL *T'CHALLA'S* FAULT. I WAS NOT TRYING TO HARM QUEEN SHURI. I WAS TRYING TO GET HER ATTENTION.
SHE SHOULD KNOW THAT HER BROTHER WILL RUIN US ALL. HE HAS ALREADY RUINED ME.
INSTEAD OF RULING WAKANADA, T'CHALLA IS PREOCCUPIED WITH THE AVENGERS.
HE HAS ALLOWED THEM INTO OUR COUNTRY AND SO HE HAS ALLOWED THEIR *ENEMIES* INTO OUR COUNTRY...
...WHAT NAMOR WROUGHT UPON US IS JUST THE BEGINNING.

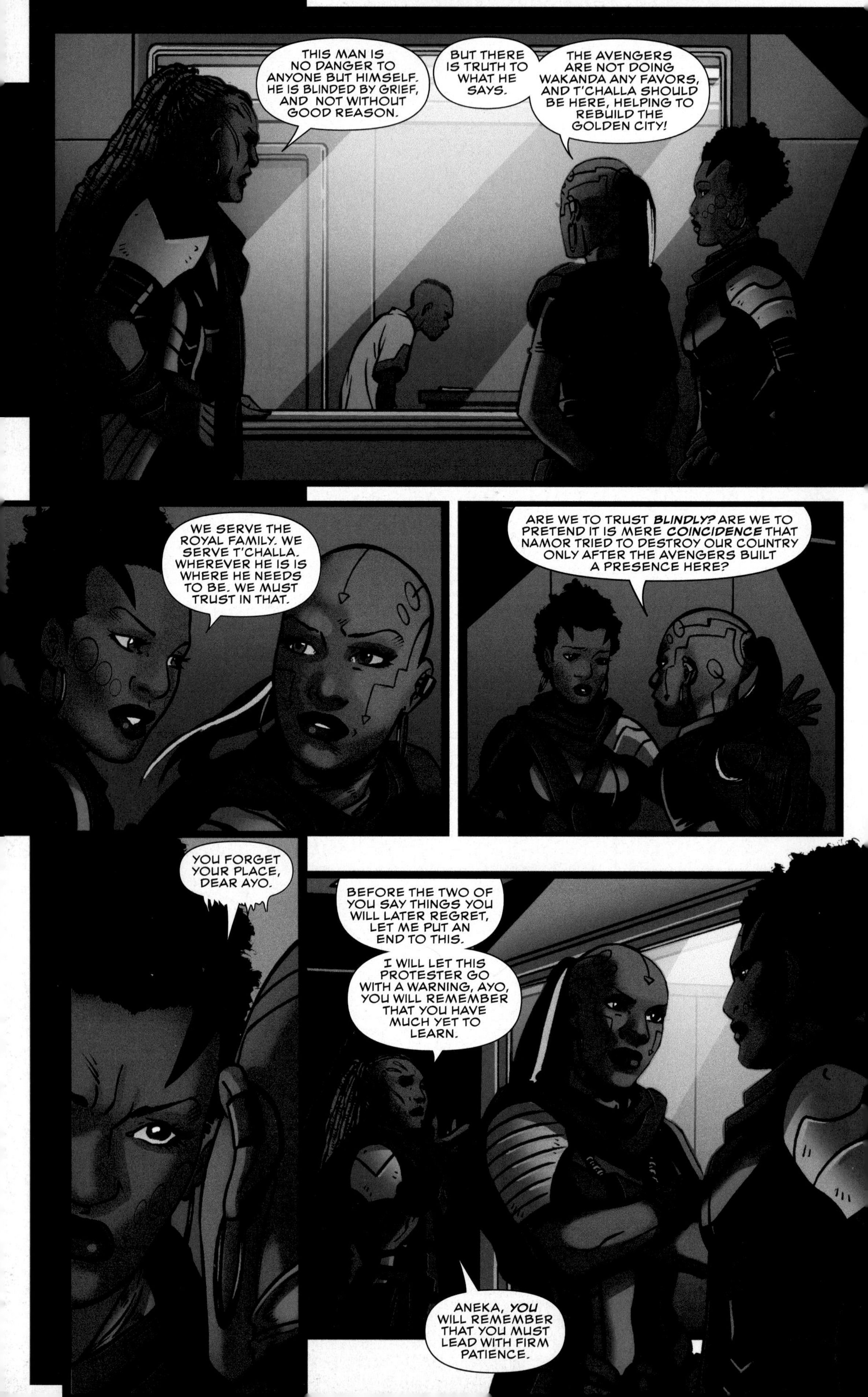
THIS MAN IS NO DANGER TO ANYONE BUT HIMSELF. HE IS BLINDED BY GRIEF, AND NOT WITHOUT GOOD REASON.
BUT THERE IS TRUTH TO WHAT HE SAYS.
THE AVENGERS ARE NOT DOING WAKANDA ANY FAVORS, AND T'CHALLA SHOULD BE HERE, HELPING TO REBUILD THE GOLDEN CITY!
WE SERVE THE ROYAL FAMILY. WE SERVE T'CHALLA. WHEREVER HE IS IS WHERE HE NEEDS TO BE. WE MUST TRUST IN THAT.
ARE WE TO TRUST *BLINDLY?* ARE WE TO PRETEND IT IS MERE *COINCIDENCE* THAT NAMOR TRIED TO DESTROY OUR COUNTRY ONLY AFTER THE AVENGERS BUILT A PRESENCE HERE?
YOU FORGET YOUR PLACE, DEAR AYO.
BEFORE THE TWO OF YOU SAY THINGS YOU WILL LATER REGRET, LET ME PUT AN END TO THIS.
I WILL LET THIS PROTESTER GO WITH A WARNING, AYO, YOU WILL REMEMBER THAT YOU HAVE MUCH YET TO LEARN.
ANEKA, *YOU* WILL REMEMBER THAT YOU MUST LEAD WITH FIRM PATIENCE.

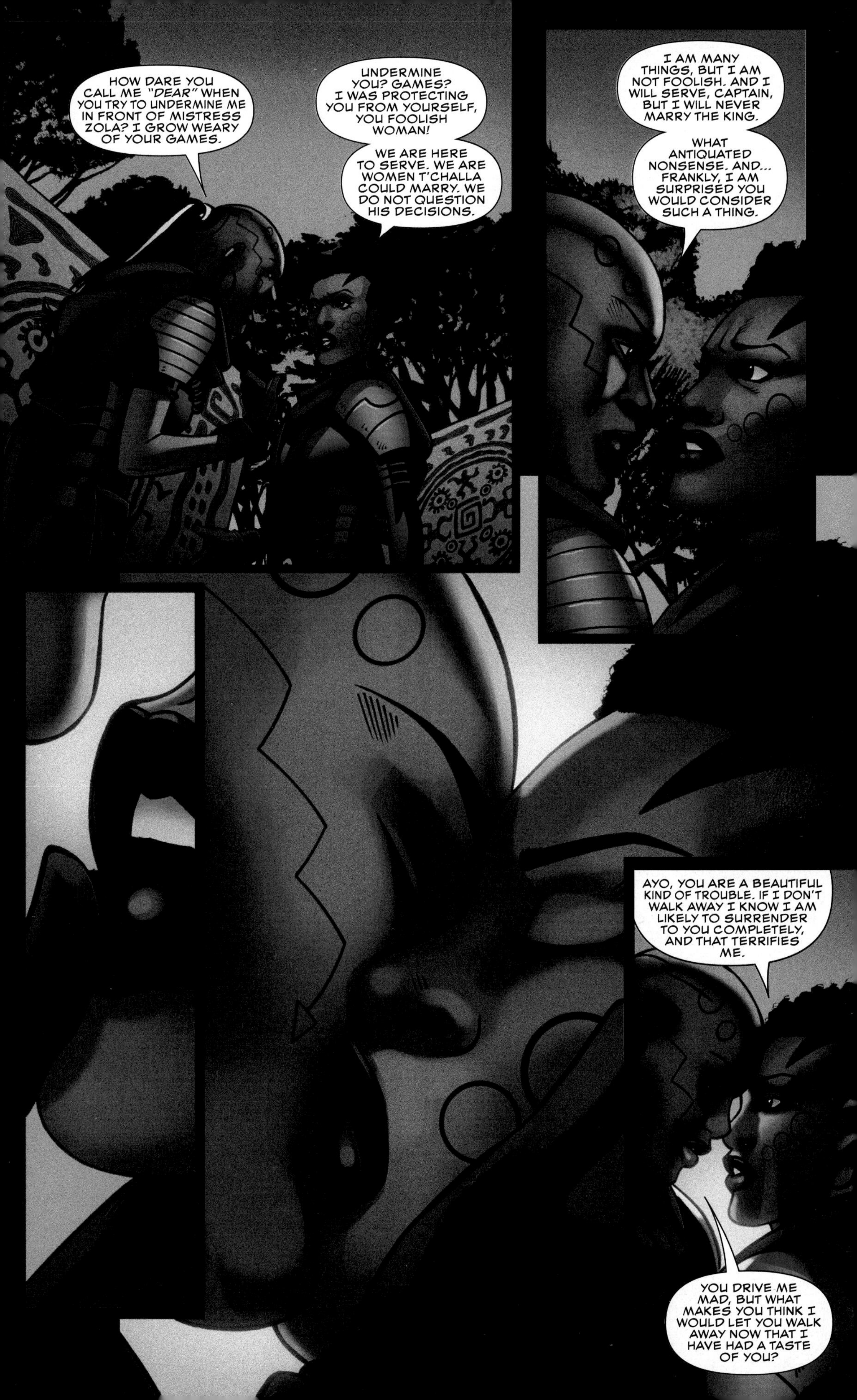
HOW DARE YOU CALL ME "DEAR" WHEN YOU TRY TO UNDERMINE ME IN FRONT OF MISTRESS ZOLA? I GROW WEARY OF YOUR GAMES.
UNDERMINE YOU? GAMES? I WAS PROTECTING YOU FROM YOURSELF, YOU FOOLISH WOMAN!
WE ARE HERE TO SERVE. WE ARE WOMEN T'CHALLA COULD MARRY. WE DO NOT QUESTION HIS DECISIONS.
I AM MANY THINGS, BUT I AM NOT FOOLISH. AND I WILL SERVE, CAPTAIN, BUT I WILL NEVER MARRY THE KING.
WHAT ANTIQUATED NONSENSE. AND... FRANKLY, I AM SURPRISED YOU WOULD CONSIDER SUCH A THING.
AYO, YOU ARE A BEAUTIFUL KIND OF TROUBLE. IF I DON'T WALK AWAY I KNOW I AM LIKELY TO SURRENDER TO YOU COMPLETELY, AND THAT TERRIFIES ME.
YOU DRIVE ME MAD, BUT WHAT MAKES YOU THINK I WOULD LET YOU WALK AWAY NOW THAT I HAVE HAD A TASTE OF YOU?

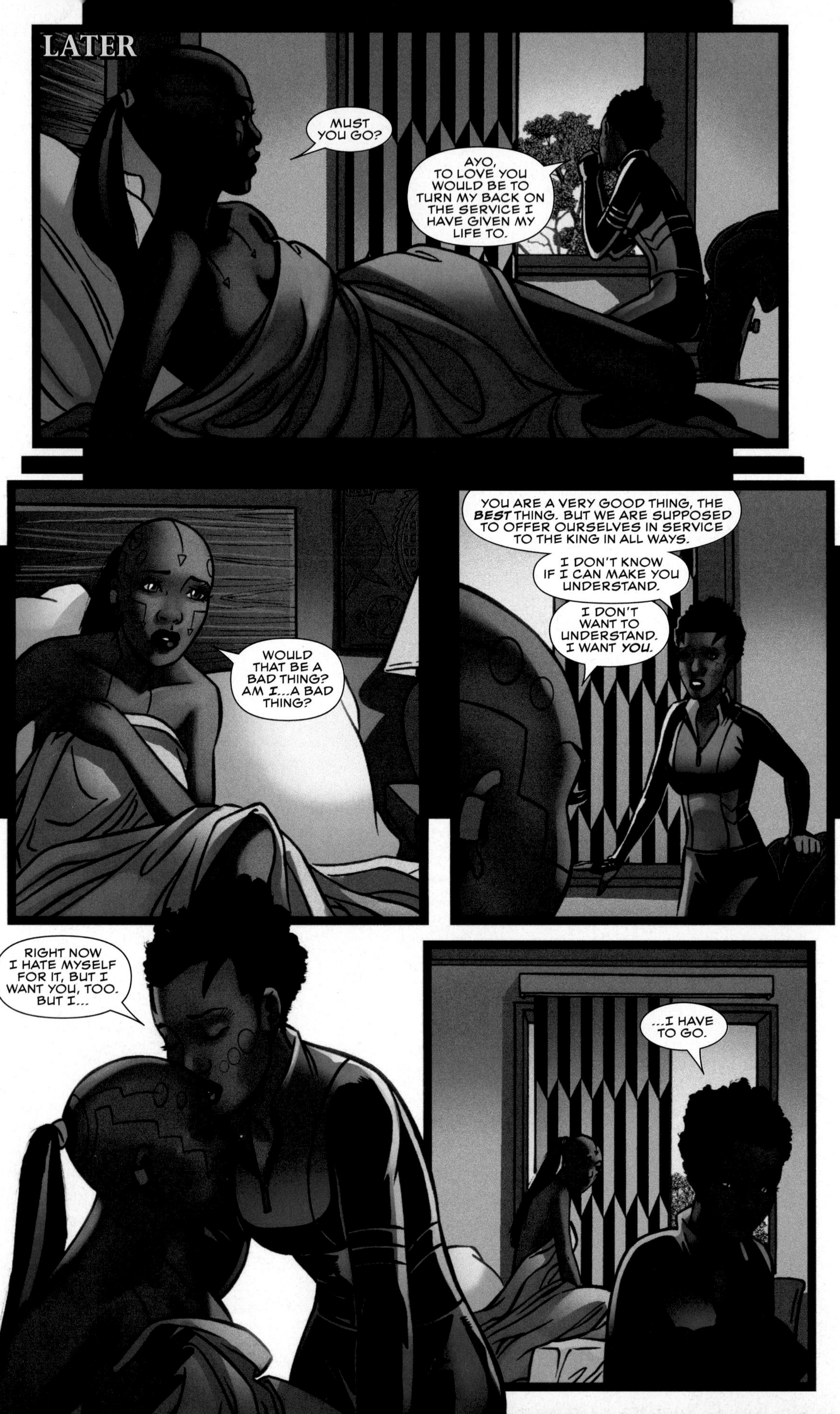
LATER
MUST YOU GO?
AYO, TO LOVE YOU WOULD BE TO TURN MY BACK ON THE SERVICE I HAVE GIVEN MY LIFE TO.
WOULD THAT BE A BAD THING? AM *I*...A BAD THING?
YOU ARE A VERY GOOD THING, THE *BEST* THING. BUT WE ARE SUPPOSED TO OFFER OURSELVES IN SERVICE TO THE KING IN ALL WAYS.
I DON'T KNOW IF I CAN MAKE YOU UNDERSTAND.
I DON'T WANT TO UNDERSTAND. I WANT *YOU*.
RIGHT NOW I HATE MYSELF FOR IT, BUT I WANT YOU, TOO. BUT I...
...I HAVE TO GO.

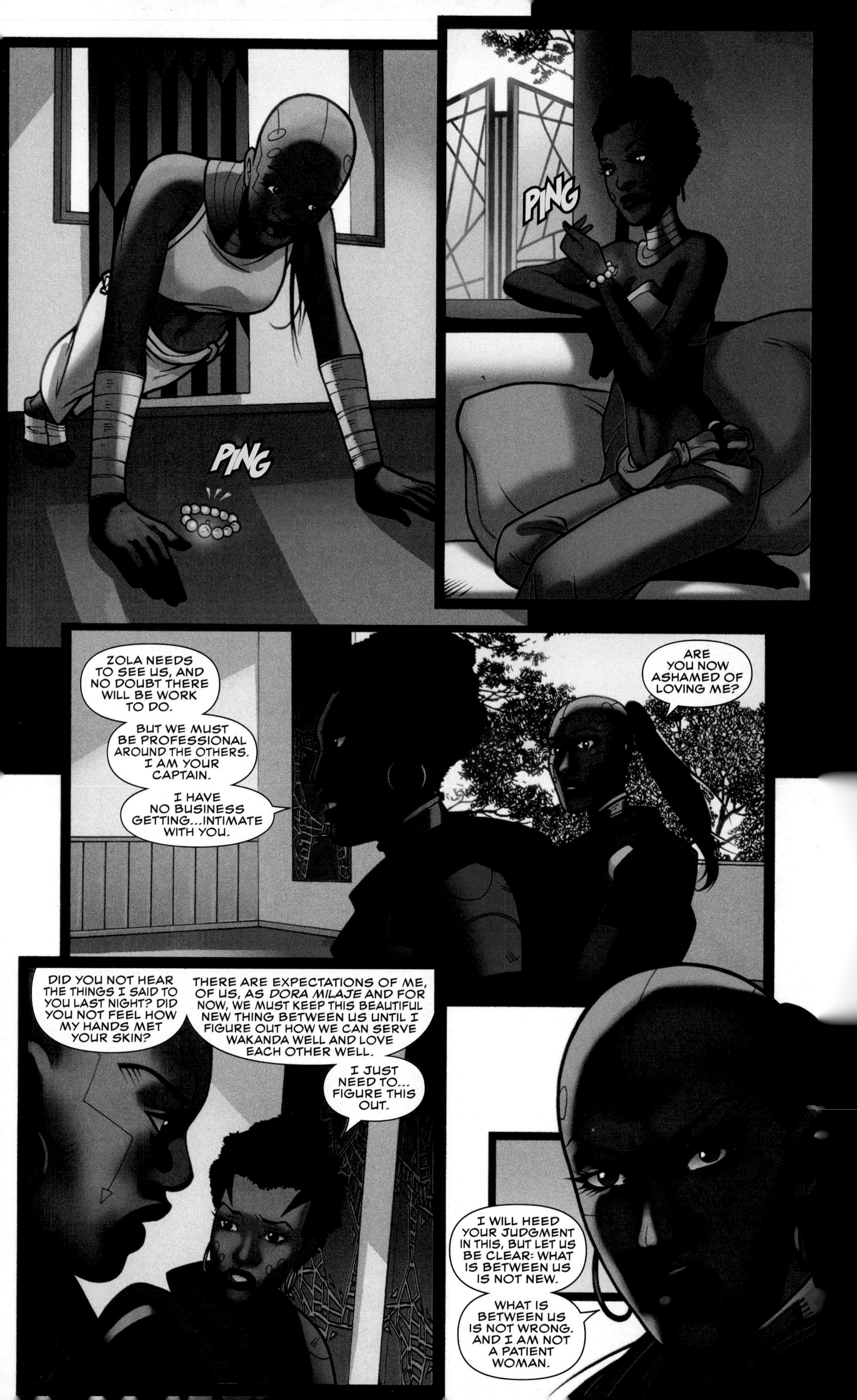
PING
PING
ZOLA NEEDS TO SEE US, AND NO DOUBT THERE WILL BE WORK TO DO.
BUT WE MUST BE PROFESSIONAL AROUND THE OTHERS. I AM YOUR CAPTAIN.
I HAVE NO BUSINESS GETTING...INTIMATE WITH YOU.
ARE YOU NOW ASHAMED OF LOVING ME?
DID YOU NOT HEAR THE THINGS I SAID TO YOU LAST NIGHT? DID YOU NOT FEEL HOW MY HANDS MET YOUR SKIN?
THERE ARE EXPECTATIONS OF ME, OF US, AS *DORA MILAJE* AND FOR NOW, WE MUST KEEP THIS BEAUTIFUL NEW THING BETWEEN US UNTIL I FIGURE OUT HOW WE CAN SERVE WAKANDA WELL AND LOVE EACH OTHER WELL.
I JUST NEED TO... FIGURE THIS OUT.
I WILL HEED YOUR JUDGMENT IN THIS, BUT LET US BE CLEAR: WHAT IS BETWEEN US IS NOT NEW.
WHAT IS BETWEEN US IS NOT WRONG. AND I AM NOT A PATIENT WOMAN.

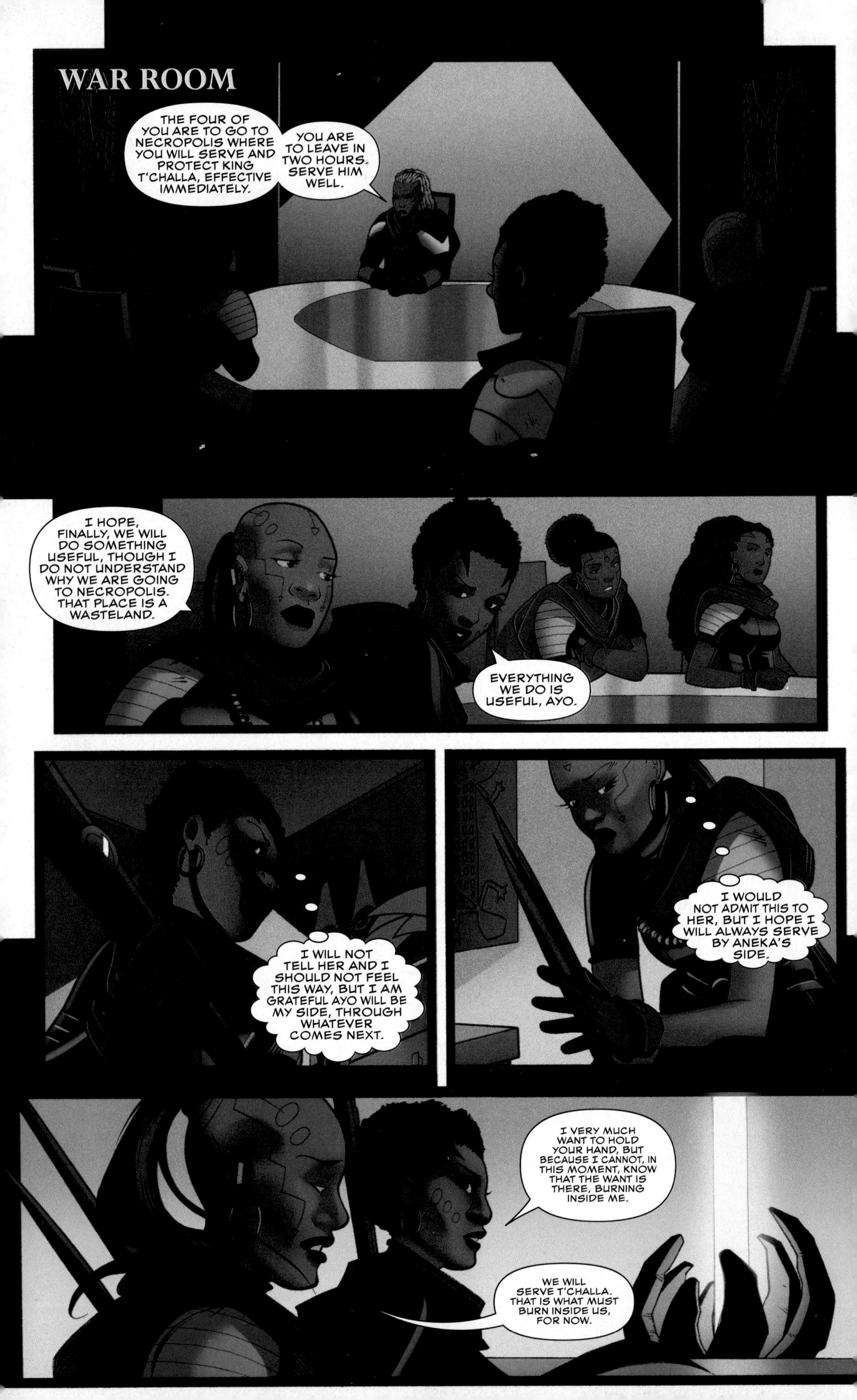
WAR ROOM
THE FOUR OF YOU ARE TO GO TO NECROPOLIS WHERE YOU WILL SERVE AND PROTECT KING T'CHALLA, EFFECTIVE IMMEDIATELY.
YOU ARE TO LEAVE IN TWO HOURS. SERVE HIM WELL.
I HOPE, FINALLY, WE WILL DO SOMETHING USEFUL, THOUGH I DO NOT UNDERSTAND WHY WE ARE GOING TO NECROPOLIS. THAT PLACE IS A WASTELAND.
EVERYTHING WE DO IS USEFUL, AYO.
I WILL NOT TELL HER AND I SHOULD NOT FEEL THIS WAY, BUT I AM GRATEFUL AYO WILL BE MY SIDE, THROUGH WHATEVER COMES NEXT.
I WOULD NOT ADMIT THIS TO HER, BUT I HOPE I WILL ALWAYS SERVE BY ANEKA'S SIDE.
I VERY MUCH WANT TO HOLD YOUR HAND, BUT BECAUSE I CANNOT, IN THIS MOMENT, KNOW THE WANT IS THERE, BURNING INSIDE ME.
WE WILL SERVE T'CHALLA. THAT IS WHAT MUST BURN INSIDE US, FOR NOW.

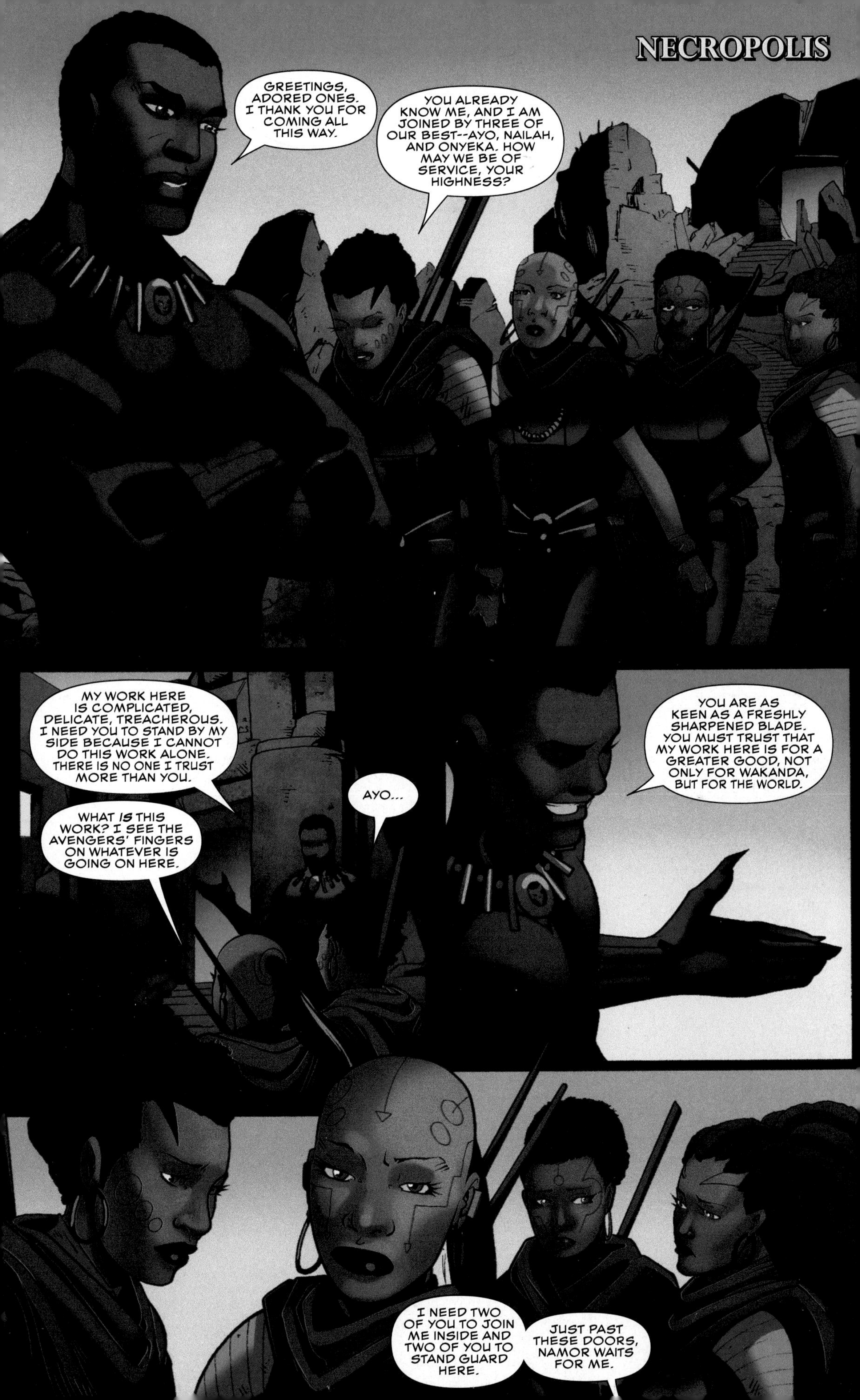
NECROPOLIS
GREETINGS, ADORED ONES. I THANK YOU FOR COMING ALL THIS WAY.
YOU ALREADY KNOW ME, AND I AM JOINED BY THREE OF OUR BEST--AYO, NAILAH, AND ONYEKA. HOW MAY WE BE OF SERVICE, YOUR HIGHNESS?
MY WORK HERE IS COMPLICATED, DELICATE, TREACHEROUS. I NEED YOU TO STAND BY MY SIDE BECAUSE I CANNOT DO THIS WORK ALONE. THERE IS NO ONE I TRUST MORE THAN YOU.
WHAT IS THIS WORK? I SEE THE AVENGERS' FINGERS ON WHATEVER IS GOING ON HERE.
AYO...
YOU ARE AS KEEN AS A FRESHLY SHARPENED BLADE. YOU MUST TRUST THAT MY WORK HERE IS FOR A GREATER GOOD, NOT ONLY FOR WAKANDA, BUT FOR THE WORLD.
I NEED TWO OF YOU TO JOIN ME INSIDE AND TWO OF YOU TO STAND GUARD HERE.
JUST PAST THESE DOORS, NAMOR WAITS FOR ME.

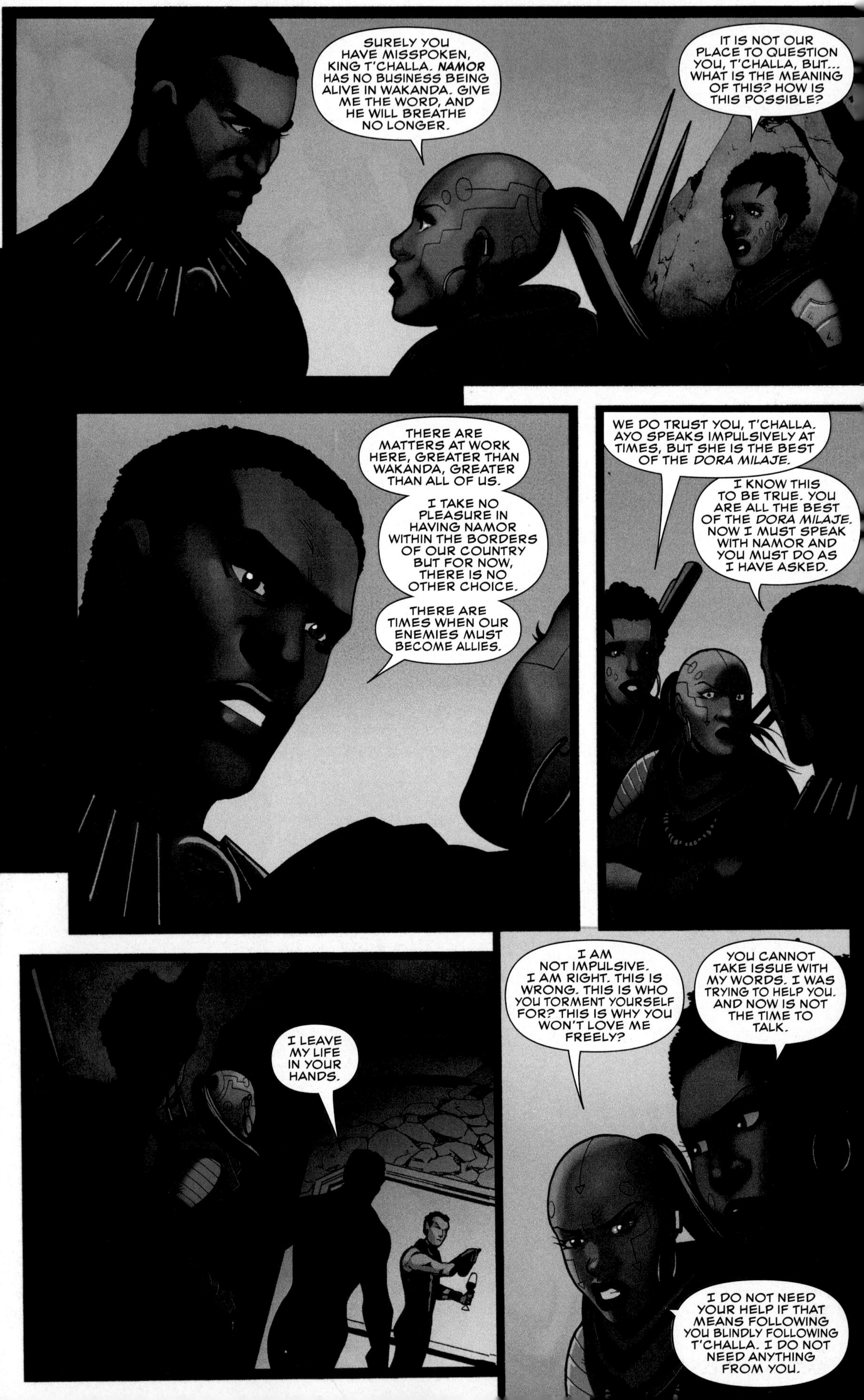
SURELY YOU HAVE MISSPOKEN, KING T'CHALLA. NAMOR HAS NO BUSINESS BEING ALIVE IN WAKANDA. GIVE ME THE WORD, AND HE WILL BREATHE NO LONGER.
IT IS NOT OUR PLACE TO QUESTION YOU, T'CHALLA, BUT... WHAT IS THE MEANING OF THIS? HOW IS THIS POSSIBLE?
THERE ARE MATTERS AT WORK HERE, GREATER THAN WAKANDA, GREATER THAN ALL OF US.
I TAKE NO PLEASURE IN HAVING NAMOR WITHIN THE BORDERS OF OUR COUNTRY BUT FOR NOW, THERE IS NO OTHER CHOICE.
THERE ARE TIMES WHEN OUR ENEMIES MUST BECOME ALLIES.
WE DO TRUST YOU, T'CHALLA. AYO SPEAKS IMPULSIVELY AT TIMES, BUT SHE IS THE BEST OF THE DORA MILAJE.
I KNOW THIS TO BE TRUE. YOU ARE ALL THE BEST OF THE DORA MILAJE. NOW I MUST SPEAK WITH NAMOR AND YOU MUST DO AS I HAVE ASKED.
I LEAVE MY LIFE IN YOUR HANDS.
I AM NOT IMPULSIVE. I AM RIGHT. THIS IS WRONG. THIS IS WHO YOU TORMENT YOURSELF FOR? THIS IS WHY YOU WON'T LOVE ME FREELY?
YOU CANNOT TAKE ISSUE WITH MY WORDS. I WAS TRYING TO HELP YOU. AND NOW IS NOT THE TIME TO TALK.
I DO NOT NEED YOUR HELP IF THAT MEANS FOLLOWING YOU BLINDLY FOLLOWING T'CHALLA. I DO NOT NEED ANYTHING FROM YOU.

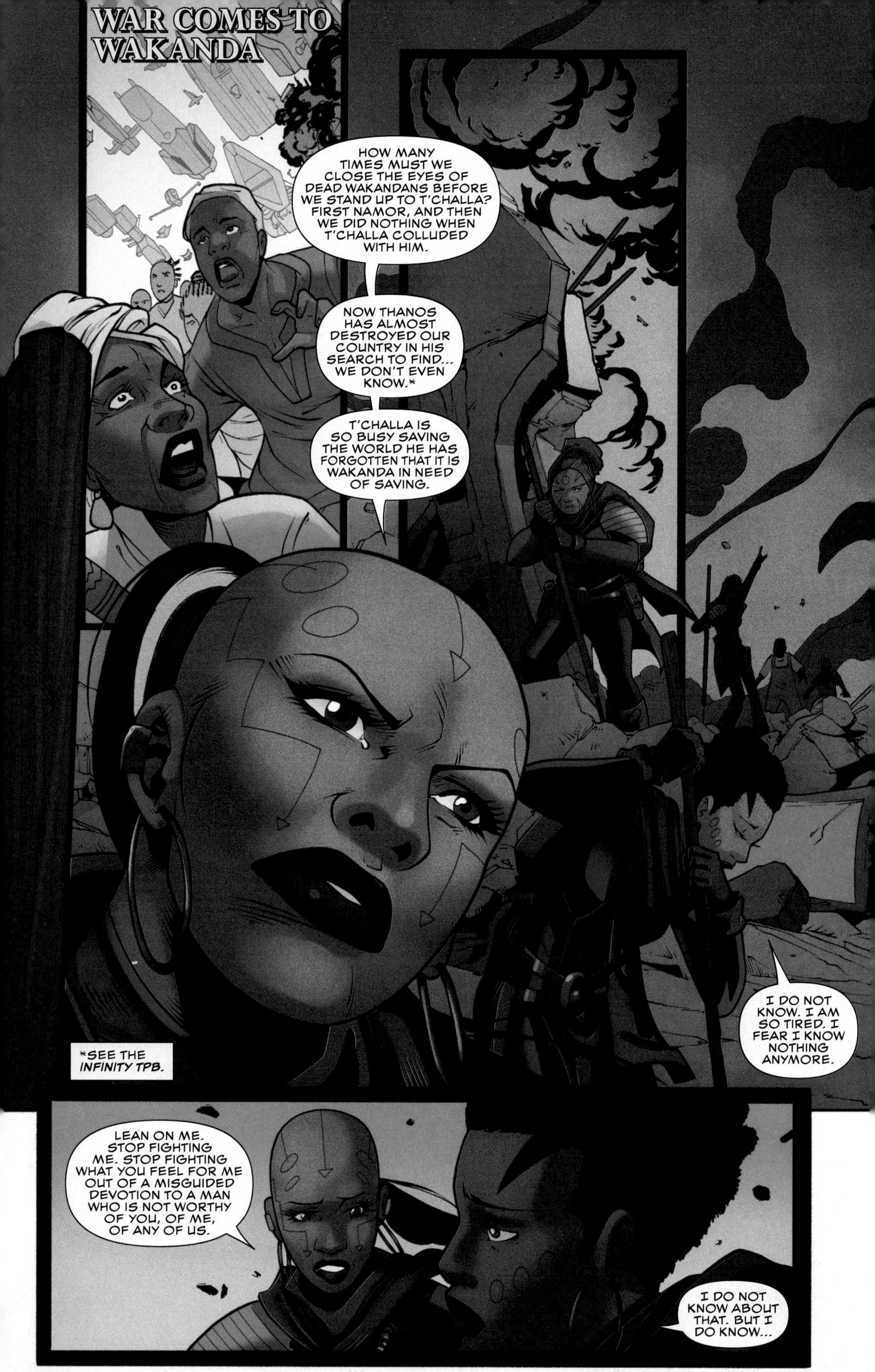
WAR COMES TO WAKANDA
HOW MANY TIMES MUST WE CLOSE THE EYES OF DEAD WAKANDANS BEFORE WE STAND UP TO T'CHALLA? FIRST NAMOR, AND THEN WE DID NOTHING WHEN T'CHALLA COLLUDED WITH HIM.
NOW THANOS HAS ALMOST DESTROYED OUR COUNTRY IN HIS SEARCH TO FIND... WE DON'T EVEN KNOW.*
T'CHALLA IS SO BUSY SAVING THE WORLD HE HAS FORGOTTEN THAT IT IS WAKANDA IN NEED OF SAVING.
*SEE THE *INFINITY TPB.*
I DO NOT KNOW. I AM SO TIRED. I FEAR I KNOW NOTHING ANYMORE.
LEAN ON ME. STOP FIGHTING ME. STOP FIGHTING WHAT YOU FEEL FOR ME OUT OF A MISGUIDED DEVOTION TO A MAN WHO IS NOT WORTHY OF YOU, OF ME, OF ANY OF US.
I DO NOT KNOW ABOUT THAT. BUT I DO KNOW...

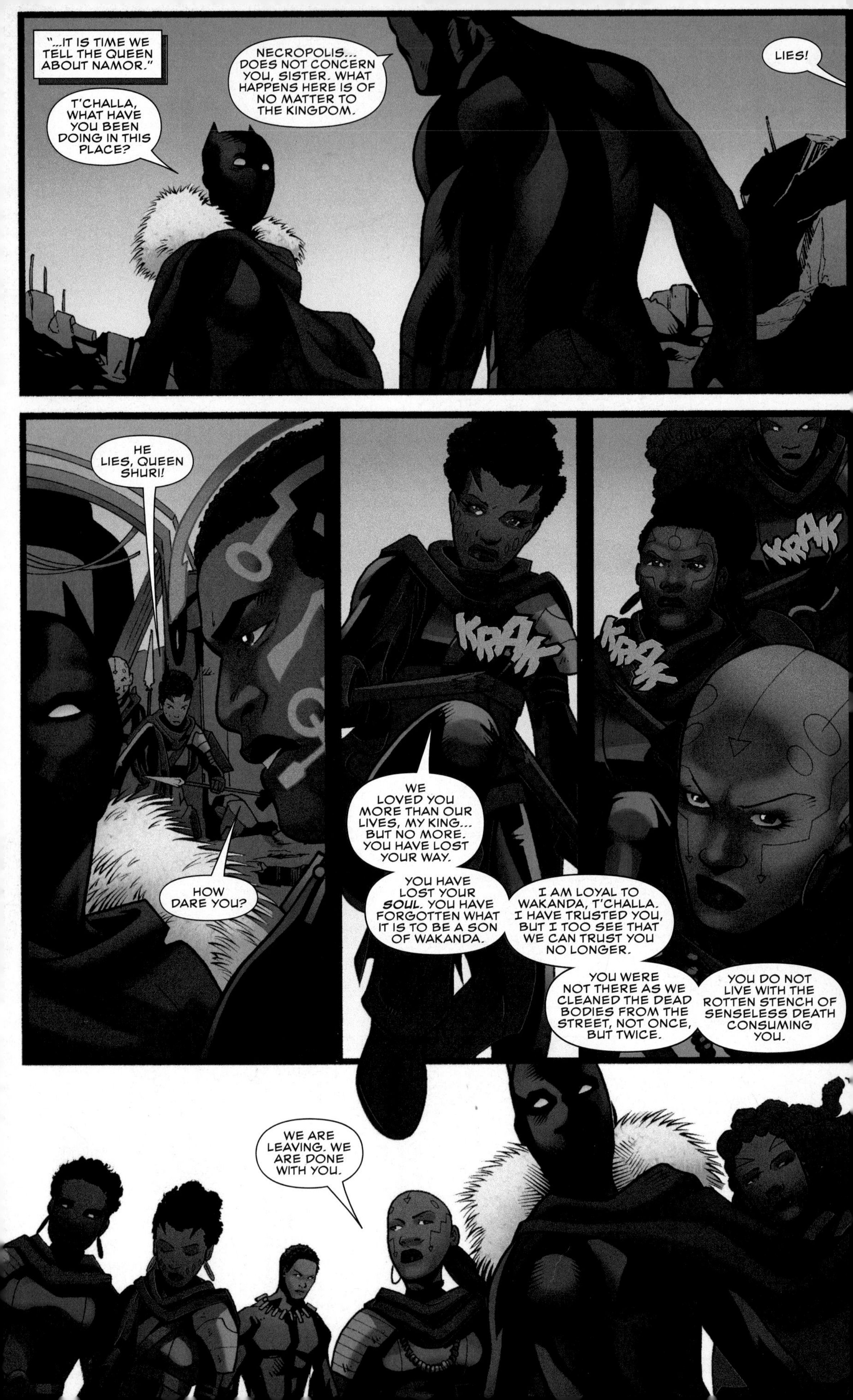
"...IT IS TIME WE TELL THE QUEEN ABOUT NAMOR."
T'CHALLA, WHAT HAVE YOU BEEN DOING IN THIS PLACE?
NECROPOLIS... DOES NOT CONCERN YOU, SISTER. WHAT HAPPENS HERE IS OF NO MATTER TO THE KINGDOM.
LIES!
HE LIES, QUEEN SHURI!
HOW DARE YOU?
KRAK
WE LOVED YOU MORE THAN OUR LIVES, MY KING... BUT NO MORE. YOU HAVE LOST YOUR WAY.
YOU HAVE LOST YOUR *SOUL*. YOU HAVE FORGOTTEN WHAT IT IS TO BE A SON OF WAKANDA.
KRAK
KRAK
I AM LOYAL TO WAKANDA, T'CHALLA. I HAVE TRUSTED YOU, BUT I TOO SEE THAT WE CAN TRUST YOU NO LONGER.
YOU WERE NOT THERE AS WE CLEANED THE DEAD BODIES FROM THE STREET, NOT ONCE, BUT TWICE.
YOU DO NOT LIVE WITH THE ROTTEN STENCH OF SENSELESS DEATH CONSUMING YOU.
WE ARE LEAVING. WE ARE DONE WITH YOU.

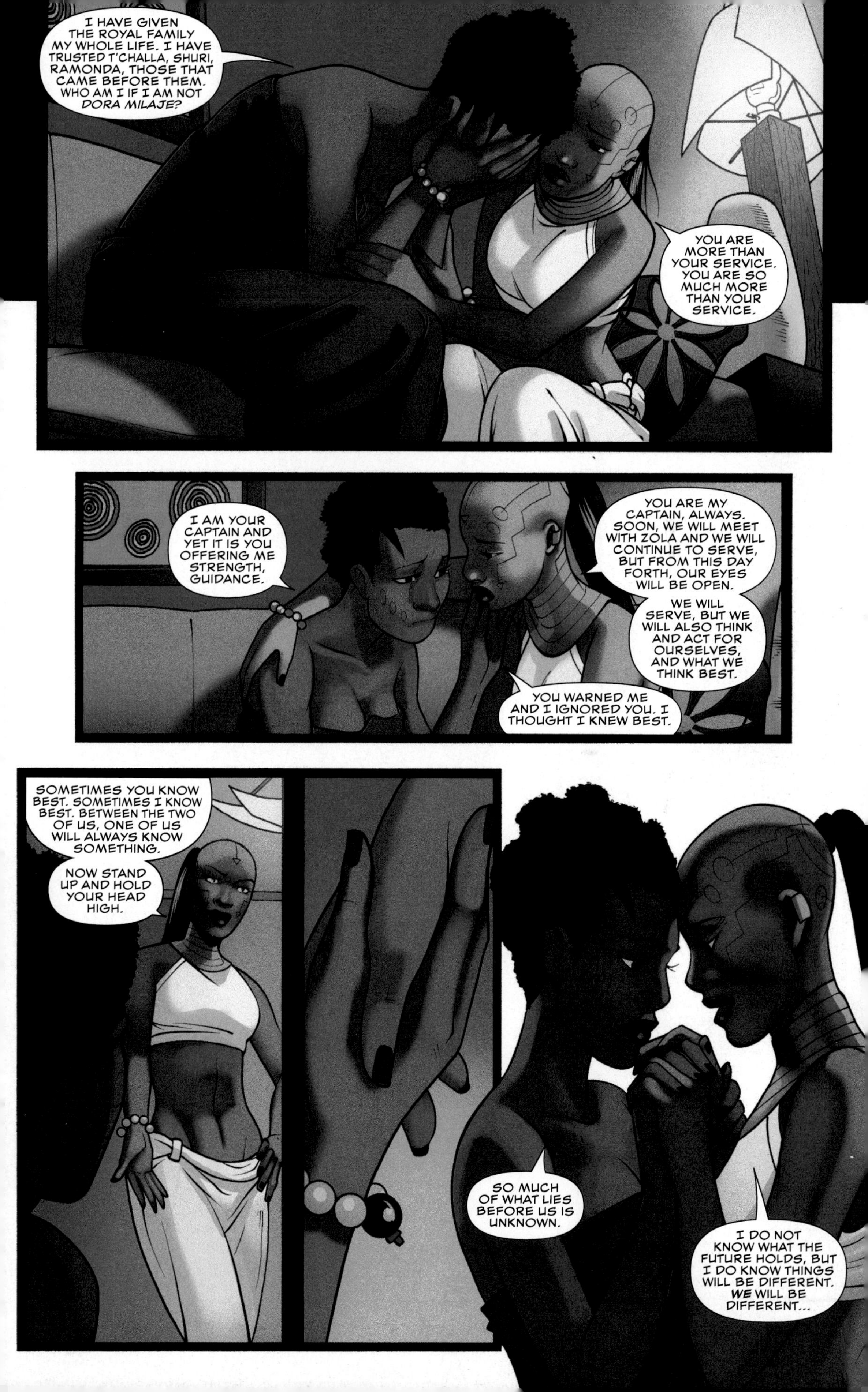
I HAVE GIVEN THE ROYAL FAMILY MY WHOLE LIFE. I HAVE TRUSTED T'CHALLA, SHURI, RAMONDA, THOSE THAT CAME BEFORE THEM. WHO AM I IF I AM NOT *DORA MILAJE?*
YOU ARE MORE THAN YOUR SERVICE. YOU ARE SO MUCH MORE THAN YOUR SERVICE.
I AM YOUR CAPTAIN AND YET IT IS YOU OFFERING ME STRENGTH, GUIDANCE.
YOU ARE MY CAPTAIN, ALWAYS. SOON, WE WILL MEET WITH ZOLA AND WE WILL CONTINUE TO SERVE, BUT FROM THIS DAY FORTH, OUR EYES WILL BE OPEN.
WE WILL SERVE, BUT WE WILL ALSO THINK AND ACT FOR OURSELVES, AND WHAT WE THINK BEST.
YOU WARNED ME AND I IGNORED YOU. I THOUGHT I KNEW BEST.
SOMETIMES YOU KNOW BEST. SOMETIMES I KNOW BEST. BETWEEN THE TWO OF US, ONE OF US WILL ALWAYS KNOW SOMETHING.
NOW STAND UP AND HOLD YOUR HEAD HIGH.
SO MUCH OF WHAT LIES BEFORE US IS UNKNOWN.
I DO NOT KNOW WHAT THE FUTURE HOLDS, BUT I DO KNOW THINGS WILL BE DIFFERENT. *WE* WILL BE DIFFERENT...

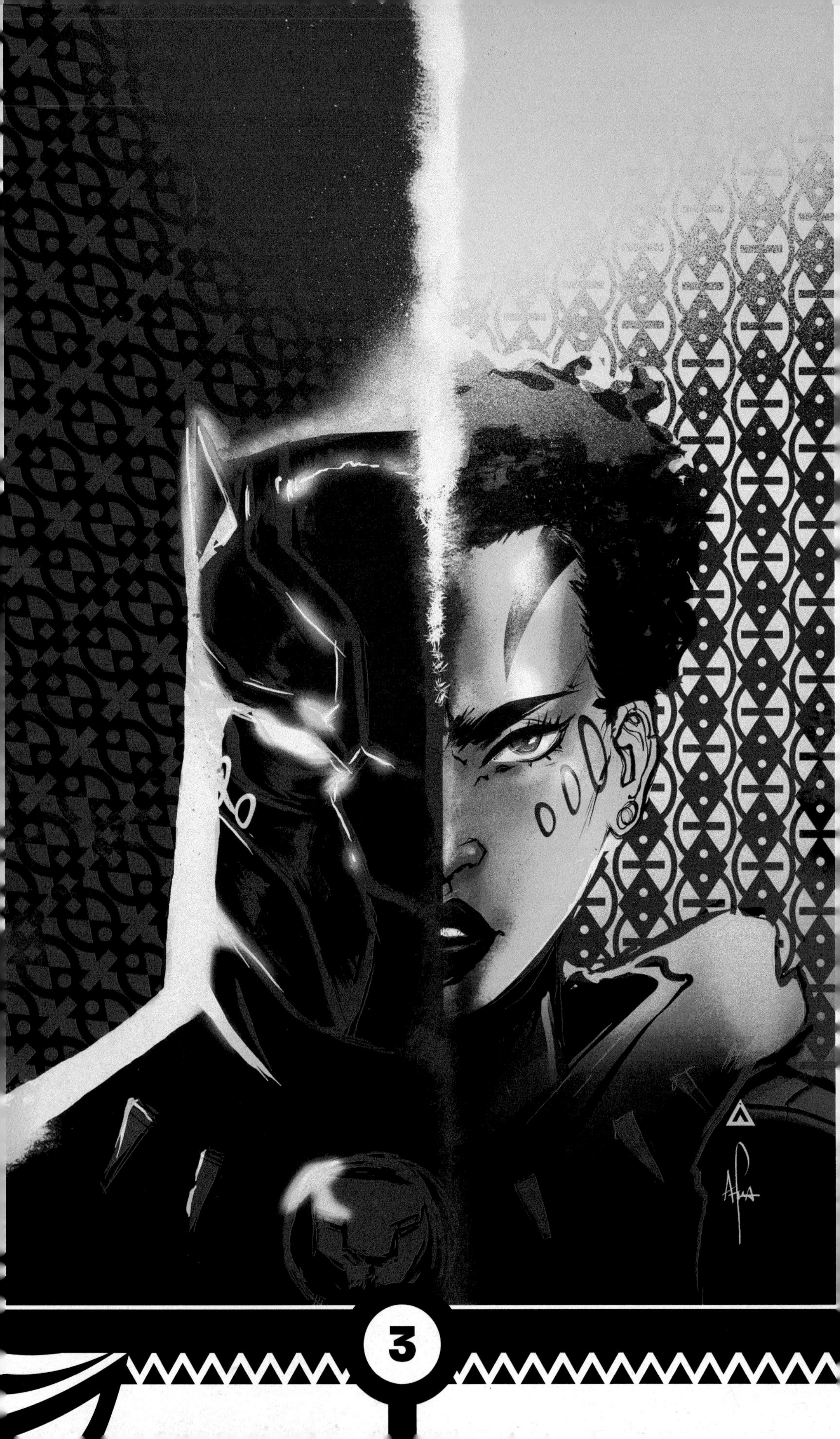
3

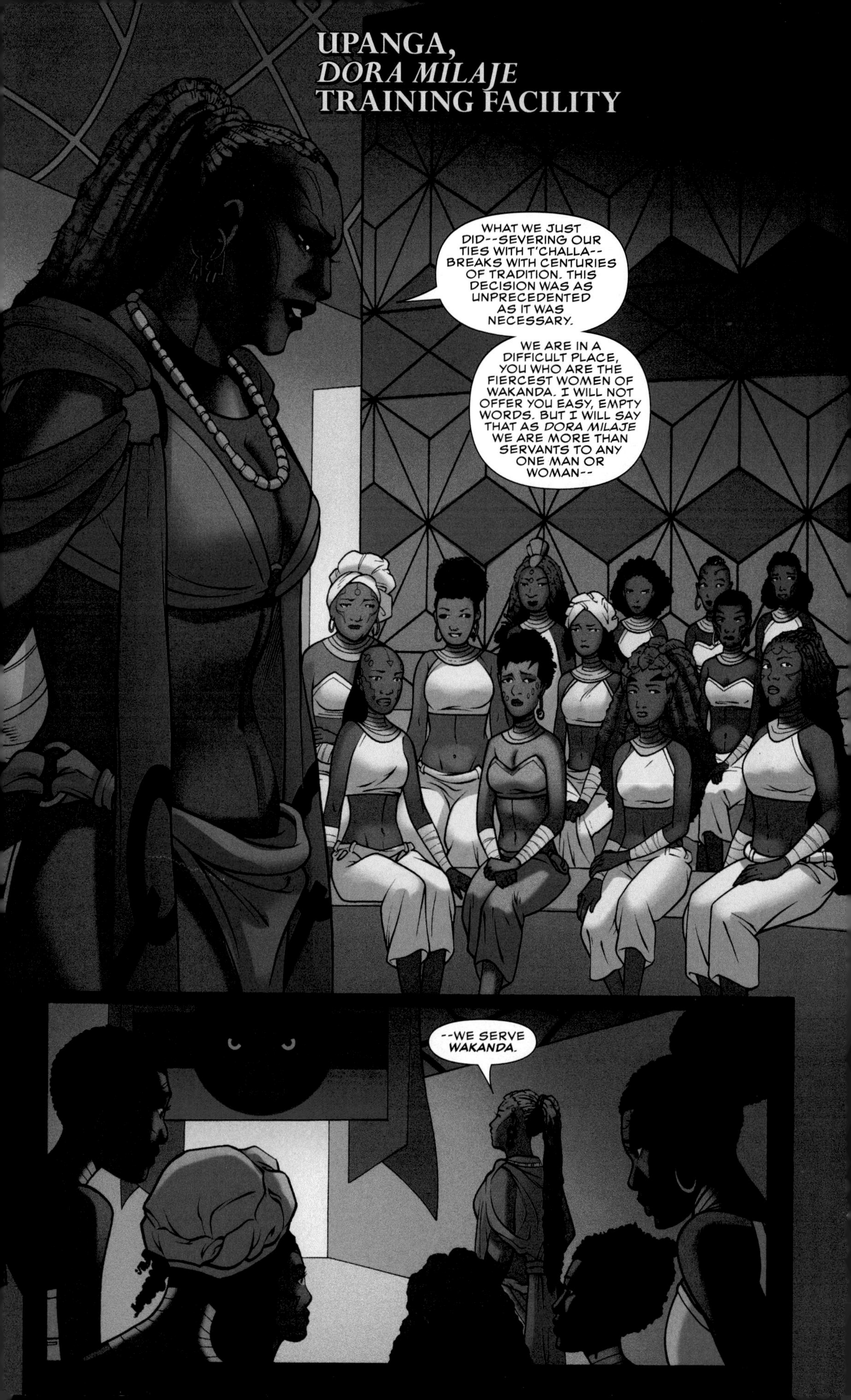
UPANGA, *DORA MILAJE* TRAINING FACILITY
WHAT WE JUST DID--SEVERING OUR TIES WITH T'CHALLA--BREAKS WITH CENTURIES OF TRADITION. THIS DECISION WAS AS UNPRECEDENTED AS IT WAS NECESSARY.
WE ARE IN A DIFFICULT PLACE, YOU WHO ARE THE FIERCEST WOMEN OF WAKANDA. I WILL NOT OFFER YOU EASY, EMPTY WORDS. BUT I WILL SAY THAT AS *DORA MILAJE* WE ARE MORE THAN SERVANTS TO ANY ONE MAN OR WOMAN--
--WE SERVE ***WAKANDA.***

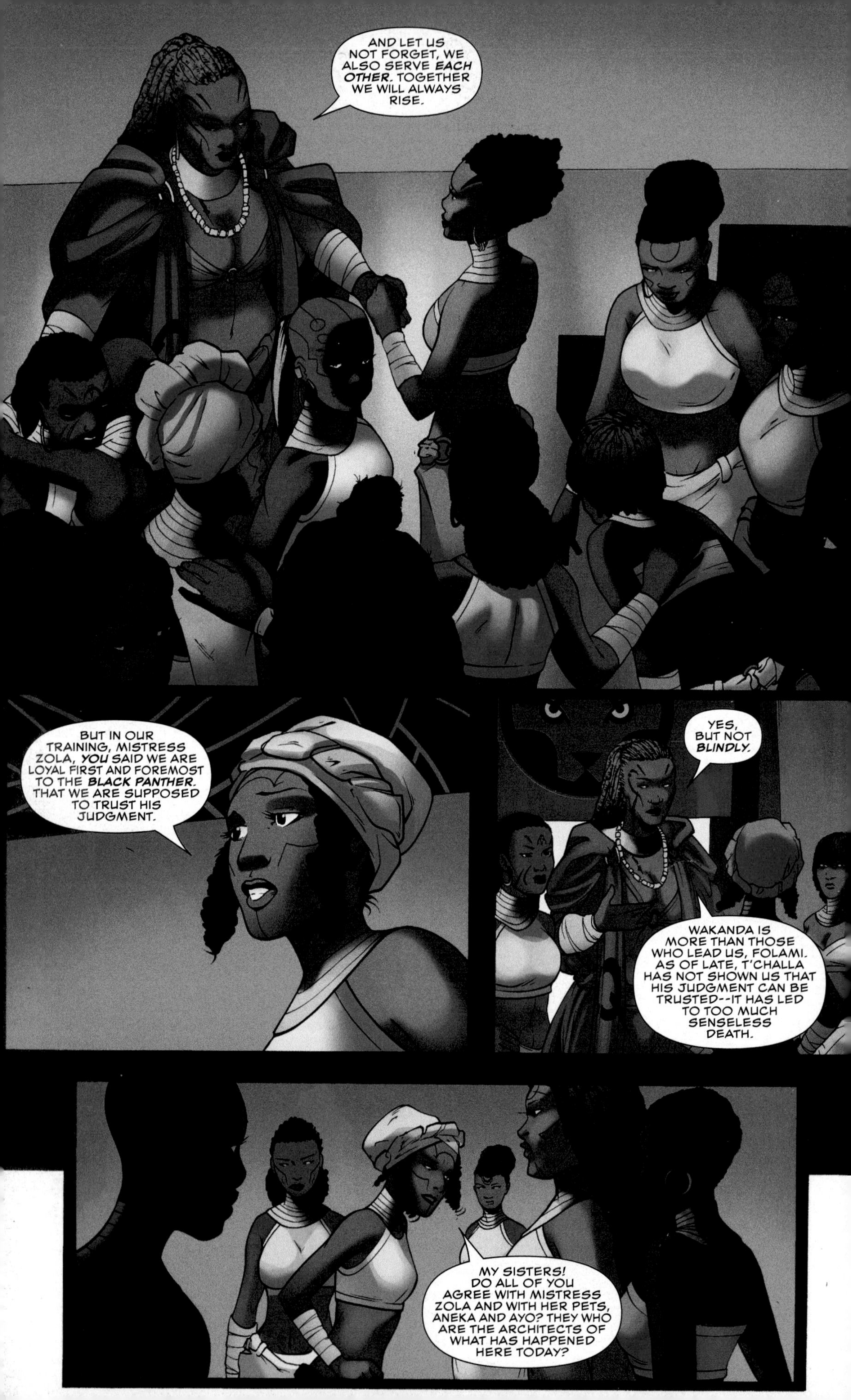
AND LET US NOT FORGET, WE ALSO SERVE EACH OTHER. TOGETHER WE WILL ALWAYS RISE.
BUT IN OUR TRAINING, MISTRESS ZOLA, YOU SAID WE ARE LOYAL FIRST AND FOREMOST TO THE BLACK PANTHER. THAT WE ARE SUPPOSED TO TRUST HIS JUDGMENT.
YES, BUT NOT BLINDLY.
WAKANDA IS MORE THAN THOSE WHO LEAD US, FOLAMI. AS OF LATE, T'CHALLA HAS NOT SHOWN US THAT HIS JUDGMENT CAN BE TRUSTED--IT HAS LED TO TOO MUCH SENSELESS DEATH.
MY SISTERS! DO ALL OF YOU AGREE WITH MISTRESS ZOLA AND WITH HER PETS, ANEKA AND AYO? THEY WHO ARE THE ARCHITECTS OF WHAT HAS HAPPENED HERE TODAY?

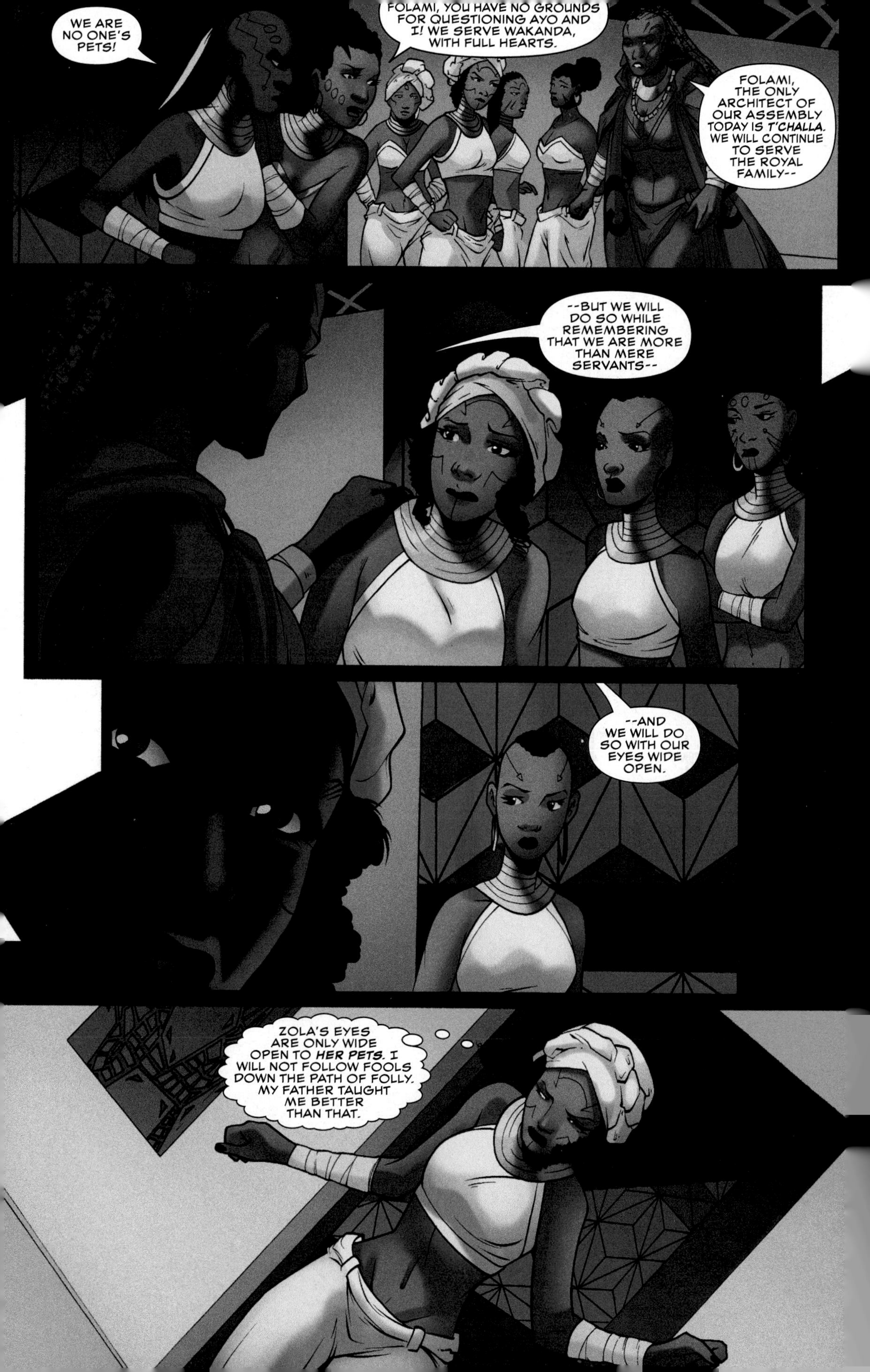
WE ARE NO ONE'S PETS!
FOLAMI, YOU HAVE NO GROUNDS FOR QUESTIONING AYO AND I! WE SERVE WAKANDA, WITH FULL HEARTS.
FOLAMI, THE ONLY ARCHITECT OF OUR ASSEMBLY TODAY IS T'CHALLA. WE WILL CONTINUE TO SERVE THE ROYAL FAMILY--
--BUT WE WILL DO SO WHILE REMEMBERING THAT WE ARE MORE THAN MERE SERVANTS--
--AND WE WILL DO SO WITH OUR EYES WIDE OPEN.
ZOLA'S EYES ARE ONLY WIDE OPEN TO HER PETS. I WILL NOT FOLLOW FOOLS DOWN THE PATH OF FOLLY. MY FATHER TAUGHT ME BETTER THAN THAT.

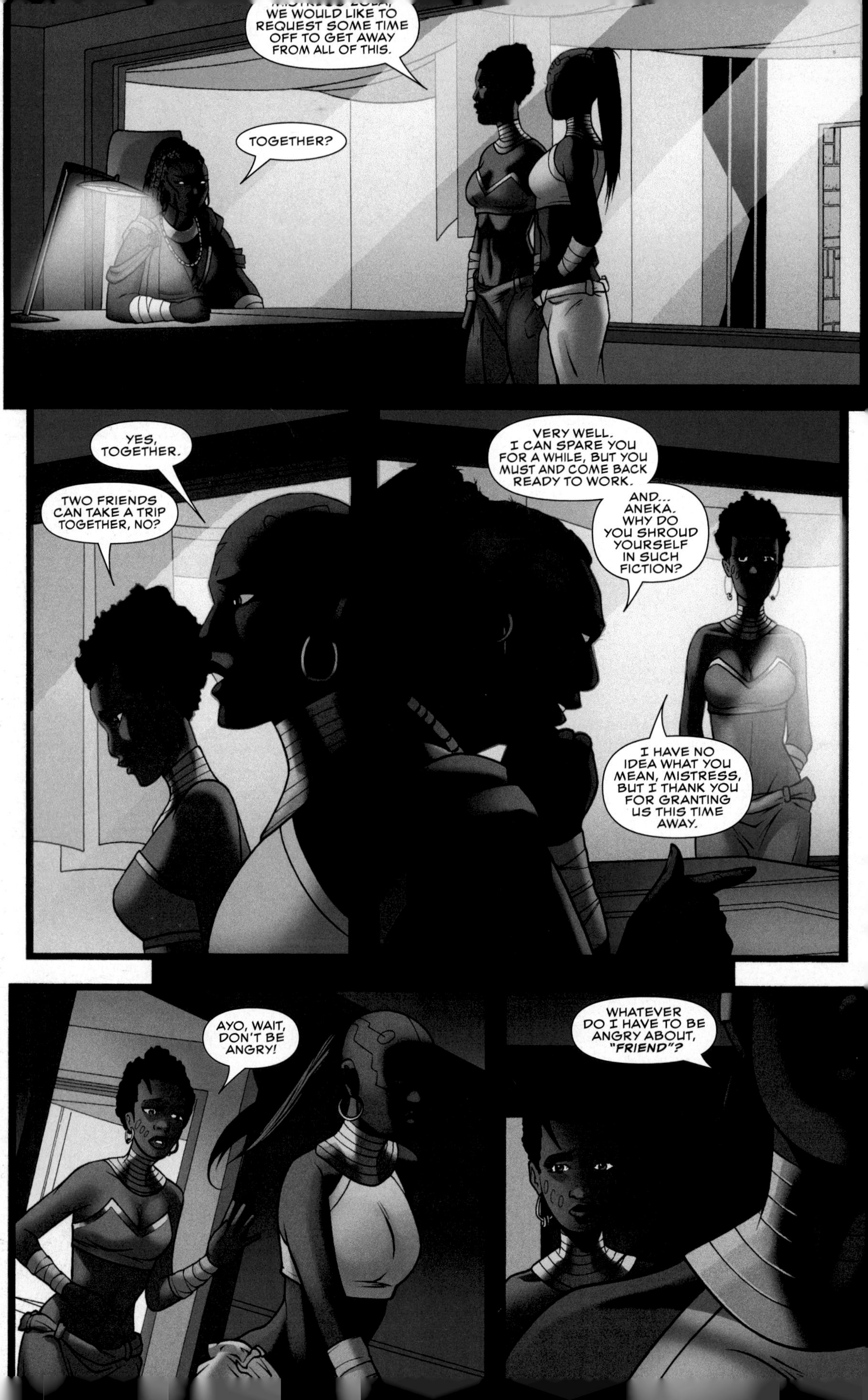

WE WOULD LIKE TO REQUEST SOME TIME OFF TO GET AWAY FROM ALL OF THIS.
TOGETHER?
YES, TOGETHER.
TWO FRIENDS CAN TAKE A TRIP TOGETHER, NO?
VERY WELL. I CAN SPARE YOU FOR A WHILE, BUT YOU MUST AND COME BACK READY TO WORK.
AND... ANEKA. WHY DO YOU SHROUD YOURSELF IN SUCH FICTION?
I HAVE NO IDEA WHAT YOU MEAN, MISTRESS, BUT I THANK YOU FOR GRANTING US THIS TIME AWAY.
AYO, WAIT, DON'T BE ANGRY!
WHATEVER DO I HAVE TO BE ANGRY ABOUT, "FRIEND"?

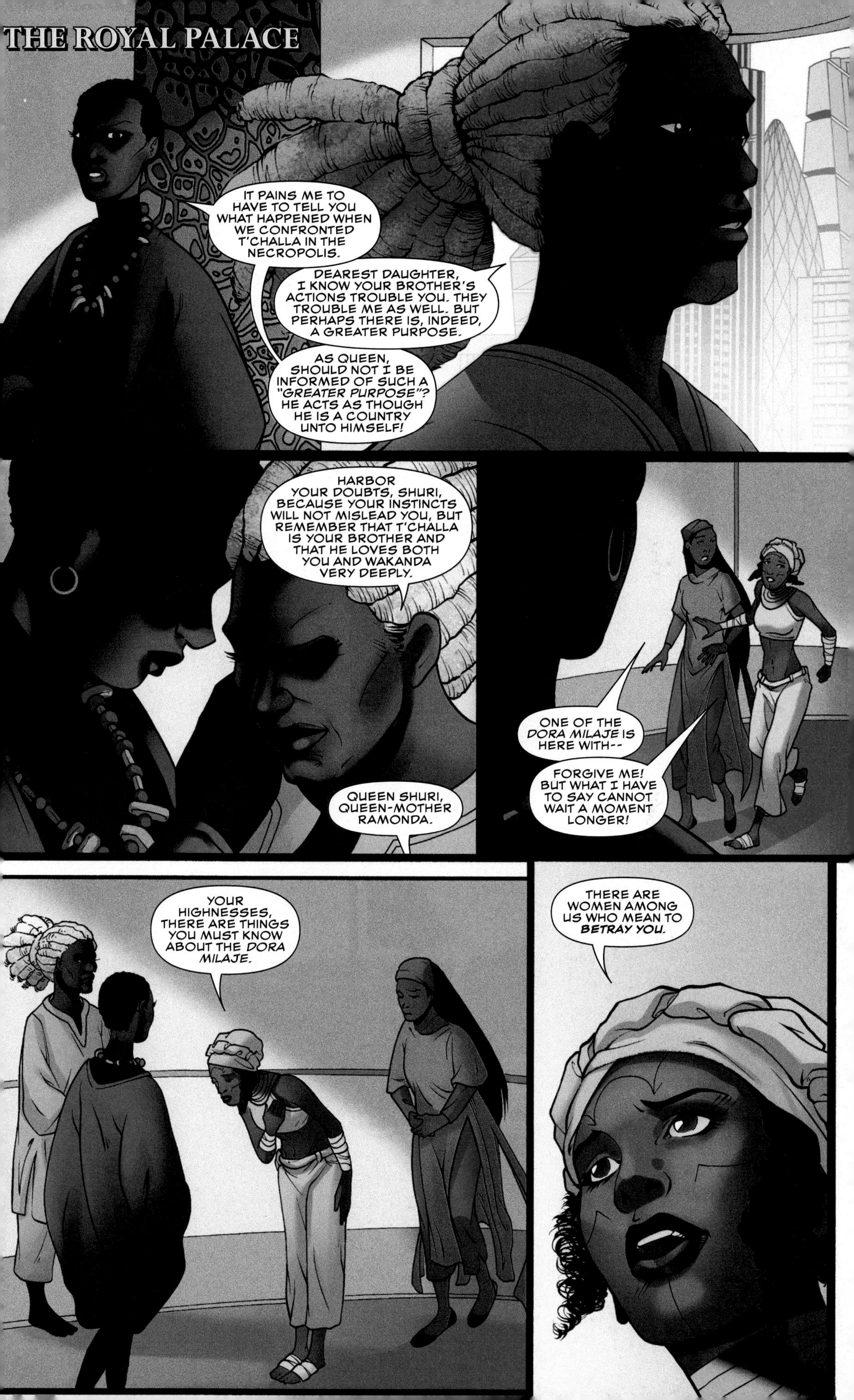
THE ROYAL PALACE
IT PAINS ME TO HAVE TO TELL YOU WHAT HAPPENED WHEN WE CONFRONTED T'CHALLA IN THE NECROPOLIS.
DEAREST DAUGHTER, I KNOW YOUR BROTHER'S ACTIONS TROUBLE YOU. THEY TROUBLE ME AS WELL. BUT PERHAPS THERE IS, INDEED, A GREATER PURPOSE.
AS QUEEN, SHOULD NOT I BE INFORMED OF SUCH A "GREATER PURPOSE"? HE ACTS AS THOUGH HE IS A COUNTRY UNTO HIMSELF!
HARBOR YOUR DOUBTS, SHURI, BECAUSE YOUR INSTINCTS WILL NOT MISLEAD YOU, BUT REMEMBER THAT T'CHALLA IS YOUR BROTHER AND THAT HE LOVES BOTH YOU AND WAKANDA VERY DEEPLY.
QUEEN SHURI, QUEEN-MOTHER RAMONDA.
ONE OF THE DORA MILAJE IS HERE WITH--
FORGIVE ME! BUT WHAT I HAVE TO SAY CANNOT WAIT A MOMENT LONGER!
YOUR HIGHNESSES, THERE ARE THINGS YOU MUST KNOW ABOUT THE DORA MILAJE.
THERE ARE WOMEN AMONG US WHO MEAN TO BETRAY YOU.

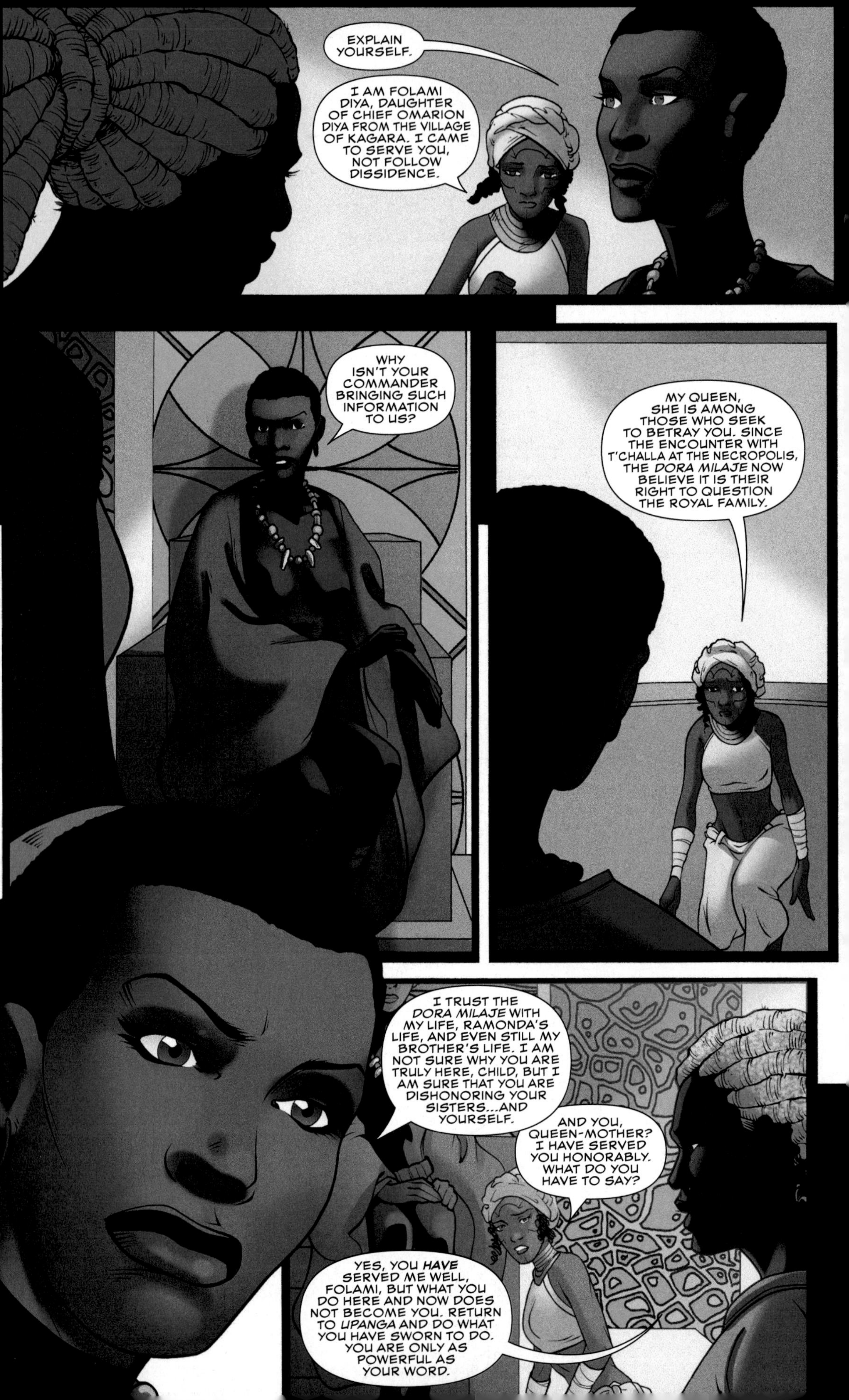
EXPLAIN YOURSELF.
I AM FOLAMI DIYA, DAUGHTER OF CHIEF OMARION DIYA FROM THE VILLAGE OF KAGARA. I CAME TO SERVE YOU, NOT FOLLOW DISSIDENCE.
WHY ISN'T YOUR COMMANDER BRINGING SUCH INFORMATION TO US?
MY QUEEN, SHE IS AMONG THOSE WHO SEEK TO BETRAY YOU. SINCE THE ENCOUNTER WITH T'CHALLA AT THE NECROPOLIS, THE *DORA MILAJE* NOW BELIEVE IT IS THEIR RIGHT TO QUESTION THE ROYAL FAMILY.
I TRUST THE *DORA MILAJE* WITH MY LIFE, RAMONDA'S LIFE, AND EVEN STILL MY BROTHER'S LIFE. I AM NOT SURE WHY YOU ARE TRULY HERE, CHILD, BUT I AM SURE THAT YOU ARE DISHONORING YOUR SISTERS...AND YOURSELF.
AND YOU, QUEEN-MOTHER? I HAVE SERVED YOU HONORABLY. WHAT DO YOU HAVE TO SAY?
YES, YOU ***HAVE*** SERVED ME WELL, FOLAMI, BUT WHAT YOU DO HERE AND NOW DOES NOT BECOME YOU. RETURN TO *UPANGA* AND DO WHAT YOU HAVE SWORN TO DO. YOU ARE ONLY AS POWERFUL AS YOUR WORD.

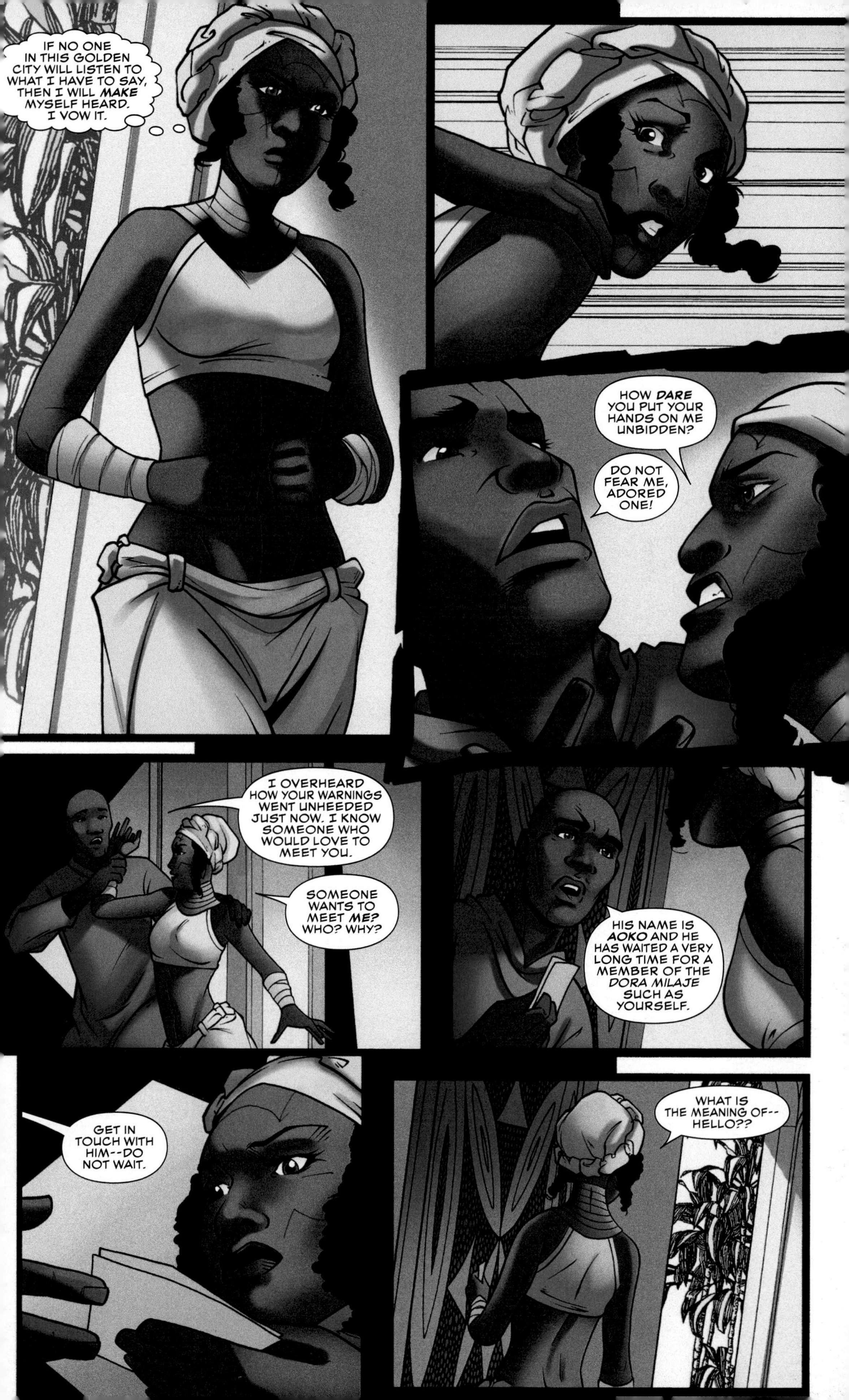
IF NO ONE IN THIS GOLDEN CITY WILL LISTEN TO WHAT I HAVE TO SAY, THEN I WILL MAKE MYSELF HEARD. I VOW IT.
HOW DARE YOU PUT YOUR HANDS ON ME UNBIDDEN?
DO NOT FEAR ME, ADORED ONE!
I OVERHEARD HOW YOUR WARNINGS WENT UNHEEDED JUST NOW. I KNOW SOMEONE WHO WOULD LOVE TO MEET YOU.
SOMEONE WANTS TO MEET ME? WHO? WHY?
HIS NAME IS AOKO AND HE HAS WAITED A VERY LONG TIME FOR A MEMBER OF THE DORA MILAJE SUCH AS YOURSELF.
GET IN TOUCH WITH HIM--DO NOT WAIT.
WHAT IS THE MEANING OF-- HELLO??

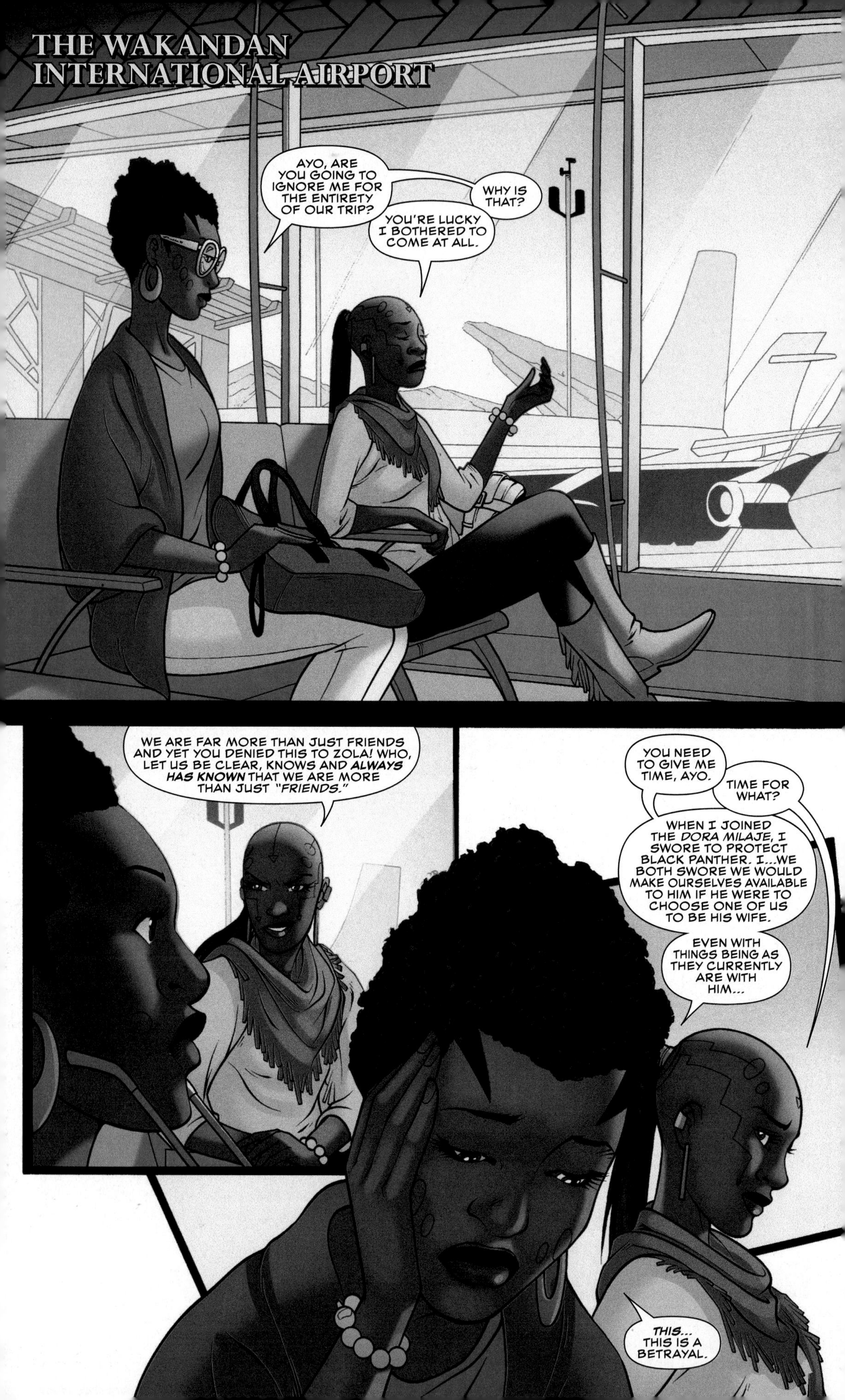

THE WAKANDAN INTERNATIONAL AIRPORT
AYO, ARE YOU GOING TO IGNORE ME FOR THE ENTIRETY OF OUR TRIP?
WHY IS THAT?
YOU'RE LUCKY I BOTHERED TO COME AT ALL.
WE ARE FAR MORE THAN JUST FRIENDS AND YET YOU DENIED THIS TO ZOLA! WHO, LET US BE CLEAR, KNOWS AND ALWAYS HAS KNOWN THAT WE ARE MORE THAN JUST "FRIENDS."
YOU NEED TO GIVE ME TIME, AYO.
TIME FOR WHAT?
WHEN I JOINED THE DORA MILAJE, I SWORE TO PROTECT BLACK PANTHER. I...WE BOTH SWORE WE WOULD MAKE OURSELVES AVAILABLE TO HIM IF HE WERE TO CHOOSE ONE OF US TO BE HIS WIFE.
EVEN WITH THINGS BEING AS THEY CURRENTLY ARE WITH HIM...
THIS... THIS IS A BETRAYAL.

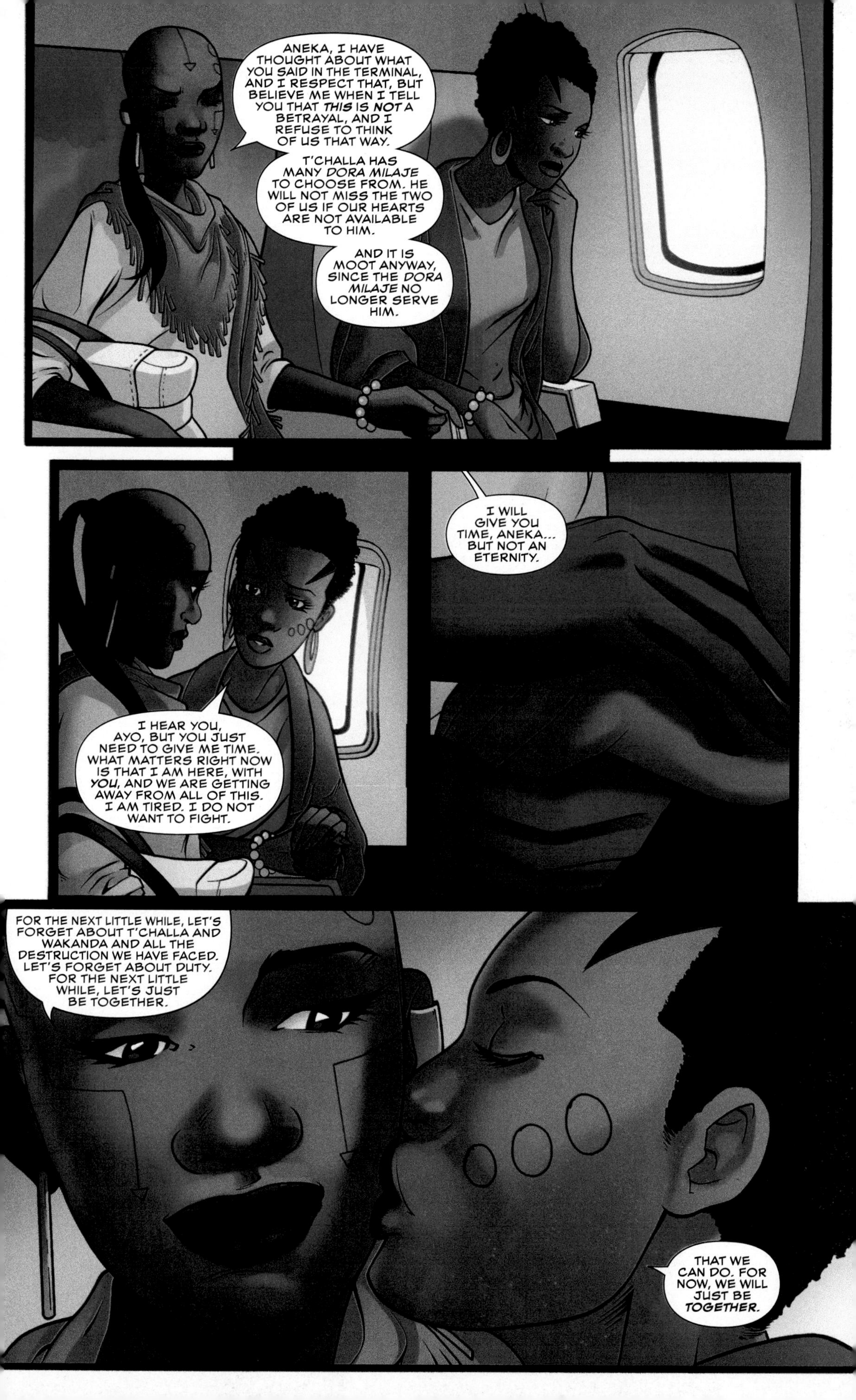
ANEKA, I HAVE THOUGHT ABOUT WHAT YOU SAID IN THE TERMINAL, AND I RESPECT THAT, BUT BELIEVE ME WHEN I TELL YOU THAT *THIS* IS *NOT* A BETRAYAL, AND I REFUSE TO THINK OF US THAT WAY.
T'CHALLA HAS MANY *DORA MILAJE* TO CHOOSE FROM. HE WILL NOT MISS THE TWO OF US IF OUR HEARTS ARE NOT AVAILABLE TO HIM.
AND IT IS MOOT ANYWAY, SINCE THE *DORA MILAJE* NO LONGER SERVE HIM.
I HEAR YOU, AYO, BUT YOU JUST NEED TO GIVE ME TIME. WHAT MATTERS RIGHT NOW IS THAT I AM HERE, WITH *YOU*, AND WE ARE GETTING AWAY FROM ALL OF THIS. I AM TIRED. I DO NOT WANT TO FIGHT.
I WILL GIVE YOU TIME, ANEKA... BUT NOT AN ETERNITY.
FOR THE NEXT LITTLE WHILE, LET'S FORGET ABOUT T'CHALLA AND WAKANDA AND ALL THE DESTRUCTION WE HAVE FACED. LET'S FORGET ABOUT DUTY. FOR THE NEXT LITTLE WHILE, LET'S JUST BE TOGETHER.
THAT WE CAN DO. FOR NOW, WE WILL JUST BE *TOGETHER*.

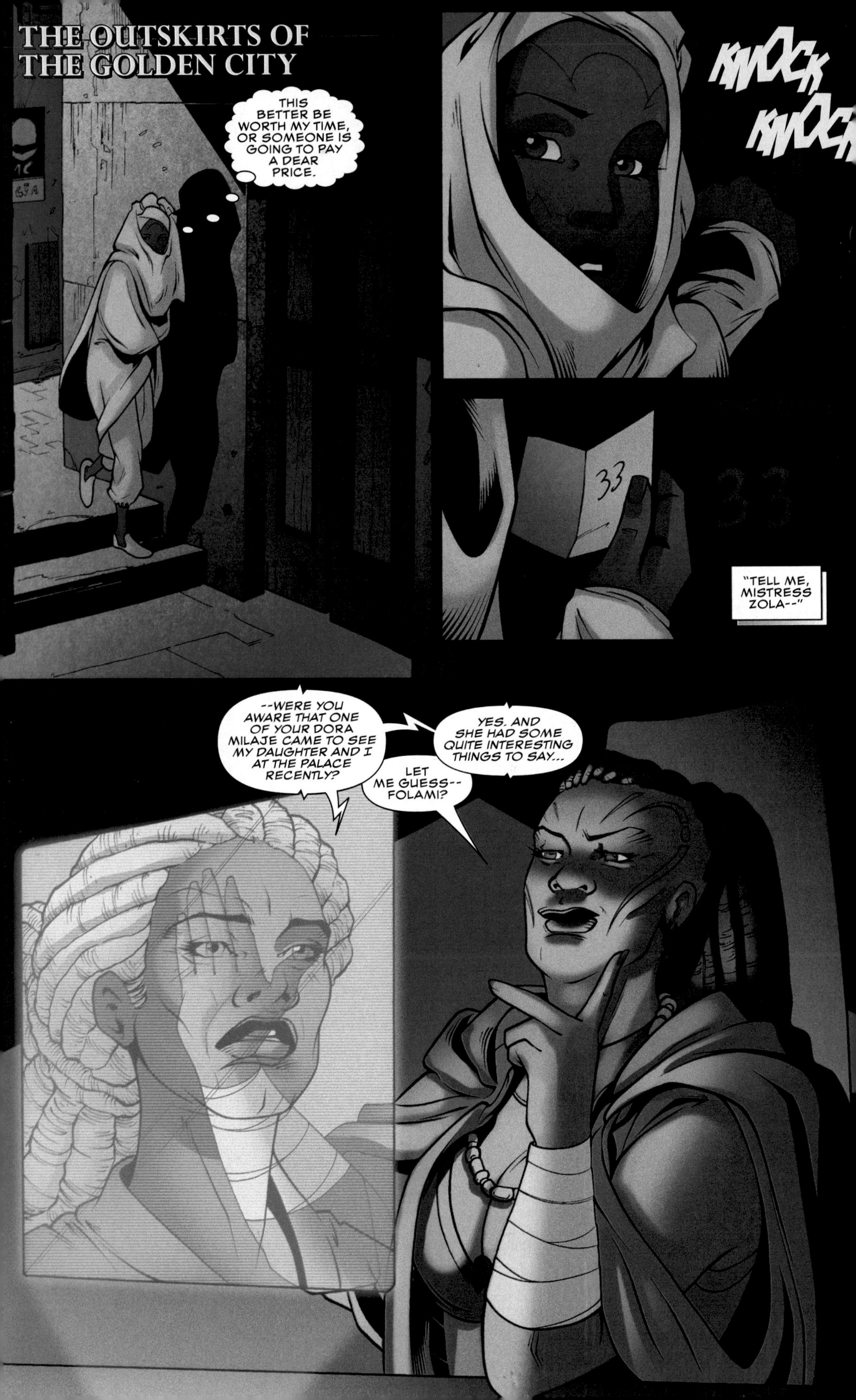
THE OUTSKIRTS OF THE GOLDEN CITY
THIS BETTER BE WORTH MY TIME, OR SOMEONE IS GOING TO PAY A DEAR PRICE.
KNOCK KNOCK
"TELL ME, MISTRESS ZOLA--"
--WERE YOU AWARE THAT ONE OF YOUR DORA MILAJE CAME TO SEE MY DAUGHTER AND I AT THE PALACE RECENTLY?
YES. AND SHE HAD SOME QUITE INTERESTING THINGS TO SAY...
LET ME GUESS--FOLAMI?

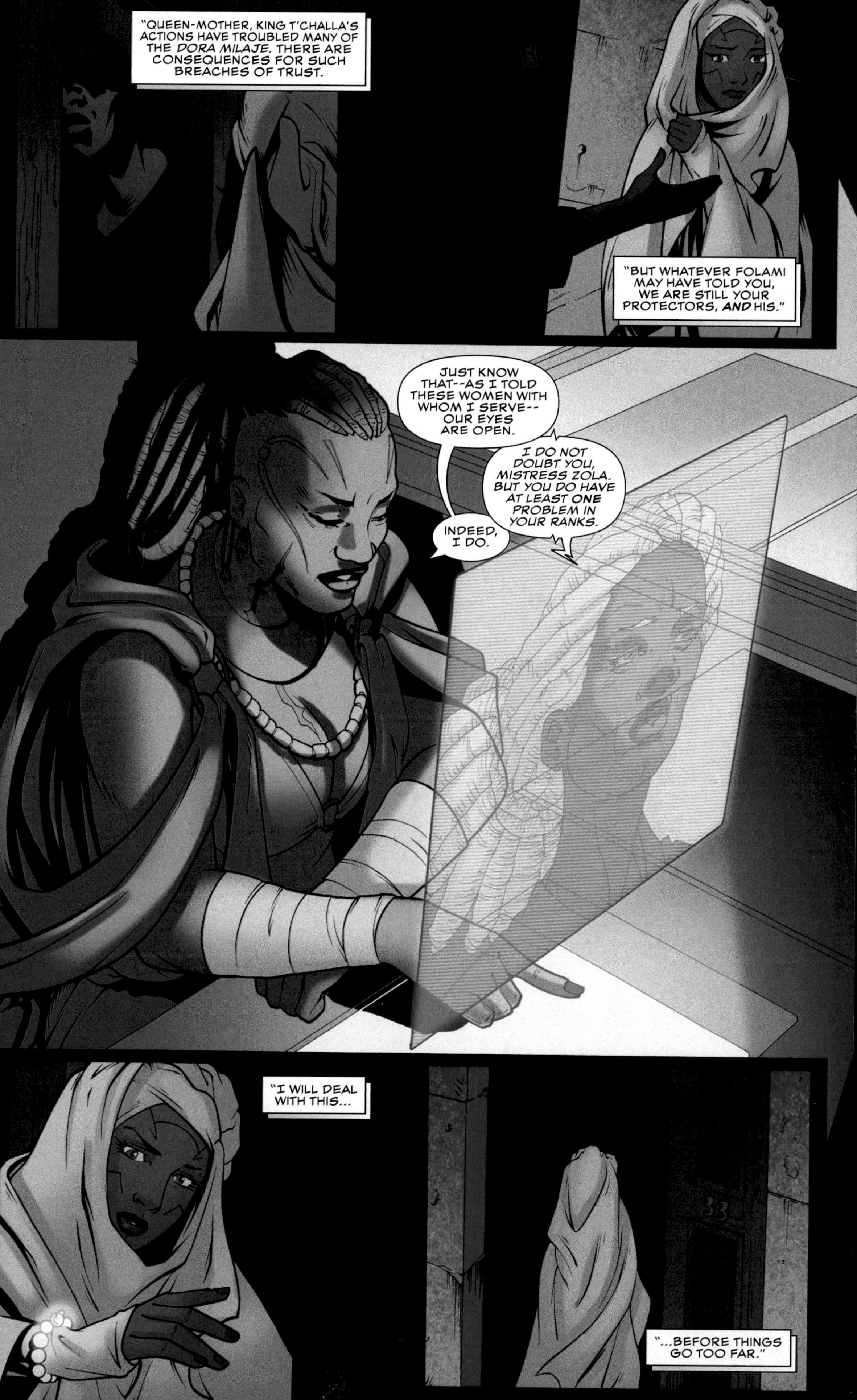
"QUEEN-MOTHER, KING T'CHALLA'S ACTIONS HAVE TROUBLED MANY OF THE *DORA MILAJE*. THERE ARE CONSEQUENCES FOR SUCH BREACHES OF TRUST.
"BUT WHATEVER FOLAMI MAY HAVE TOLD YOU, WE ARE STILL YOUR PROTECTORS, ***AND*** HIS."
JUST KNOW THAT--AS I TOLD THESE WOMEN WITH WHOM I SERVE--OUR EYES ARE OPEN.
*I DO NOT DOUBT YOU, MISTRESS ZOLA. BUT YOU DO HAVE AT LEAST* ***ONE*** *PROBLEM IN YOUR RANKS.*
INDEED, I DO.
"I WILL DEAL WITH THIS...
"...BEFORE THINGS GO TOO FAR."

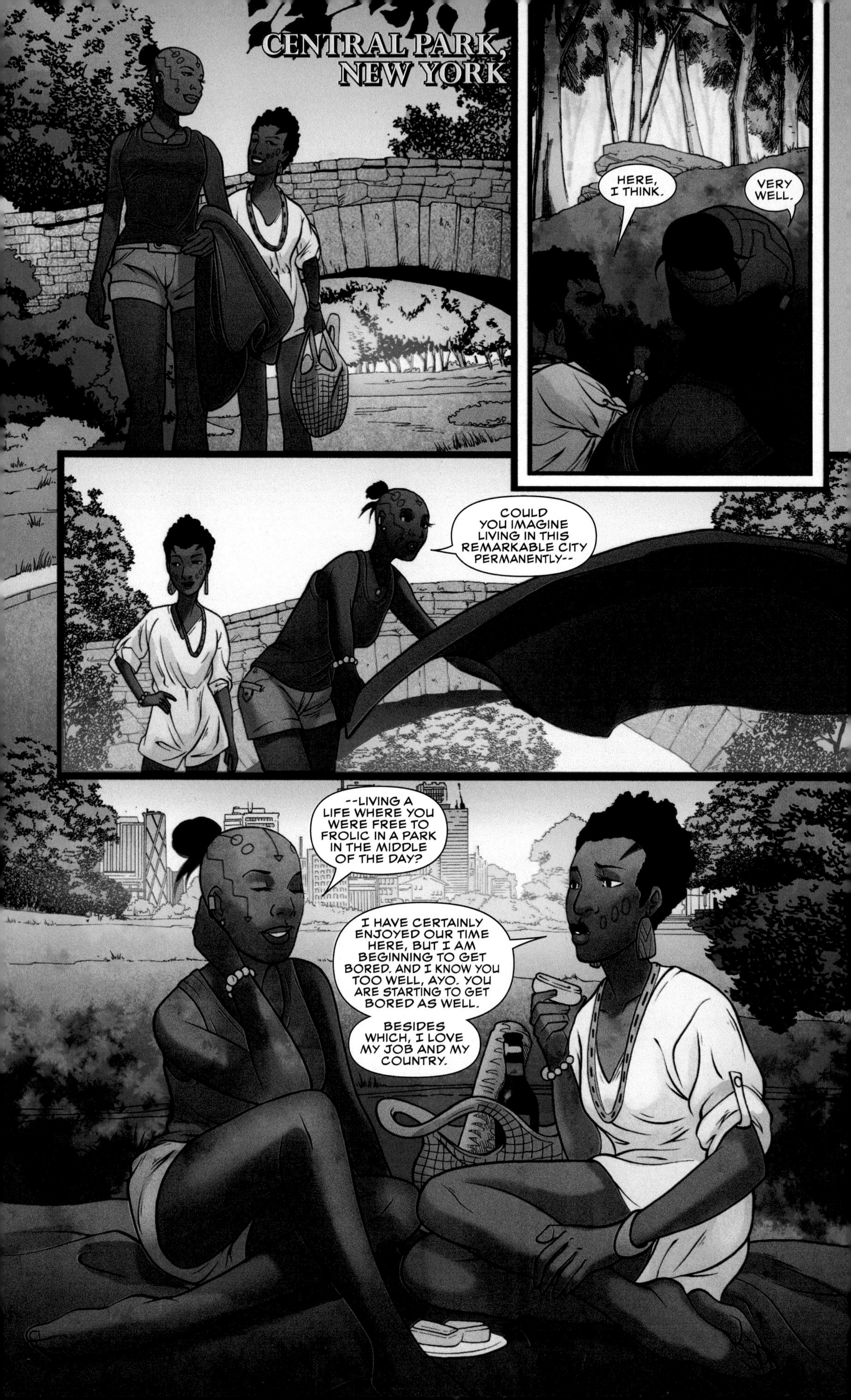
CENTRAL PARK, NEW YORK
HERE, I THINK.
VERY WELL.
COULD YOU IMAGINE LIVING IN THIS REMARKABLE CITY PERMANENTLY--
--LIVING A LIFE WHERE YOU WERE FREE TO FROLIC IN A PARK IN THE MIDDLE OF THE DAY?
I HAVE CERTAINLY ENJOYED OUR TIME HERE, BUT I AM BEGINNING TO GET BORED. AND I KNOW YOU TOO WELL, AYO. YOU ARE STARTING TO GET BORED AS WELL.
BESIDES WHICH, I LOVE MY JOB AND MY COUNTRY.

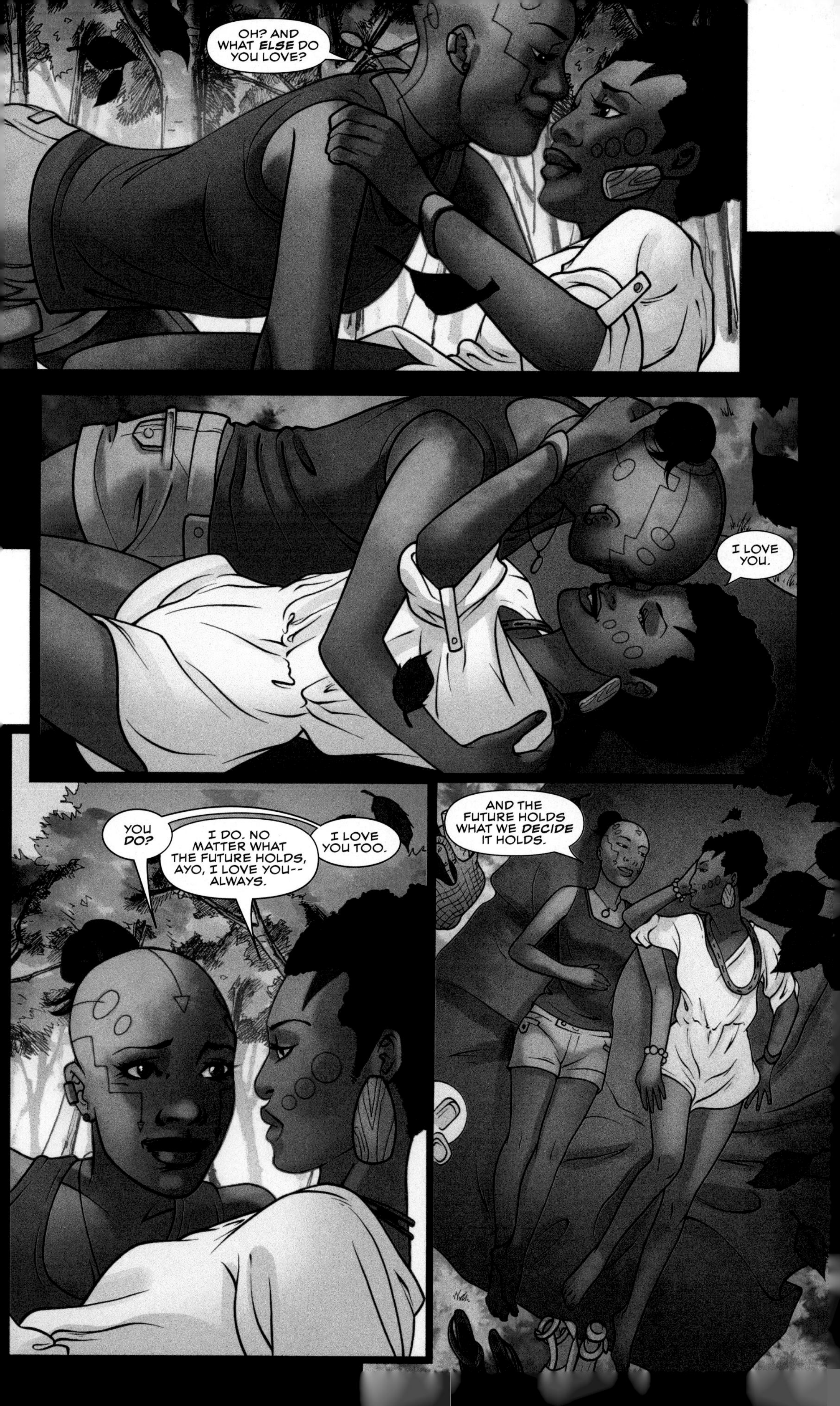
OH? AND WHAT *ELSE* DO YOU LOVE?
I LOVE YOU.
YOU *DO?*
I DO. NO MATTER WHAT THE FUTURE HOLDS, AYO, I LOVE YOU-- ALWAYS.
I LOVE YOU TOO.
AND THE FUTURE HOLDS WHAT WE *DECIDE* IT HOLDS.

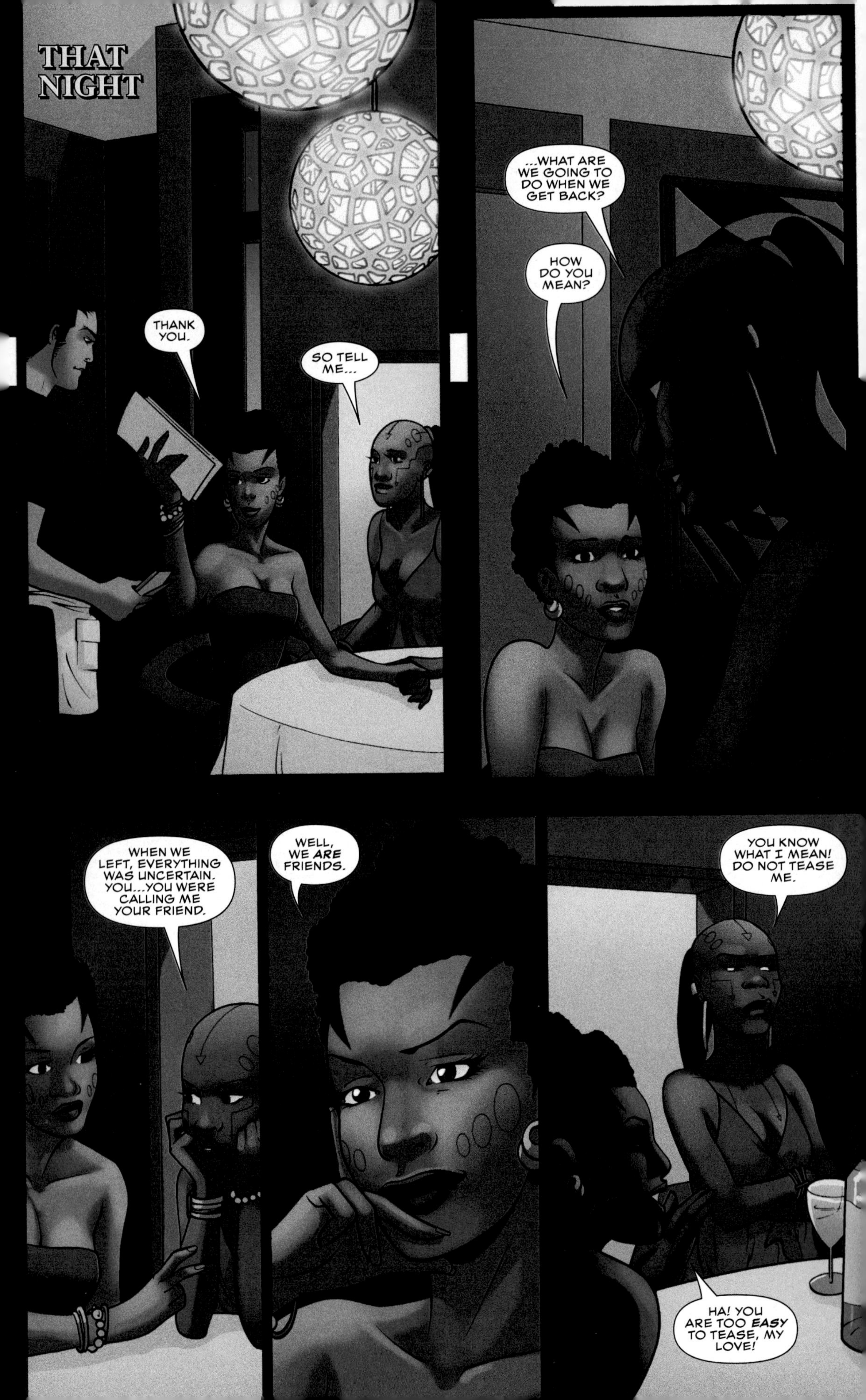
THAT NIGHT
THANK YOU.
SO TELL ME...
...WHAT ARE WE GOING TO DO WHEN WE GET BACK?
HOW DO YOU MEAN?
WHEN WE LEFT, EVERYTHING WAS UNCERTAIN. YOU...YOU WERE CALLING ME YOUR FRIEND.
WELL, WE ARE FRIENDS.
YOU KNOW WHAT I MEAN! DO NOT TEASE ME.
HA! YOU ARE TOO EASY TO TEASE, MY LOVE!

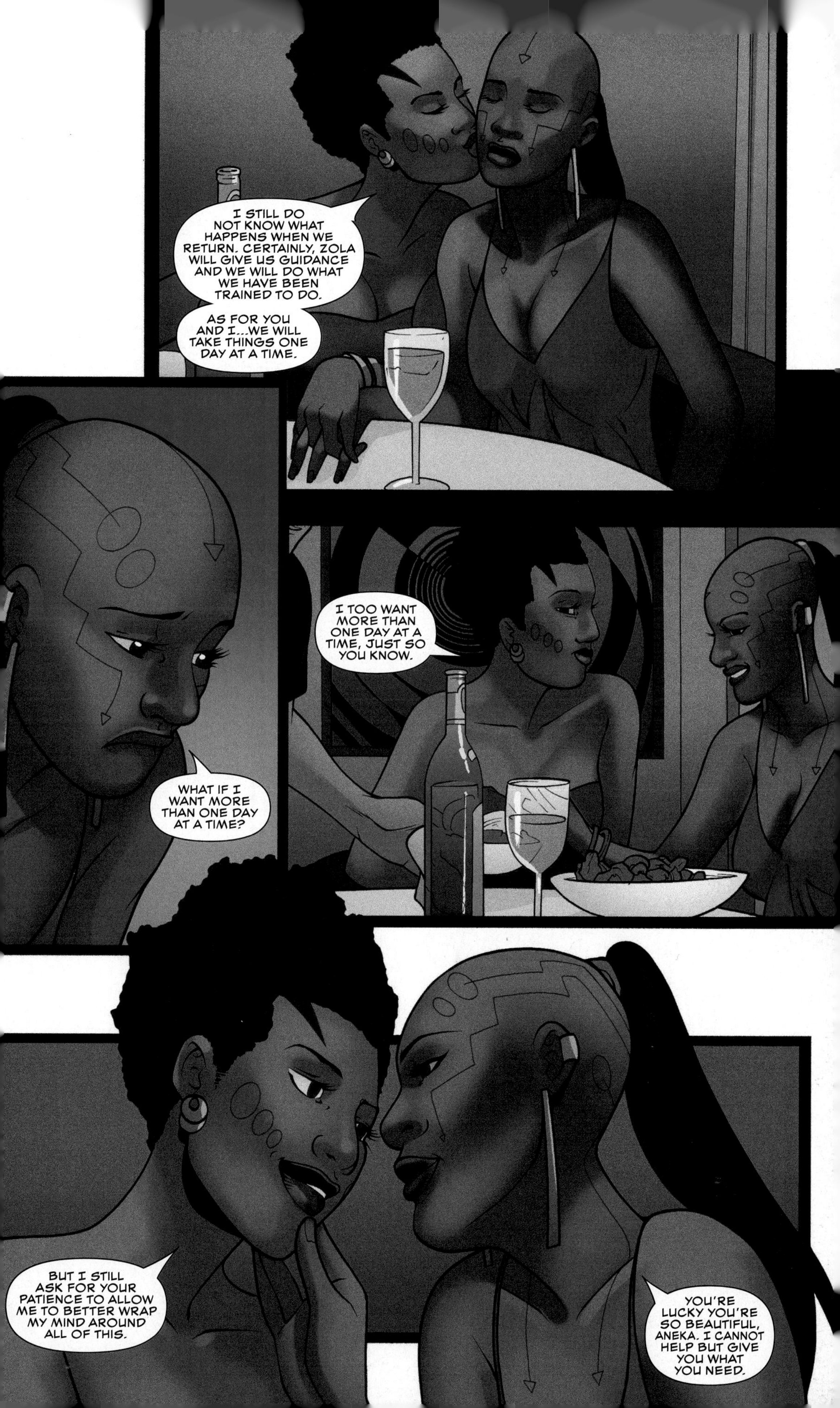
I STILL DO NOT KNOW WHAT HAPPENS WHEN WE RETURN. CERTAINLY, ZOLA WILL GIVE US GUIDANCE AND WE WILL DO WHAT WE HAVE BEEN TRAINED TO DO.
AS FOR YOU AND I...WE WILL TAKE THINGS ONE DAY AT A TIME.
WHAT IF I WANT MORE THAN ONE DAY AT A TIME?
I TOO WANT MORE THAN ONE DAY AT A TIME, JUST SO YOU KNOW.
BUT I STILL ASK FOR YOUR PATIENCE TO ALLOW ME TO BETTER WRAP MY MIND AROUND ALL OF THIS.
YOU'RE LUCKY YOU'RE SO BEAUTIFUL, ANEKA. I CANNOT HELP BUT GIVE YOU WHAT YOU NEED.

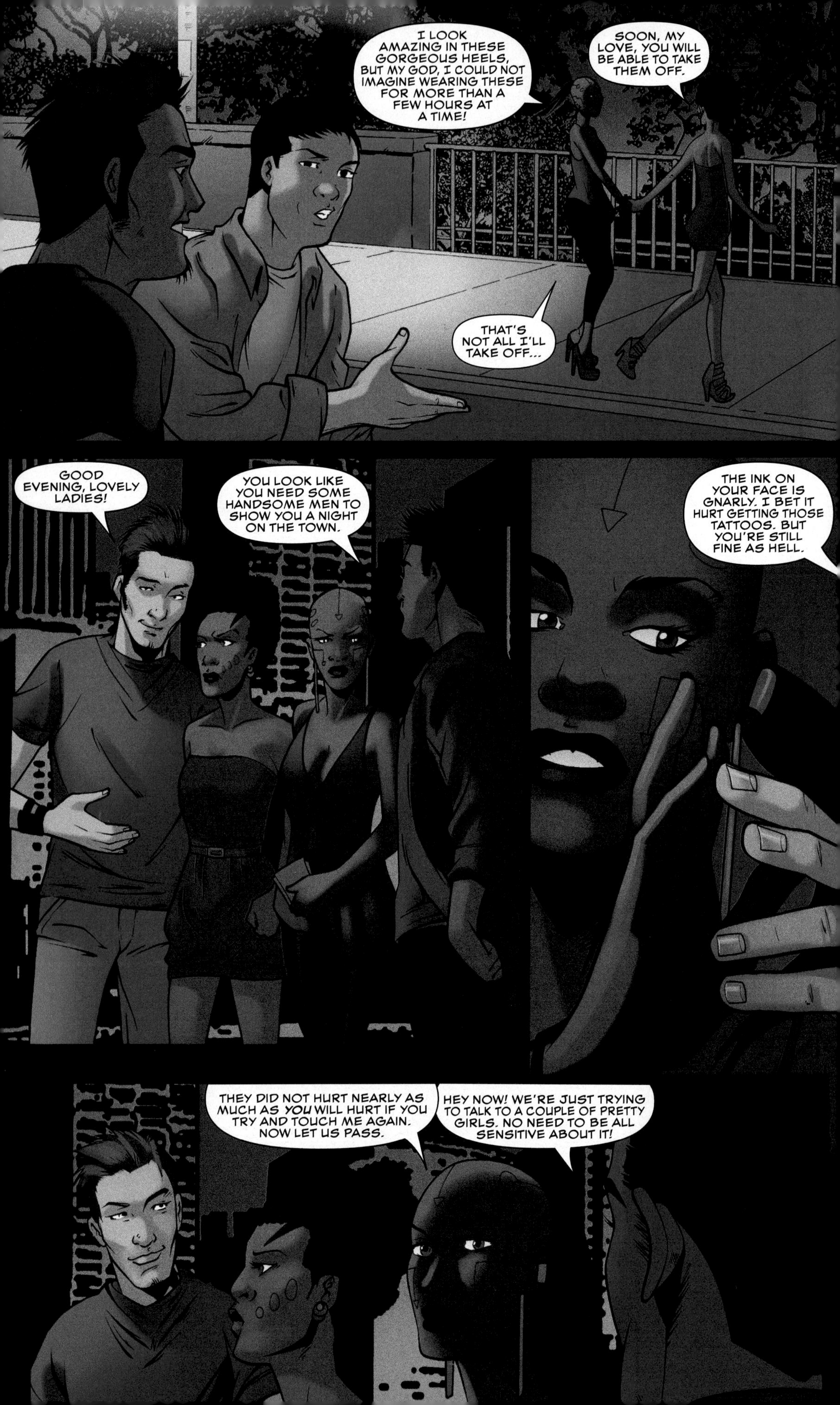
I LOOK AMAZING IN THESE GORGEOUS HEELS, BUT MY GOD, I COULD NOT IMAGINE WEARING THESE FOR MORE THAN A FEW HOURS AT A TIME!
SOON, MY LOVE, YOU WILL BE ABLE TO TAKE THEM OFF.
THAT'S NOT ALL I'LL TAKE OFF...
GOOD EVENING, LOVELY LADIES!
YOU LOOK LIKE YOU NEED SOME HANDSOME MEN TO SHOW YOU A NIGHT ON THE TOWN.
THE INK ON YOUR FACE IS GNARLY. I BET IT HURT GETTING THOSE TATTOOS. BUT YOU'RE STILL FINE AS HELL.
THEY DID NOT HURT NEARLY AS MUCH AS *YOU* WILL HURT IF YOU TRY AND TOUCH ME AGAIN. NOW LET US PASS.
HEY NOW! WE'RE JUST TRYING TO TALK TO A COUPLE OF PRETTY GIRLS. NO NEED TO BE ALL SENSITIVE ABOUT IT!

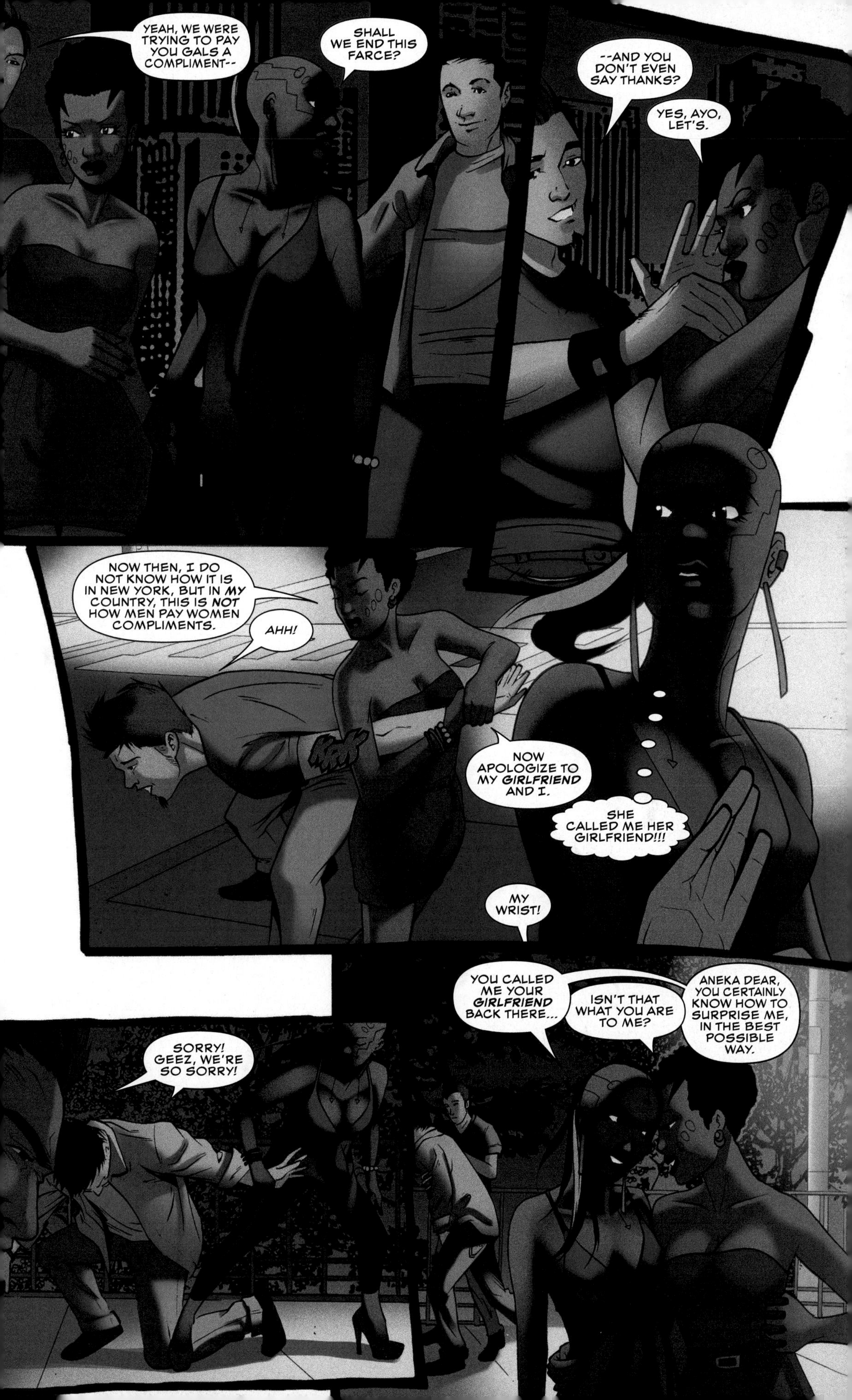
YEAH, WE WERE TRYING TO PAY YOU GALS A COMPLIMENT--
SHALL WE END THIS FARCE?
--AND YOU DON'T EVEN SAY THANKS?
YES, AYO, LET'S.
NOW THEN, I DO NOT KNOW HOW IT IS IN NEW YORK, BUT IN MY COUNTRY, THIS IS NOT HOW MEN PAY WOMEN COMPLIMENTS.
AHH!
NOW APOLOGIZE TO MY GIRLFRIEND AND I.
SHE CALLED ME HER GIRLFRIEND!!!
MY WRIST!
SORRY! GEEZ, WE'RE SO SORRY!
YOU CALLED ME YOUR GIRLFRIEND BACK THERE...
ISN'T THAT WHAT YOU ARE TO ME?
ANEKA DEAR, YOU CERTAINLY KNOW HOW TO SURPRISE ME, IN THE BEST POSSIBLE WAY.

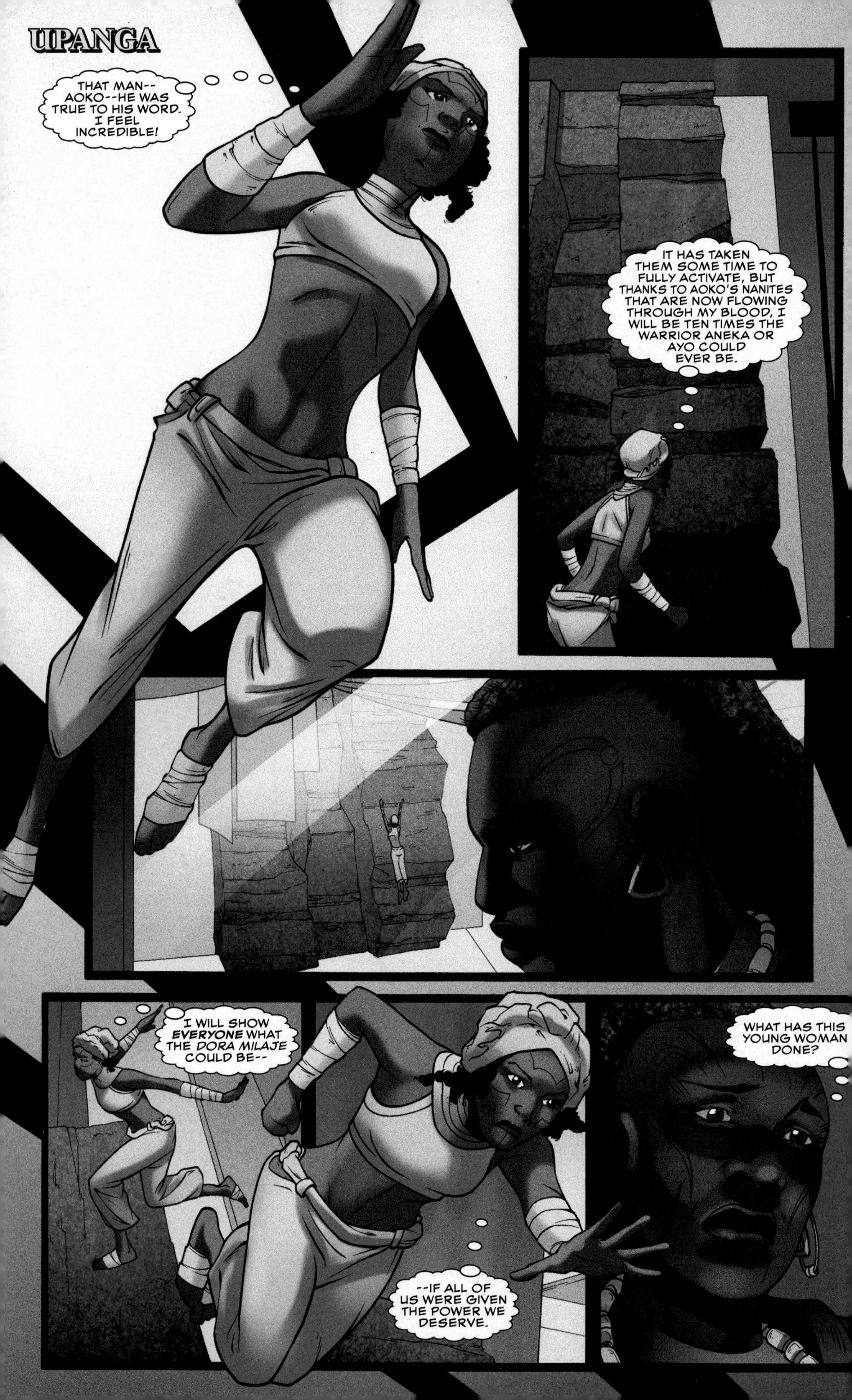
UPANGA
THAT MAN-- AOKO--HE WAS TRUE TO HIS WORD. I FEEL INCREDIBLE!
IT HAS TAKEN THEM SOME TIME TO FULLY ACTIVATE, BUT THANKS TO AOKO'S NANITES THAT ARE NOW FLOWING THROUGH MY BLOOD, I WILL BE TEN TIMES THE WARRIOR ANEKA OR AYO COULD EVER BE.
I WILL SHOW *EVERYONE* WHAT THE *DORA MILAJE* COULD BE--
--IF ALL OF US WERE GIVEN THE POWER WE DESERVE.
WHAT HAS THIS YOUNG WOMAN DONE?

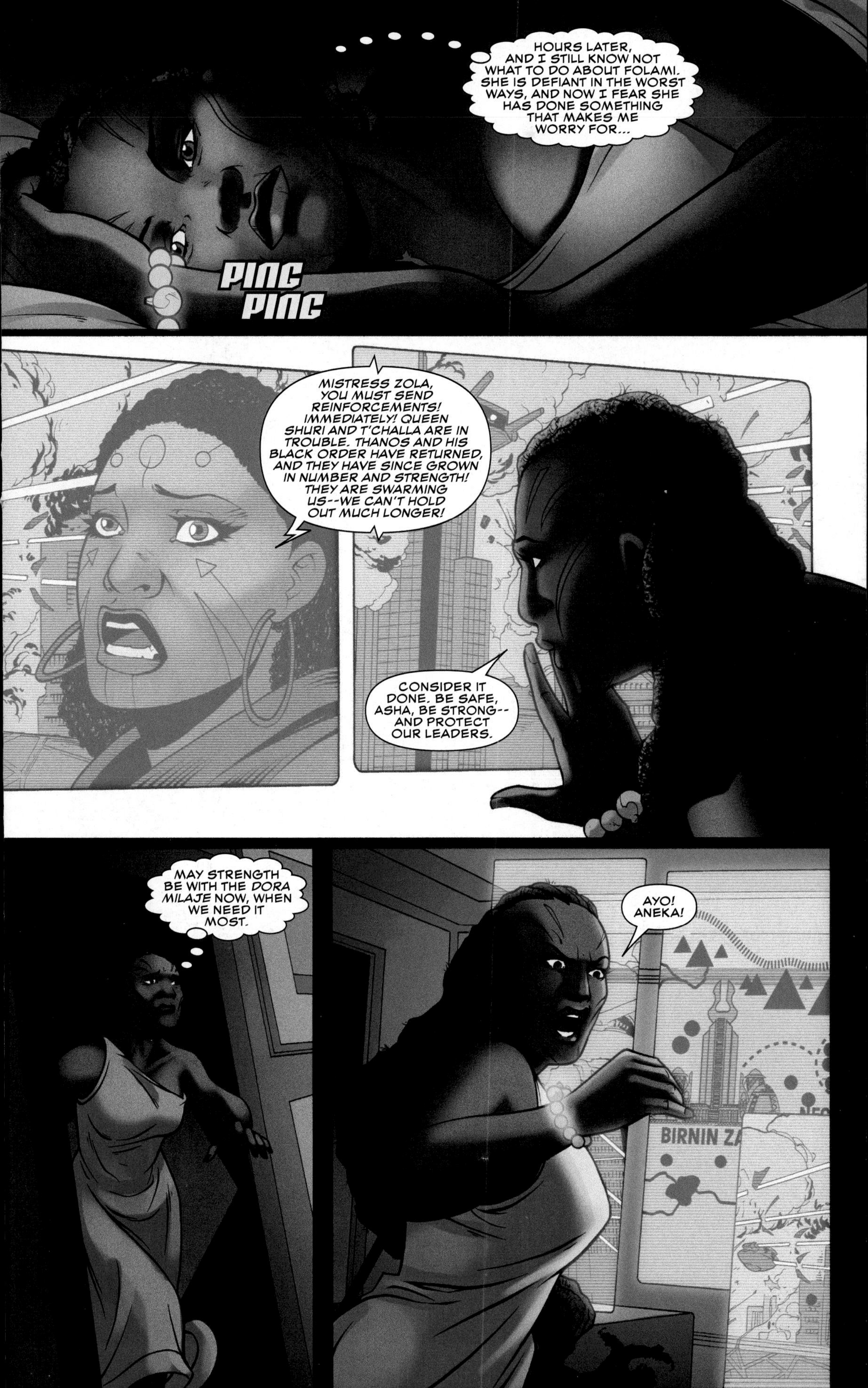

HOURS LATER, AND I STILL KNOW NOT WHAT TO DO ABOUT FOLAMI. SHE IS DEFIANT IN THE WORST WAYS, AND NOW I FEAR SHE HAS DONE SOMETHING THAT MAKES ME WORRY FOR...
PING PING
MISTRESS ZOLA, YOU MUST SEND REINFORCEMENTS! IMMEDIATELY! QUEEN SHURI AND T'CHALLA ARE IN TROUBLE. THANOS AND HIS BLACK ORDER HAVE RETURNED, AND THEY HAVE SINCE GROWN IN NUMBER AND STRENGTH! THEY ARE SWARMING US--WE CAN'T HOLD OUT MUCH LONGER!
CONSIDER IT DONE. BE SAFE, ASHA, BE STRONG--AND PROTECT OUR LEADERS.
MAY STRENGTH BE WITH THE *DORA MILAJE* NOW, WHEN WE NEED IT MOST.
AYO! ANEKA!
BIRNIN ZA

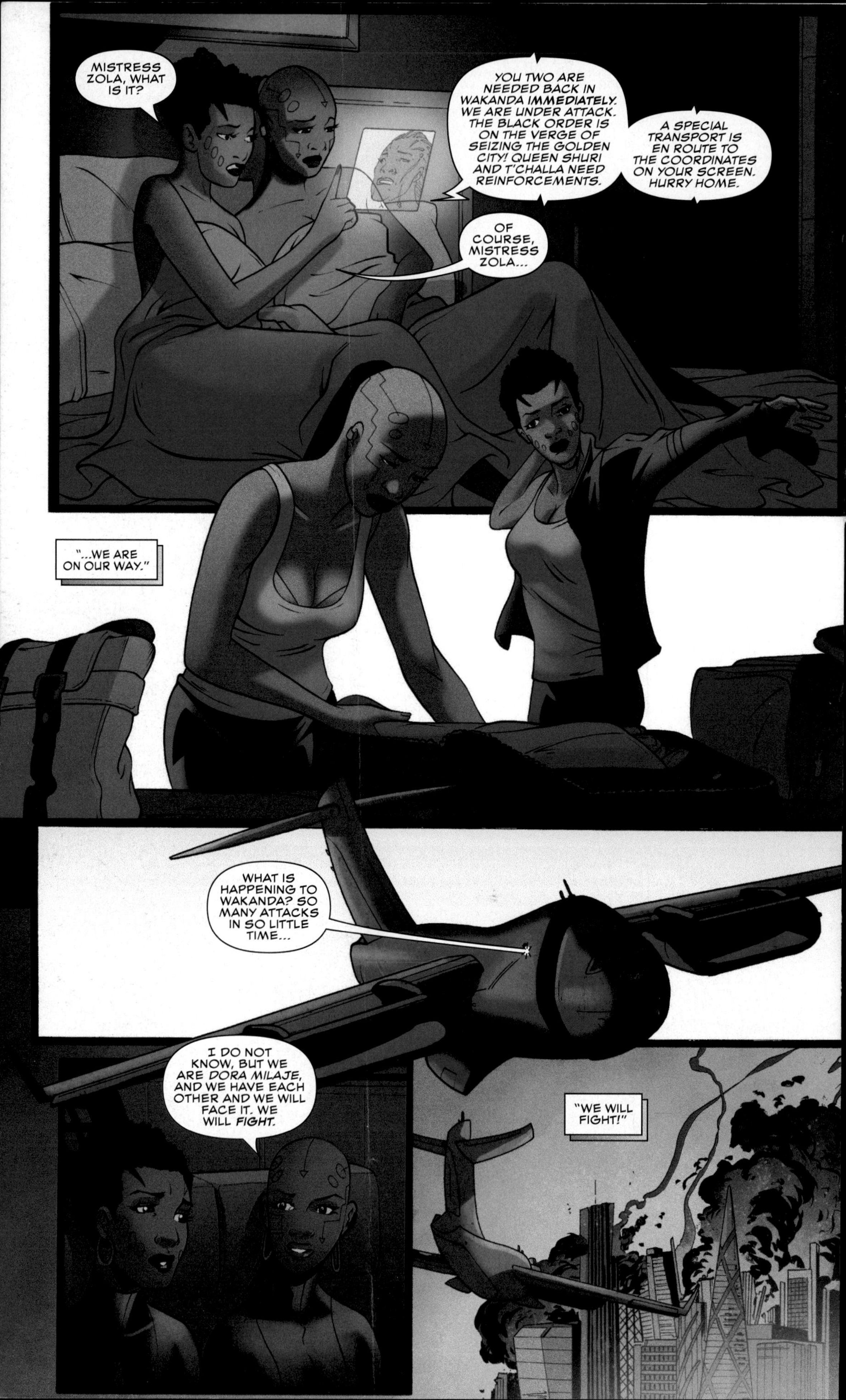
MISTRESS ZOLA, WHAT IS IT?
YOU TWO ARE NEEDED BACK IN WAKANDA IMMEDIATELY. WE ARE UNDER ATTACK. THE BLACK ORDER IS ON THE VERGE OF SEIZING THE GOLDEN CITY! QUEEN SHURI AND T'CHALLA NEED REINFORCEMENTS.
A SPECIAL TRANSPORT IS EN ROUTE TO THE COORDINATES ON YOUR SCREEN. HURRY HOME.
OF COURSE, MISTRESS ZOLA...
"...WE ARE ON OUR WAY."
WHAT IS HAPPENING TO WAKANDA? SO MANY ATTACKS IN SO LITTLE TIME...
I DO NOT KNOW, BUT WE ARE DORA MILAJE, AND WE HAVE EACH OTHER AND WE WILL FACE IT. WE WILL FIGHT.
"WE WILL FIGHT!"

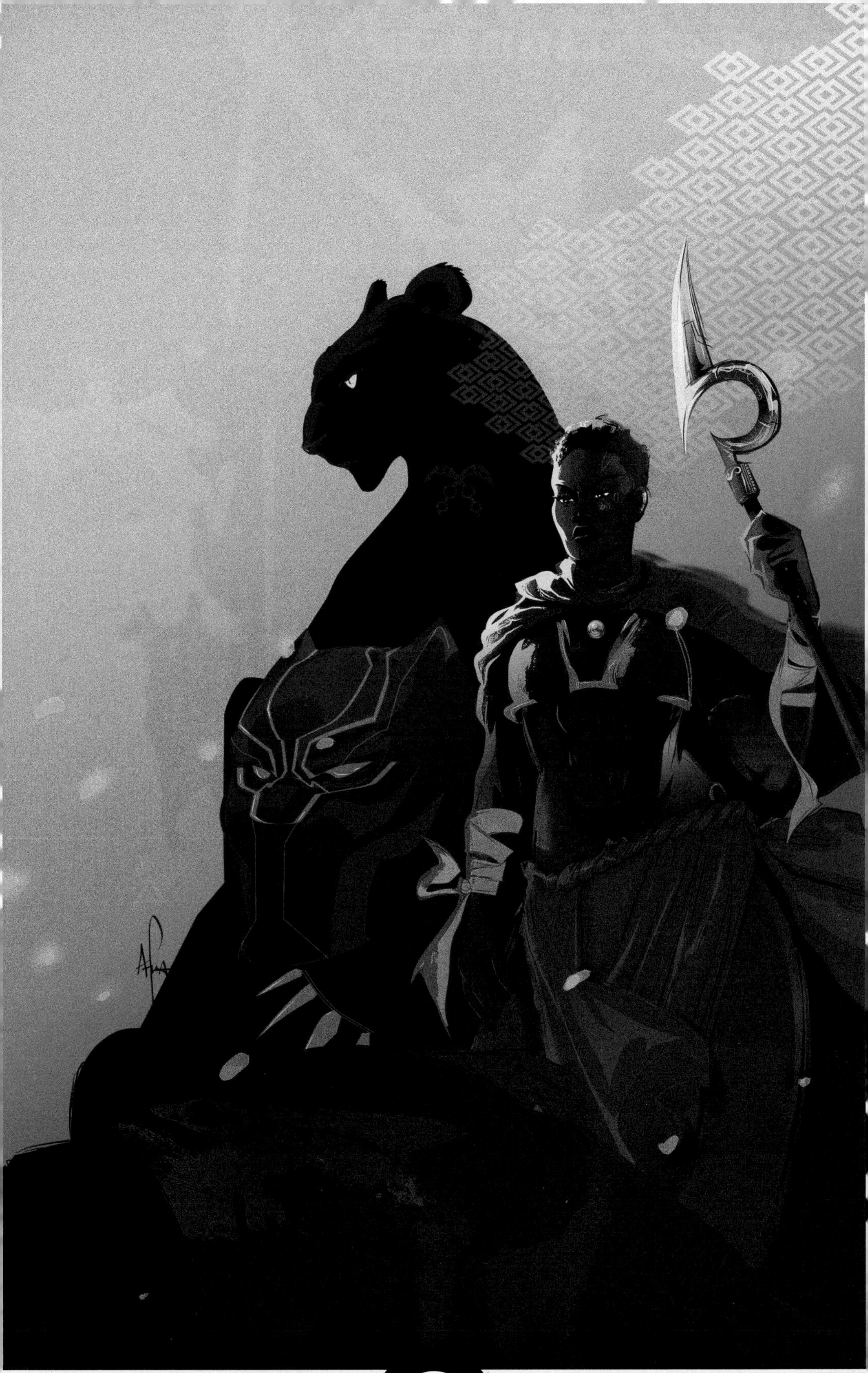

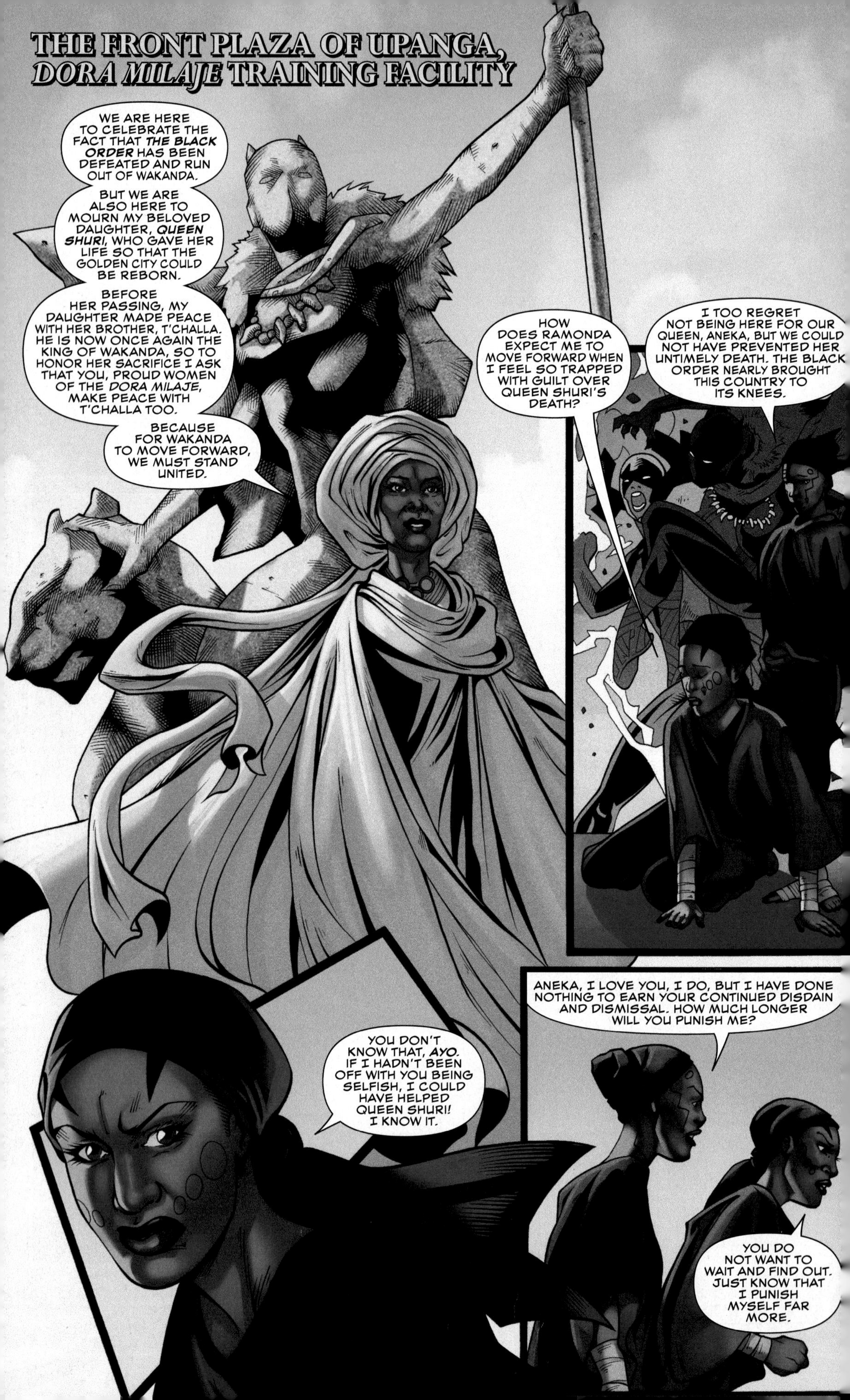
THE FRONT PLAZA OF UPANGA, DORA MILAJE TRAINING FACILITY
WE ARE HERE TO CELEBRATE THE FACT THAT THE BLACK ORDER HAS BEEN DEFEATED AND RUN OUT OF WAKANDA.
BUT WE ARE ALSO HERE TO MOURN MY BELOVED DAUGHTER, QUEEN SHURI, WHO GAVE HER LIFE SO THAT THE GOLDEN CITY COULD BE REBORN.
BEFORE HER PASSING, MY DAUGHTER MADE PEACE WITH HER BROTHER, T'CHALLA. HE IS NOW ONCE AGAIN THE KING OF WAKANDA, SO TO HONOR HER SACRIFICE I ASK THAT YOU, PROUD WOMEN OF THE DORA MILAJE, MAKE PEACE WITH T'CHALLA TOO.
BECAUSE FOR WAKANDA TO MOVE FORWARD, WE MUST STAND UNITED.
HOW DOES RAMONDA EXPECT ME TO MOVE FORWARD WHEN I FEEL SO TRAPPED WITH GUILT OVER QUEEN SHURI'S DEATH?
I TOO REGRET NOT BEING HERE FOR OUR QUEEN, ANEKA, BUT WE COULD NOT HAVE PREVENTED HER UNTIMELY DEATH. THE BLACK ORDER NEARLY BROUGHT THIS COUNTRY TO ITS KNEES.
YOU DON'T KNOW THAT, AYO. IF I HADN'T BEEN OFF WITH YOU BEING SELFISH, I COULD HAVE HELPED QUEEN SHURI! I KNOW IT.
ANEKA, I LOVE YOU, I DO, BUT I HAVE DONE NOTHING TO EARN YOUR CONTINUED DISDAIN AND DISMISSAL. HOW MUCH LONGER WILL YOU PUNISH ME?
YOU DO NOT WANT TO WAIT AND FIND OUT. JUST KNOW THAT I PUNISH MYSELF FAR MORE.

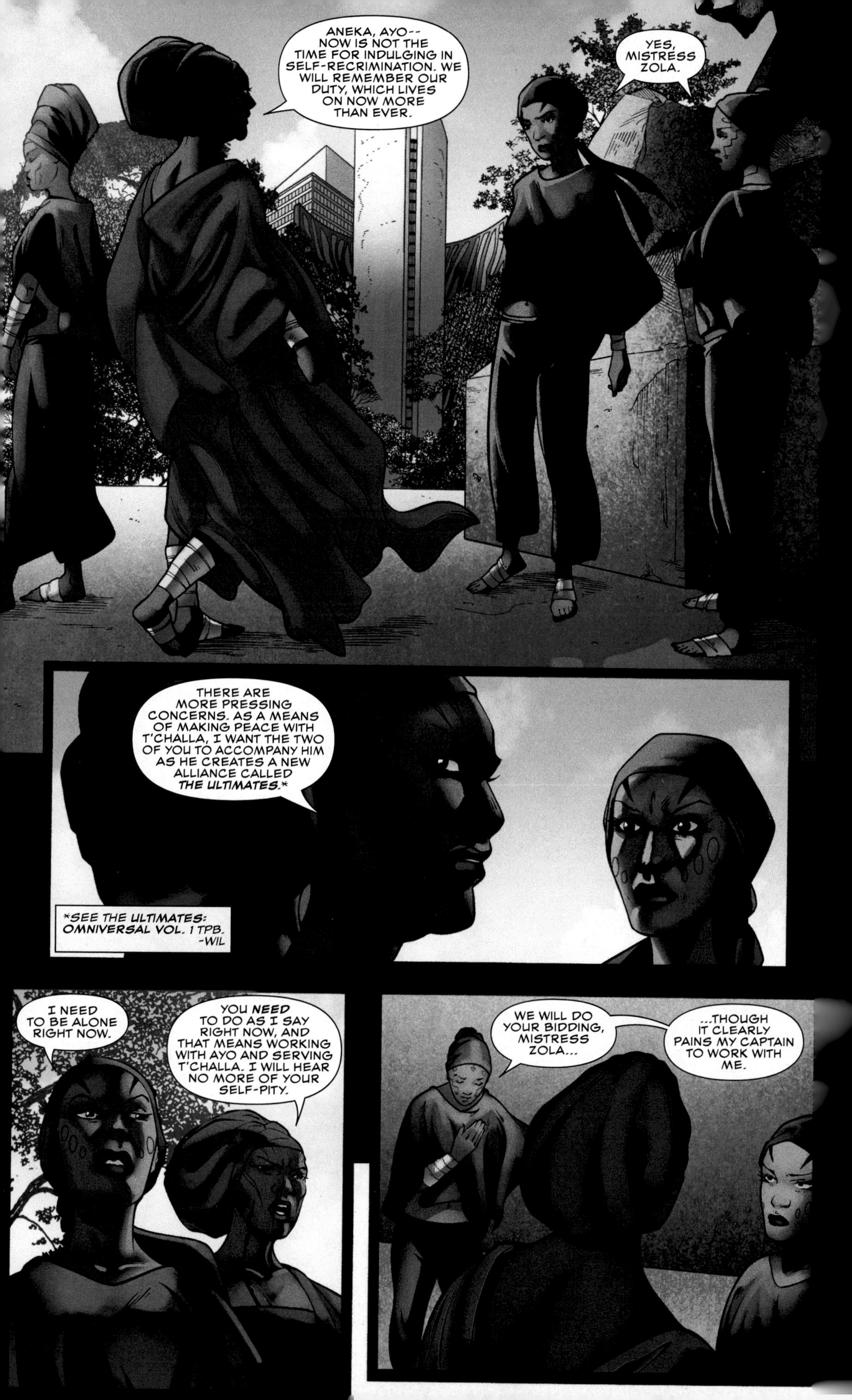
ANEKA, AYO-- NOW IS NOT THE TIME FOR INDULGING IN SELF-RECRIMINATION. WE WILL REMEMBER OUR DUTY, WHICH LIVES ON NOW MORE THAN EVER.
YES, MISTRESS ZOLA.
THERE ARE MORE PRESSING CONCERNS. AS A MEANS OF MAKING PEACE WITH T'CHALLA, I WANT THE TWO OF YOU TO ACCOMPANY HIM AS HE CREATES A NEW ALLIANCE CALLED THE ULTIMATES.*
*SEE THE ULTIMATES: OMNIVERSAL VOL. 1 TPB. -WIL
I NEED TO BE ALONE RIGHT NOW.
YOU NEED TO DO AS I SAY RIGHT NOW, AND THAT MEANS WORKING WITH AYO AND SERVING T'CHALLA. I WILL HEAR NO MORE OF YOUR SELF-PITY.
WE WILL DO YOUR BIDDING, MISTRESS ZOLA...
...THOUGH IT CLEARLY PAINS MY CAPTAIN TO WORK WITH ME.

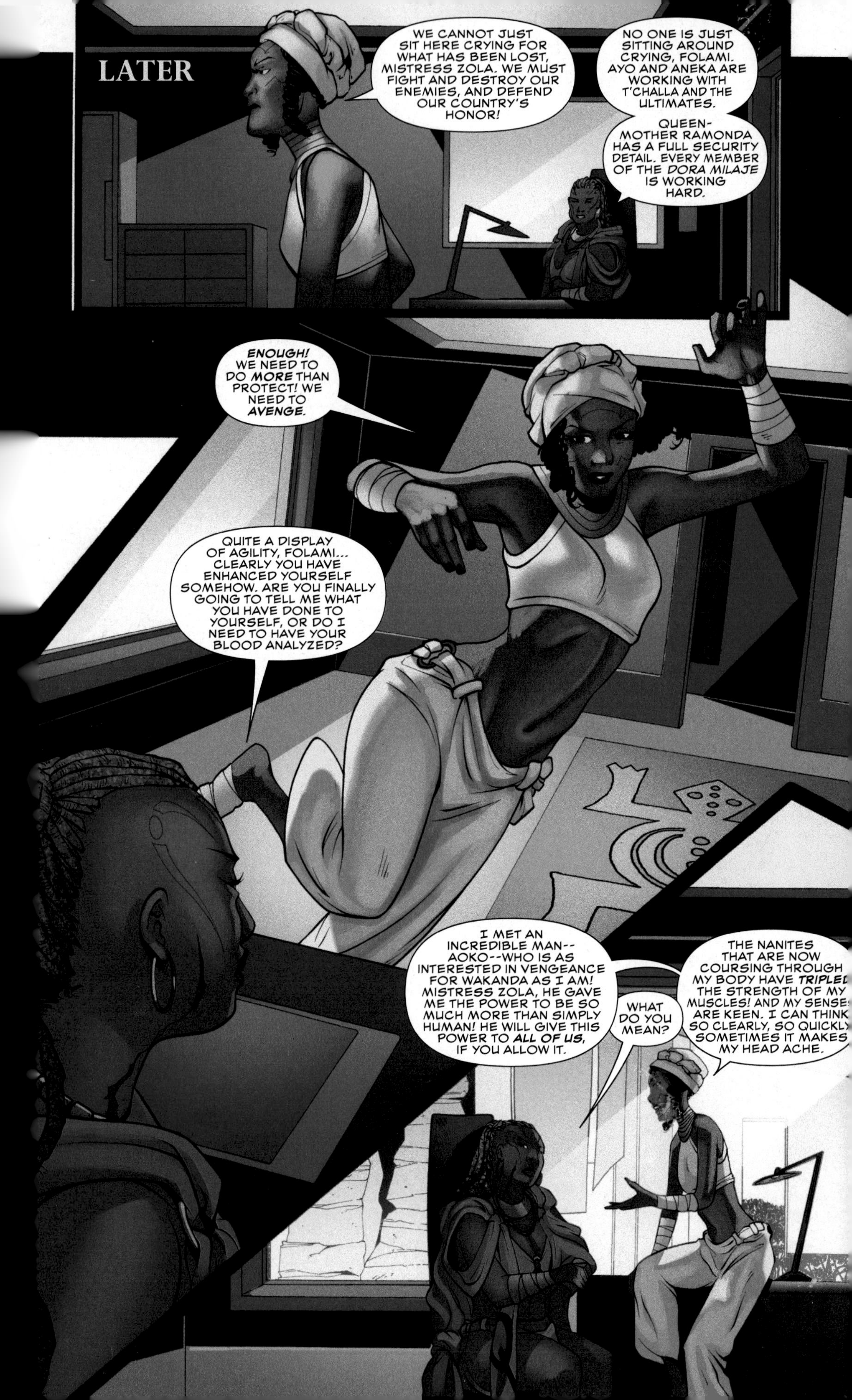
LATER
WE CANNOT JUST SIT HERE CRYING FOR WHAT HAS BEEN LOST, MISTRESS ZOLA. WE MUST FIGHT AND DESTROY OUR ENEMIES, AND DEFEND OUR COUNTRY'S HONOR!
NO ONE IS JUST SITTING AROUND CRYING, FOLAMI. AYO AND ANEKA ARE WORKING WITH T'CHALLA AND THE ULTIMATES.
QUEEN-MOTHER RAMONDA HAS A FULL SECURITY DETAIL. EVERY MEMBER OF THE DORA MILAJE IS WORKING HARD.
ENOUGH! WE NEED TO DO MORE THAN PROTECT! WE NEED TO AVENGE.
QUITE A DISPLAY OF AGILITY, FOLAMI... CLEARLY YOU HAVE ENHANCED YOURSELF SOMEHOW. ARE YOU FINALLY GOING TO TELL ME WHAT YOU HAVE DONE TO YOURSELF, OR DO I NEED TO HAVE YOUR BLOOD ANALYZED?
I MET AN INCREDIBLE MAN--AOKO--WHO IS AS INTERESTED IN VENGEANCE FOR WAKANDA AS I AM! MISTRESS ZOLA, HE GAVE ME THE POWER TO BE SO MUCH MORE THAN SIMPLY HUMAN! HE WILL GIVE THIS POWER TO ALL OF US, IF YOU ALLOW IT.
WHAT DO YOU MEAN?
THE NANITES THAT ARE NOW COURSING THROUGH MY BODY HAVE TRIPLED THE STRENGTH OF MY MUSCLES! AND MY SENSES ARE KEEN. I CAN THINK SO CLEARLY, SO QUICKLY SOMETIMES IT MAKES MY HEAD ACHE.

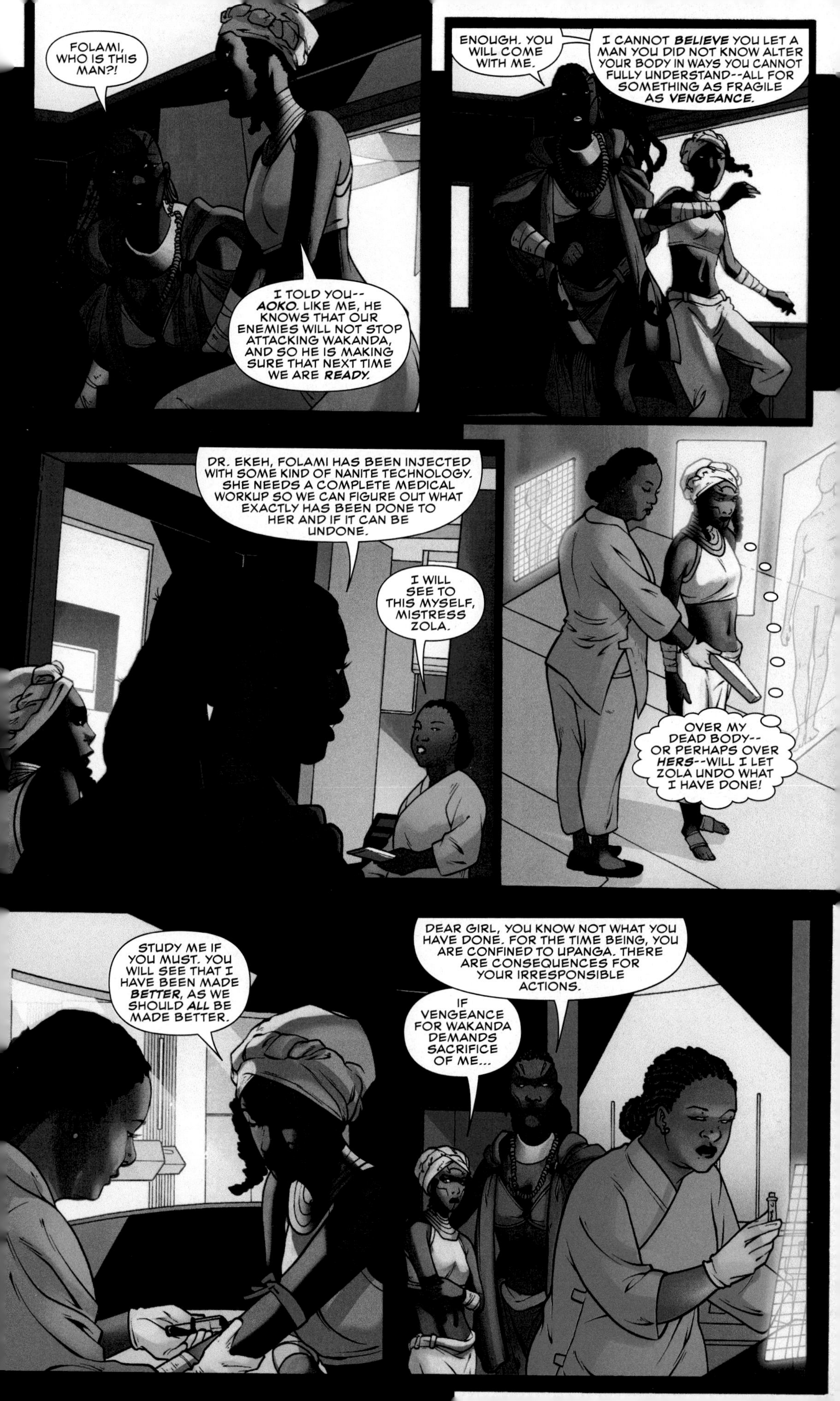
FOLAMI, WHO IS THIS MAN?!
I TOLD YOU-- AOKO. LIKE ME, HE KNOWS THAT OUR ENEMIES WILL NOT STOP ATTACKING WAKANDA, AND SO HE IS MAKING SURE THAT NEXT TIME WE ARE READY.
ENOUGH. YOU WILL COME WITH ME.
I CANNOT BELIEVE YOU LET A MAN YOU DID NOT KNOW ALTER YOUR BODY IN WAYS YOU CANNOT FULLY UNDERSTAND--ALL FOR SOMETHING AS FRAGILE AS VENGEANCE.
DR. EKEH, FOLAMI HAS BEEN INJECTED WITH SOME KIND OF NANITE TECHNOLOGY. SHE NEEDS A COMPLETE MEDICAL WORKUP SO WE CAN FIGURE OUT WHAT EXACTLY HAS BEEN DONE TO HER AND IF IT CAN BE UNDONE.
I WILL SEE TO THIS MYSELF, MISTRESS ZOLA.
OVER MY DEAD BODY-- OR PERHAPS OVER HERS--WILL I LET ZOLA UNDO WHAT I HAVE DONE!
STUDY ME IF YOU MUST. YOU WILL SEE THAT I HAVE BEEN MADE BETTER, AS WE SHOULD ALL BE MADE BETTER.
DEAR GIRL, YOU KNOW NOT WHAT YOU HAVE DONE. FOR THE TIME BEING, YOU ARE CONFINED TO UPANGA. THERE ARE CONSEQUENCES FOR YOUR IRRESPONSIBLE ACTIONS.
IF VENGEANCE FOR WAKANDA DEMANDS SACRIFICE OF ME...

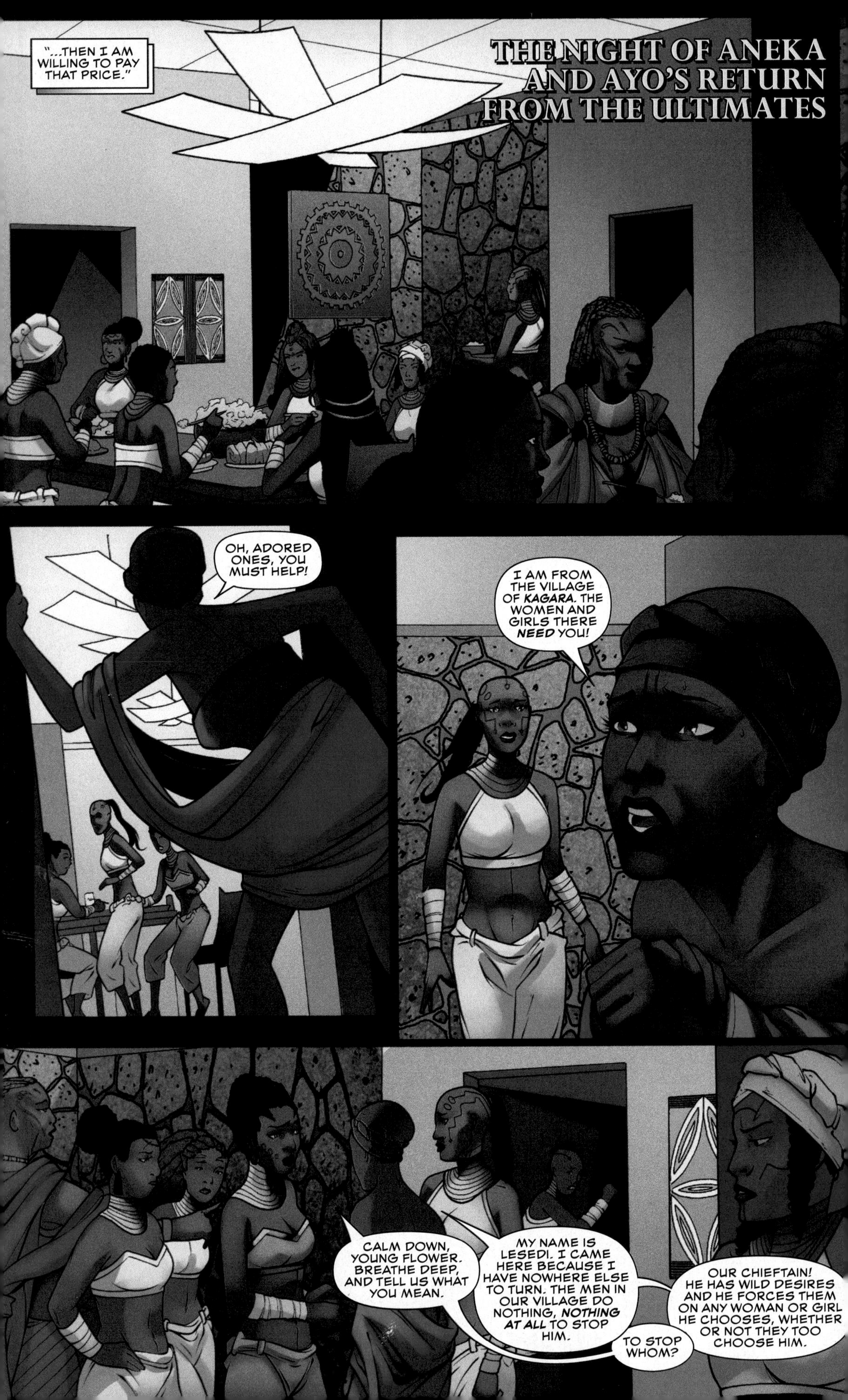
"...THEN I AM WILLING TO PAY THAT PRICE."
THE NIGHT OF ANEKA AND AYO'S RETURN FROM THE ULTIMATES
OH, ADORED ONES, YOU MUST HELP!
I AM FROM THE VILLAGE OF *KAGARA*. THE WOMEN AND GIRLS THERE *NEED* YOU!
CALM DOWN, YOUNG FLOWER. BREATHE DEEP, AND TELL US WHAT YOU MEAN.
MY NAME IS LESEDI. I CAME HERE BECAUSE I HAVE NOWHERE ELSE TO TURN. THE MEN IN OUR VILLAGE DO NOTHING, ***NOTHING AT ALL*** TO STOP HIM.
TO STOP WHOM?
OUR CHIEFTAIN! HE HAS WILD DESIRES AND HE FORCES THEM ON ANY WOMAN OR GIRL HE CHOOSES, WHETHER OR NOT THEY TOO CHOOSE HIM.

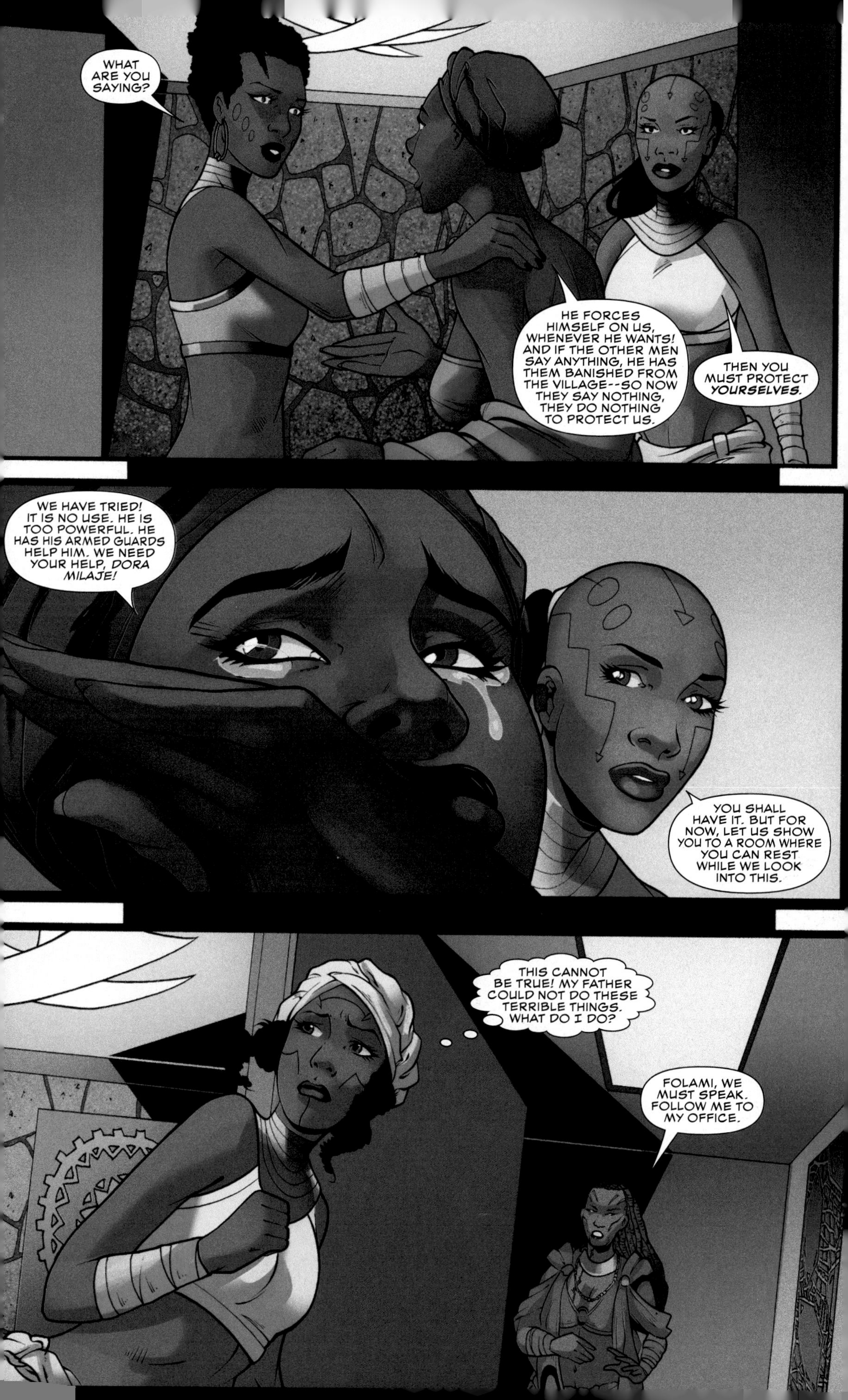
WHAT ARE YOU SAYING?
HE FORCES HIMSELF ON US, WHENEVER HE WANTS! AND IF THE OTHER MEN SAY ANYTHING, HE HAS THEM BANISHED FROM THE VILLAGE--SO NOW THEY SAY NOTHING, THEY DO NOTHING TO PROTECT US.
THEN YOU MUST PROTECT *YOURSELVES.*
WE HAVE TRIED! IT IS NO USE. HE IS TOO POWERFUL. HE HAS HIS ARMED GUARDS HELP HIM. WE NEED YOUR HELP, *DORA MILAJE!*
YOU SHALL HAVE IT. BUT FOR NOW, LET US SHOW YOU TO A ROOM WHERE YOU CAN REST WHILE WE LOOK INTO THIS.
THIS CANNOT BE TRUE! MY FATHER COULD NOT DO THESE TERRIBLE THINGS. WHAT DO I DO?
FOLAMI, WE MUST SPEAK. FOLLOW ME TO MY OFFICE.

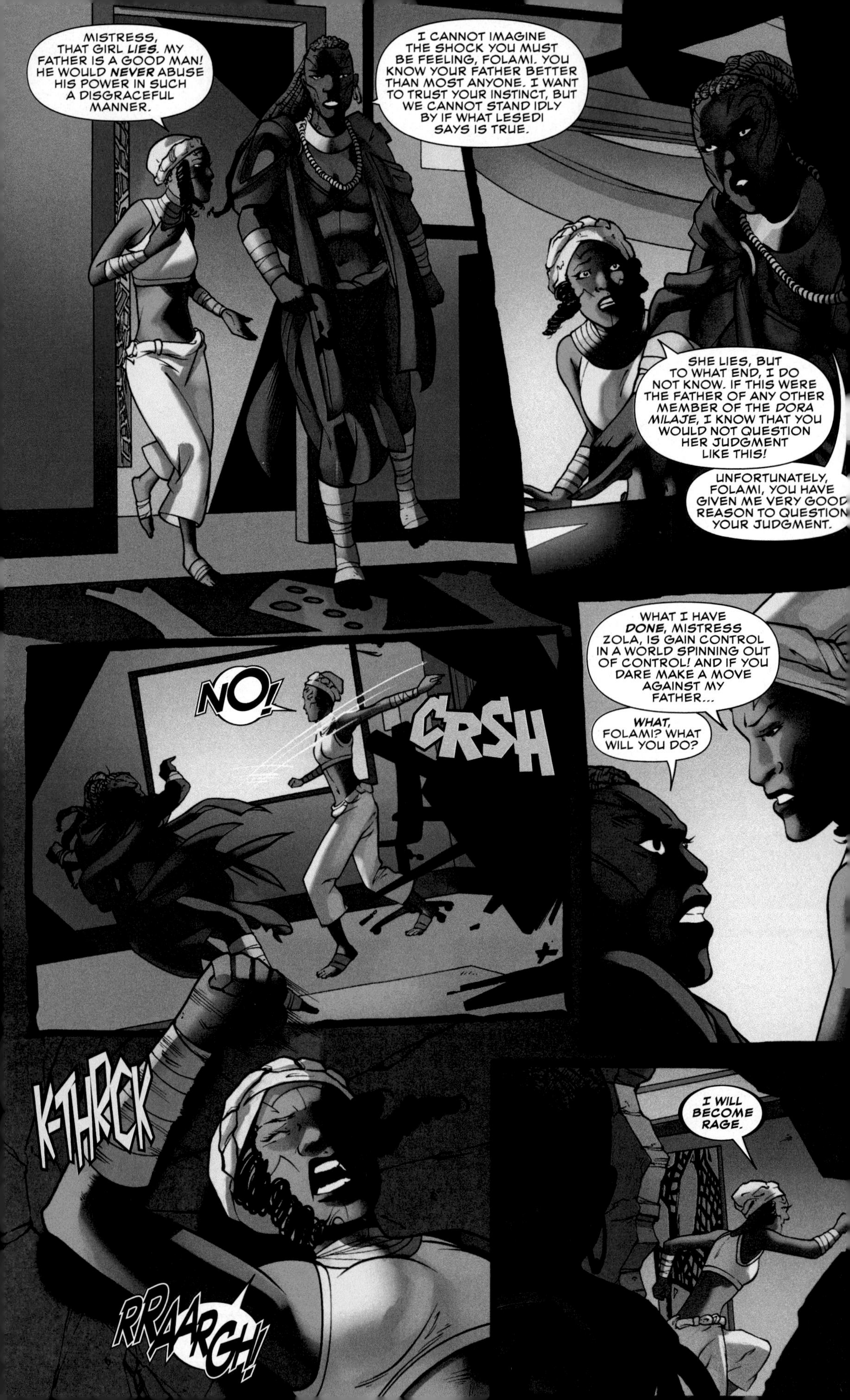
MISTRESS, THAT GIRL LIES. MY FATHER IS A GOOD MAN! HE WOULD NEVER ABUSE HIS POWER IN SUCH A DISGRACEFUL MANNER.
I CANNOT IMAGINE THE SHOCK YOU MUST BE FEELING, FOLAMI. YOU KNOW YOUR FATHER BETTER THAN MOST ANYONE. I WANT TO TRUST YOUR INSTINCT, BUT WE CANNOT STAND IDLY BY IF WHAT LESEDI SAYS IS TRUE.
SHE LIES, BUT TO WHAT END, I DO NOT KNOW. IF THIS WERE THE FATHER OF ANY OTHER MEMBER OF THE DORA MILAJE, I KNOW THAT YOU WOULD NOT QUESTION HER JUDGMENT LIKE THIS!
UNFORTUNATELY, FOLAMI, YOU HAVE GIVEN ME VERY GOOD REASON TO QUESTION YOUR JUDGMENT.
NO!
CRSH
WHAT I HAVE DONE, MISTRESS ZOLA, IS GAIN CONTROL IN A WORLD SPINNING OUT OF CONTROL! AND IF YOU DARE MAKE A MOVE AGAINST MY FATHER...
WHAT, FOLAMI? WHAT WILL YOU DO?
K-THRCK
RRAARGH!
I WILL BECOME RAGE.

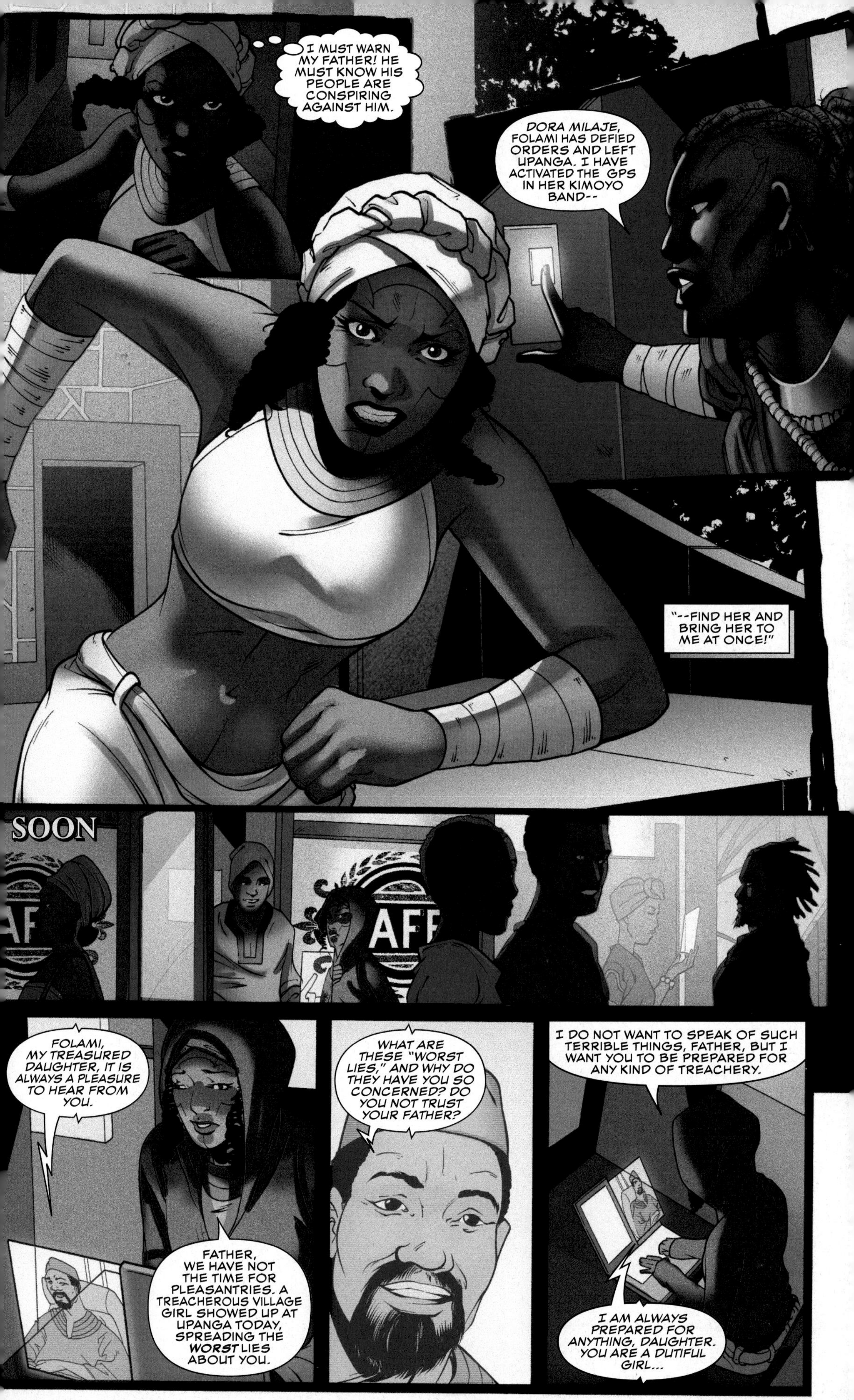

I MUST WARN MY FATHER! HE MUST KNOW HIS PEOPLE ARE CONSPIRING AGAINST HIM.
DORA MILAJE, FOLAMI HAS DEFIED ORDERS AND LEFT UPANGA. I HAVE ACTIVATED THE GPS IN HER KIMOYO BAND--
"--FIND HER AND BRING HER TO ME AT ONCE!"
SOON
FOLAMI, MY TREASURED DAUGHTER, IT IS ALWAYS A PLEASURE TO HEAR FROM YOU.
FATHER, WE HAVE NOT THE TIME FOR PLEASANTRIES. A TREACHEROUS VILLAGE GIRL SHOWED UP AT UPANGA TODAY, SPREADING THE WORST LIES ABOUT YOU.
WHAT ARE THESE "WORST LIES," AND WHY DO THEY HAVE YOU SO CONCERNED? DO YOU NOT TRUST YOUR FATHER?
I DO NOT WANT TO SPEAK OF SUCH TERRIBLE THINGS, FATHER, BUT I WANT YOU TO BE PREPARED FOR ANY KIND OF TREACHERY.
I AM ALWAYS PREPARED FOR ANYTHING, DAUGHTER. YOU ARE A DUTIFUL GIRL...

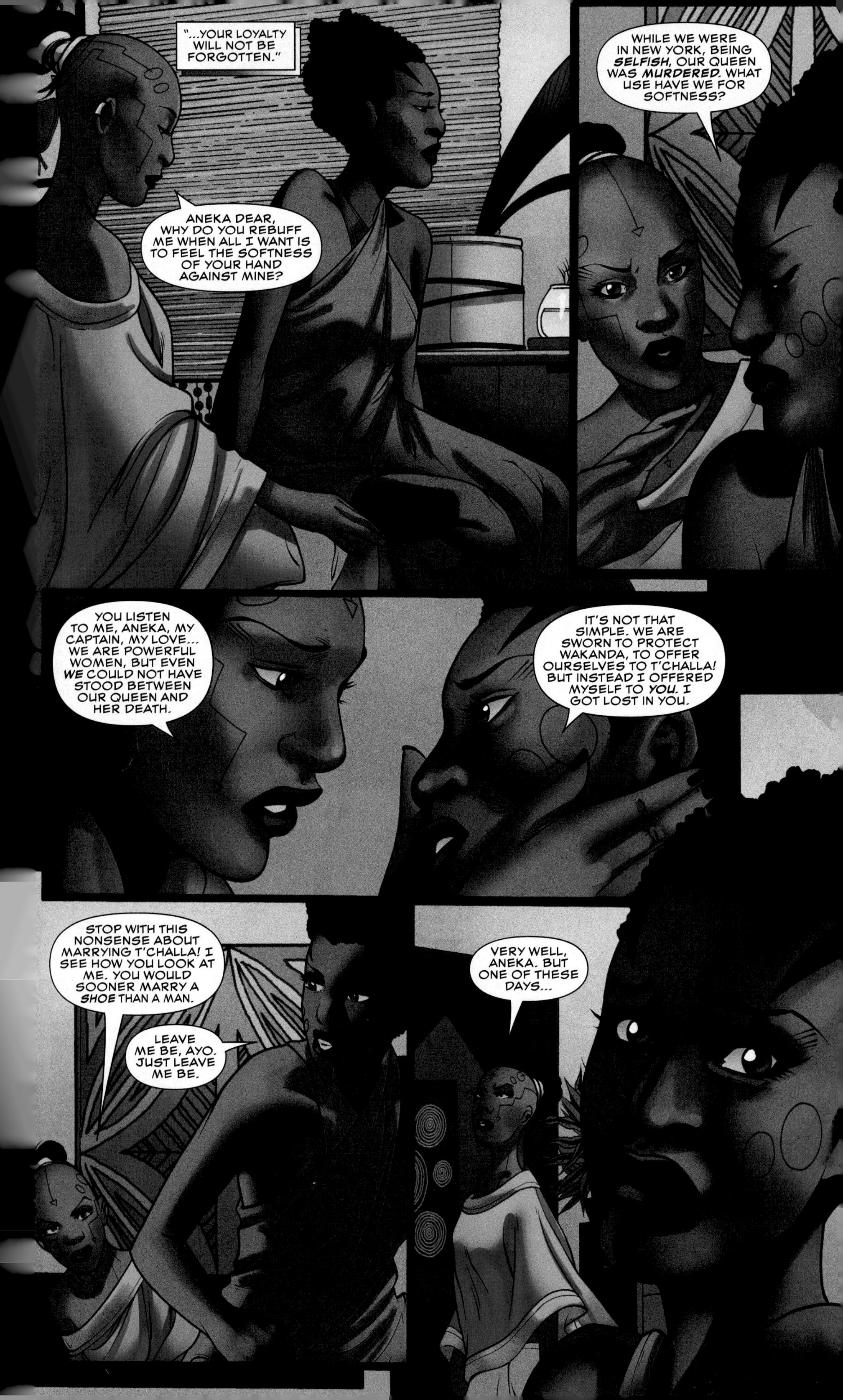

"...YOUR LOYALTY WILL NOT BE FORGOTTEN."
ANEKA DEAR, WHY DO YOU REBUFF ME WHEN ALL I WANT IS TO FEEL THE SOFTNESS OF YOUR HAND AGAINST MINE?
WHILE WE WERE IN NEW YORK, BEING SELFISH, OUR QUEEN WAS MURDERED. WHAT USE HAVE WE FOR SOFTNESS?
YOU LISTEN TO ME, ANEKA, MY CAPTAIN, MY LOVE... WE ARE POWERFUL WOMEN, BUT EVEN WE COULD NOT HAVE STOOD BETWEEN OUR QUEEN AND HER DEATH.
IT'S NOT THAT SIMPLE. WE ARE SWORN TO PROTECT WAKANDA, TO OFFER OURSELVES TO T'CHALLA! BUT INSTEAD I OFFERED MYSELF TO YOU. I GOT LOST IN YOU.
STOP WITH THIS NONSENSE ABOUT MARRYING T'CHALLA! I SEE HOW YOU LOOK AT ME. YOU WOULD SOONER MARRY A SHOE THAN A MAN.
LEAVE ME BE, AYO. JUST LEAVE ME BE.
VERY WELL, ANEKA. BUT ONE OF THESE DAYS...

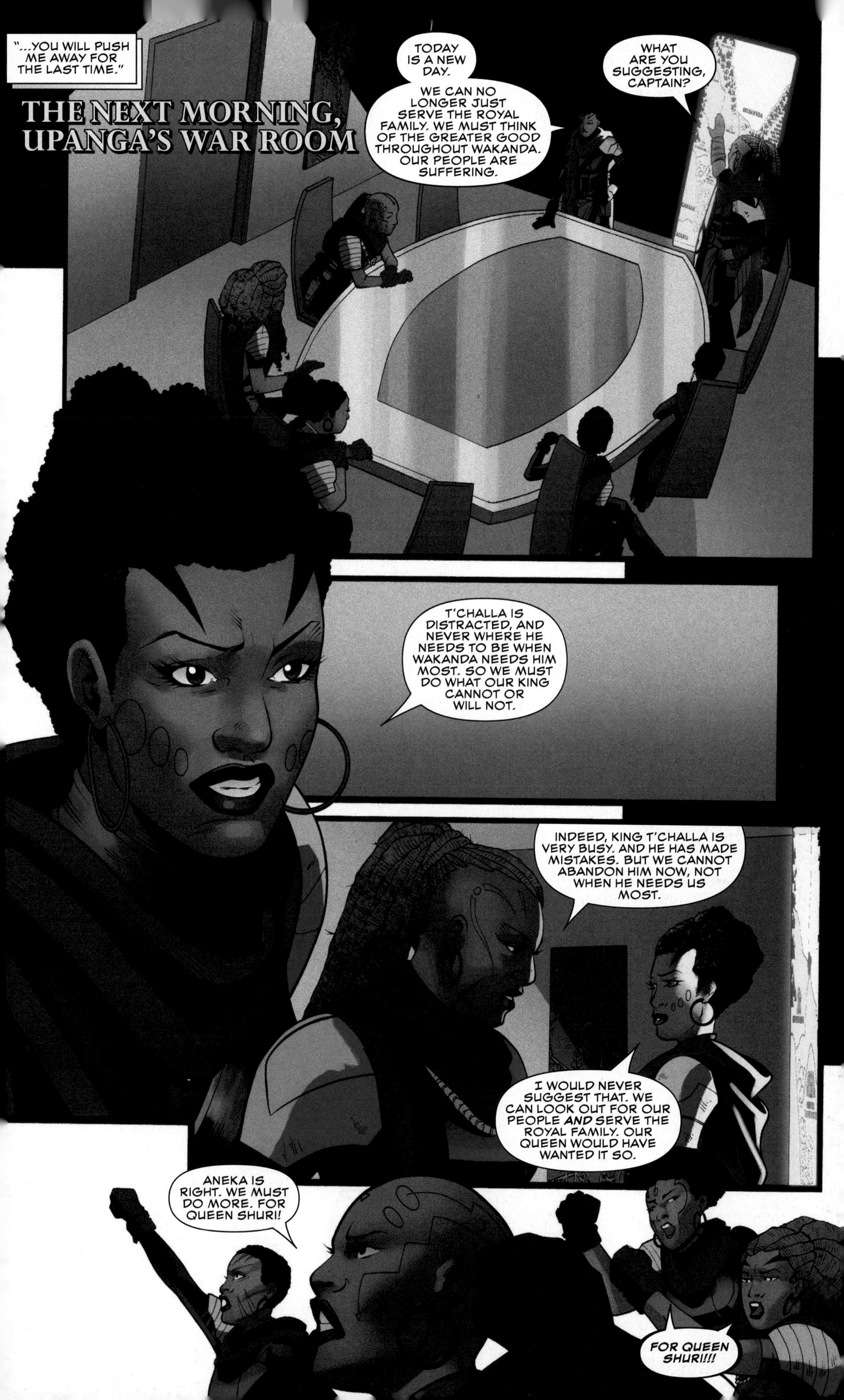
"...YOU WILL PUSH ME AWAY FOR THE LAST TIME."
THE NEXT MORNING, UPANGA'S WAR ROOM
TODAY IS A NEW DAY.
WE CAN NO LONGER JUST SERVE THE ROYAL FAMILY. WE MUST THINK OF THE GREATER GOOD THROUGHOUT WAKANDA. OUR PEOPLE ARE SUFFERING.
WHAT ARE YOU SUGGESTING, CAPTAIN?
T'CHALLA IS DISTRACTED, AND NEVER WHERE HE NEEDS TO BE WHEN WAKANDA NEEDS HIM MOST. SO WE MUST DO WHAT OUR KING CANNOT OR WILL NOT.
INDEED, KING T'CHALLA IS VERY BUSY. AND HE HAS MADE MISTAKES. BUT WE CANNOT ABANDON HIM NOW, NOT WHEN HE NEEDS US MOST.
I WOULD NEVER SUGGEST THAT. WE CAN LOOK OUT FOR OUR PEOPLE AND SERVE THE ROYAL FAMILY. OUR QUEEN WOULD HAVE WANTED IT SO.
ANEKA IS RIGHT. WE MUST DO MORE. FOR QUEEN SHURI!
FOR QUEEN SHURI!!!

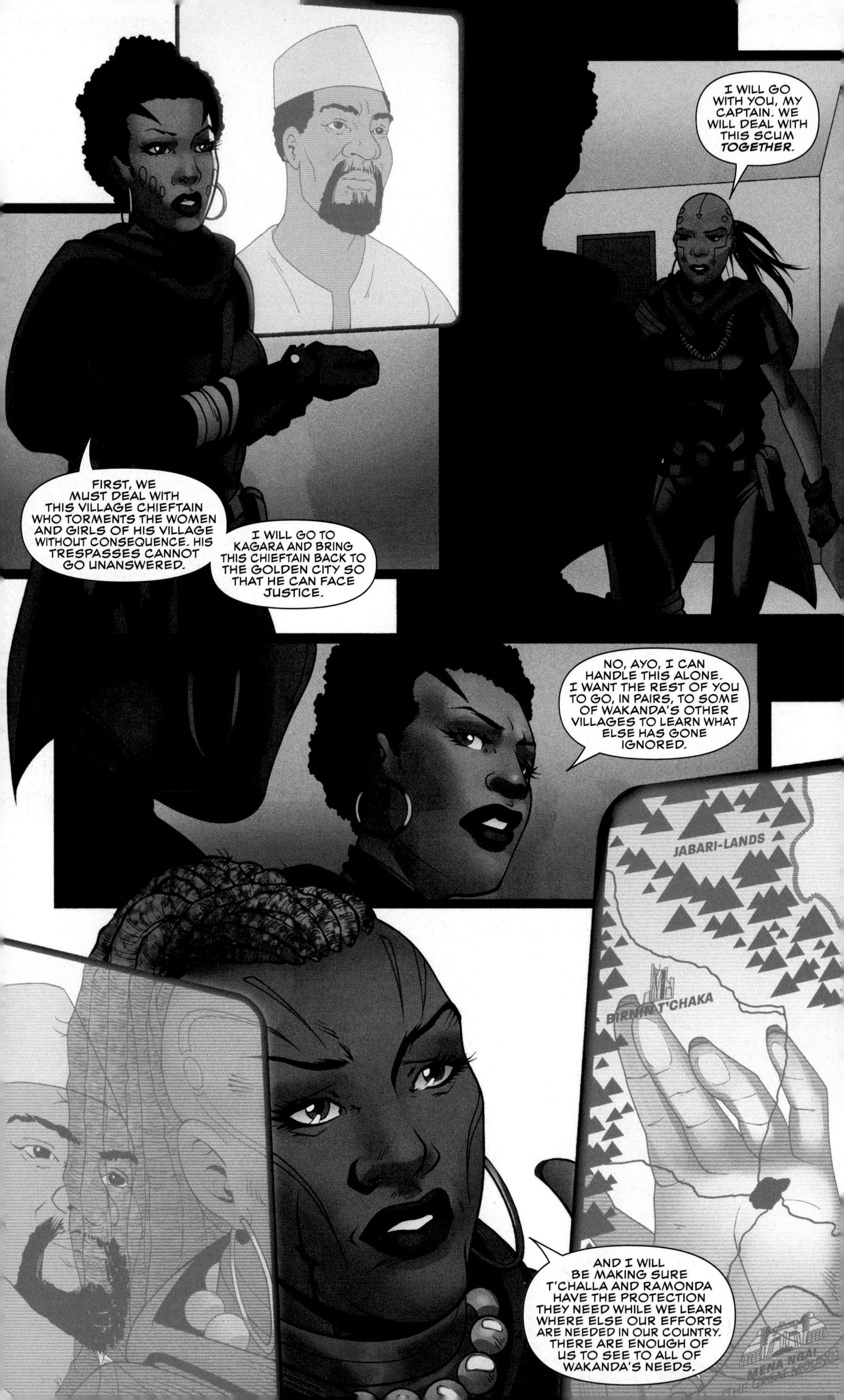
FIRST, WE MUST DEAL WITH THIS VILLAGE CHIEFTAIN WHO TORMENTS THE WOMEN AND GIRLS OF HIS VILLAGE WITHOUT CONSEQUENCE. HIS TRESPASSES CANNOT GO UNANSWERED.
I WILL GO TO KAGARA AND BRING THIS CHIEFTAIN BACK TO THE GOLDEN CITY SO THAT HE CAN FACE JUSTICE.
I WILL GO WITH YOU, MY CAPTAIN. WE WILL DEAL WITH THIS SCUM *TOGETHER*.
NO, AYO, I CAN HANDLE THIS ALONE. I WANT THE REST OF YOU TO GO, IN PAIRS, TO SOME OF WAKANDA'S OTHER VILLAGES TO LEARN WHAT ELSE HAS GONE IGNORED.
JABARI-LANDS
BIRNIN T'CHAKA
MENA NGAI
AND I WILL BE MAKING SURE T'CHALLA AND RAMONDA HAVE THE PROTECTION THEY NEED WHILE WE LEARN WHERE ELSE OUR EFFORTS ARE NEEDED IN OUR COUNTRY. THERE ARE ENOUGH OF US TO SEE TO ALL OF WAKANDA'S NEEDS.

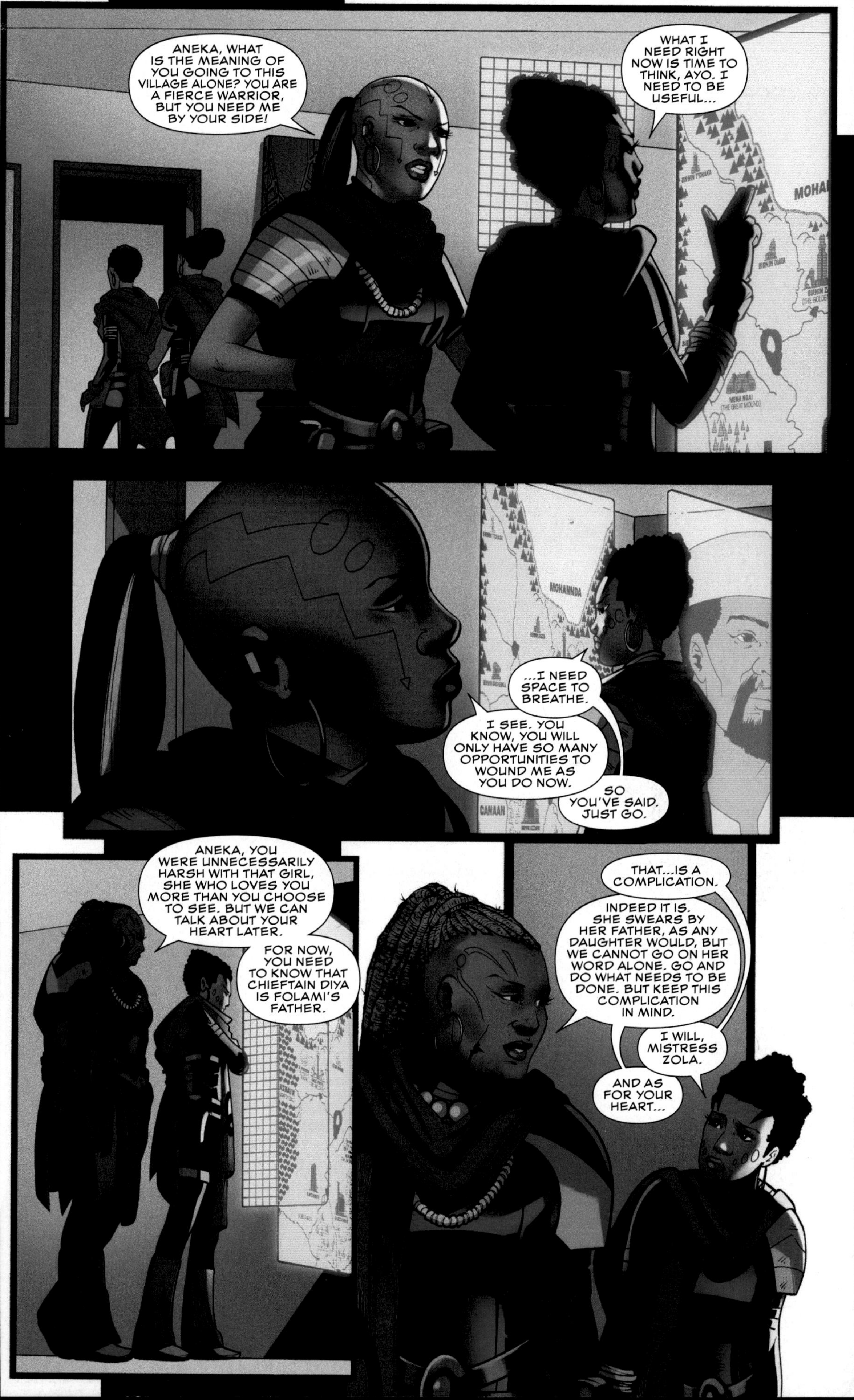
ANEKA, WHAT IS THE MEANING OF YOU GOING TO THIS VILLAGE ALONE? YOU ARE A FIERCE WARRIOR, BUT YOU NEED ME BY YOUR SIDE!
WHAT I NEED RIGHT NOW IS TIME TO THINK, AYO. I NEED TO BE USEFUL...
MOHANNDA
...I NEED SPACE TO BREATHE.
I SEE. YOU KNOW, YOU WILL ONLY HAVE SO MANY OPPORTUNITIES TO WOUND ME AS YOU DO NOW.
SO YOU'VE SAID. JUST GO.
CANAAN
ANEKA, YOU WERE UNNECESSARILY HARSH WITH THAT GIRL, SHE WHO LOVES YOU MORE THAN YOU CHOOSE TO SEE. BUT WE CAN TALK ABOUT YOUR HEART LATER.
FOR NOW, YOU NEED TO KNOW THAT CHIEFTAIN DIYA IS FOLAMI'S FATHER.
THAT...IS A COMPLICATION.
INDEED IT IS. SHE SWEARS BY HER FATHER, AS ANY DAUGHTER WOULD, BUT WE CANNOT GO ON HER WORD ALONE. GO AND DO WHAT NEEDS TO BE DONE. BUT KEEP THIS COMPLICATION IN MIND.
I WILL, MISTRESS ZOLA.
AND AS FOR YOUR HEART...

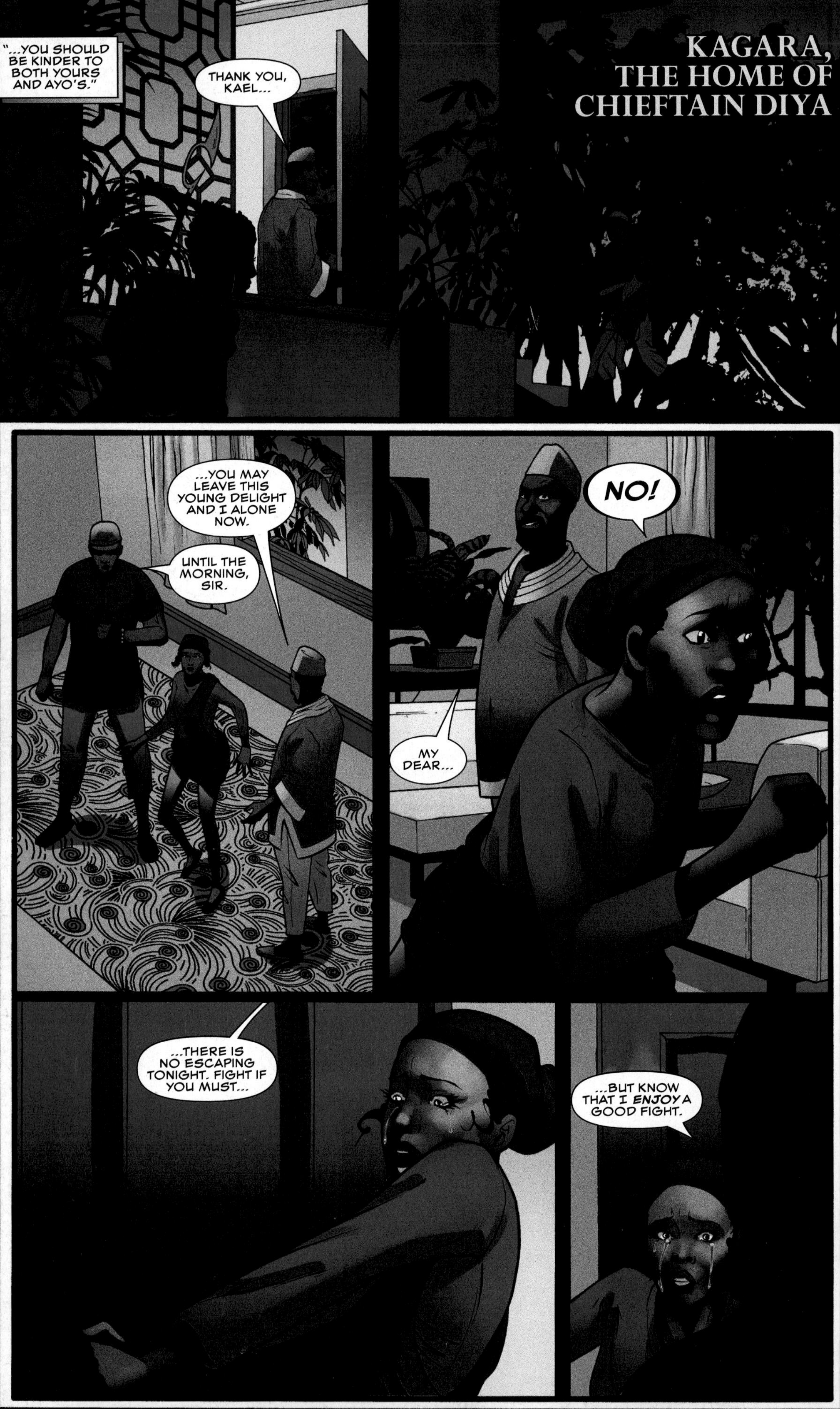
"...YOU SHOULD BE KINDER TO BOTH YOURS AND AYO'S."
THANK YOU, KAEL...
KAGARA, THE HOME OF CHIEFTAIN DIYA
...YOU MAY LEAVE THIS YOUNG DELIGHT AND I ALONE NOW.
UNTIL THE MORNING, SIR.
NO!
MY DEAR...
...THERE IS NO ESCAPING TONIGHT. FIGHT IF YOU MUST...
...BUT KNOW THAT I *ENJOY* A GOOD FIGHT.

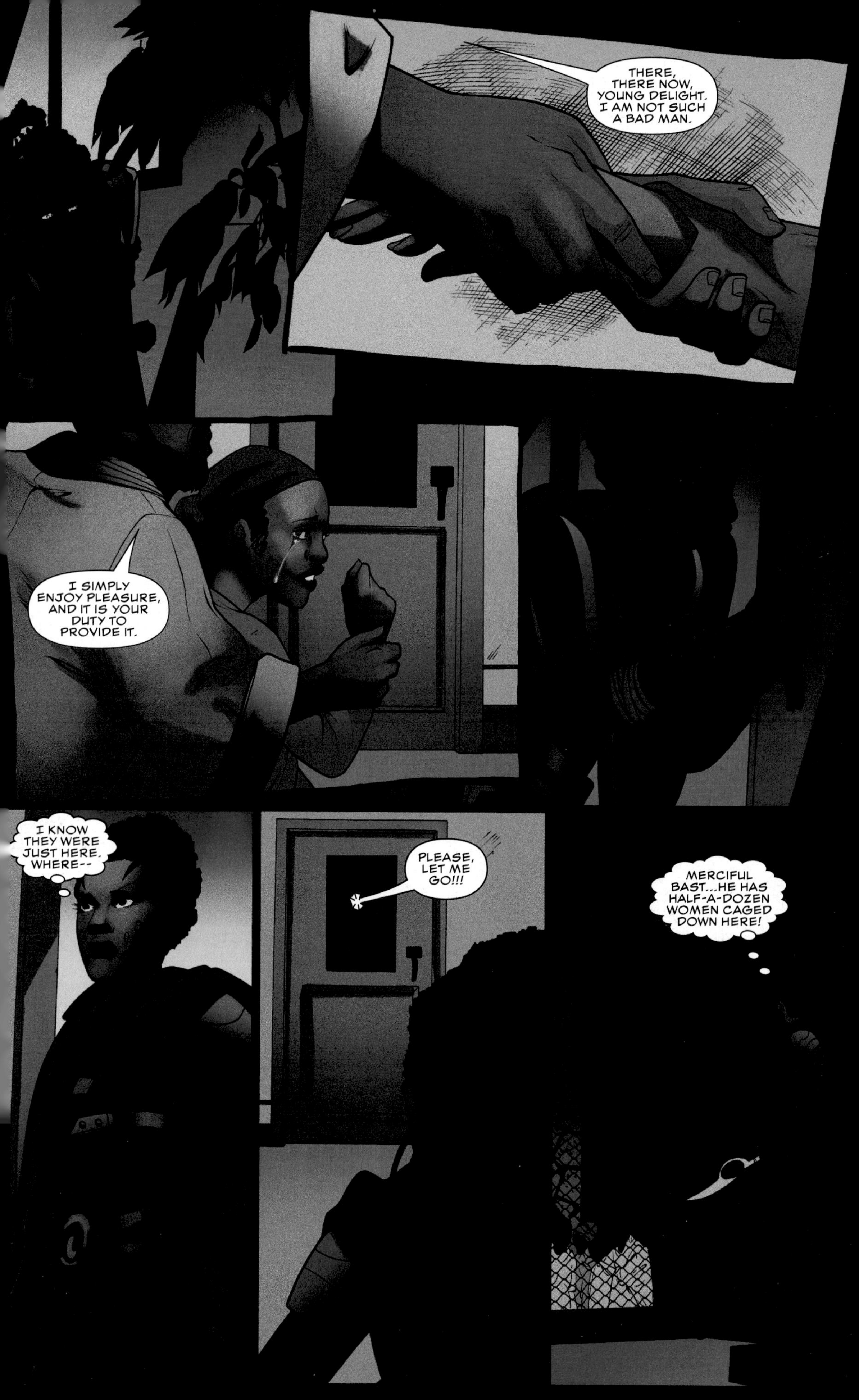
THERE, THERE NOW, YOUNG DELIGHT. I AM NOT SUCH A BAD MAN.
I SIMPLY ENJOY PLEASURE, AND IT IS YOUR DUTY TO PROVIDE IT.
I KNOW THEY WERE JUST HERE. WHERE--
PLEASE, LET ME GO!!!
MERCIFUL BAST...HE HAS HALF-A-DOZEN WOMEN CAGED DOWN HERE!

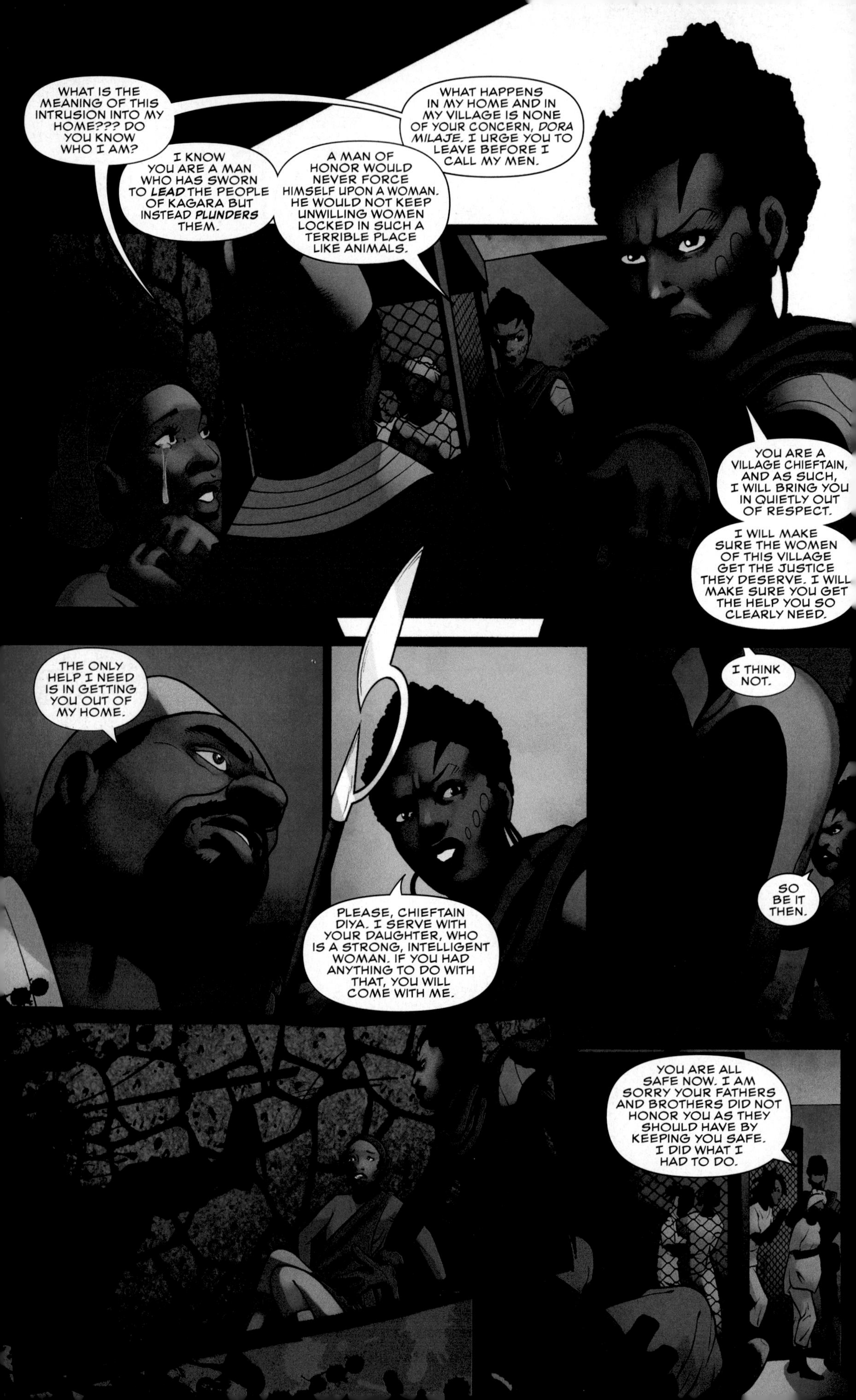
WHAT IS THE MEANING OF THIS INTRUSION INTO MY HOME??? DO YOU KNOW WHO I AM?
WHAT HAPPENS IN MY HOME AND IN MY VILLAGE IS NONE OF YOUR CONCERN, DORA MILAJE. I URGE YOU TO LEAVE BEFORE I CALL MY MEN.
I KNOW YOU ARE A MAN WHO HAS SWORN TO LEAD THE PEOPLE OF KAGARA BUT INSTEAD PLUNDERS THEM.
A MAN OF HONOR WOULD NEVER FORCE HIMSELF UPON A WOMAN. HE WOULD NOT KEEP UNWILLING WOMEN LOCKED IN SUCH A TERRIBLE PLACE LIKE ANIMALS.
YOU ARE A VILLAGE CHIEFTAIN, AND AS SUCH, I WILL BRING YOU IN QUIETLY OUT OF RESPECT.
I WILL MAKE SURE THE WOMEN OF THIS VILLAGE GET THE JUSTICE THEY DESERVE. I WILL MAKE SURE YOU GET THE HELP YOU SO CLEARLY NEED.
THE ONLY HELP I NEED IS IN GETTING YOU OUT OF MY HOME.
PLEASE, CHIEFTAIN DIYA. I SERVE WITH YOUR DAUGHTER, WHO IS A STRONG, INTELLIGENT WOMAN. IF YOU HAD ANYTHING TO DO WITH THAT, YOU WILL COME WITH ME.
I THINK NOT.
SO BE IT THEN.
YOU ARE ALL SAFE NOW. I AM SORRY YOUR FATHERS AND BROTHERS DID NOT HONOR YOU AS THEY SHOULD HAVE BY KEEPING YOU SAFE. I DID WHAT I HAD TO DO.

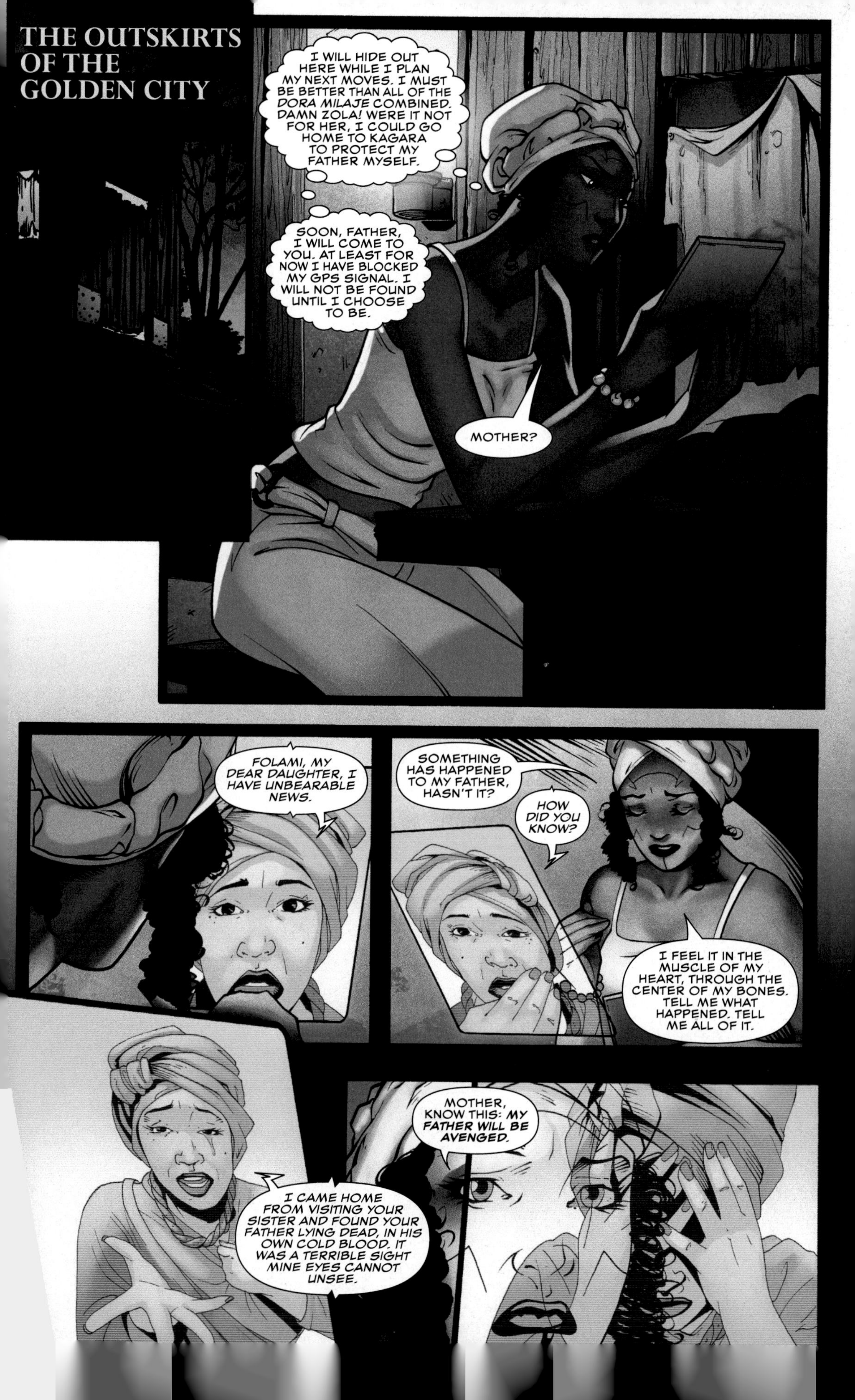
THE OUTSKIRTS OF THE GOLDEN CITY
I WILL HIDE OUT HERE WHILE I PLAN MY NEXT MOVES. I MUST BE BETTER THAN ALL OF THE DORA MILAJE COMBINED. DAMN ZOLA! WERE IT NOT FOR HER, I COULD GO HOME TO KAGARA TO PROTECT MY FATHER MYSELF.
SOON, FATHER, I WILL COME TO YOU. AT LEAST FOR NOW I HAVE BLOCKED MY GPS SIGNAL. I WILL NOT BE FOUND UNTIL I CHOOSE TO BE.
MOTHER?
FOLAMI, MY DEAR DAUGHTER, I HAVE UNBEARABLE NEWS.
SOMETHING HAS HAPPENED TO MY FATHER, HASN'T IT?
HOW DID YOU KNOW?
I FEEL IT IN THE MUSCLE OF MY HEART, THROUGH THE CENTER OF MY BONES. TELL ME WHAT HAPPENED. TELL ME ALL OF IT.
I CAME HOME FROM VISITING YOUR SISTER AND FOUND YOUR FATHER LYING DEAD, IN HIS OWN COLD BLOOD. IT WAS A TERRIBLE SIGHT MINE EYES CANNOT UNSEE.
MOTHER, KNOW THIS: MY FATHER WILL BE AVENGED.

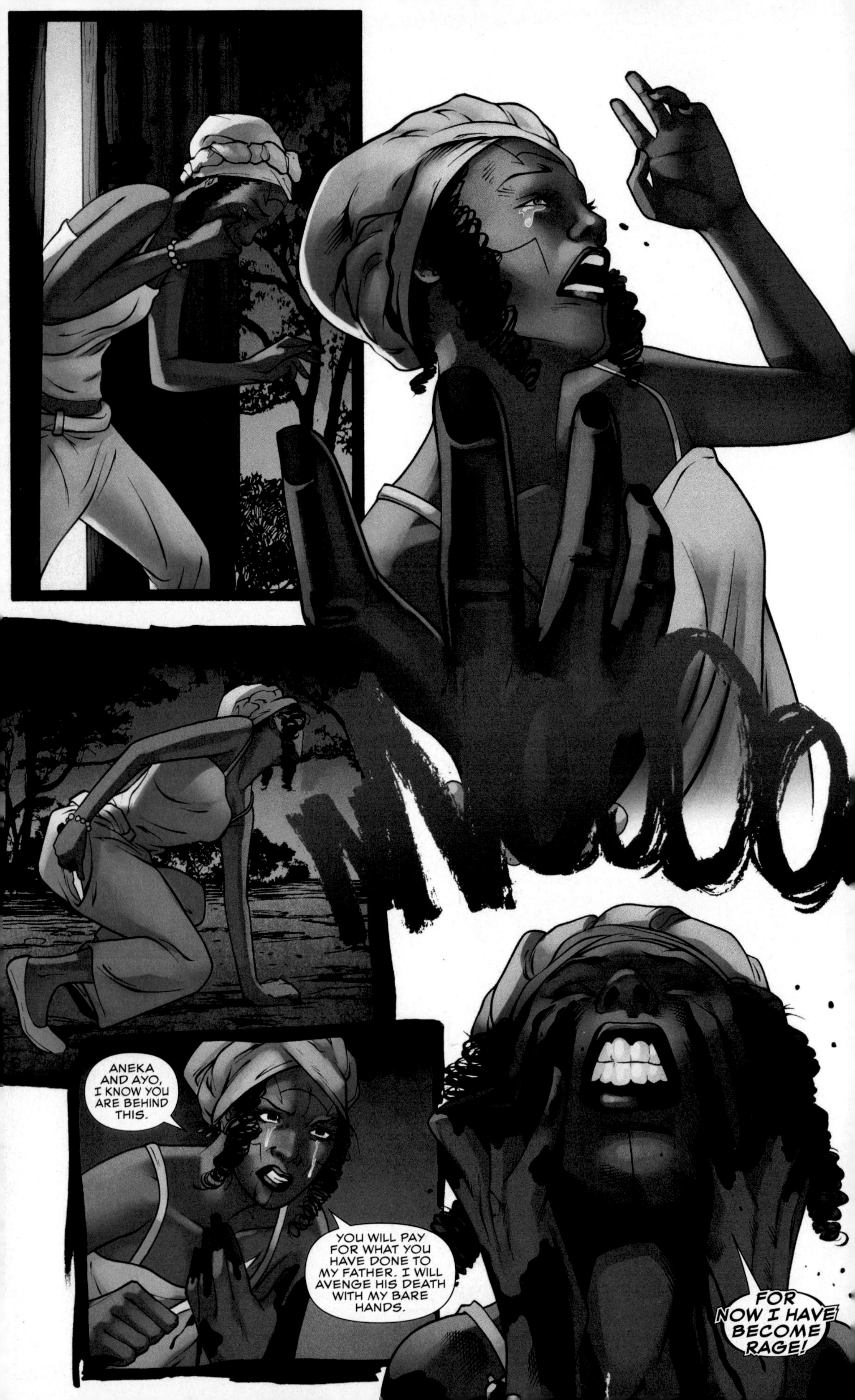
ANEKA AND AYO, I KNOW YOU ARE BEHIND THIS.
YOU WILL PAY FOR WHAT YOU HAVE DONE TO MY FATHER. I WILL AVENGE HIS DEATH WITH MY BARE HANDS.
FOR NOW I HAVE BECOME RAGE!

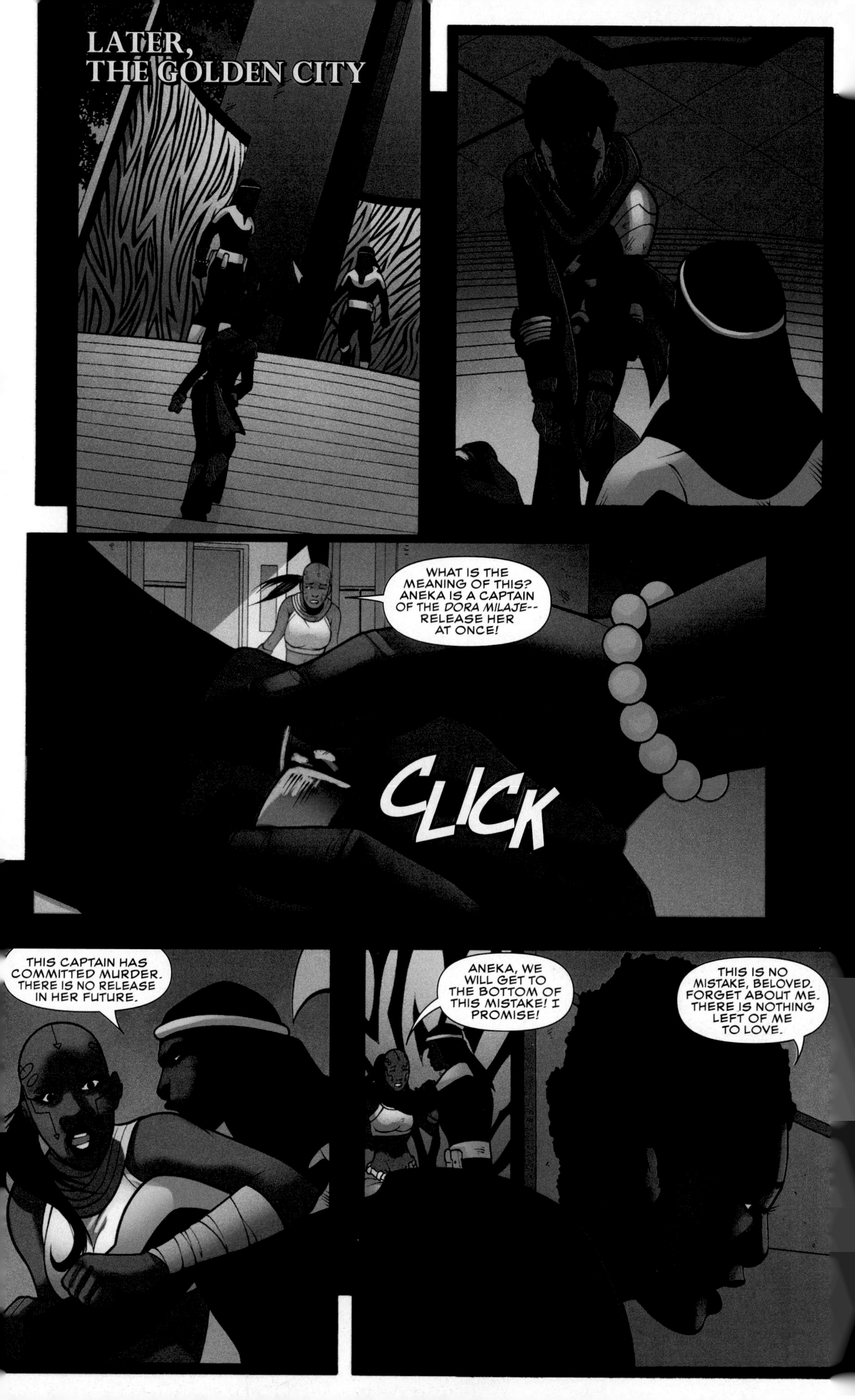
LATER,
THE GOLDEN CITY
WHAT IS THE MEANING OF THIS? ANEKA IS A CAPTAIN OF THE *DORA MILAJE*-- RELEASE HER AT ONCE!
CLICK
THIS CAPTAIN HAS COMMITTED MURDER. THERE IS NO RELEASE IN HER FUTURE.
ANEKA, WE WILL GET TO THE BOTTOM OF THIS MISTAKE! I PROMISE!
THIS IS NO MISTAKE, BELOVED. FORGET ABOUT ME. THERE IS NOTHING LEFT OF ME TO LOVE.

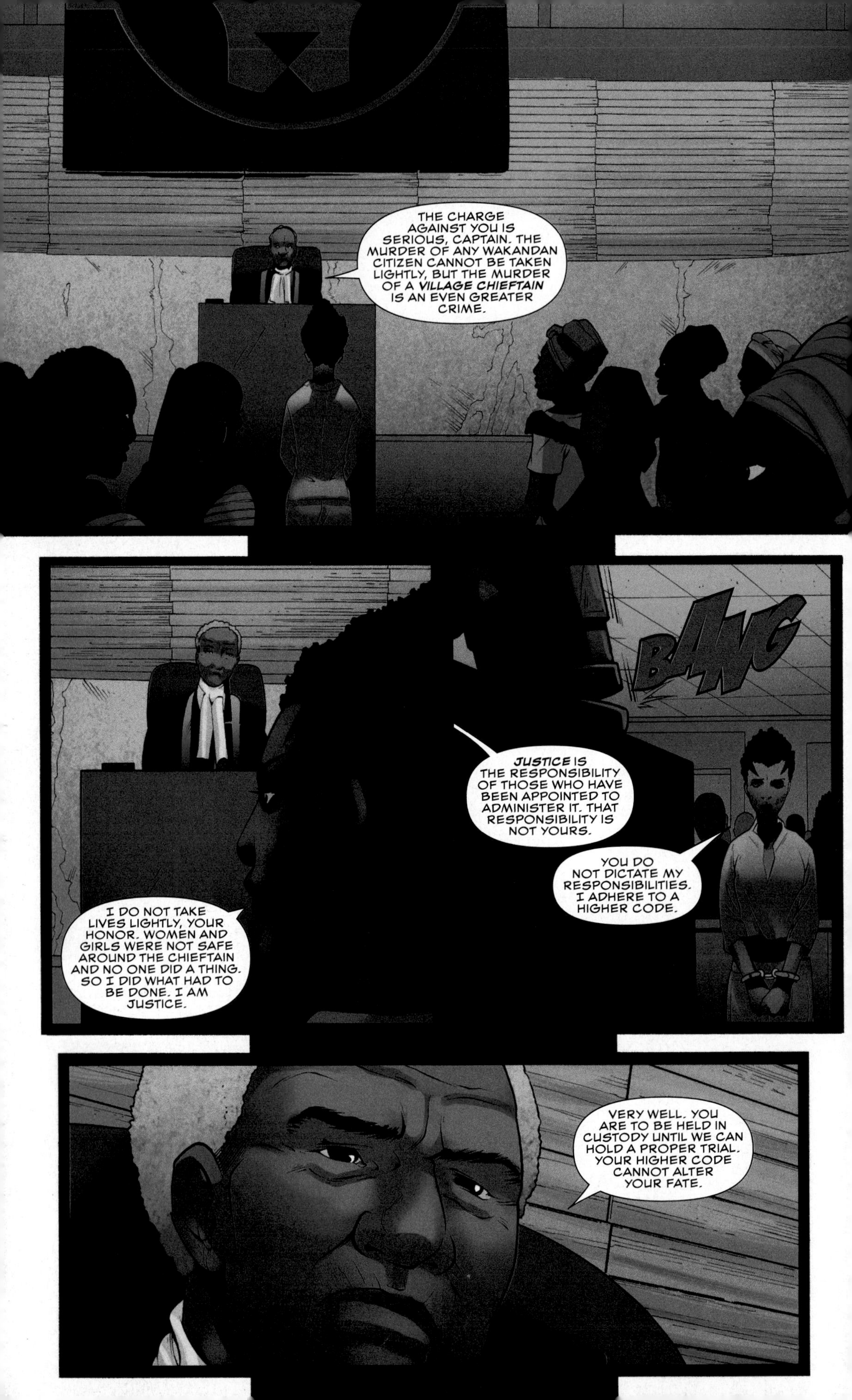
THE CHARGE AGAINST YOU IS SERIOUS, CAPTAIN. THE MURDER OF ANY WAKANDAN CITIZEN CANNOT BE TAKEN LIGHTLY, BUT THE MURDER OF A *VILLAGE CHIEFTAIN* IS AN EVEN GREATER CRIME.
BANG
I DO NOT TAKE LIVES LIGHTLY, YOUR HONOR. WOMEN AND GIRLS WERE NOT SAFE AROUND THE CHIEFTAIN AND NO ONE DID A THING. SO I DID WHAT HAD TO BE DONE. I AM JUSTICE.
*JUSTICE* IS THE RESPONSIBILITY OF THOSE WHO HAVE BEEN APPOINTED TO ADMINISTER IT. THAT RESPONSIBILITY IS NOT YOURS.
YOU DO NOT DICTATE MY RESPONSIBILITIES. I ADHERE TO A HIGHER CODE.
VERY WELL. YOU ARE TO BE HELD IN CUSTODY UNTIL WE CAN HOLD A PROPER TRIAL. YOUR HIGHER CODE CANNOT ALTER YOUR FATE.

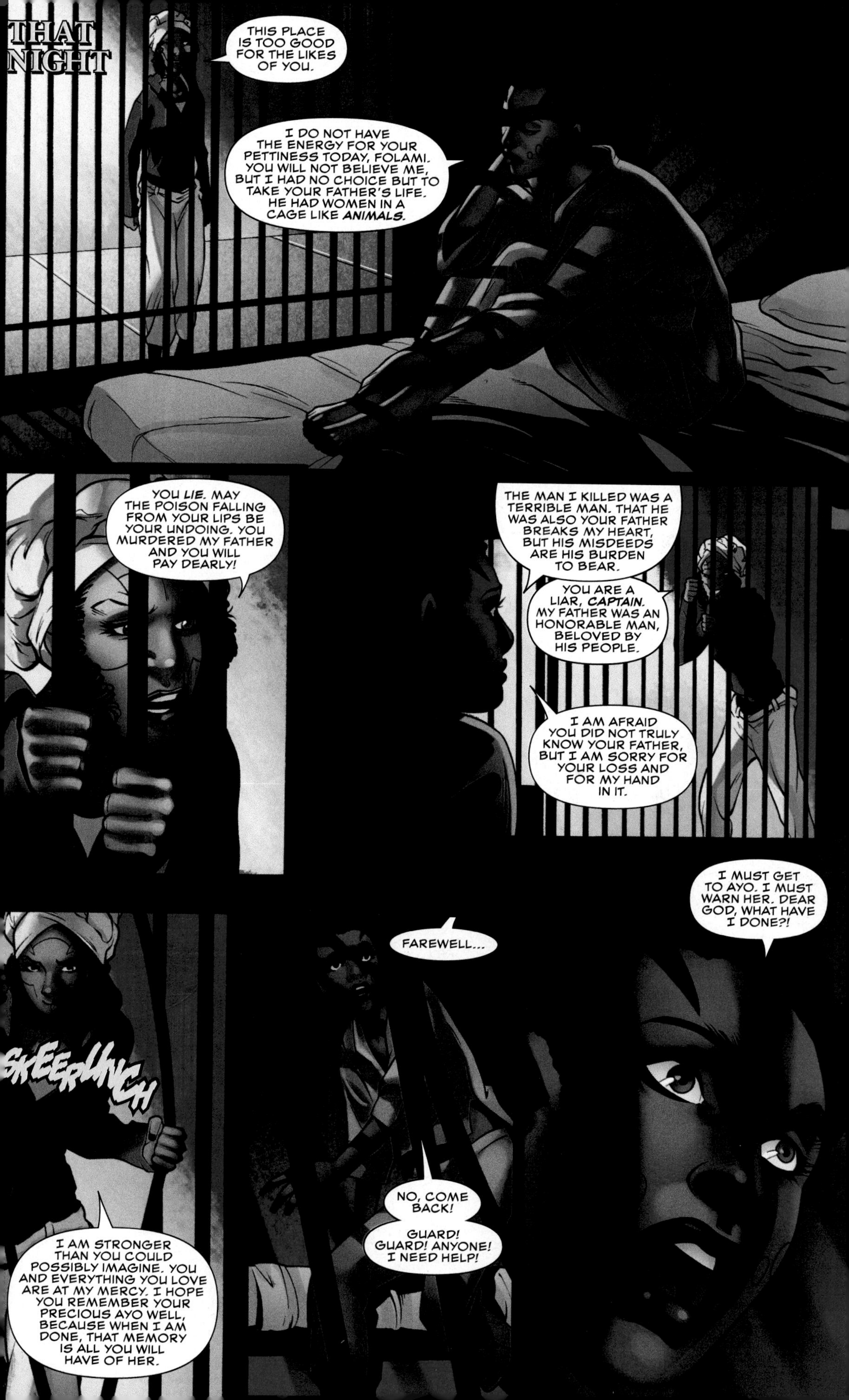
THAT NIGHT
THIS PLACE IS TOO GOOD FOR THE LIKES OF YOU.
I DO NOT HAVE THE ENERGY FOR YOUR PETTINESS TODAY, FOLAMI. YOU WILL NOT BELIEVE ME, BUT I HAD NO CHOICE BUT TO TAKE YOUR FATHER'S LIFE. HE HAD WOMEN IN A CAGE LIKE ANIMALS.
YOU LIE. MAY THE POISON FALLING FROM YOUR LIPS BE YOUR UNDOING. YOU MURDERED MY FATHER AND YOU WILL PAY DEARLY!
THE MAN I KILLED WAS A TERRIBLE MAN. THAT HE WAS ALSO YOUR FATHER BREAKS MY HEART, BUT HIS MISDEEDS ARE HIS BURDEN TO BEAR.
YOU ARE A LIAR, CAPTAIN. MY FATHER WAS AN HONORABLE MAN, BELOVED BY HIS PEOPLE.
I AM AFRAID YOU DID NOT TRULY KNOW YOUR FATHER, BUT I AM SORRY FOR YOUR LOSS AND FOR MY HAND IN IT.
SKEERUNCH
I AM STRONGER THAN YOU COULD POSSIBLY IMAGINE. YOU AND EVERYTHING YOU LOVE ARE AT MY MERCY. I HOPE YOU REMEMBER YOUR PRECIOUS AYO WELL, BECAUSE WHEN I AM DONE, THAT MEMORY IS ALL YOU WILL HAVE OF HER.
FAREWELL...
NO, COME BACK!
GUARD! GUARD! ANYONE! I NEED HELP!
I MUST GET TO AYO. I MUST WARN HER. DEAR GOD, WHAT HAVE I DONE?!

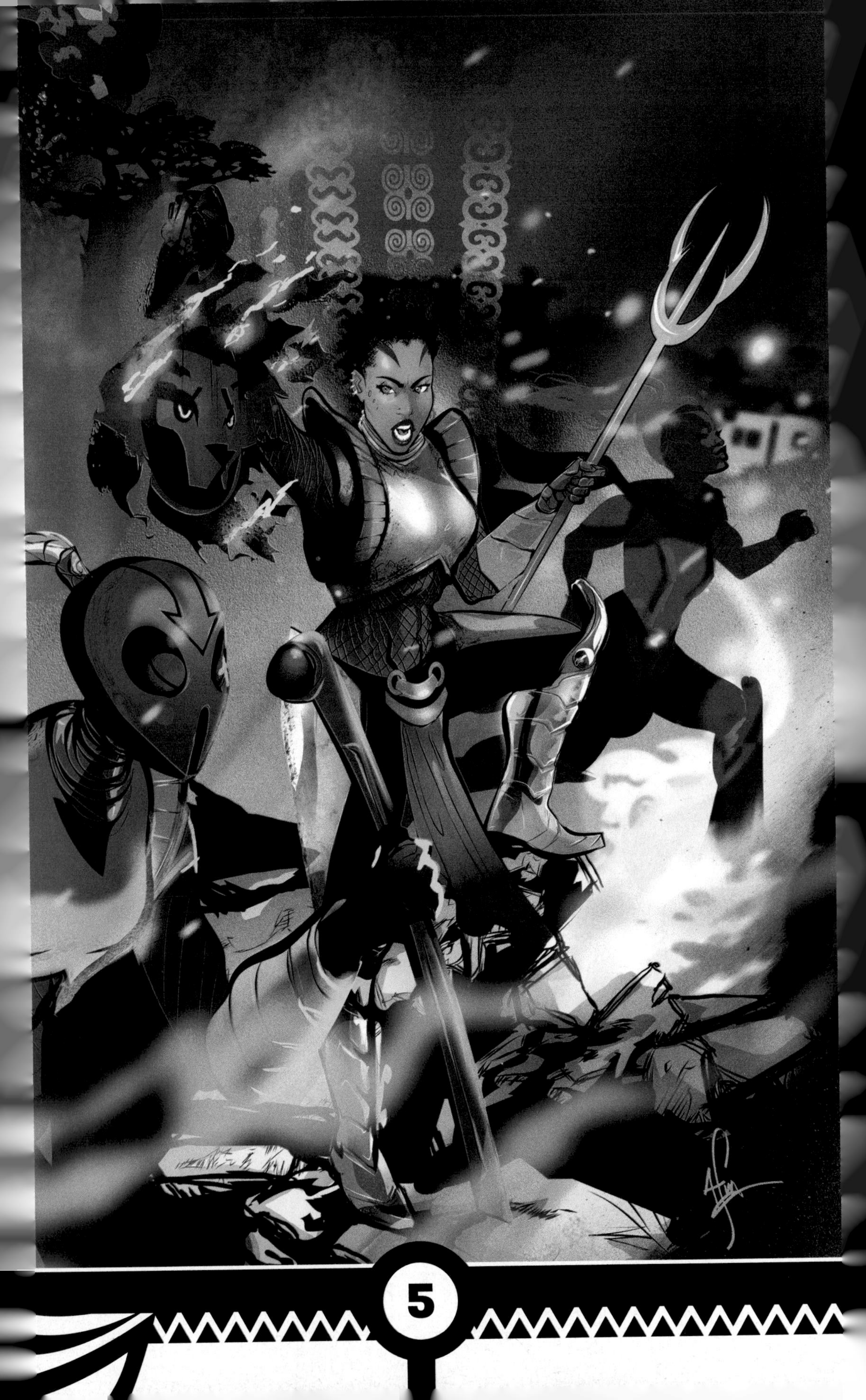

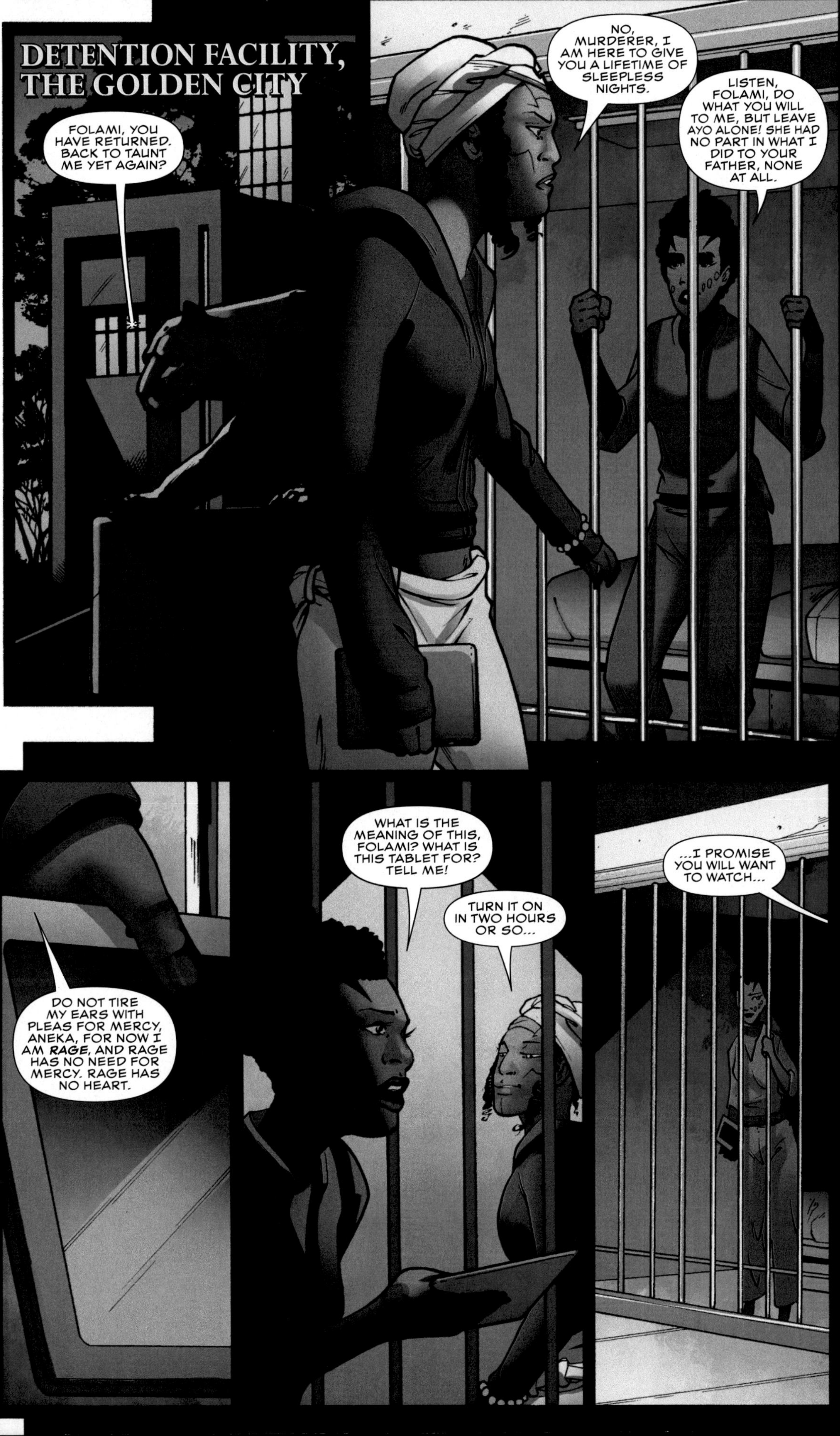
DETENTION FACILITY, THE GOLDEN CITY
FOLAMI, YOU HAVE RETURNED. BACK TO TAUNT ME YET AGAIN?
NO, MURDERER, I AM HERE TO GIVE YOU A LIFETIME OF SLEEPLESS NIGHTS.
LISTEN, FOLAMI, DO WHAT YOU WILL TO ME, BUT LEAVE AYO ALONE! SHE HAD NO PART IN WHAT I DID TO YOUR FATHER, NONE AT ALL.
DO NOT TIRE MY EARS WITH PLEAS FOR MERCY, ANEKA, FOR NOW I AM *RAGE*, AND RAGE HAS NO NEED FOR MERCY. RAGE HAS NO HEART.
WHAT IS THE MEANING OF THIS, FOLAMI? WHAT IS THIS TABLET FOR? TELL ME!
TURN IT ON IN TWO HOURS OR SO...
...I PROMISE YOU WILL WANT TO WATCH...

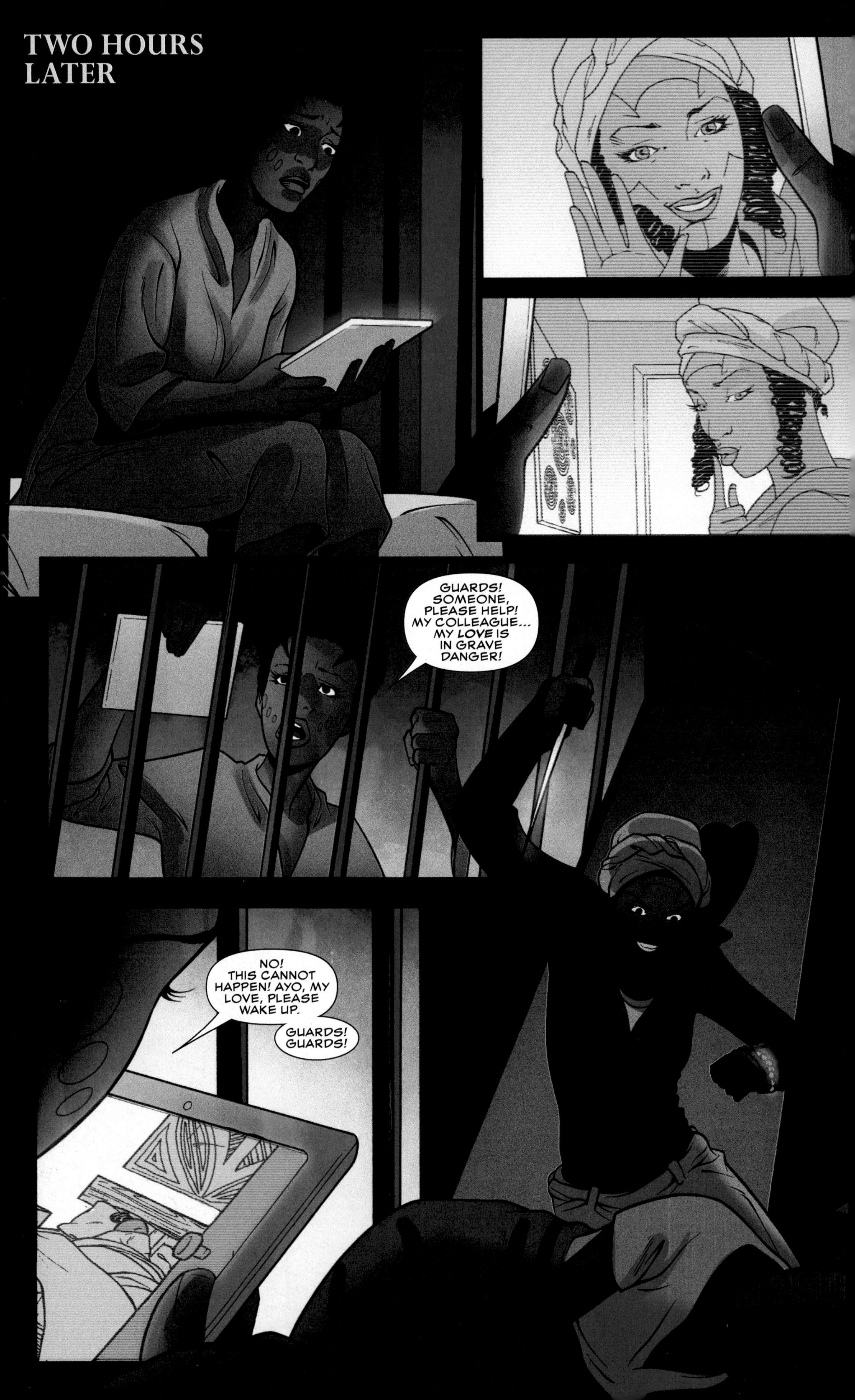
TWO HOURS LATER
GUARDS! SOMEONE, PLEASE HELP! MY COLLEAGUE... MY LOVE IS IN GRAVE DANGER!
NO! THIS CANNOT HAPPEN! AYO, MY LOVE, PLEASE WAKE UP.
GUARDS! GUARDS!

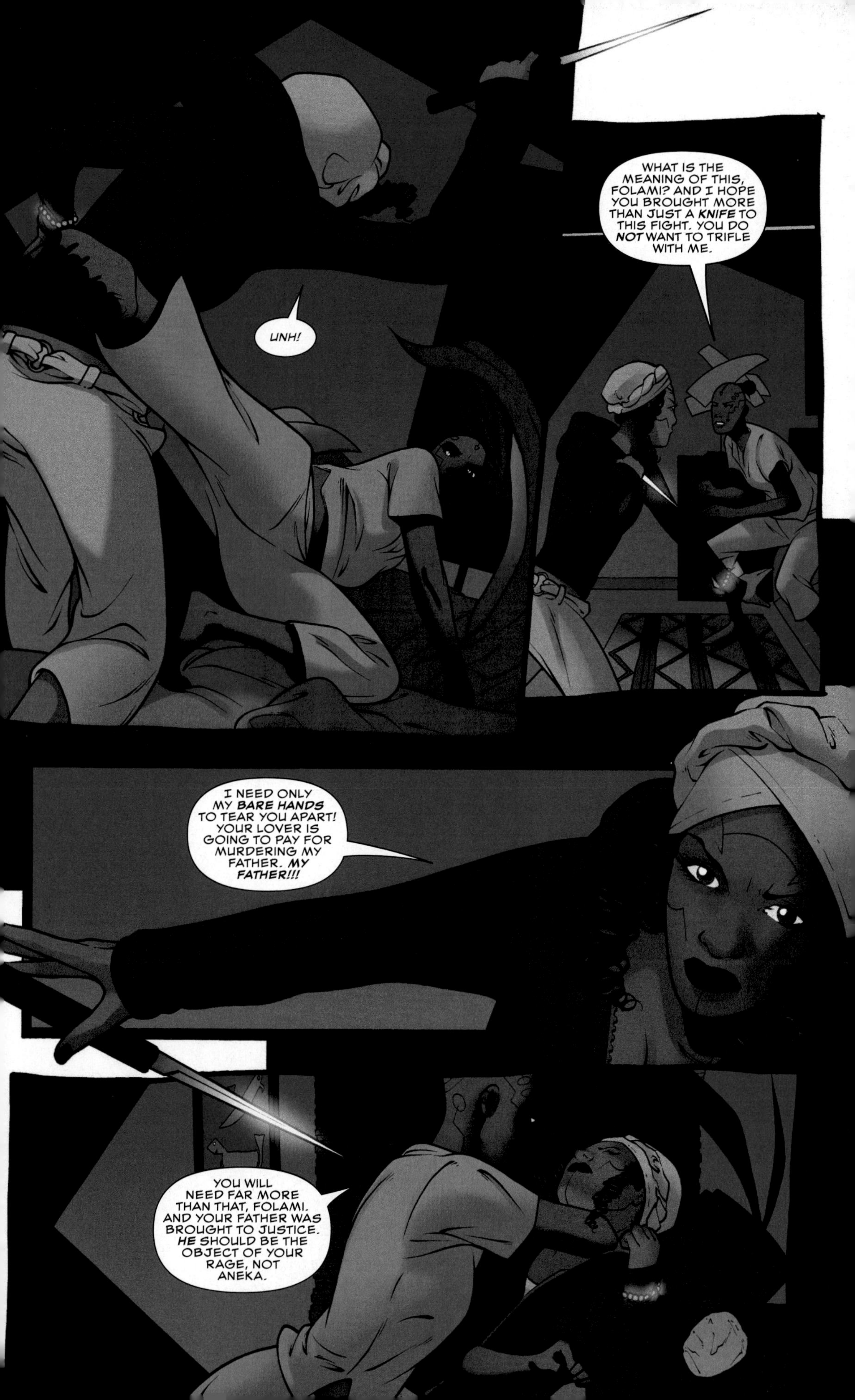
WHAT IS THE MEANING OF THIS, FOLAMI? AND I HOPE YOU BROUGHT MORE THAN JUST A KNIFE TO THIS FIGHT. YOU DO NOT WANT TO TRIFLE WITH ME.
UNH!
I NEED ONLY MY BARE HANDS TO TEAR YOU APART! YOUR LOVER IS GOING TO PAY FOR MURDERING MY FATHER. MY FATHER!!!
YOU WILL NEED FAR MORE THAN THAT, FOLAMI. AND YOUR FATHER WAS BROUGHT TO JUSTICE. HE SHOULD BE THE OBJECT OF YOUR RAGE, NOT ANEKA.

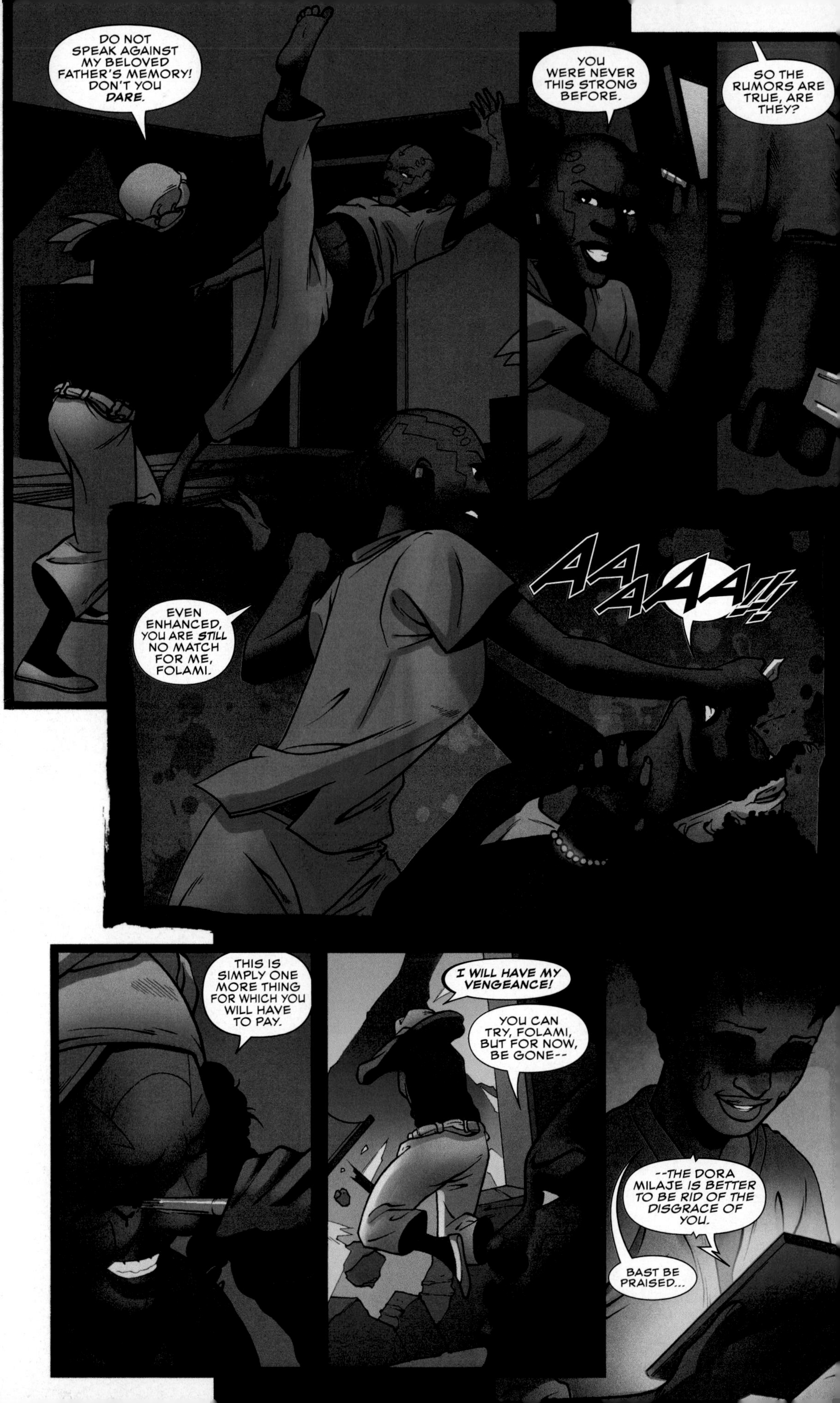
DO NOT SPEAK AGAINST MY BELOVED FATHER'S MEMORY! DON'T YOU *DARE*.
YOU WERE NEVER THIS STRONG BEFORE.
SO THE RUMORS ARE TRUE, ARE THEY?
EVEN ENHANCED, YOU ARE *STILL* NO MATCH FOR ME, FOLAMI.
AAAAA!!!
THIS IS SIMPLY ONE MORE THING FOR WHICH YOU WILL HAVE TO PAY.
*I WILL HAVE MY VENGEANCE!*
YOU CAN TRY, FOLAMI, BUT FOR NOW, BE GONE--
--THE DORA MILAJE IS BETTER TO BE RID OF THE DISGRACE OF YOU.
BAST BE PRAISED...

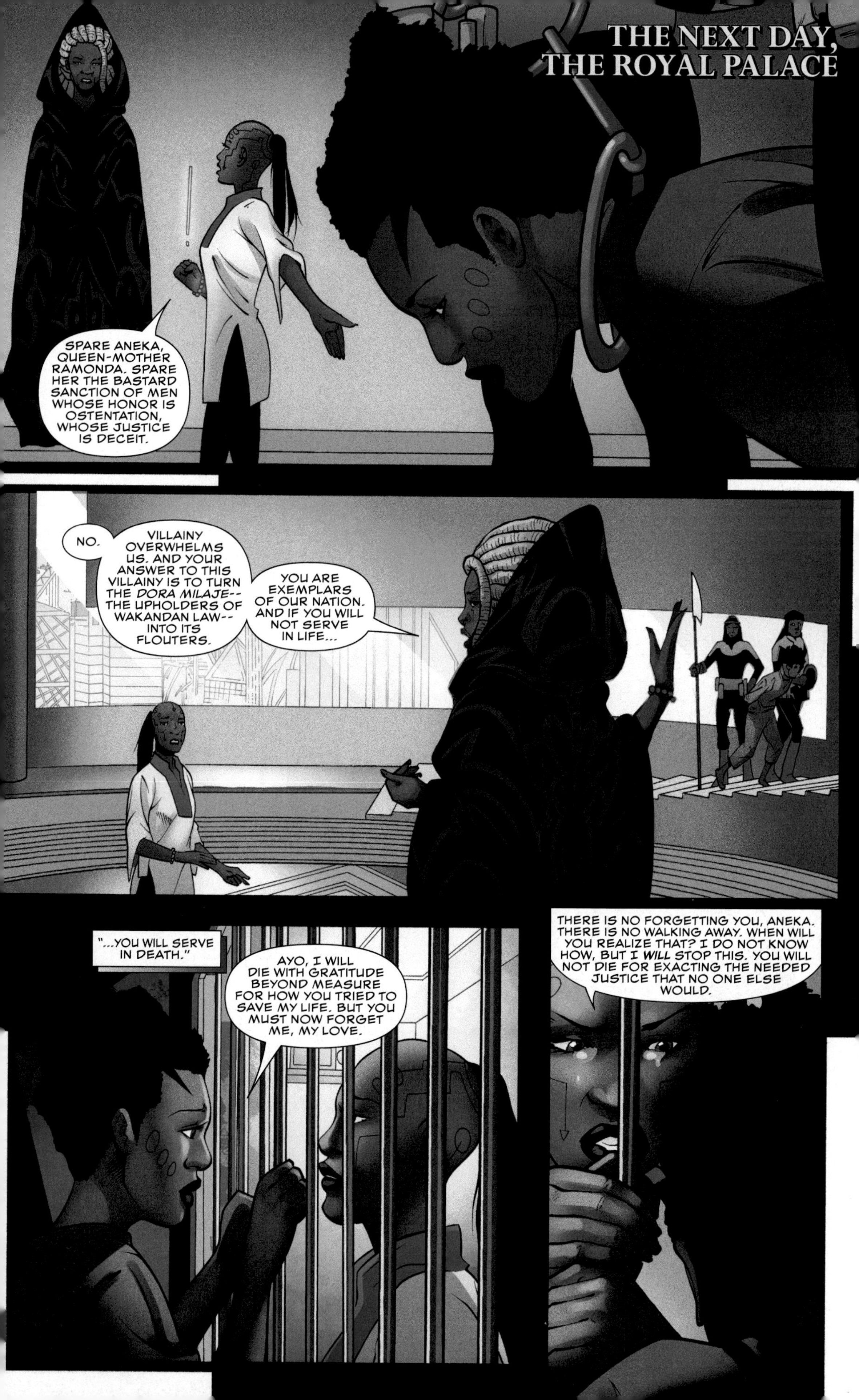
THE NEXT DAY, THE ROYAL PALACE
SPARE ANEKA, QUEEN-MOTHER RAMONDA. SPARE HER THE BASTARD SANCTION OF MEN WHOSE HONOR IS OSTENTATION, WHOSE JUSTICE IS DECEIT.
NO.
VILLAINY OVERWHELMS US. AND YOUR ANSWER TO THIS VILLAINY IS TO TURN THE *DORA MILAJE*-- THE UPHOLDERS OF WAKANDAN LAW-- INTO ITS FLOUTERS.
YOU ARE EXEMPLARS OF OUR NATION. AND IF YOU WILL NOT SERVE IN LIFE...
"...YOU WILL SERVE IN DEATH."
AYO, I WILL DIE WITH GRATITUDE BEYOND MEASURE FOR HOW YOU TRIED TO SAVE MY LIFE. BUT YOU MUST NOW FORGET ME, MY LOVE.
THERE IS NO FORGETTING YOU, ANEKA. THERE IS NO WALKING AWAY. WHEN WILL YOU REALIZE THAT? I DO NOT KNOW HOW, BUT I ***WILL*** STOP THIS. YOU WILL NOT DIE FOR EXACTING THE NEEDED JUSTICE THAT NO ONE ELSE WOULD.

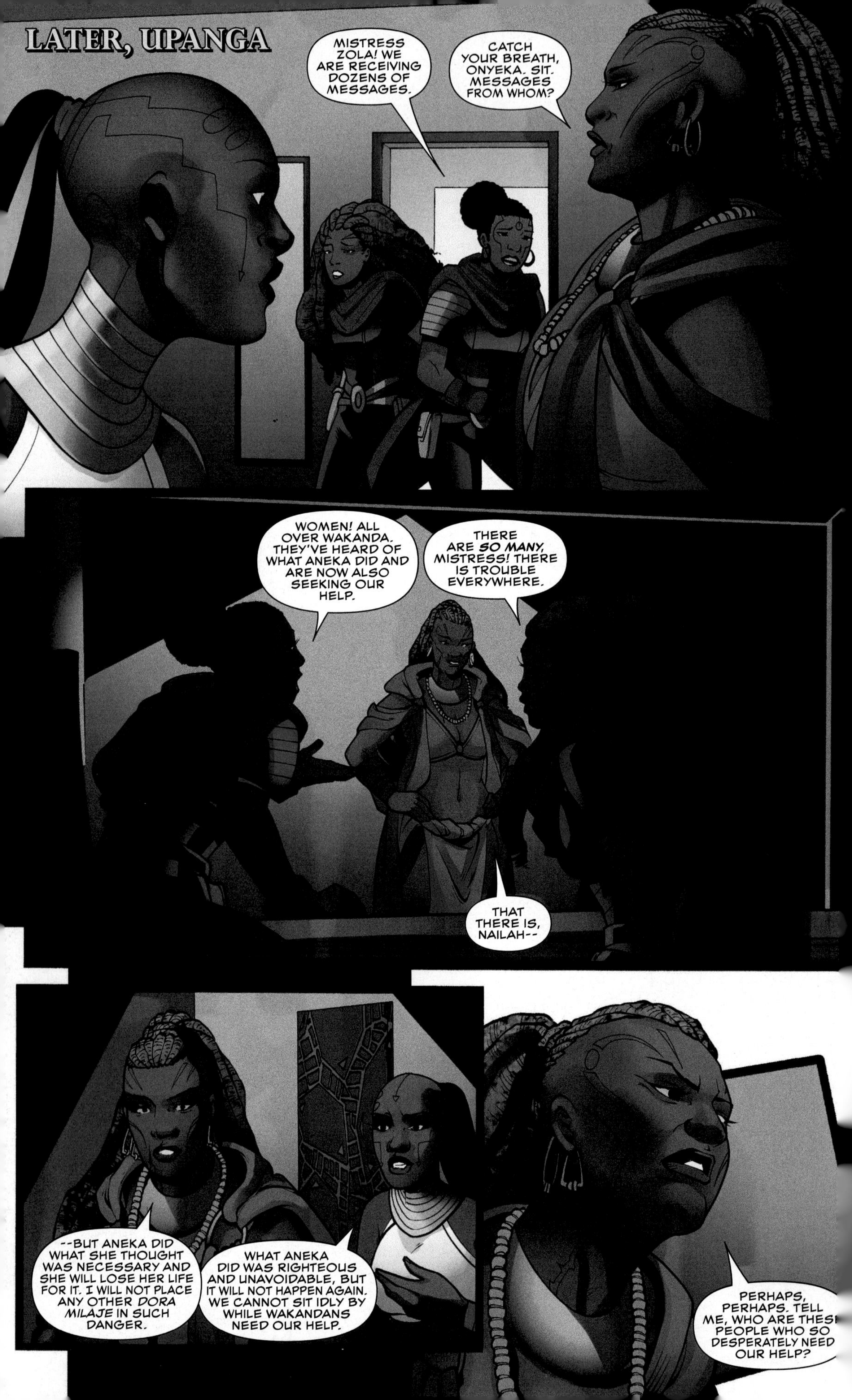
LATER, UPANGA
MISTRESS ZOLA! WE ARE RECEIVING DOZENS OF MESSAGES.
CATCH YOUR BREATH, ONYEKA. SIT. MESSAGES FROM WHOM?
WOMEN! ALL OVER WAKANDA. THEY'VE HEARD OF WHAT ANEKA DID AND ARE NOW ALSO SEEKING OUR HELP.
THERE ARE *SO MANY*, MISTRESS! THERE IS TROUBLE EVERYWHERE.
THAT THERE IS, NAILAH--
--BUT ANEKA DID WHAT SHE THOUGHT WAS NECESSARY AND SHE WILL LOSE HER LIFE FOR IT. I WILL NOT PLACE ANY OTHER *DORA MILAJE* IN SUCH DANGER.
WHAT ANEKA DID WAS RIGHTEOUS AND UNAVOIDABLE, BUT IT WILL NOT HAPPEN AGAIN. WE CANNOT SIT IDLY BY WHILE WAKANDANS NEED OUR HELP.
PERHAPS, PERHAPS. TELL ME, WHO ARE THES PEOPLE WHO SO DESPERATELY NEED OUR HELP?

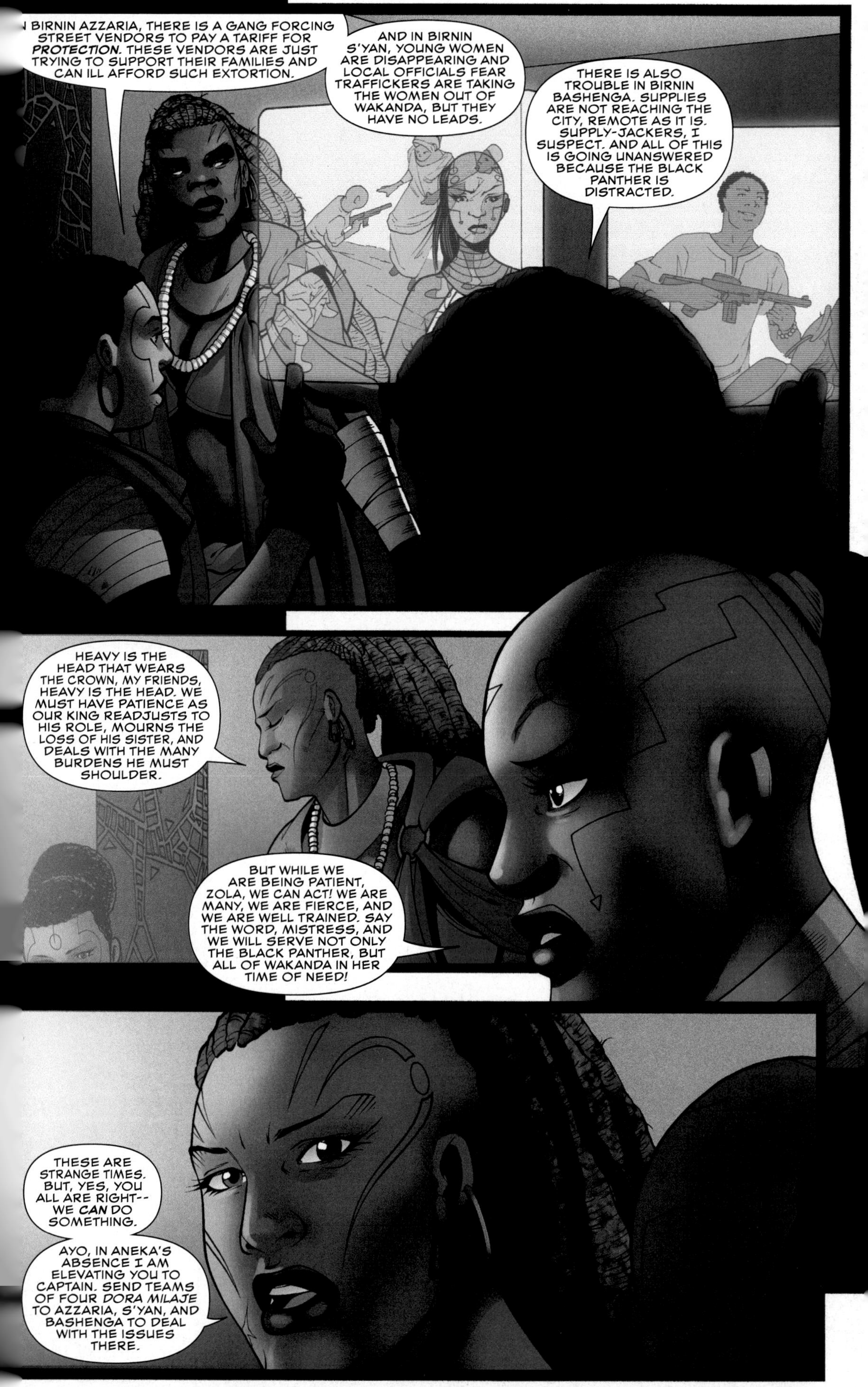
N BIRNIN AZZARIA, THERE IS A GANG FORCING STREET VENDORS TO PAY A TARIFF FOR *PROTECTION*. THESE VENDORS ARE JUST TRYING TO SUPPORT THEIR FAMILIES AND CAN ILL AFFORD SUCH EXTORTION.
AND IN BIRNIN S'YAN, YOUNG WOMEN ARE DISAPPEARING AND LOCAL OFFICIALS FEAR TRAFFICKERS ARE TAKING THE WOMEN OUT OF WAKANDA, BUT THEY HAVE NO LEADS.
THERE IS ALSO TROUBLE IN BIRNIN BASHENGA. SUPPLIES ARE NOT REACHING THE CITY, REMOTE AS IT IS. SUPPLY-JACKERS, I SUSPECT. AND ALL OF THIS IS GOING UNANSWERED BECAUSE THE BLACK PANTHER IS DISTRACTED.
HEAVY IS THE HEAD THAT WEARS THE CROWN, MY FRIENDS, HEAVY IS THE HEAD. WE MUST HAVE PATIENCE AS OUR KING READJUSTS TO HIS ROLE, MOURNS THE LOSS OF HIS SISTER, AND DEALS WITH THE MANY BURDENS HE MUST SHOULDER.
BUT WHILE WE ARE BEING PATIENT, ZOLA, WE CAN ACT! WE ARE MANY, WE ARE FIERCE, AND WE ARE WELL TRAINED. SAY THE WORD, MISTRESS, AND WE WILL SERVE NOT ONLY THE BLACK PANTHER, BUT ALL OF WAKANDA IN HER TIME OF NEED!
THESE ARE STRANGE TIMES. BUT, YES, YOU ALL ARE RIGHT-- WE *CAN* DO SOMETHING.
AYO, IN ANEKA'S ABSENCE I AM ELEVATING YOU TO CAPTAIN. SEND TEAMS OF FOUR *DORA MILAJE* TO AZZARIA, S'YAN, AND BASHENGA TO DEAL WITH THE ISSUES THERE.

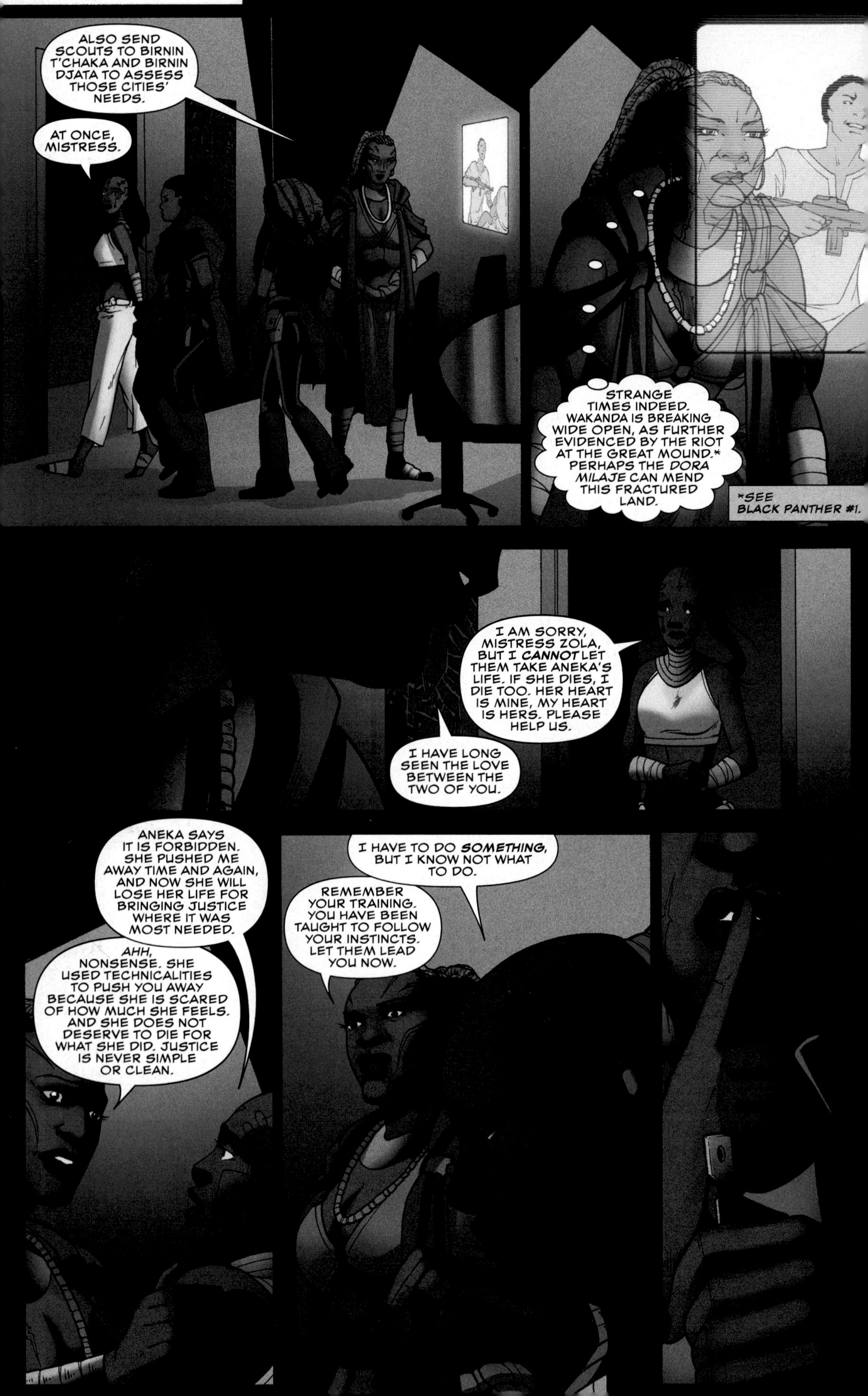
ALSO SEND SCOUTS TO BIRNIN T'CHAKA AND BIRNIN DJATA TO ASSESS THOSE CITIES' NEEDS.
AT ONCE, MISTRESS.
STRANGE TIMES INDEED. WAKANDA IS BREAKING WIDE OPEN, AS FURTHER EVIDENCED BY THE RIOT AT THE GREAT MOUND.* PERHAPS THE DORA MILAJE CAN MEND THIS FRACTURED LAND.
*SEE BLACK PANTHER #1.
I AM SORRY, MISTRESS ZOLA, BUT I CANNOT LET THEM TAKE ANEKA'S LIFE. IF SHE DIES, I DIE TOO. HER HEART IS MINE, MY HEART IS HERS. PLEASE HELP US.
I HAVE LONG SEEN THE LOVE BETWEEN THE TWO OF YOU.
ANEKA SAYS IT IS FORBIDDEN. SHE PUSHED ME AWAY TIME AND AGAIN, AND NOW SHE WILL LOSE HER LIFE FOR BRINGING JUSTICE WHERE IT WAS MOST NEEDED.
AHH, NONSENSE. SHE USED TECHNICALITIES TO PUSH YOU AWAY BECAUSE SHE IS SCARED OF HOW MUCH SHE FEELS. AND SHE DOES NOT DESERVE TO DIE FOR WHAT SHE DID. JUSTICE IS NEVER SIMPLE OR CLEAN.
I HAVE TO DO SOMETHING, BUT I KNOW NOT WHAT TO DO.
REMEMBER YOUR TRAINING. YOU HAVE BEEN TAUGHT TO FOLLOW YOUR INSTINCTS. LET THEM LEAD YOU NOW.

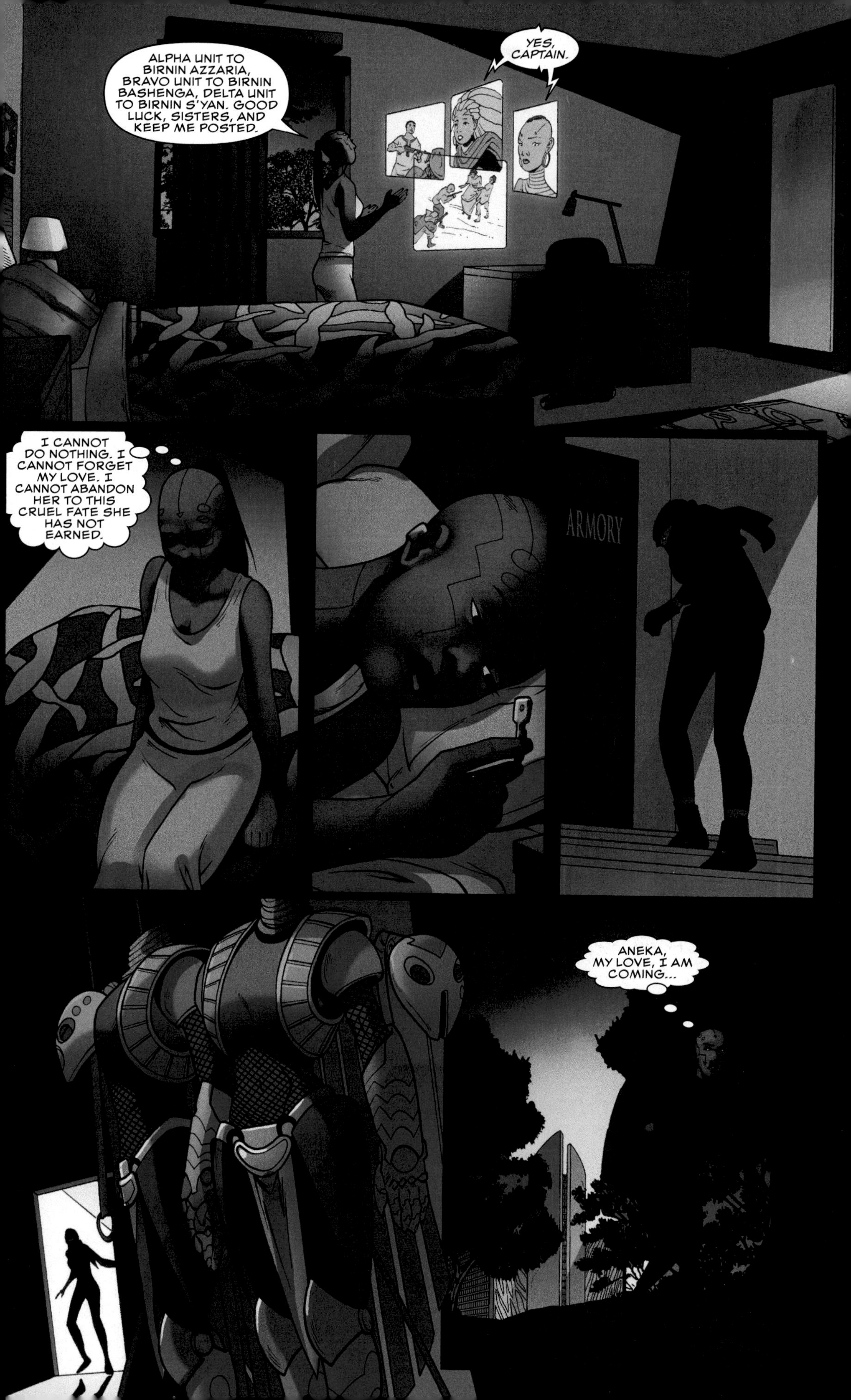
ALPHA UNIT TO BIRNIN AZZARIA, BRAVO UNIT TO BIRNIN BASHENGA, DELTA UNIT TO BIRNIN S'YAN. GOOD LUCK, SISTERS, AND KEEP ME POSTED.
YES, CAPTAIN.
I CANNOT DO NOTHING. I CANNOT FORGET MY LOVE. I CANNOT ABANDON HER TO THIS CRUEL FATE SHE HAS NOT EARNED.
ARMORY
ANEKA, MY LOVE, I AM COMING...

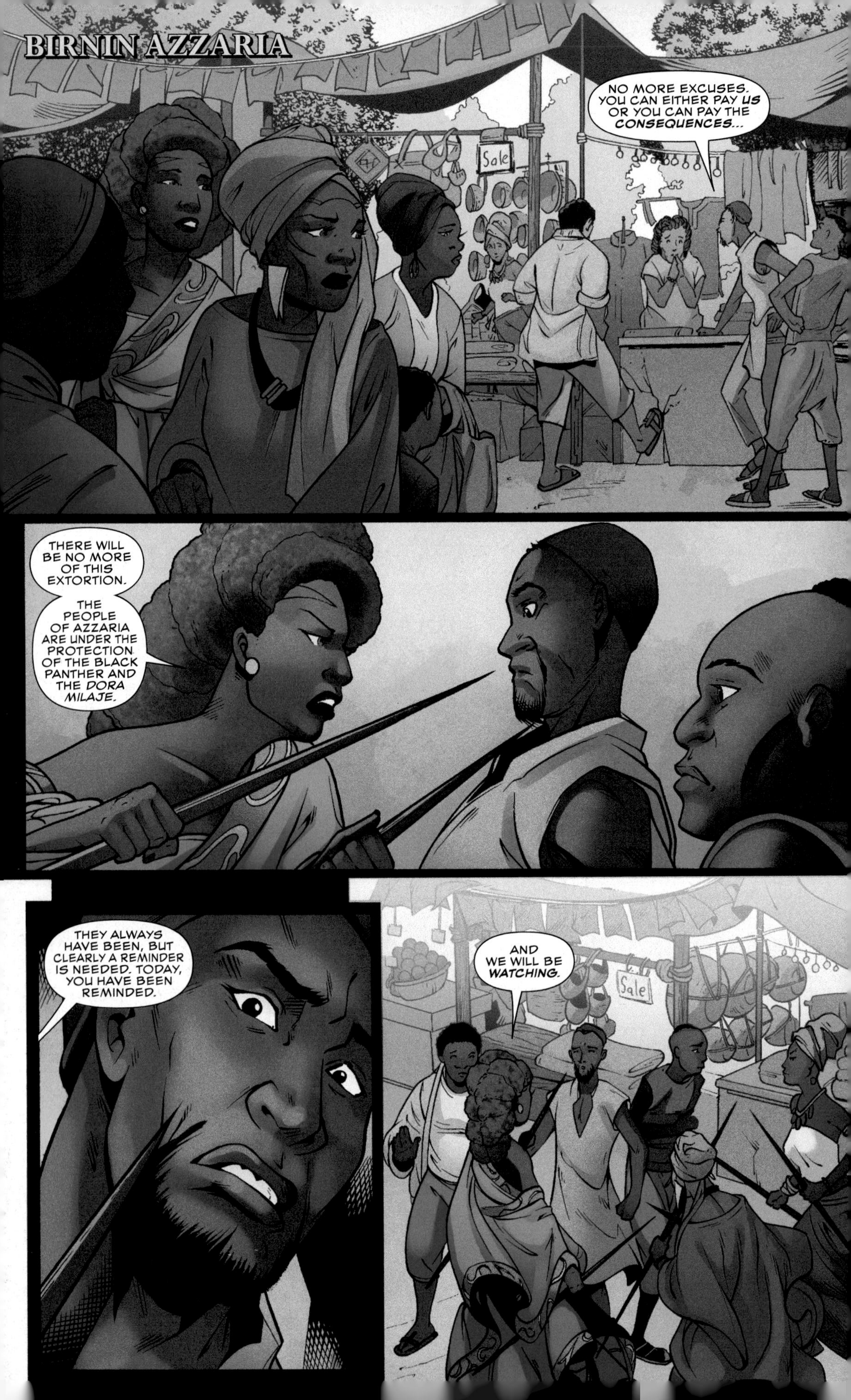
BIRNIN AZZARIA
NO MORE EXCUSES. YOU CAN EITHER PAY US OR YOU CAN PAY THE CONSEQUENCES...
Sale
THERE WILL BE NO MORE OF THIS EXTORTION.
THE PEOPLE OF AZZARIA ARE UNDER THE PROTECTION OF THE BLACK PANTHER AND THE DORA MILAJE.
THEY ALWAYS HAVE BEEN, BUT CLEARLY A REMINDER IS NEEDED. TODAY, YOU HAVE BEEN REMINDED.
AND WE WILL BE WATCHING.
Sale

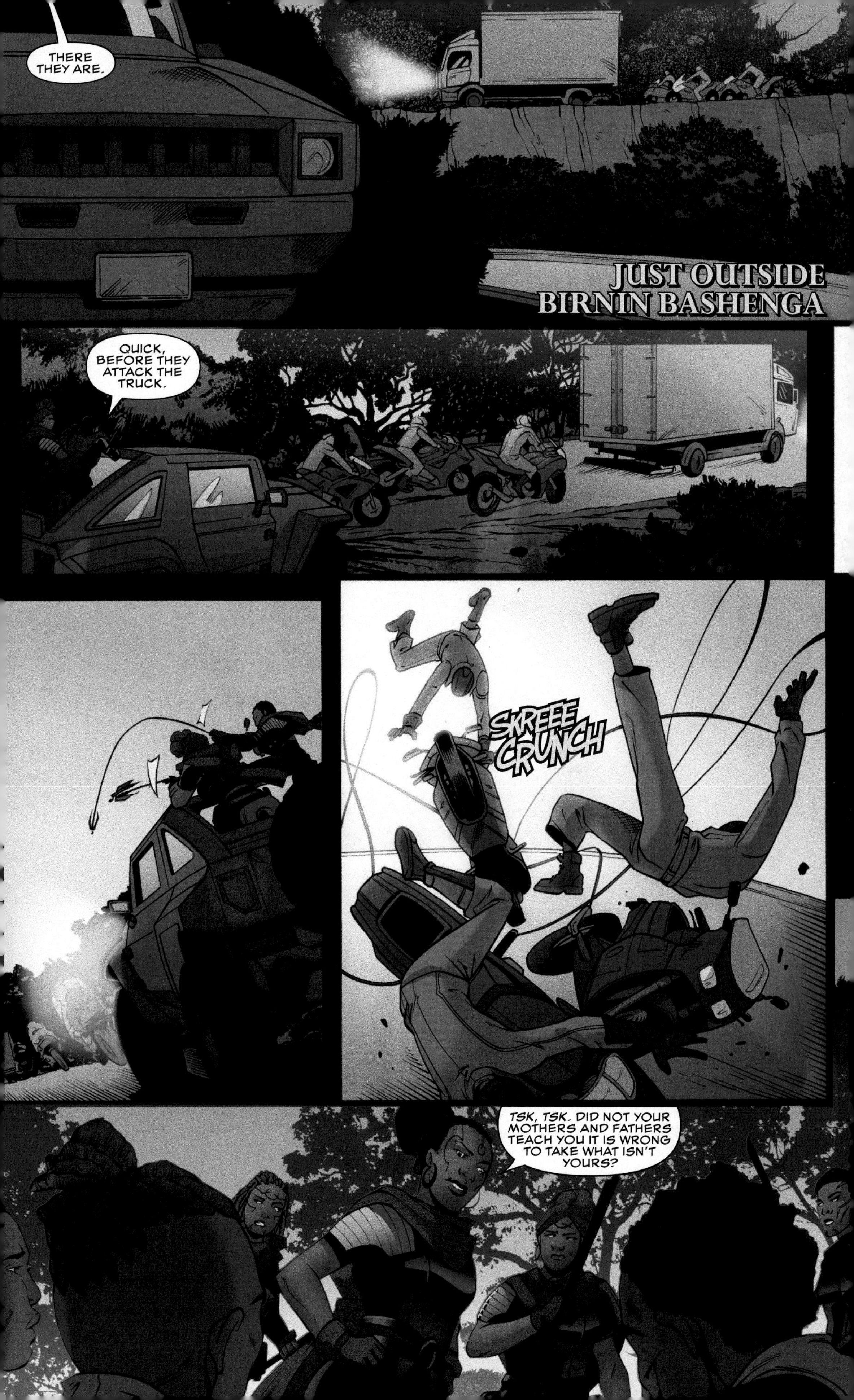
THERE THEY ARE.
JUST OUTSIDE BIRNIN BASHENGA
QUICK, BEFORE THEY ATTACK THE TRUCK.
SKREEE CRUNCH
TSK, TSK. DID NOT YOUR MOTHERS AND FATHERS TEACH YOU IT IS WRONG TO TAKE WHAT ISN'T YOURS?

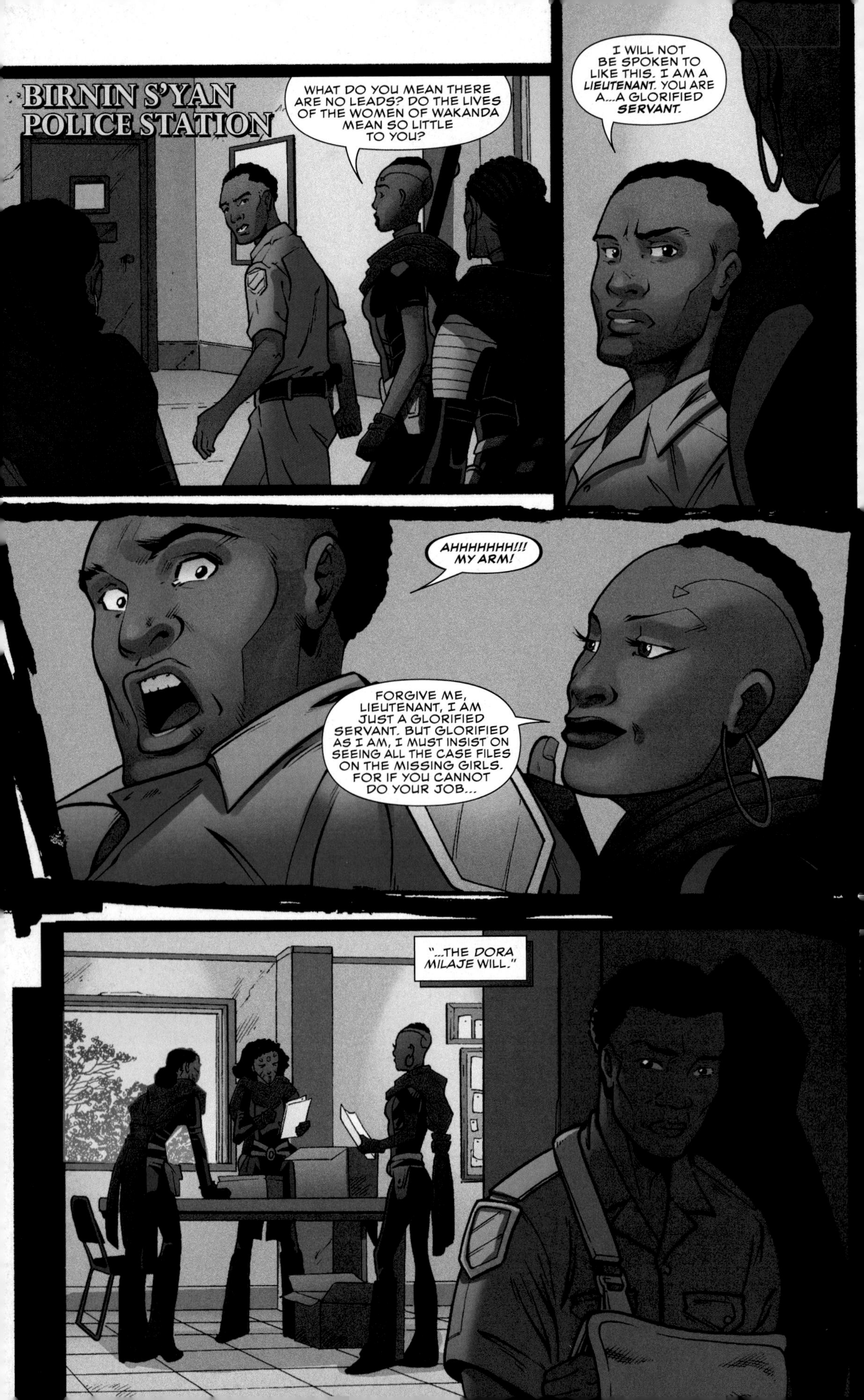
BIRNIN S'YAN POLICE STATION
WHAT DO YOU MEAN THERE ARE NO LEADS? DO THE LIVES OF THE WOMEN OF WAKANDA MEAN SO LITTLE TO YOU?
I WILL NOT BE SPOKEN TO LIKE THIS. I AM A LIEUTENANT. YOU ARE A...A GLORIFIED SERVANT.
AHHHHHHH!!! MY ARM!
FORGIVE ME, LIEUTENANT, I AM JUST A GLORIFIED SERVANT. BUT GLORIFIED AS I AM, I MUST INSIST ON SEEING ALL THE CASE FILES ON THE MISSING GIRLS. FOR IF YOU CANNOT DO YOUR JOB...
"...THE DORA MILAJE WILL."

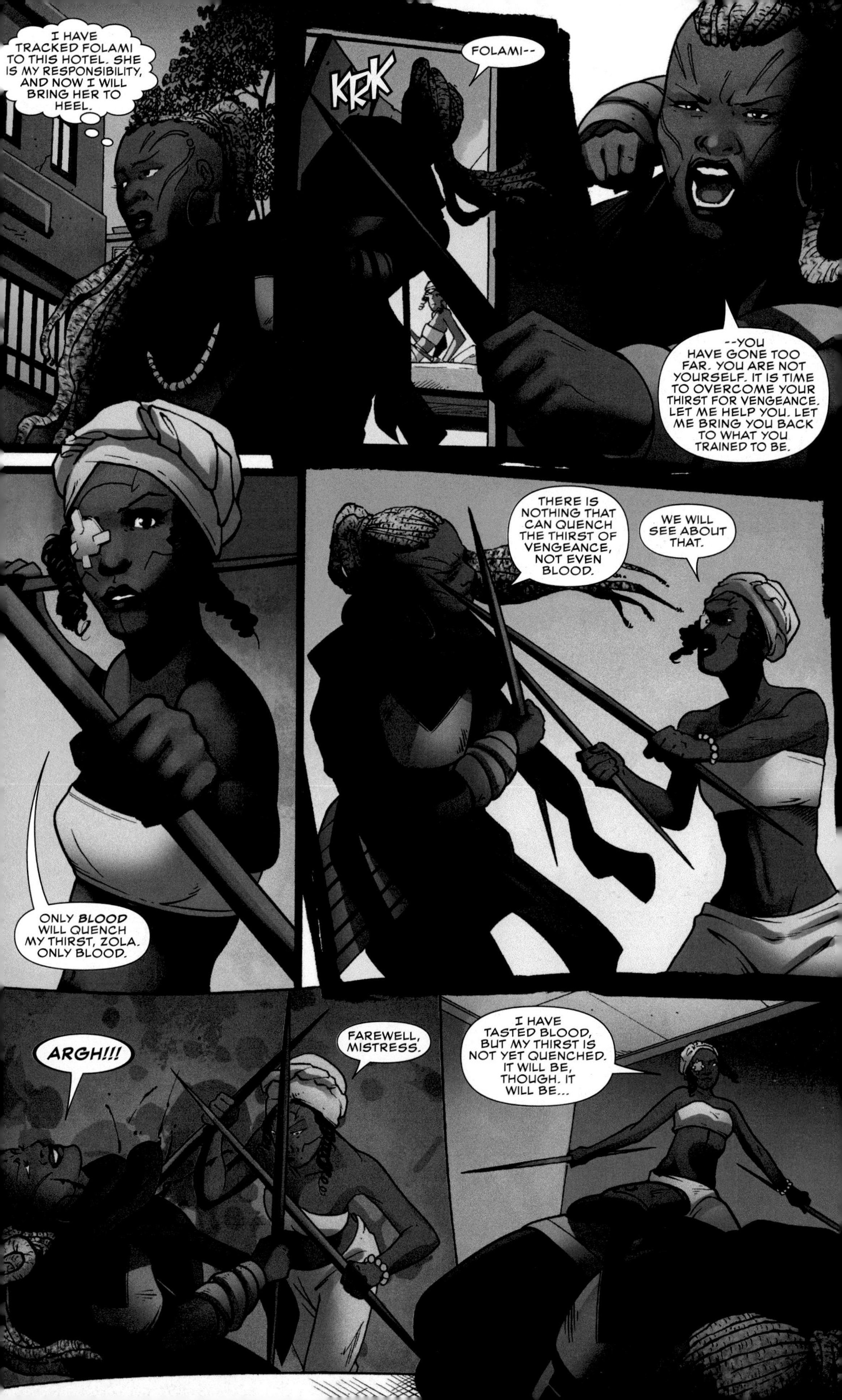

I HAVE TRACKED FOLAMI TO THIS HOTEL. SHE IS MY RESPONSIBILITY, AND NOW I WILL BRING HER TO HEEL.
KRK
FOLAMI--
--YOU HAVE GONE TOO FAR. YOU ARE NOT YOURSELF. IT IS TIME TO OVERCOME YOUR THIRST FOR VENGEANCE. LET ME HELP YOU. LET ME BRING YOU BACK TO WHAT YOU TRAINED TO BE.
ONLY BLOOD WILL QUENCH MY THIRST, ZOLA. ONLY BLOOD.
THERE IS NOTHING THAT CAN QUENCH THE THIRST OF VENGEANCE, NOT EVEN BLOOD.
WE WILL SEE ABOUT THAT.
ARGH!!!
FAREWELL, MISTRESS.
I HAVE TASTED BLOOD, BUT MY THIRST IS NOT YET QUENCHED. IT WILL BE, THOUGH. IT WILL BE...

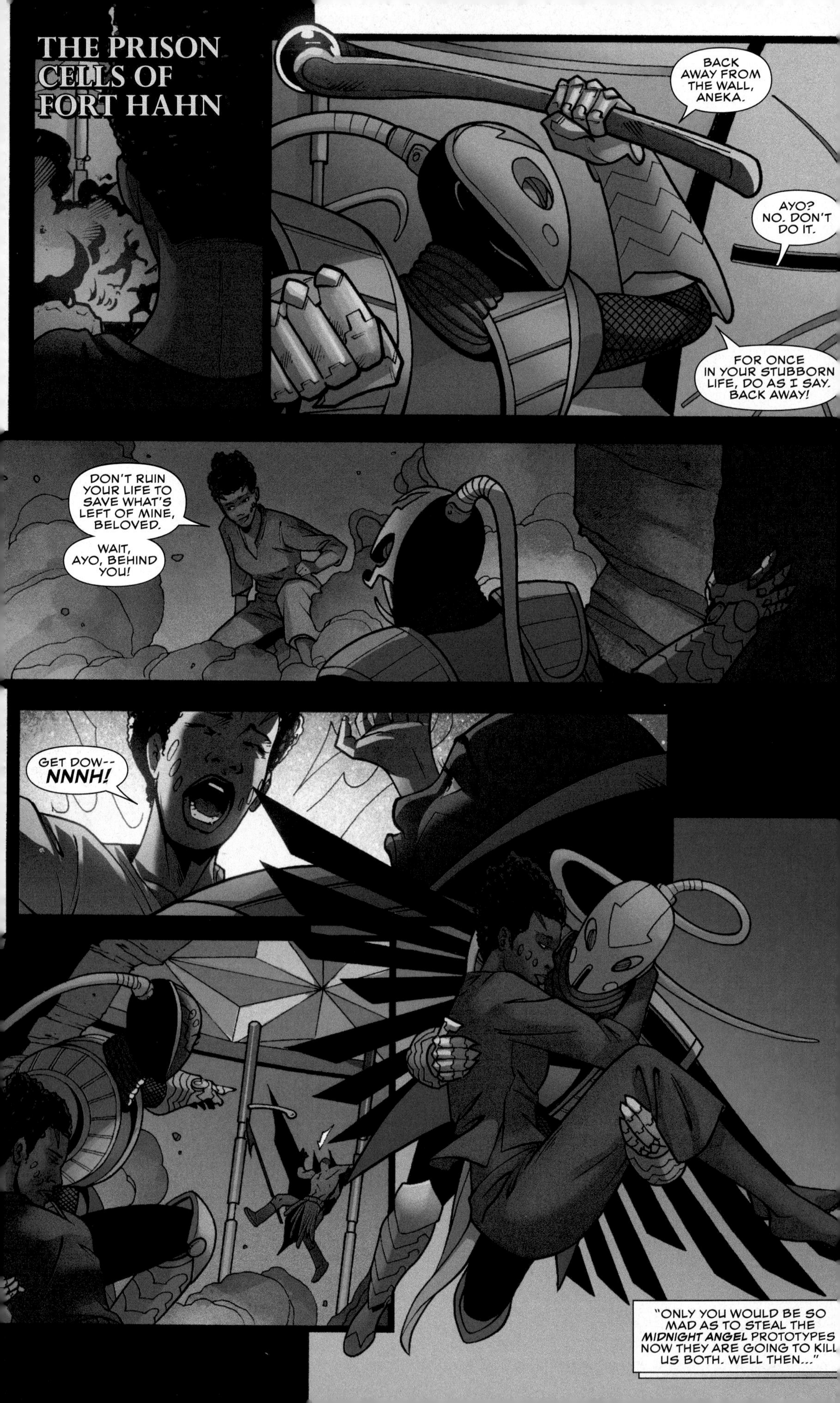
THE PRISON CELLS OF FORT HAHN
BACK AWAY FROM THE WALL, ANEKA.
AYO? NO. DON'T DO IT.
FOR ONCE IN YOUR STUBBORN LIFE, DO AS I SAY. BACK AWAY!
DON'T RUIN YOUR LIFE TO SAVE WHAT'S LEFT OF MINE, BELOVED.
WAIT, AYO, BEHIND YOU!
GET DOW-- NNNH!
"ONLY YOU WOULD BE SO MAD AS TO STEAL THE MIDNIGHT ANGEL PROTOTYPES NOW THEY ARE GOING TO KILL US BOTH. WELL THEN..."

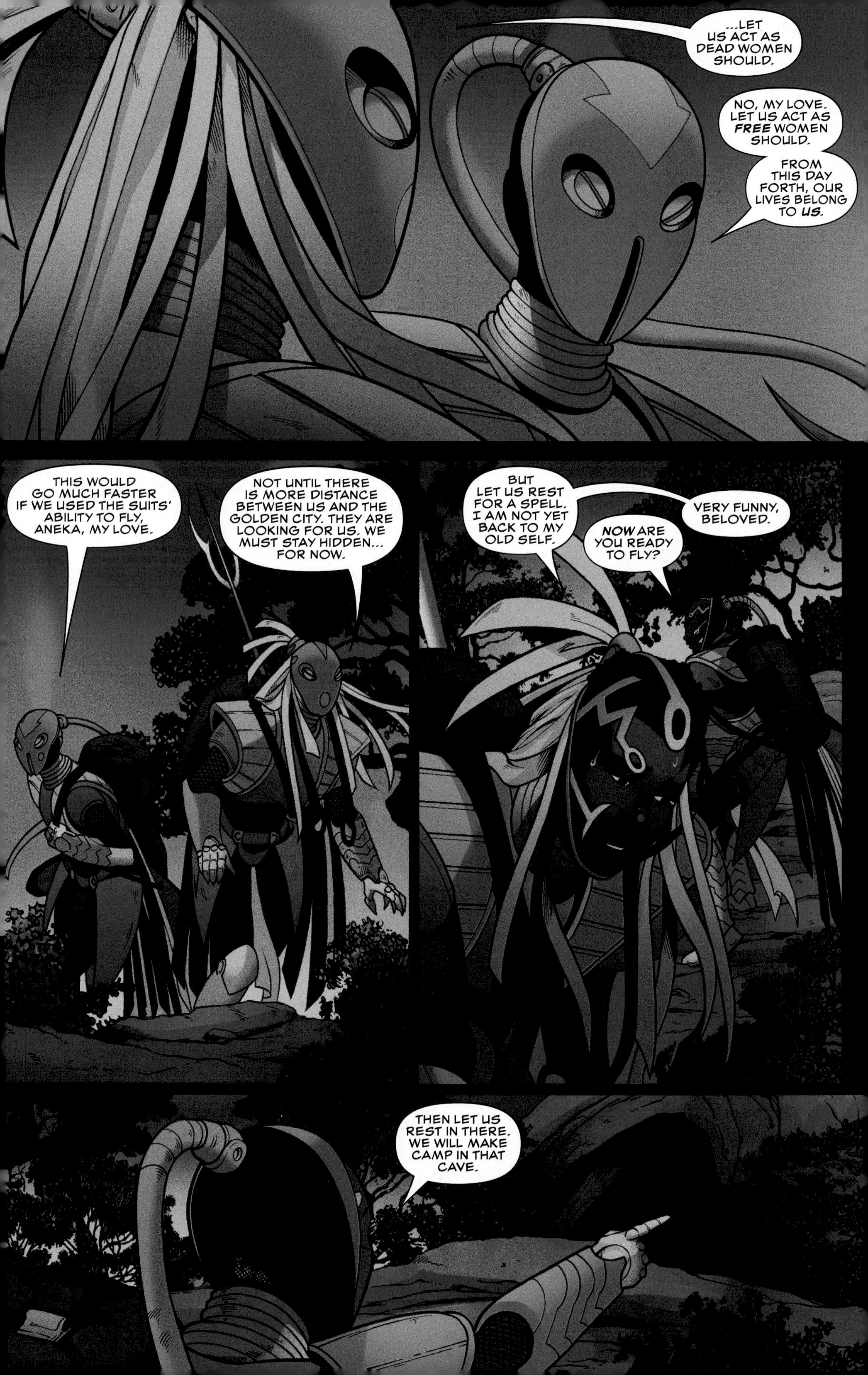
...LET US ACT AS DEAD WOMEN SHOULD.
NO, MY LOVE. LET US ACT AS FREE WOMEN SHOULD.
FROM THIS DAY FORTH, OUR LIVES BELONG TO US.
THIS WOULD GO MUCH FASTER IF WE USED THE SUITS' ABILITY TO FLY, ANEKA, MY LOVE.
NOT UNTIL THERE IS MORE DISTANCE BETWEEN US AND THE GOLDEN CITY. THEY ARE LOOKING FOR US. WE MUST STAY HIDDEN... FOR NOW.
BUT LET US REST FOR A SPELL. I AM NOT YET BACK TO MY OLD SELF.
VERY FUNNY, BELOVED.
NOW ARE YOU READY TO FLY?
THEN LET US REST IN THERE. WE WILL MAKE CAMP IN THAT CAVE.

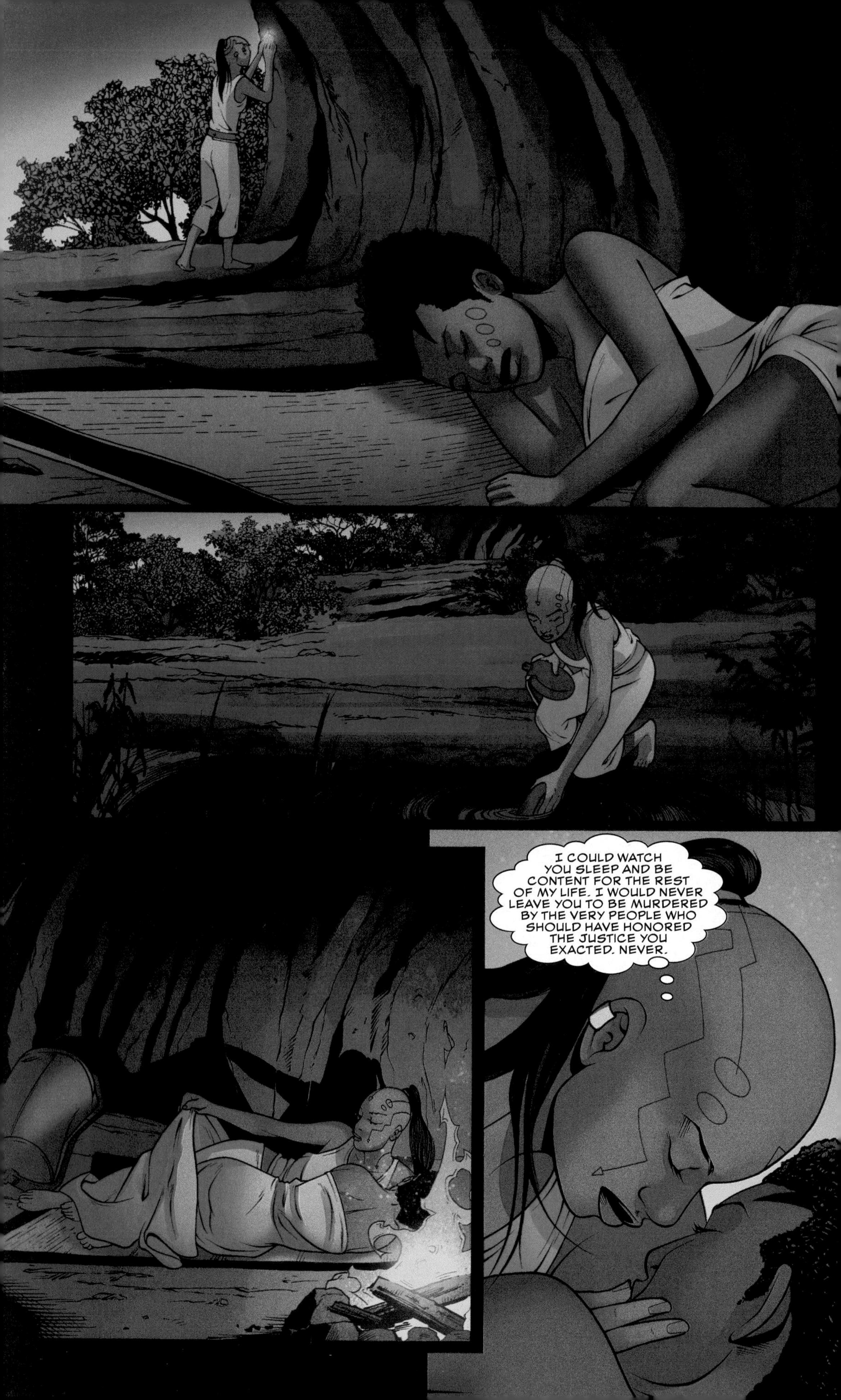
I COULD WATCH YOU SLEEP AND BE CONTENT FOR THE REST OF MY LIFE. I WOULD NEVER LEAVE YOU TO BE MURDERED BY THE VERY PEOPLE WHO SHOULD HAVE HONORED THE JUSTICE YOU EXACTED. NEVER.

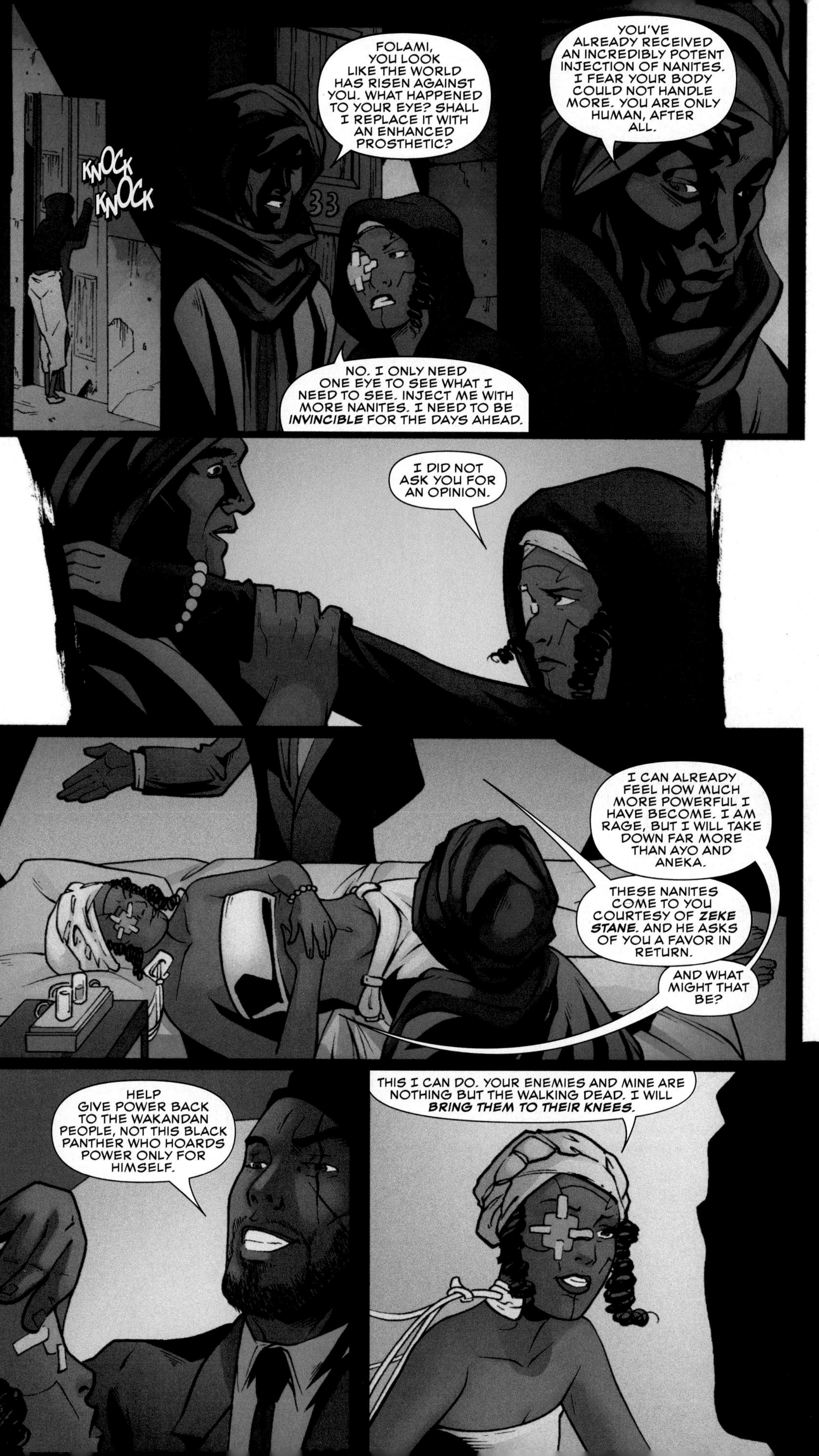
KNOCK KNOCK
FOLAMI, YOU LOOK LIKE THE WORLD HAS RISEN AGAINST YOU. WHAT HAPPENED TO YOUR EYE? SHALL I REPLACE IT WITH AN ENHANCED PROSTHETIC?
NO. I ONLY NEED ONE EYE TO SEE WHAT I NEED TO SEE. INJECT ME WITH MORE NANITES. I NEED TO BE INVINCIBLE FOR THE DAYS AHEAD.
YOU'VE ALREADY RECEIVED AN INCREDIBLY POTENT INJECTION OF NANITES. I FEAR YOUR BODY COULD NOT HANDLE MORE. YOU ARE ONLY HUMAN, AFTER ALL.
I DID NOT ASK YOU FOR AN OPINION.
I CAN ALREADY FEEL HOW MUCH MORE POWERFUL I HAVE BECOME. I AM RAGE, BUT I WILL TAKE DOWN FAR MORE THAN AYO AND ANEKA.
THESE NANITES COME TO YOU COURTESY OF ZEKE STANE. AND HE ASKS OF YOU A FAVOR IN RETURN.
AND WHAT MIGHT THAT BE?
HELP GIVE POWER BACK TO THE WAKANDAN PEOPLE, NOT THIS BLACK PANTHER WHO HOARDS POWER ONLY FOR HIMSELF.
THIS I CAN DO. YOUR ENEMIES AND MINE ARE NOTHING BUT THE WALKING DEAD. I WILL BRING THEM TO THEIR KNEES.

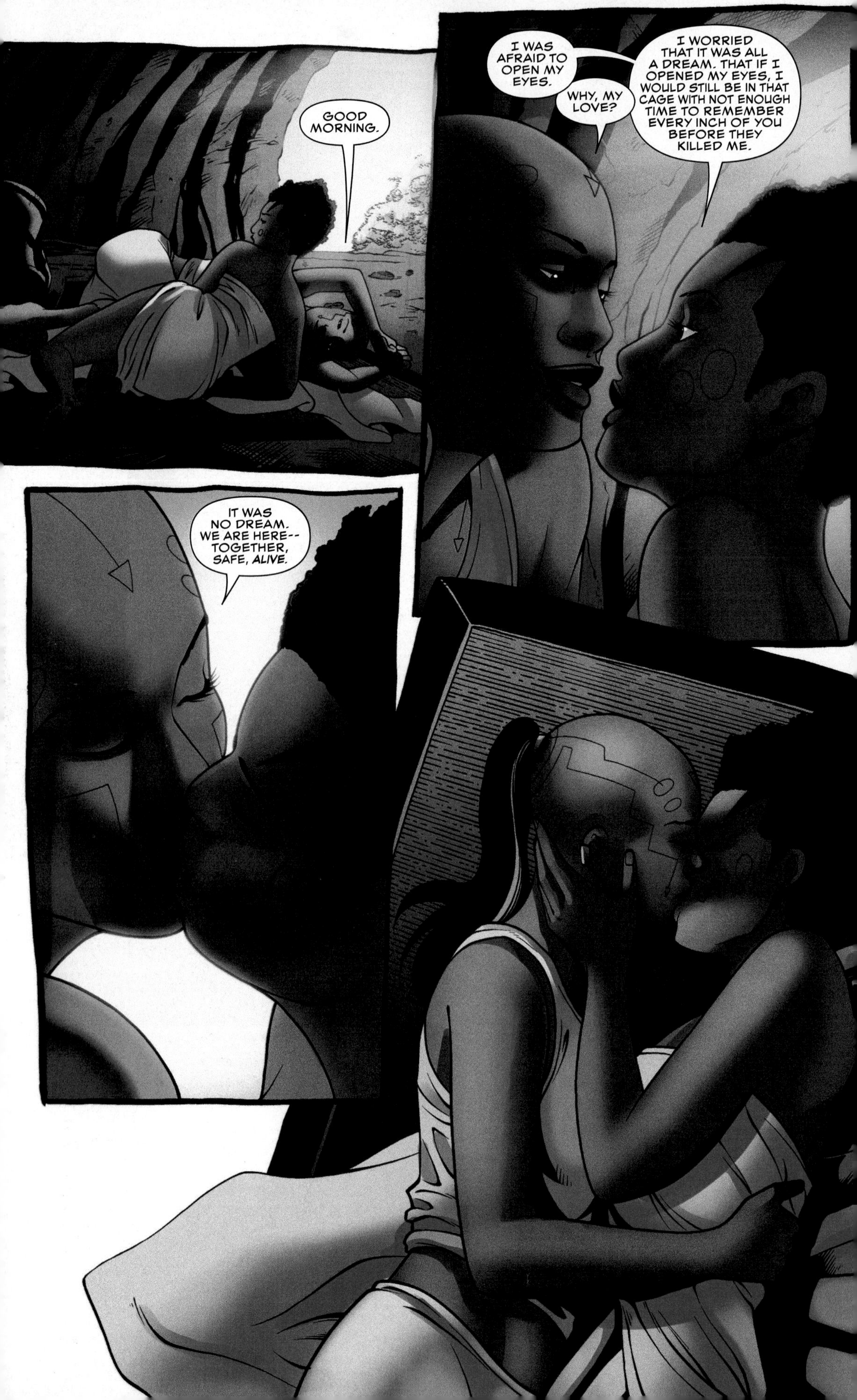
GOOD MORNING.
I WAS AFRAID TO OPEN MY EYES.
WHY, MY LOVE?
I WORRIED THAT IT WAS ALL A DREAM. THAT IF I OPENED MY EYES, I WOULD STILL BE IN THAT CAGE WITH NOT ENOUGH TIME TO REMEMBER EVERY INCH OF YOU BEFORE THEY KILLED ME.
IT WAS NO DREAM. WE ARE HERE--TOGETHER, SAFE, *ALIVE*.

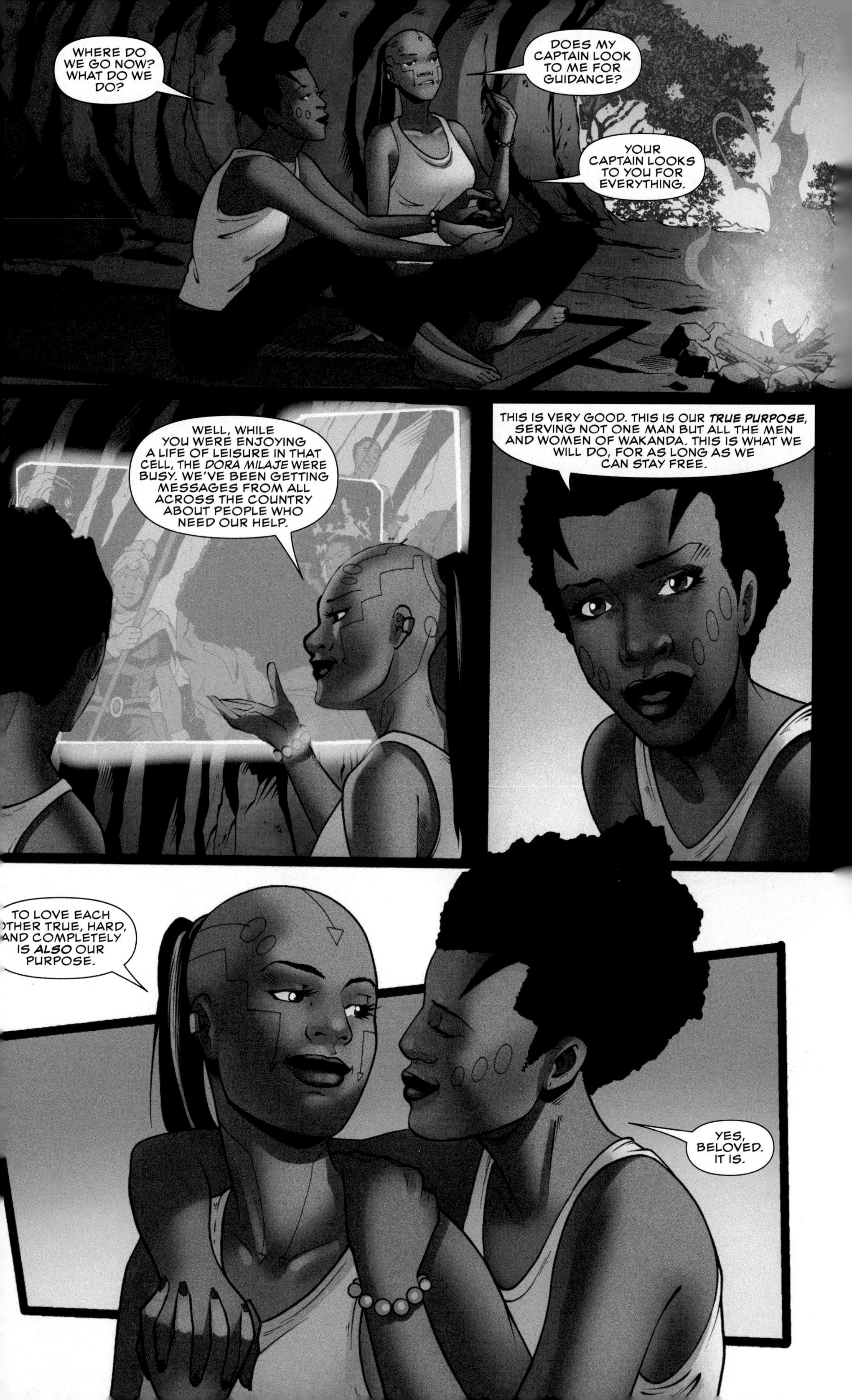
WHERE DO WE GO NOW? WHAT DO WE DO?
DOES MY CAPTAIN LOOK TO ME FOR GUIDANCE?
YOUR CAPTAIN LOOKS TO YOU FOR EVERYTHING.
WELL, WHILE YOU WERE ENJOYING A LIFE OF LEISURE IN THAT CELL, THE *DORA MILAJE* WERE BUSY. WE'VE BEEN GETTING MESSAGES FROM ALL ACROSS THE COUNTRY ABOUT PEOPLE WHO NEED OUR HELP.
THIS IS VERY GOOD. THIS IS OUR ***TRUE PURPOSE***, SERVING NOT ONE MAN BUT ALL THE MEN AND WOMEN OF WAKANDA. THIS IS WHAT WE WILL DO, FOR AS LONG AS WE CAN STAY FREE.
TO LOVE EACH THER TRUE, HARD, ND COMPLETELY IS ***ALSO*** OUR PURPOSE.
YES, BELOVED. IT IS.

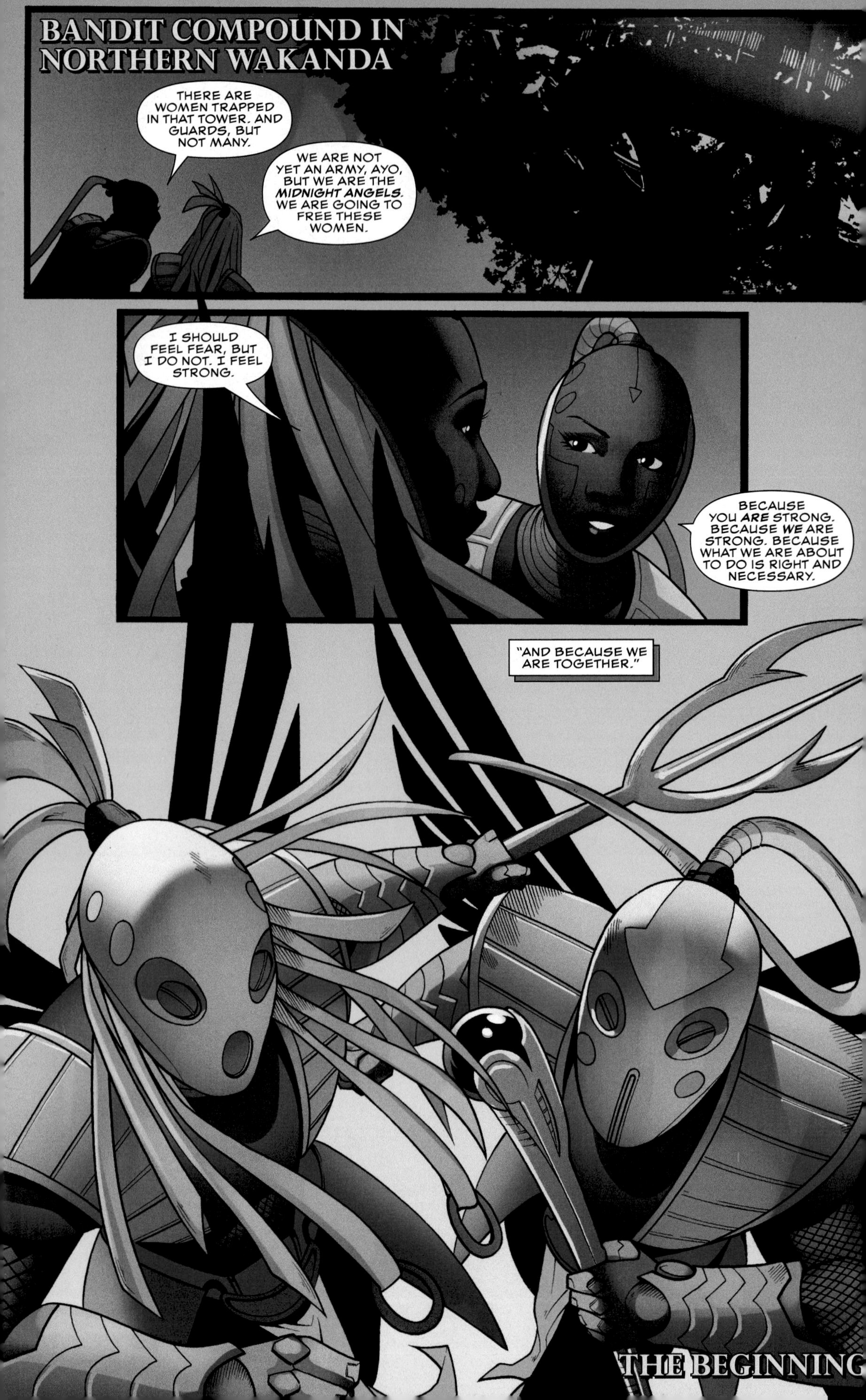

BANDIT COMPOUND IN NORTHERN WAKANDA
THERE ARE WOMEN TRAPPED IN THAT TOWER. AND GUARDS, BUT NOT MANY.
WE ARE NOT YET AN ARMY, AYO, BUT WE ARE THE *MIDNIGHT ANGELS*. WE ARE GOING TO FREE THESE WOMEN.
I SHOULD FEEL FEAR, BUT I DO NOT. I FEEL STRONG.
BECAUSE YOU *ARE* STRONG. BECAUSE *WE* ARE STRONG. BECAUSE WHAT WE ARE ABOUT TO DO IS RIGHT AND NECESSARY.
"AND BECAUSE WE ARE TOGETHER."
THE BEGINNING

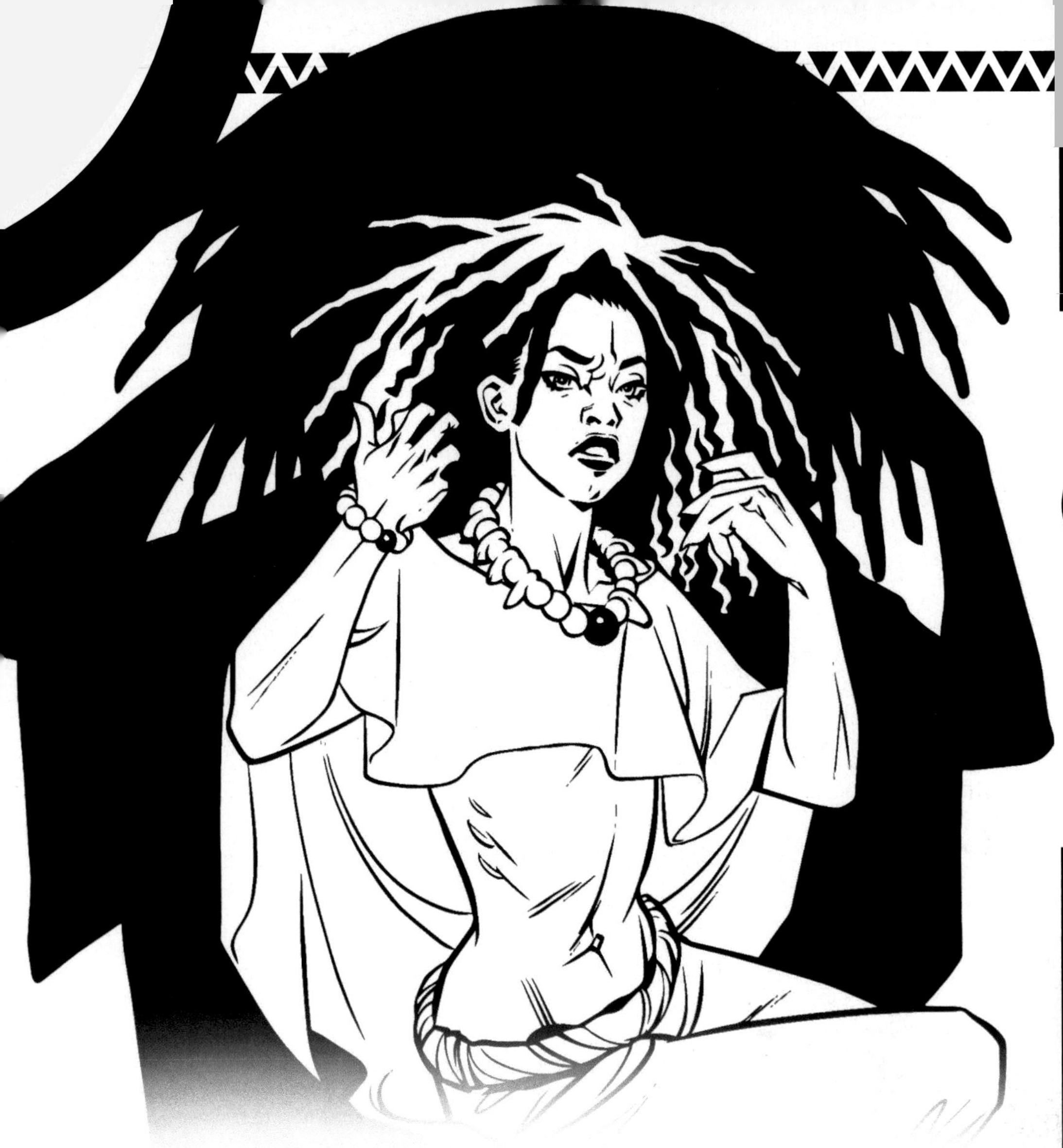

# THE PEOPLE FOR THE PEOPLE

Alongside Tetu, the mysterious **Zenzi** leads The People, a group currently trying to topple the Wakandan monarchy. An experimental treatment in her native country of Niganda gave Zenzi the ability to control and amplify people's emotions, a power she has used to great effect in stirring up the citizens of Wakanda. But who was Zenzi before the experiment? And how did she go from lab rat to revolutionary?

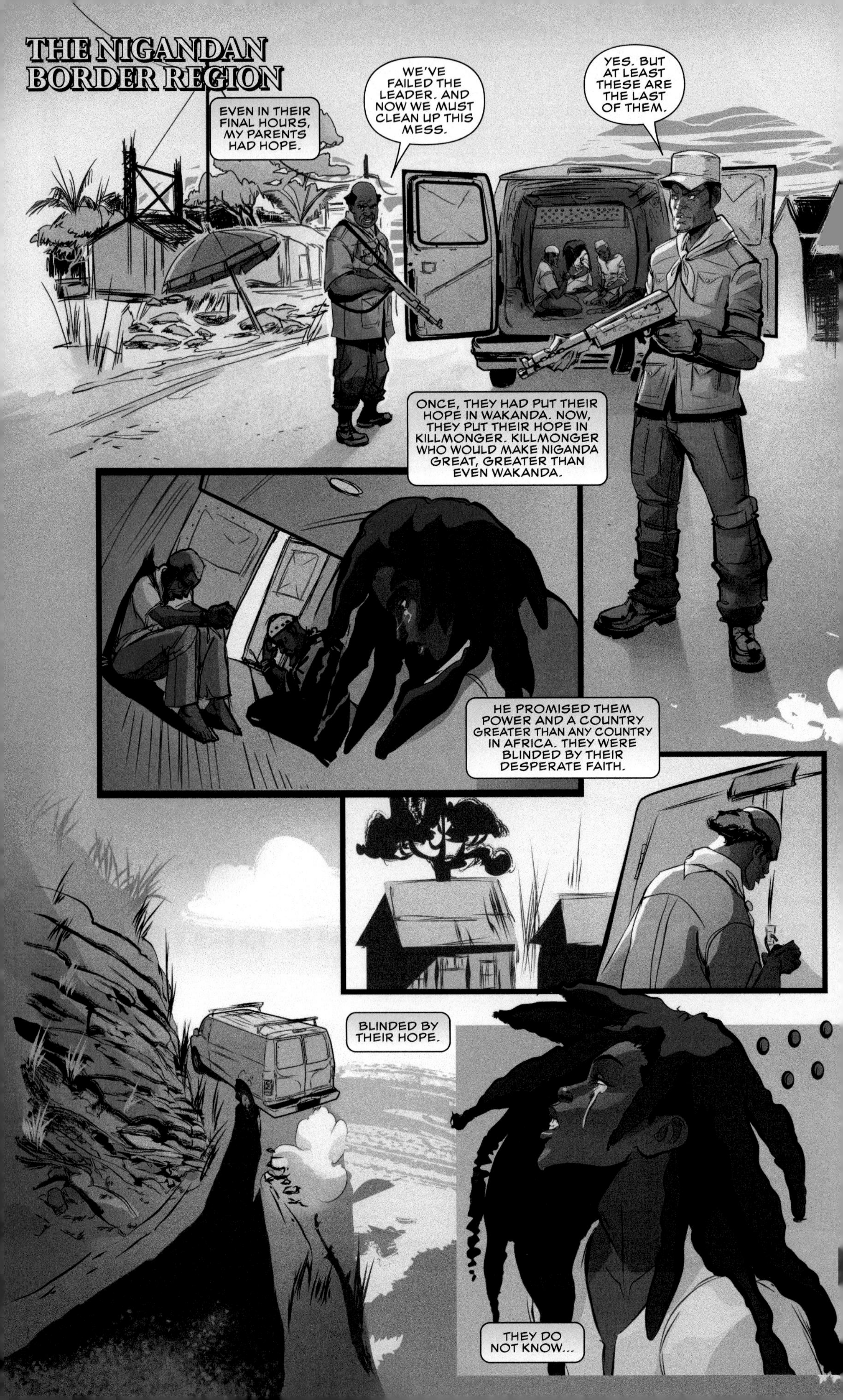
THE NIGANDAN BORDER REGION
EVEN IN THEIR FINAL HOURS, MY PARENTS HAD HOPE.
WE'VE FAILED THE LEADER. AND NOW WE MUST CLEAN UP THIS MESS.
YES. BUT AT LEAST THESE ARE THE LAST OF THEM.
ONCE, THEY HAD PUT THEIR HOPE IN WAKANDA. NOW, THEY PUT THEIR HOPE IN KILLMONGER. KILLMONGER WHO WOULD MAKE NIGANDA GREAT, GREATER THAN EVEN WAKANDA.
HE PROMISED THEM POWER AND A COUNTRY GREATER THAN ANY COUNTRY IN AFRICA. THEY WERE BLINDED BY THEIR DESPERATE FAITH.
BLINDED BY THEIR HOPE.
THEY DO NOT KNOW...

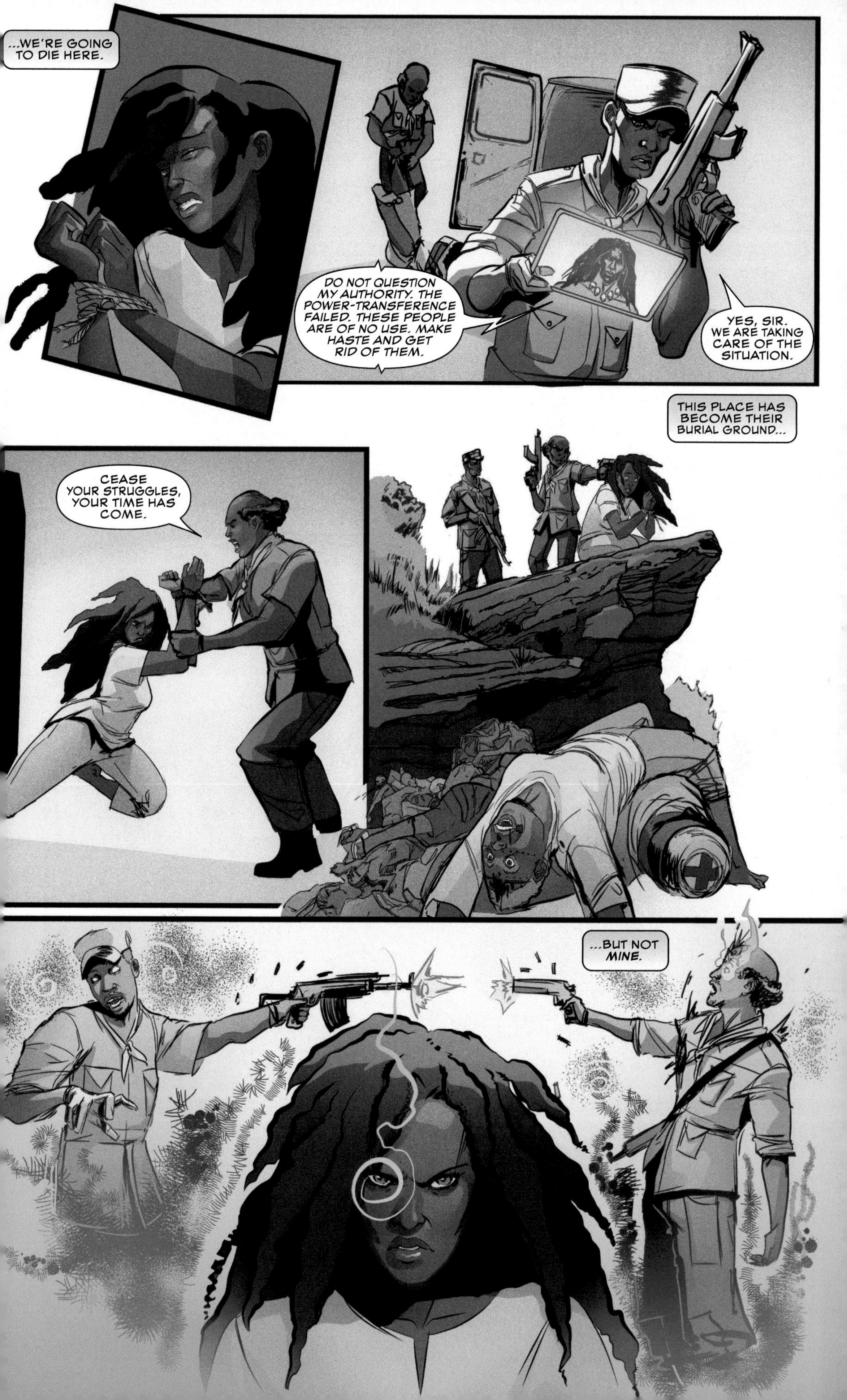

...WE'RE GOING TO DIE HERE.
DO NOT QUESTION MY AUTHORITY. THE POWER-TRANSFERENCE FAILED. THESE PEOPLE ARE OF NO USE. MAKE HASTE AND GET RID OF THEM.
YES, SIR. WE ARE TAKING CARE OF THE SITUATION.
THIS PLACE HAS BECOME THEIR BURIAL GROUND...
CEASE YOUR STRUGGLES, YOUR TIME HAS COME.
...BUT NOT MINE.

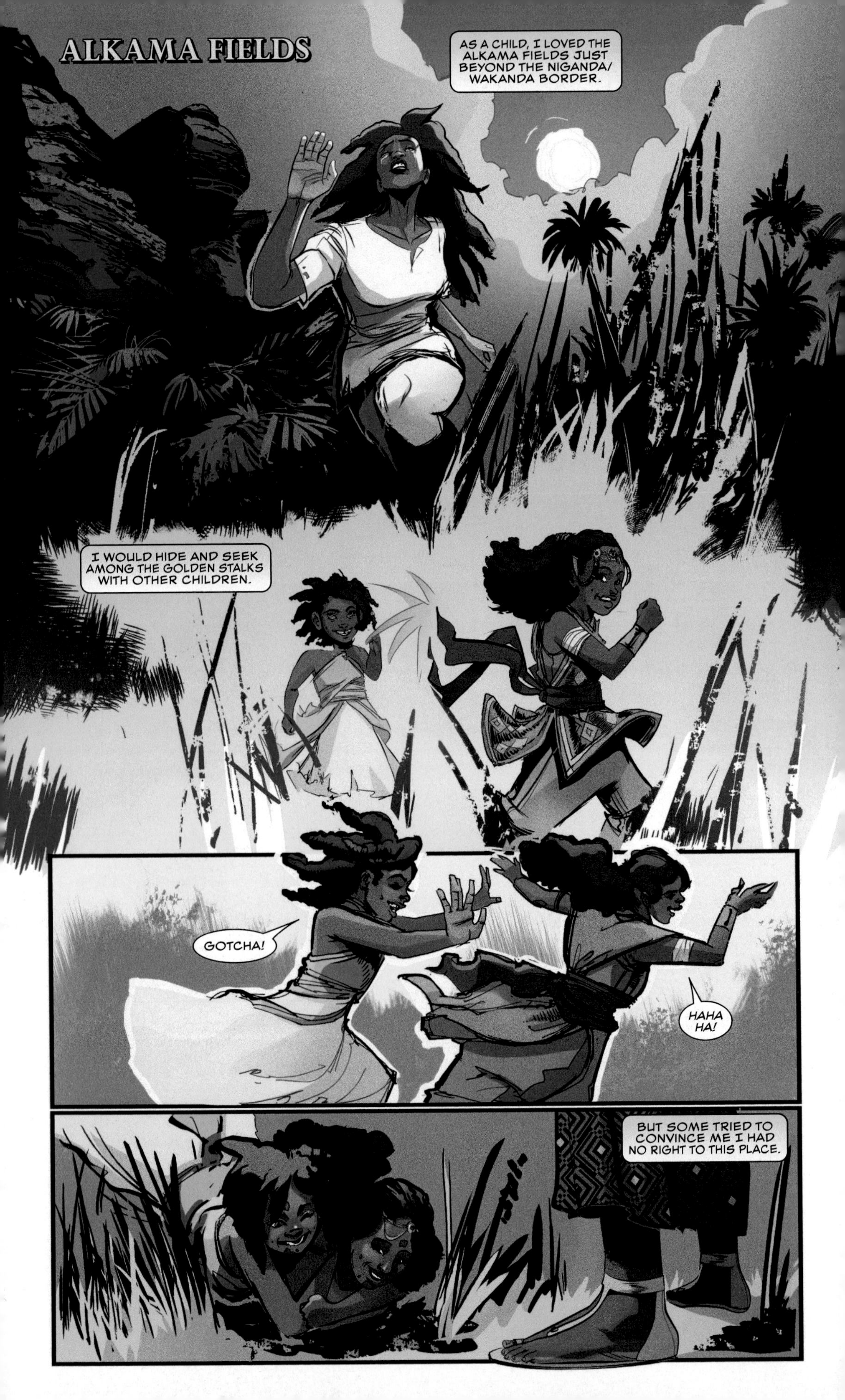
ALKAMA FIELDS
AS A CHILD, I LOVED THE ALKAMA FIELDS JUST BEYOND THE NIGANDA/ WAKANDA BORDER.
I WOULD HIDE AND SEEK AMONG THE GOLDEN STALKS WITH OTHER CHILDREN.
GOTCHA!
HAHA HA!
BUT SOME TRIED TO CONVINCE ME I HAD NO RIGHT TO THIS PLACE.

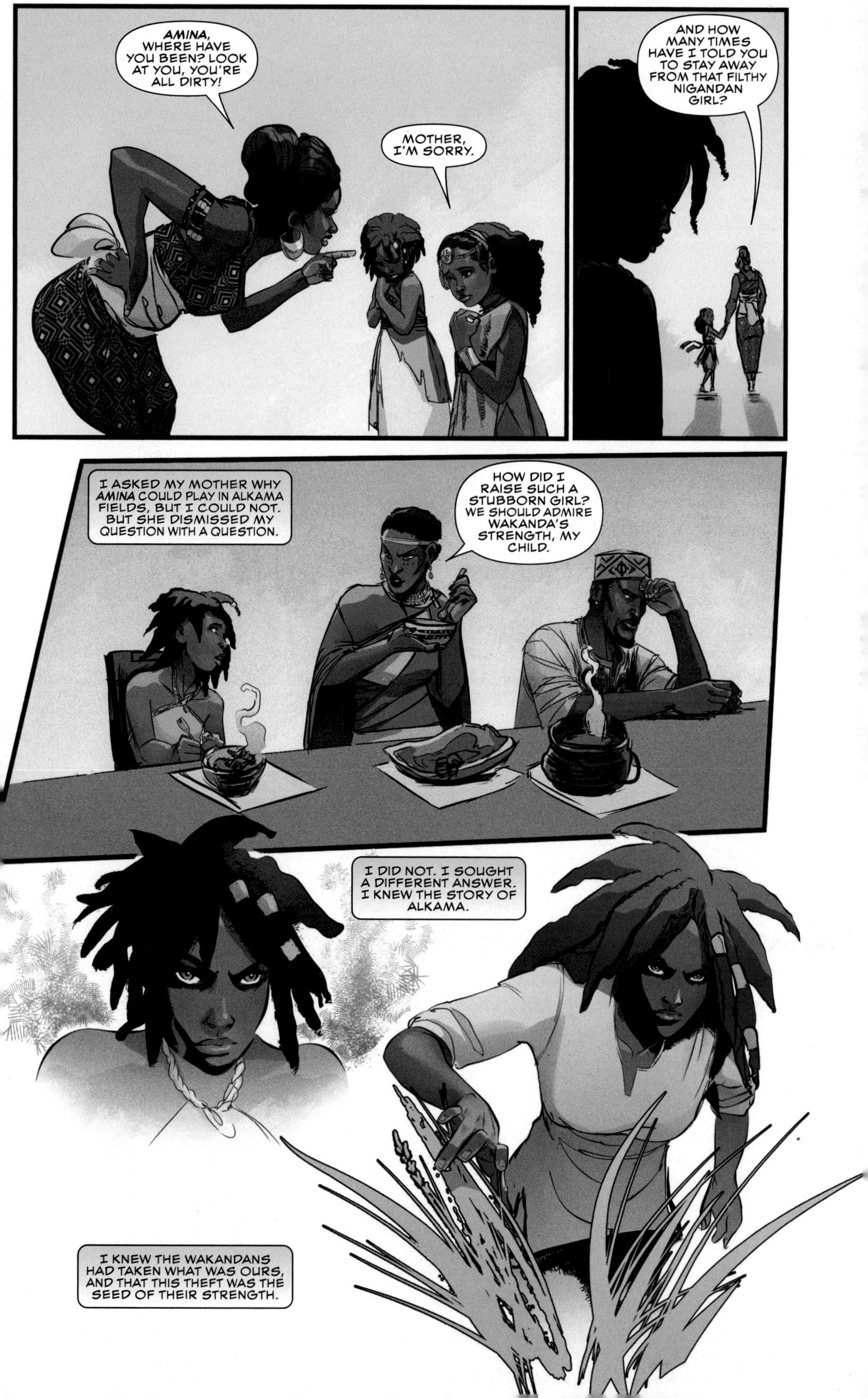
AMINA, WHERE HAVE YOU BEEN? LOOK AT YOU, YOU'RE ALL DIRTY!
MOTHER, I'M SORRY.
AND HOW MANY TIMES HAVE I TOLD YOU TO STAY AWAY FROM THAT FILTHY NIGANDAN GIRL?
I ASKED MY MOTHER WHY AMINA COULD PLAY IN ALKAMA FIELDS, BUT I COULD NOT. BUT SHE DISMISSED MY QUESTION WITH A QUESTION.
HOW DID I RAISE SUCH A STUBBORN GIRL? WE SHOULD ADMIRE WAKANDA'S STRENGTH, MY CHILD.
I DID NOT. I SOUGHT A DIFFERENT ANSWER. I KNEW THE STORY OF ALKAMA.
I KNEW THE WAKANDANS HAD TAKEN WHAT WAS OURS, AND THAT THIS THEFT WAS THE SEED OF THEIR STRENGTH.

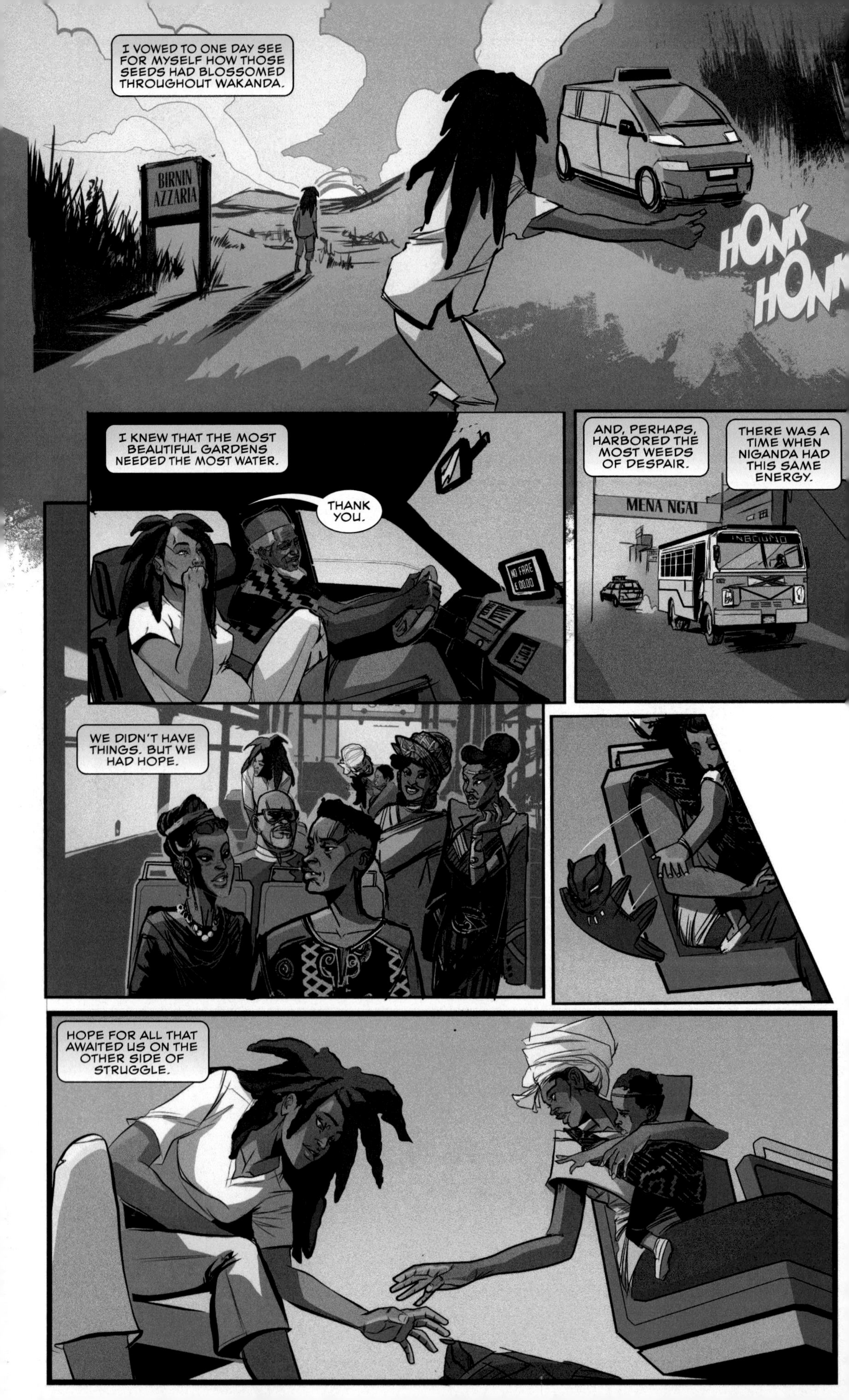
I VOWED TO ONE DAY SEE FOR MYSELF HOW THOSE SEEDS HAD BLOSSOMED THROUGHOUT WAKANDA.
BIRNIN AZZARIA
HONK HONK
I KNEW THAT THE MOST BEAUTIFUL GARDENS NEEDED THE MOST WATER.
THANK YOU.
NO FARE
AND, PERHAPS, HARBORED THE MOST WEEDS OF DESPAIR.
THERE WAS A TIME WHEN NIGANDA HAD THIS SAME ENERGY.
MENA NGAI
WE DIDN'T HAVE THINGS. BUT WE HAD HOPE.
HOPE FOR ALL THAT AWAITED US ON THE OTHER SIDE OF STRUGGLE.

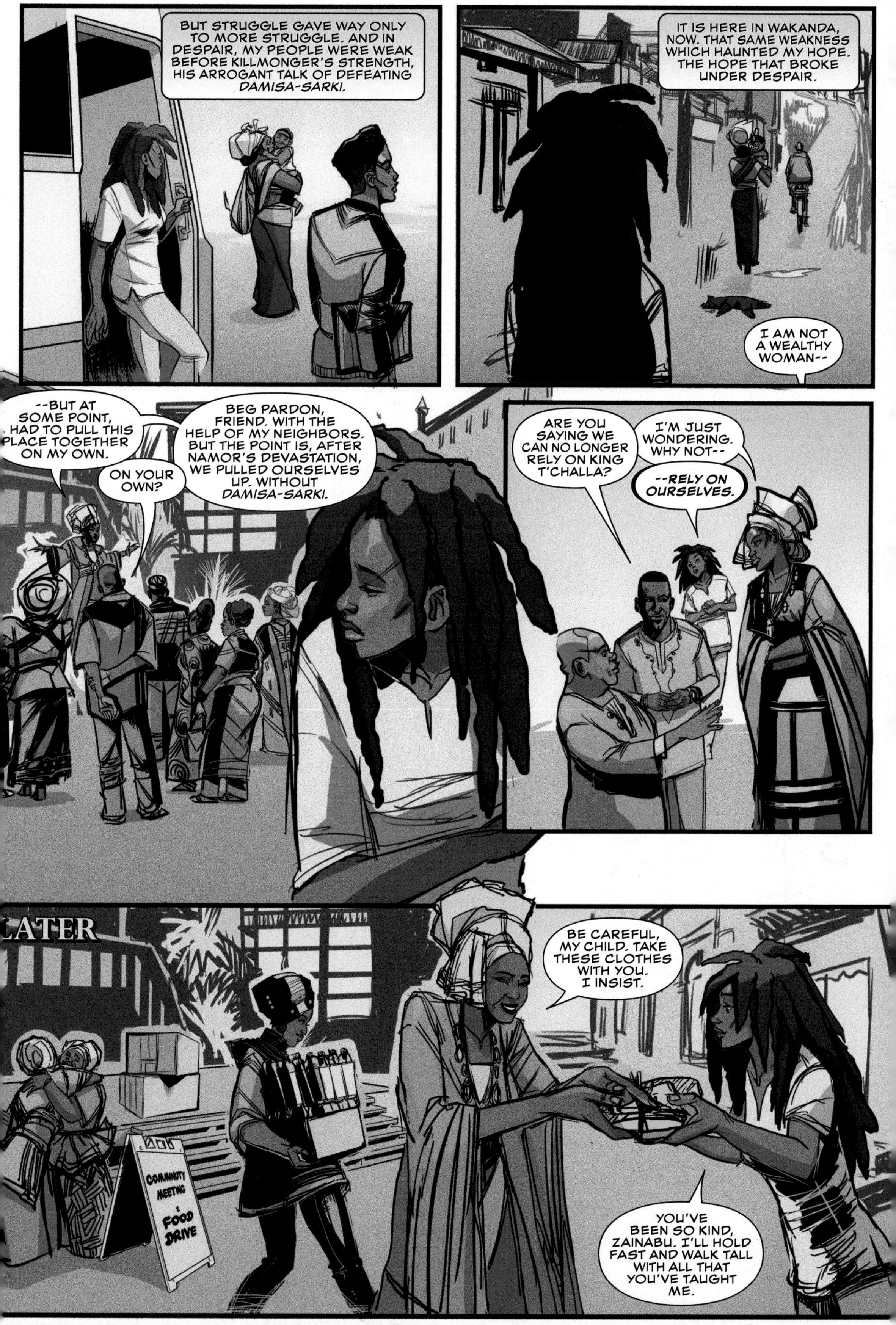

BUT STRUGGLE GAVE WAY ONLY TO MORE STRUGGLE. AND IN DESPAIR, MY PEOPLE WERE WEAK BEFORE KILLMONGER'S STRENGTH, HIS ARROGANT TALK OF DEFEATING *DAMISA-SARKI.*
IT IS HERE IN WAKANDA, NOW. THAT SAME WEAKNESS WHICH HAUNTED MY HOPE. THE HOPE THAT BROKE UNDER DESPAIR.
I AM NOT A WEALTHY WOMAN--
--BUT AT SOME POINT, I HAD TO PULL THIS PLACE TOGETHER ON MY OWN.
ON YOUR OWN?
BEG PARDON, FRIEND. WITH THE HELP OF MY NEIGHBORS. BUT THE POINT IS, AFTER NAMOR'S DEVASTATION, WE PULLED OURSELVES UP. WITHOUT *DAMISA-SARKI.*
ARE YOU SAYING WE CAN NO LONGER RELY ON KING T'CHALLA?
I'M JUST WONDERING. WHY NOT--
***--RELY ON OURSELVES.***
LATER
BE CAREFUL, MY CHILD. TAKE THESE CLOTHES WITH YOU. I INSIST.
COMMUNITY MEETING & FOOD DRIVE
YOU'VE BEEN SO KIND, ZAINABU. I'LL HOLD FAST AND WALK TALL WITH ALL THAT YOU'VE TAUGHT ME.

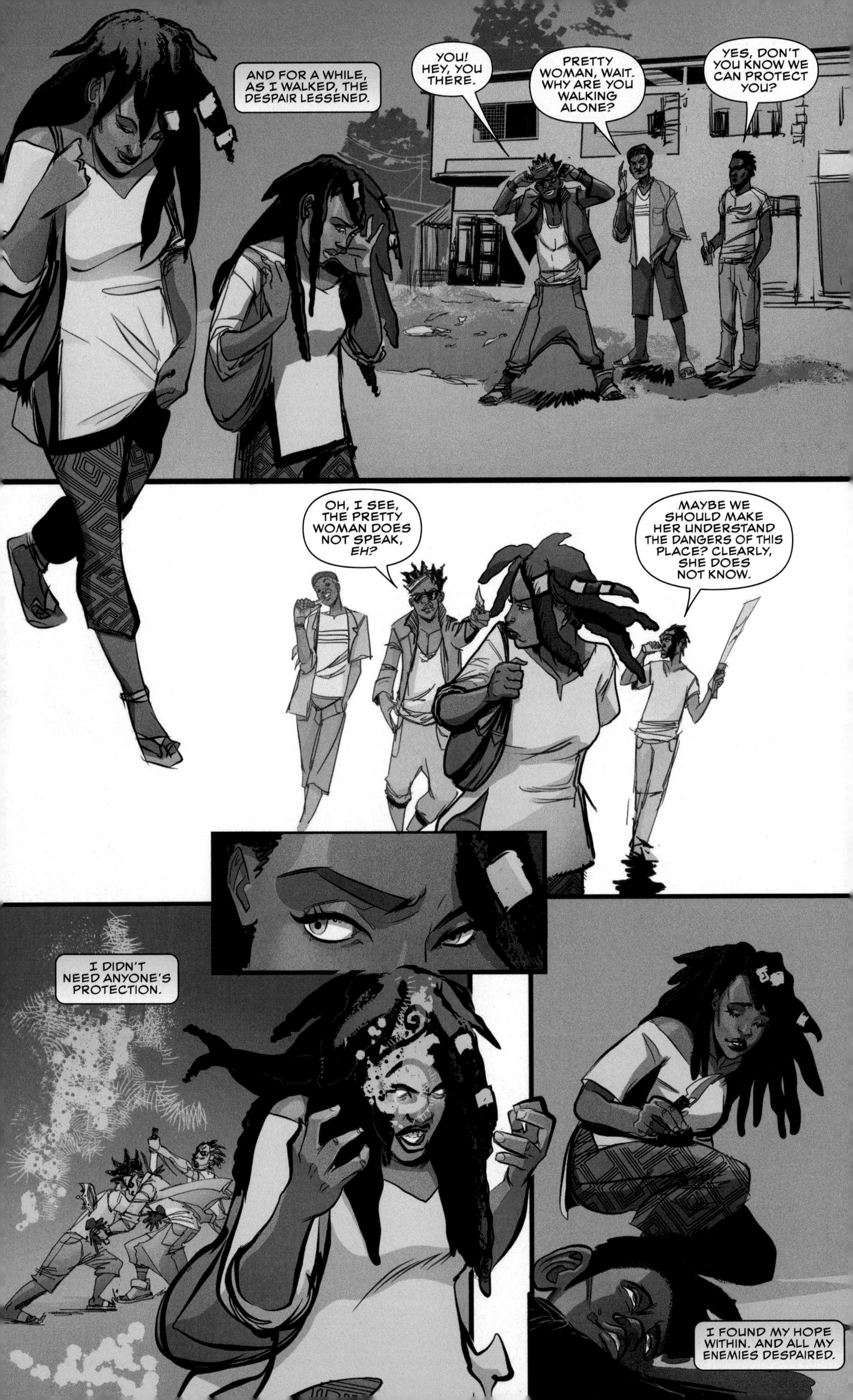
AND FOR A WHILE, AS I WALKED, THE DESPAIR LESSENED.
YOU! HEY, YOU THERE.
PRETTY WOMAN, WAIT. WHY ARE YOU WALKING ALONE?
YES, DON'T YOU KNOW WE CAN PROTECT YOU?
OH, I SEE, THE PRETTY WOMAN DOES NOT SPEAK, EH?
MAYBE WE SHOULD MAKE HER UNDERSTAND THE DANGERS OF THIS PLACE? CLEARLY, SHE DOES NOT KNOW.
I DIDN'T NEED ANYONE'S PROTECTION.
I FOUND MY HOPE WITHIN. AND ALL MY ENEMIES DESPAIRED.

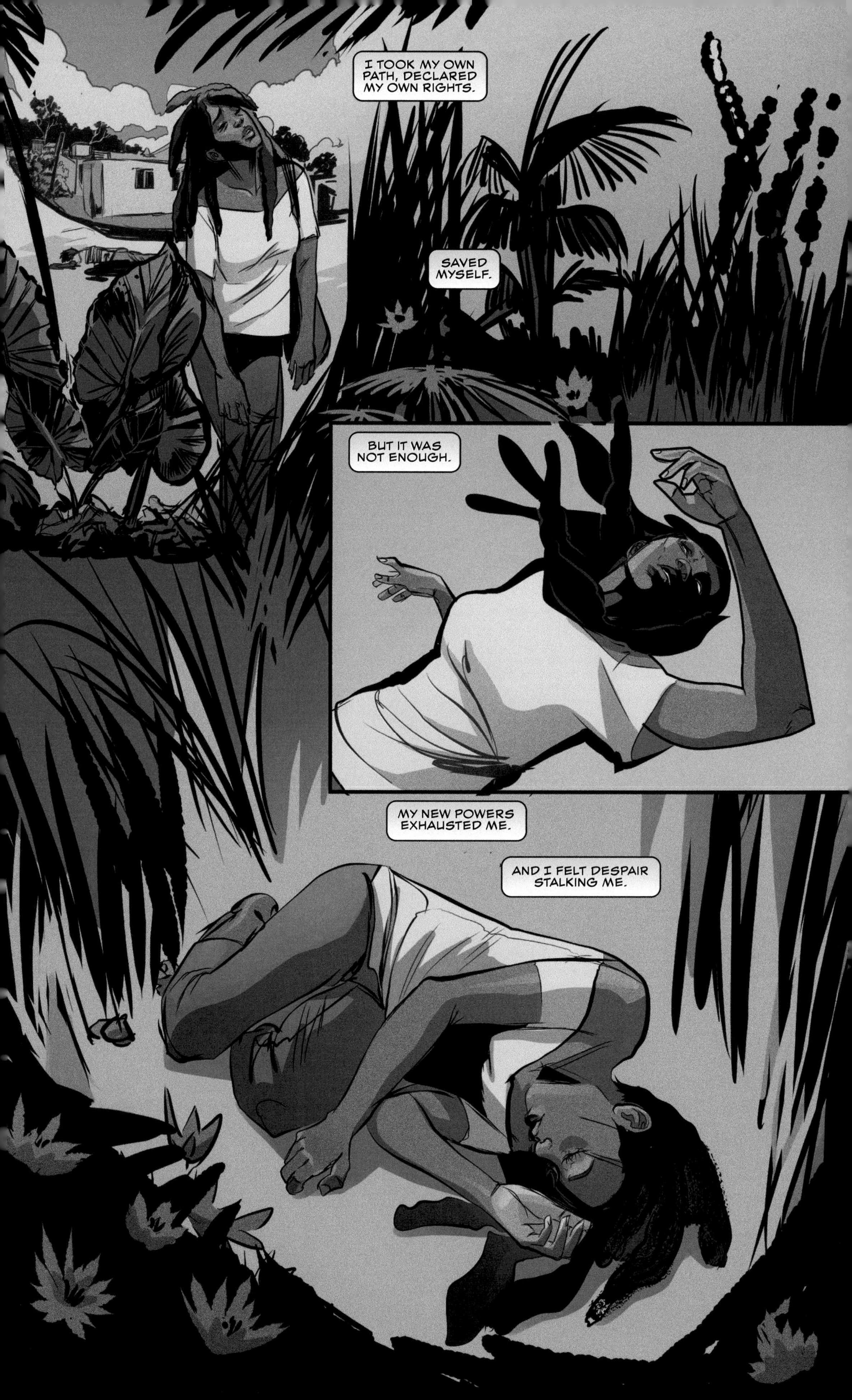
I TOOK MY OWN PATH, DECLARED MY OWN RIGHTS.
SAVED MYSELF.
BUT IT WAS NOT ENOUGH.
MY NEW POWERS EXHAUSTED ME.
AND I FELT DESPAIR STALKING ME.

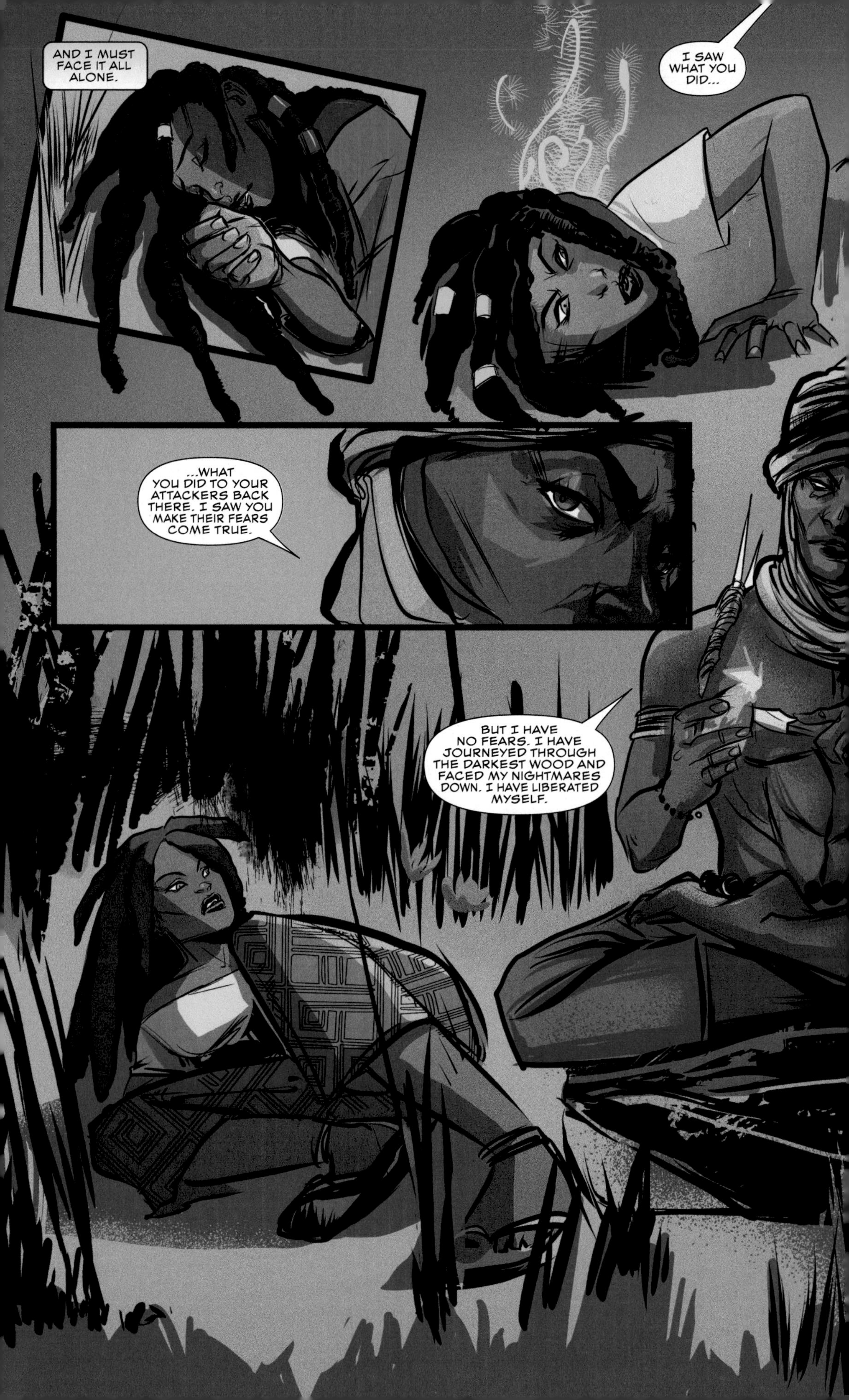
AND I MUST FACE IT ALL ALONE.
I SAW WHAT YOU DID...
...WHAT YOU DID TO YOUR ATTACKERS BACK THERE. I SAW YOU MAKE THEIR FEARS COME TRUE.
BUT I HAVE NO FEARS. I HAVE JOURNEYED THROUGH THE DARKEST WOOD AND FACED MY NIGHTMARES DOWN. I HAVE LIBERATED MYSELF.

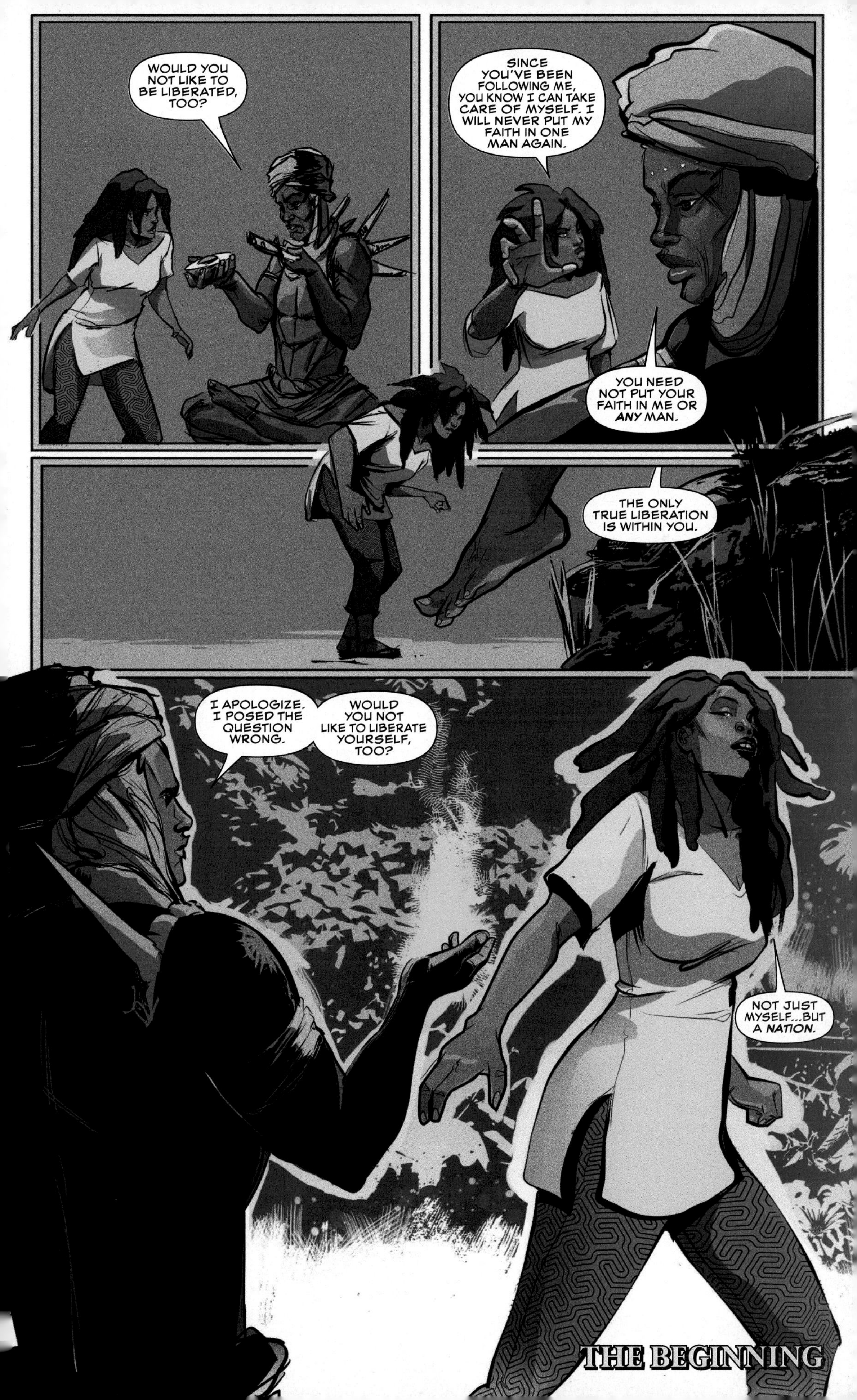
WOULD YOU NOT LIKE TO BE LIBERATED, TOO?
SINCE YOU'VE BEEN FOLLOWING ME, YOU KNOW I CAN TAKE CARE OF MYSELF. I WILL NEVER PUT MY FAITH IN ONE MAN AGAIN.
YOU NEED NOT PUT YOUR FAITH IN ME OR ANY MAN.
THE ONLY TRUE LIBERATION IS WITHIN YOU.
I APOLOGIZE. I POSED THE QUESTION WRONG.
WOULD YOU NOT LIKE TO LIBERATE YOURSELF, TOO?
NOT JUST MYSELF...BUT A NATION.
THE BEGINNING

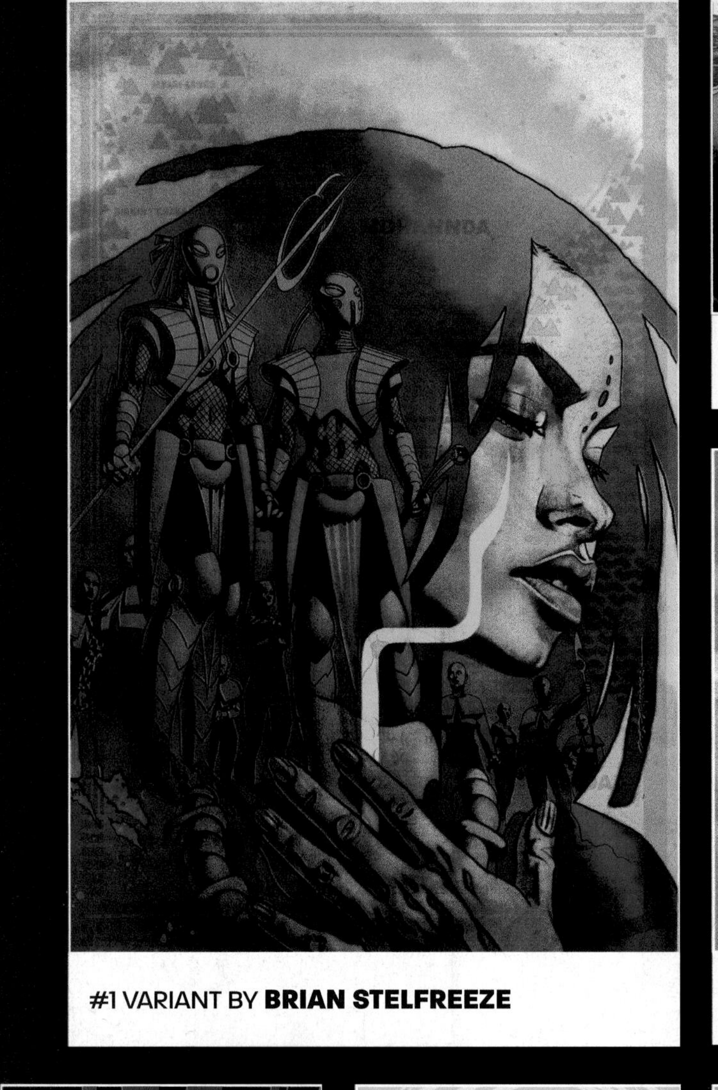

#1 VARIANT BY **BRIAN STELFREEZE**

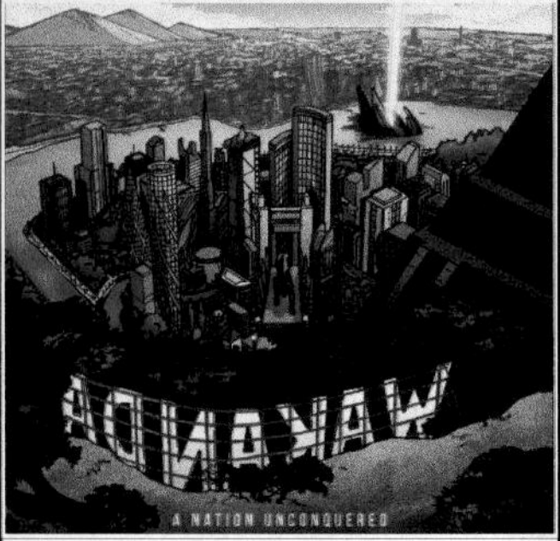
A NATION UNCONQUERED

#1 HIP-HOP VARIANT BY
**ALITHA E. MARTINEZ**
& **RACHELLE ROSENBERG**

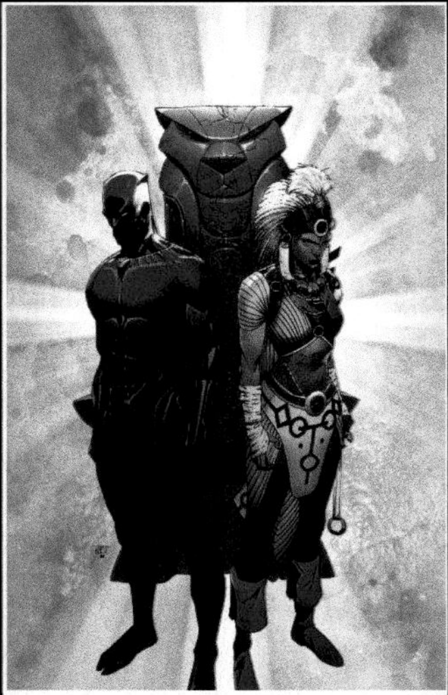

#1 DIVIDED WE STAND VARIANT
BY **KHOI PHAM** &
**FRANK D'ARMATA**

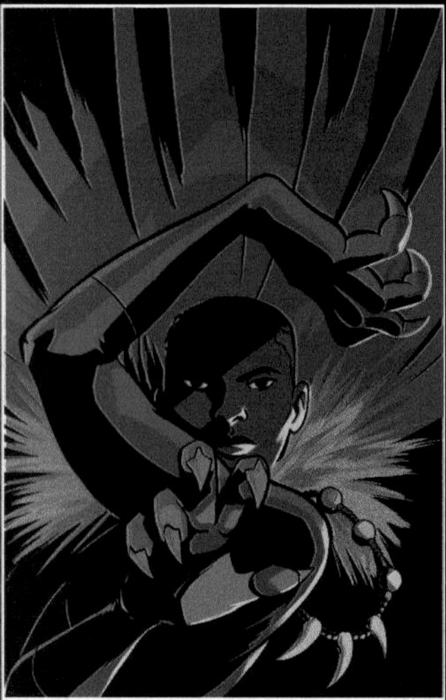

#1 BLACK PANTHER 50TH
ANNIVERSARY VARIANT BY
**NATACHA BUSTOS**

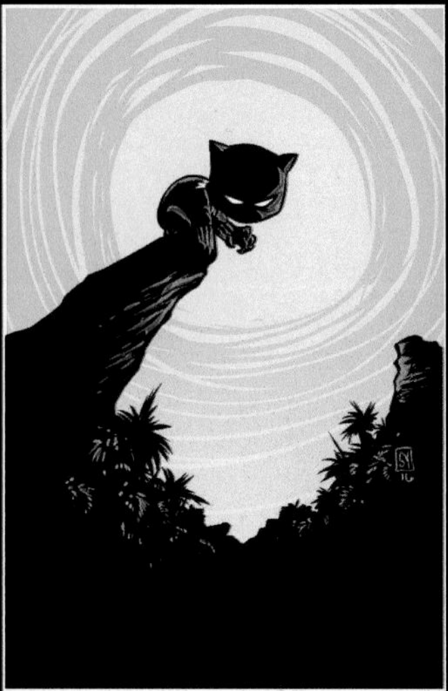

#1 VARIANT BY **SKOTTIE YOUNG**

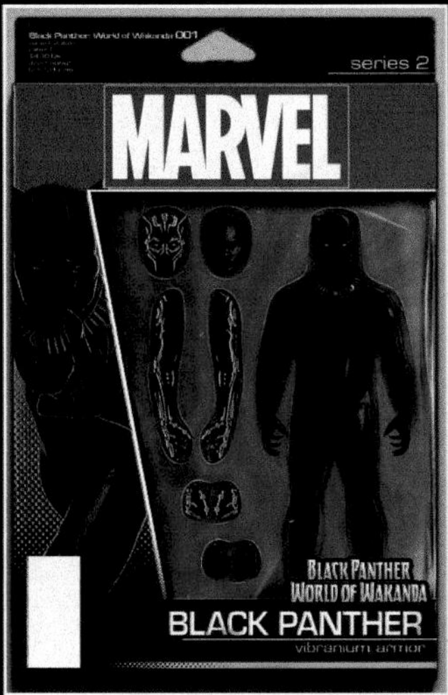
series 2
MARVEL
BLACK PANTHER
WORLD OF WAKANDA
BLACK PANTHER
vibranium armor

#1 ACTION FIGURE VARIANT BY
**JOHN TYLER CHRISTOPHER**

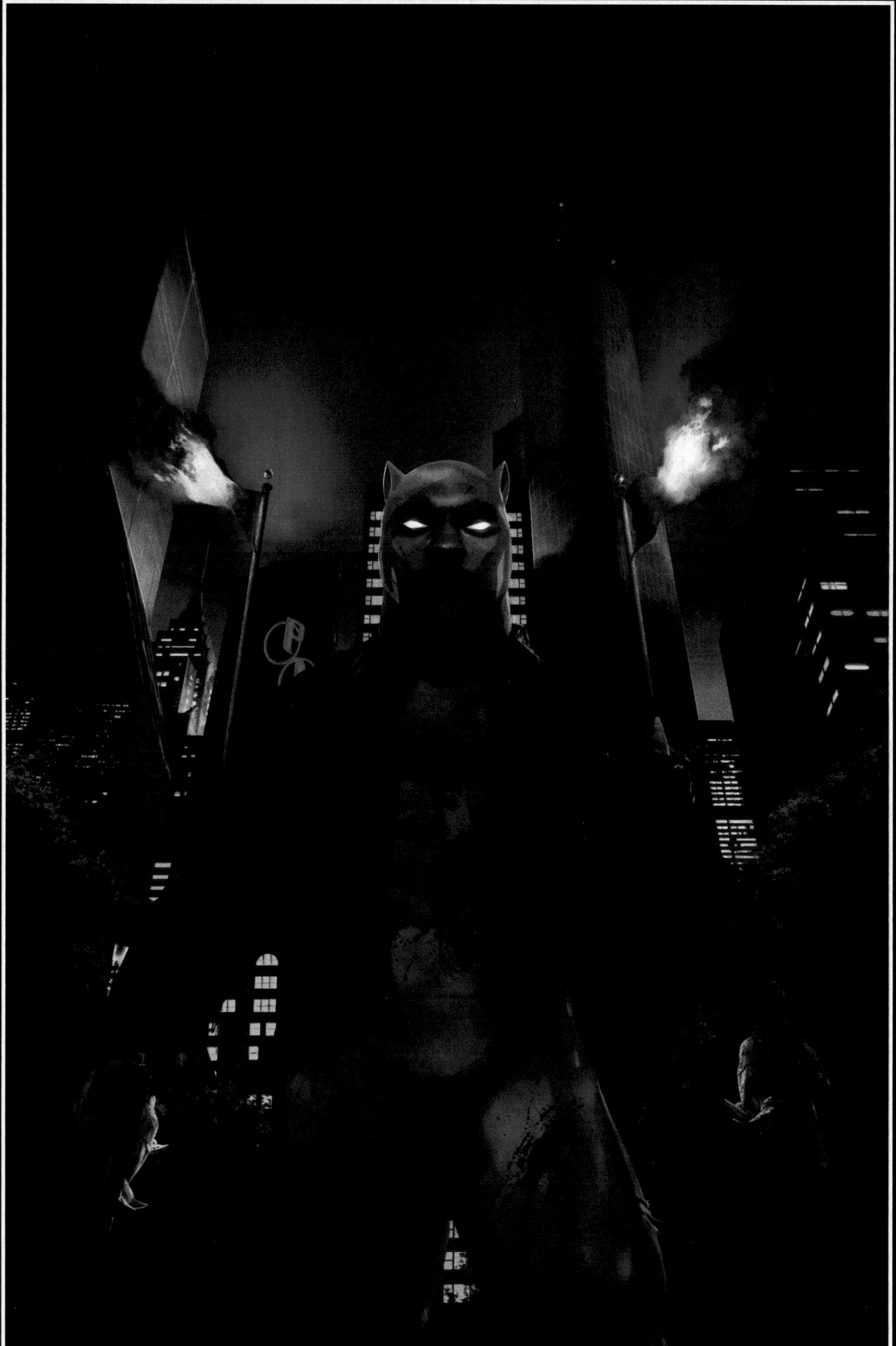

6

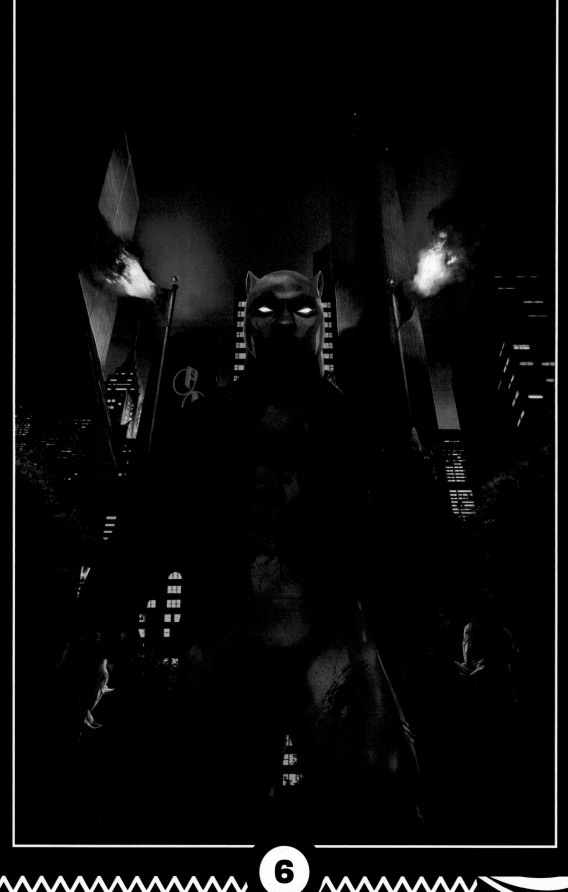

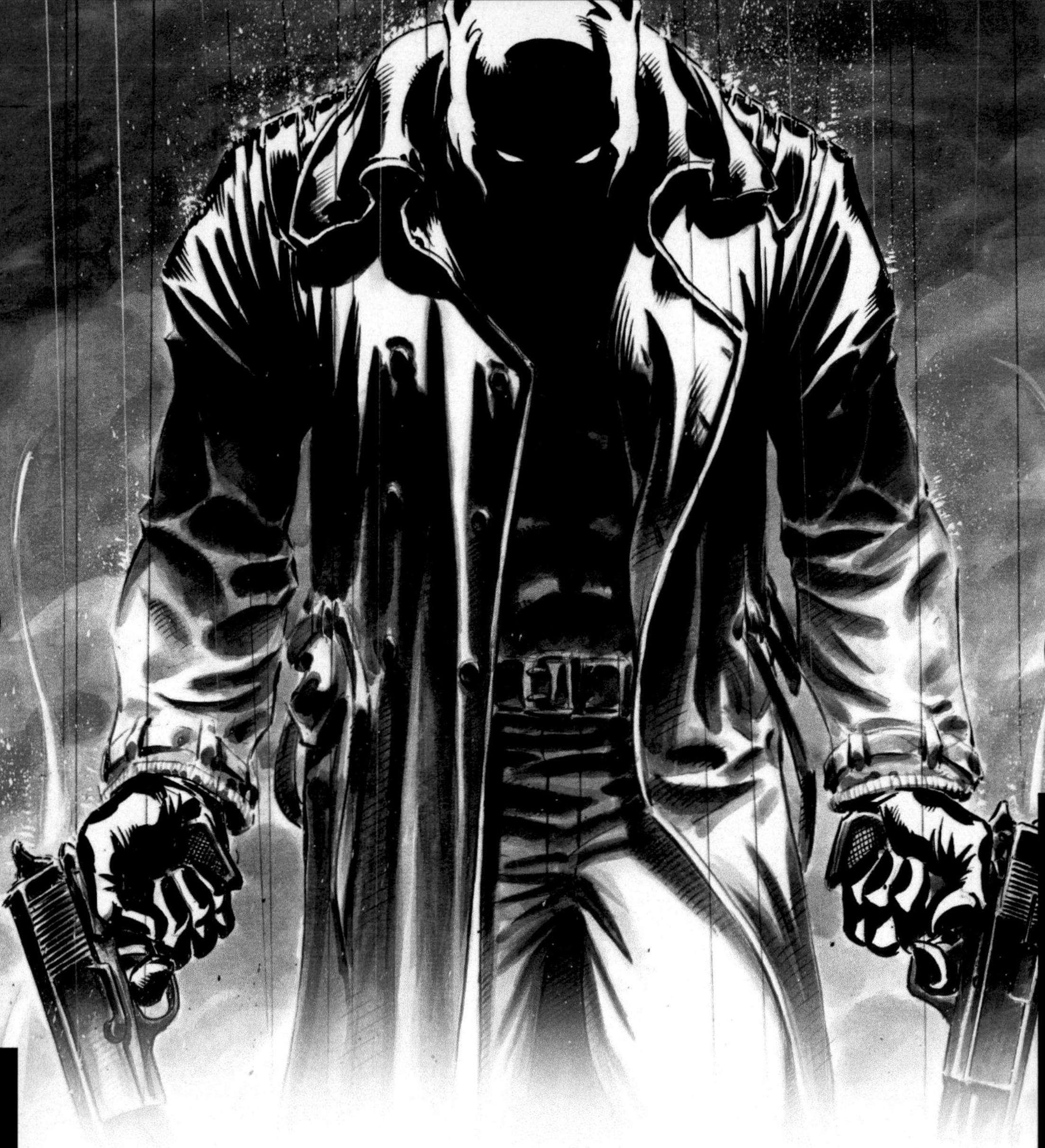

# DEATH OF THE WHITE TIGER

When NYPD officer Kevin "Kasper" Cole was unjustly suspended from the force, he discovered a spare Black Panther costume and took on the mantle of the then M.I.A. hero to continue his organized crime investigations (and to clear his name and get promoted, natch). But after receiving guidance and equipment from King T'Challa (the true Black Panther), Kasper juggled a double life as a police officer by day and the vigilante White Tiger by night (while still trying to provide for his mother and his pregnant girlfriend).

That was then...

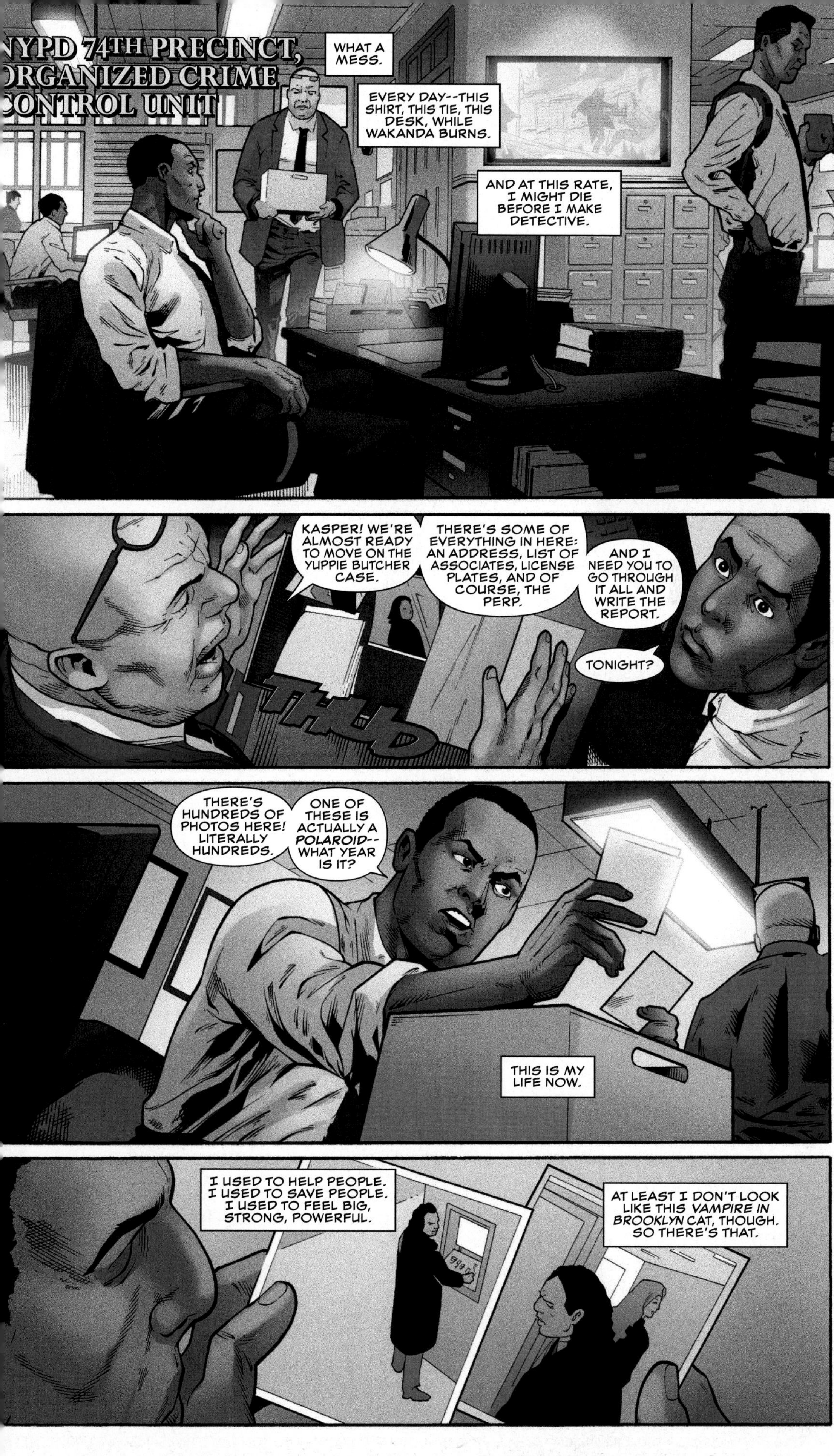

NYPD 74TH PRECINCT, ORGANIZED CRIME CONTROL UNIT
WHAT A MESS.
EVERY DAY--THIS SHIRT, THIS TIE, THIS DESK, WHILE WAKANDA BURNS.
AND AT THIS RATE, I MIGHT DIE BEFORE I MAKE DETECTIVE.
KASPER! WE'RE ALMOST READY TO MOVE ON THE YUPPIE BUTCHER CASE.
THERE'S SOME OF EVERYTHING IN HERE: AN ADDRESS, LIST OF ASSOCIATES, LICENSE PLATES, AND OF COURSE, THE PERP.
AND I NEED YOU TO GO THROUGH IT ALL AND WRITE THE REPORT.
THUD
TONIGHT?
THERE'S HUNDREDS OF PHOTOS HERE! LITERALLY HUNDREDS.
ONE OF THESE IS ACTUALLY A *POLAROID*--WHAT YEAR IS IT?
THIS IS MY LIFE NOW.
I USED TO HELP PEOPLE. I USED TO SAVE PEOPLE. I USED TO FEEL BIG, STRONG, POWERFUL.
AT LEAST I DON'T LOOK LIKE THIS *VAMPIRE IN BROOKLYN* CAT, THOUGH. SO THERE'S THAT.

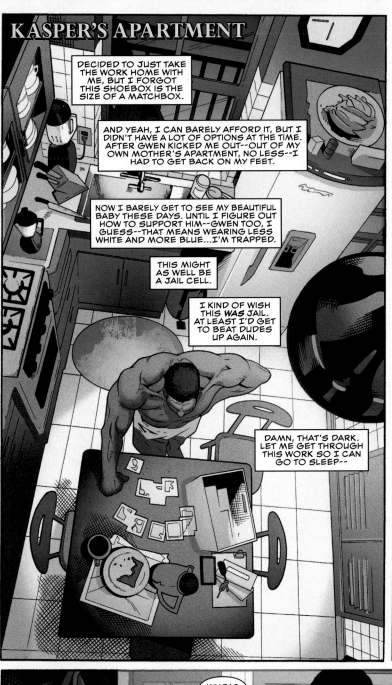

DECIDED TO JUST TAKE THE WORK HOME WITH ME, BUT I FORGOT THIS SHOEBOX IS THE SIZE OF A MATCHBOX.

AND YEAH, I CAN BARELY AFFORD IT, BUT I DIDN'T HAVE A LOT OF OPTIONS AT THE TIME. AFTER GWEN KICKED ME OUT--OUT OF MY OWN MOTHER'S APARTMENT, NO LESS--I HAD TO GET BACK ON MY FEET.

NOW I BARELY GET TO SEE MY BEAUTIFUL BABY THESE DAYS. UNTIL I FIGURE OUT HOW TO SUPPORT HIM--GWEN TOO, I GUESS--THAT MEANS WEARING LESS WHITE AND MORE BLUE...I'M TRAPPED.

THIS MIGHT AS WELL BE A JAIL CELL.

I KIND OF WISH THIS *WAS* JAIL. AT LEAST I'D GET TO BEAT DUDES UP AGAIN.

DAMN, THAT'S DARK. LET ME GET THROUGH THIS WORK SO I CAN GO TO SLEEP--

PING PING

PING PING

!$#*Ɛ^

PING PING

#$%!Ɛ@#@#Ɛ^%@

PING PING

WHO'S CALLING ME?

WELL, THE *OTHER* ME. THE SAME GUY WHO SITS AT A DESK USED TO WEAR THE COSTUME, PRETENDED TO BE WAKANDAN, HAD A SUPER HERO NAME-- *WHITE TIGER.*

AND NO ONE KNEW. AND I NEVER GOT ANY REAL CREDIT. AND I'M STILL BROKE, LOOKING AT PICTURES OF LAME BAD GUYS IN QUEENS.

IT SEEMS LIKE A LIFETIME AGO.

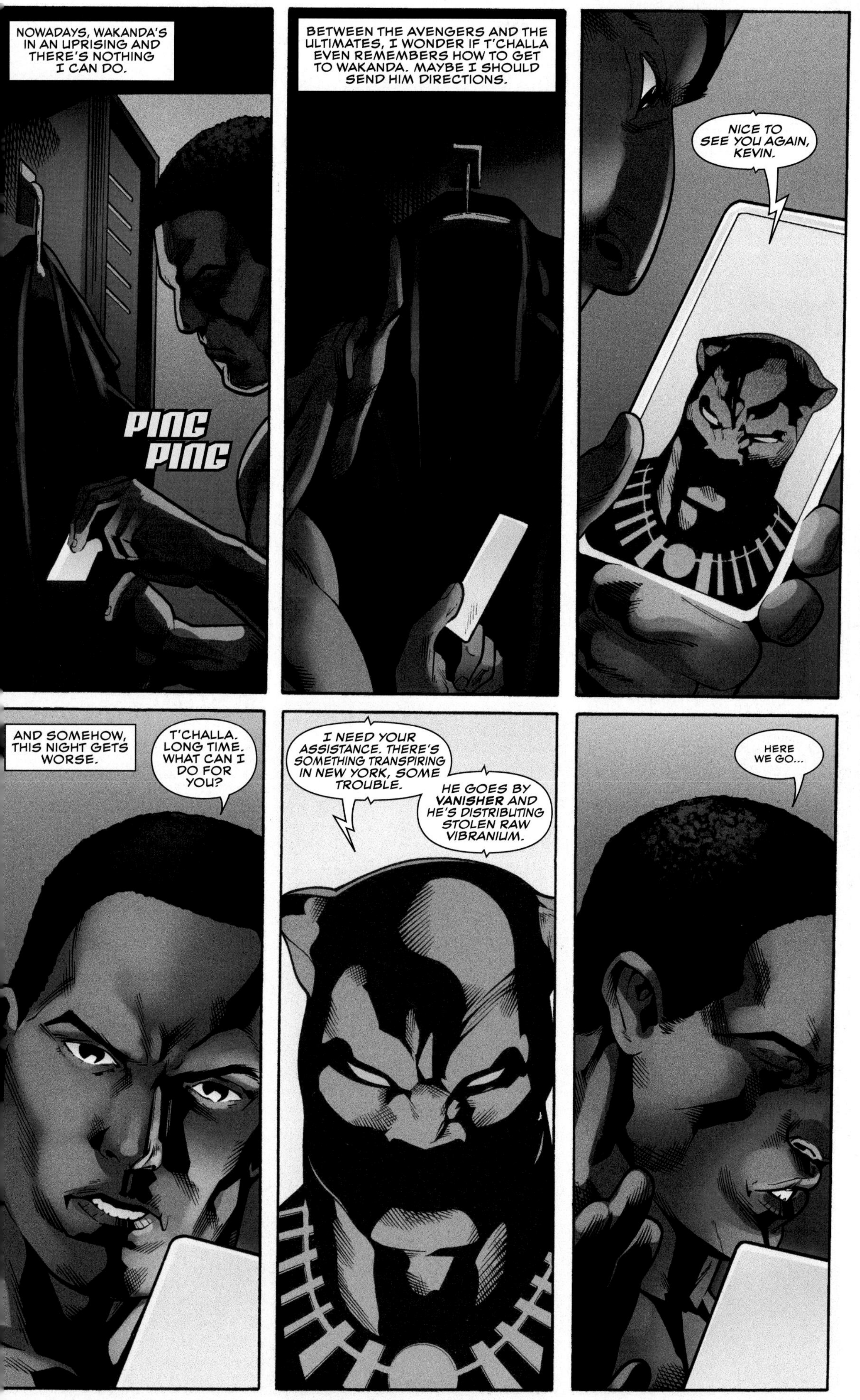
NOWADAYS, WAKANDA'S IN AN UPRISING AND THERE'S NOTHING I CAN DO.
PING PING
BETWEEN THE AVENGERS AND THE ULTIMATES, I WONDER IF T'CHALLA EVEN REMEMBERS HOW TO GET TO WAKANDA. MAYBE I SHOULD SEND HIM DIRECTIONS.
NICE TO SEE YOU AGAIN, KEVIN.
AND SOMEHOW, THIS NIGHT GETS WORSE.
T'CHALLA. LONG TIME. WHAT CAN I DO FOR YOU?
I NEED YOUR ASSISTANCE. THERE'S SOMETHING TRANSPIRING IN NEW YORK, SOME TROUBLE.
HE GOES BY VANISHER AND HE'S DISTRIBUTING STOLEN RAW VIBRANIUM.
HERE WE GO...

VANISHER IS ARMED WITH THE POWER TO TELEPORT, WHICH IS HOW HE MOVES THE VIBRANIUM SO EASILY, WHICH IS WHY HE'S SO DANGEROUS.

I NEED YOU TO STOP HIM. I KNOW IT HAS BEEN SOME TIME, BUT IF YOU DO THIS I CAN GO BACK TO FOCUSING ON THE NEW WAKANDAN GOVERNMENT.

ARE YOU SURE YOU REALLY EVEN CARE?

NO ONE CARES ABOUT WAKANDA MORE THAN I DO--DO NOT EVER FORGET THAT.

I KNOW YOU CARE...

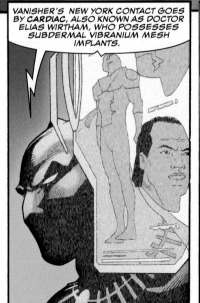

VANISHER'S NEW YORK CONTACT GOES BY CARDIAC, ALSO KNOWN AS DOCTOR ELIAS WIRTHAM, WHO POSSESSES SUBDERMAL VIBRANIUM MESH IMPLANTS.

CURIOUSLY, HE STYLES HIMSELF A VIGILANTE, BUT HIS METHODS ARE TOO BRUTAL TO REMAIN UNCHECKED.

FUNNY, I'VE BEEN LOOKING AT THIS UGLY CREEP ALL NIGHT.

LOOK FAMILIAR?

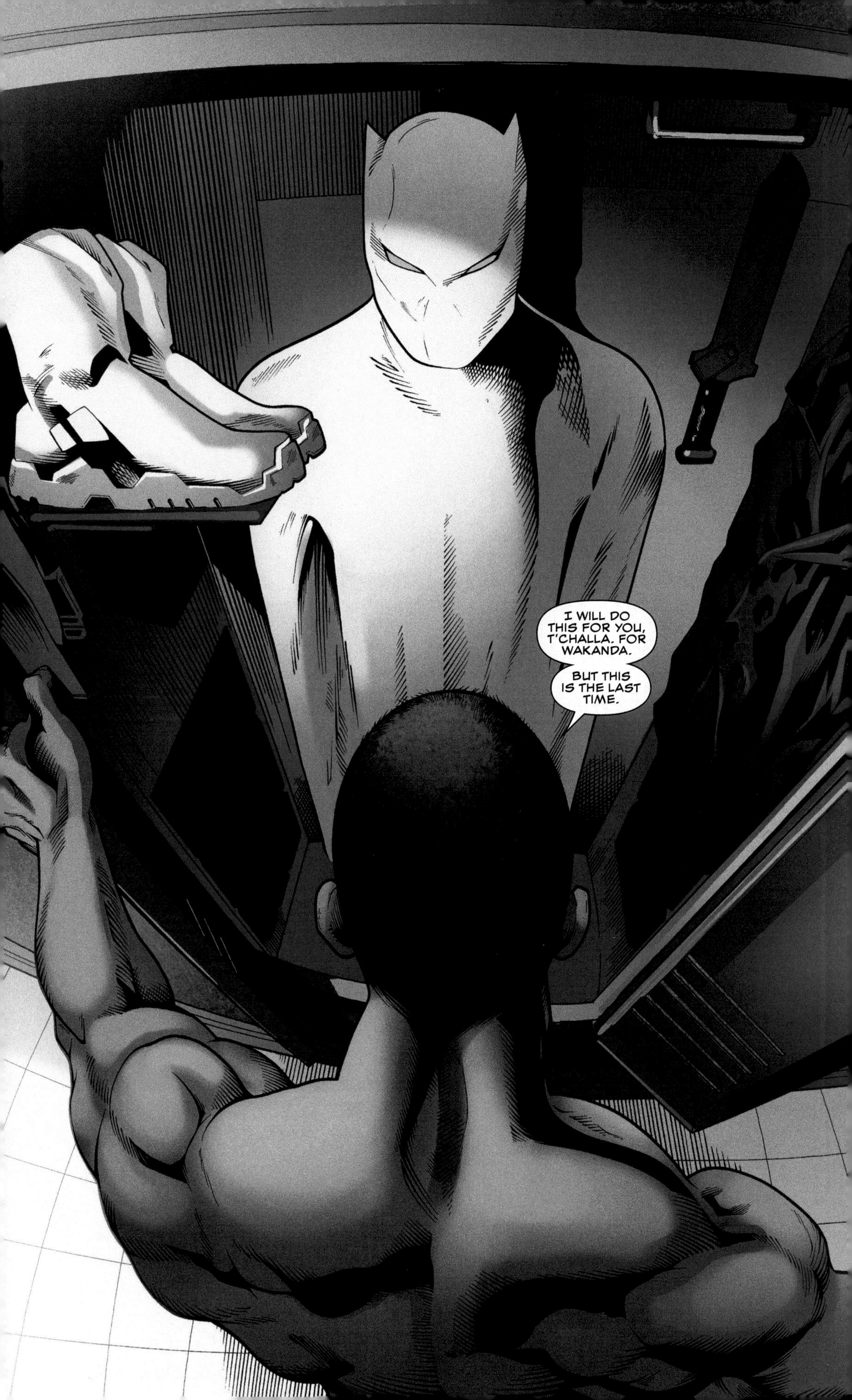
I WILL DO THIS FOR YOU, T'CHALLA. FOR WAKANDA.
BUT THIS IS THE LAST TIME.

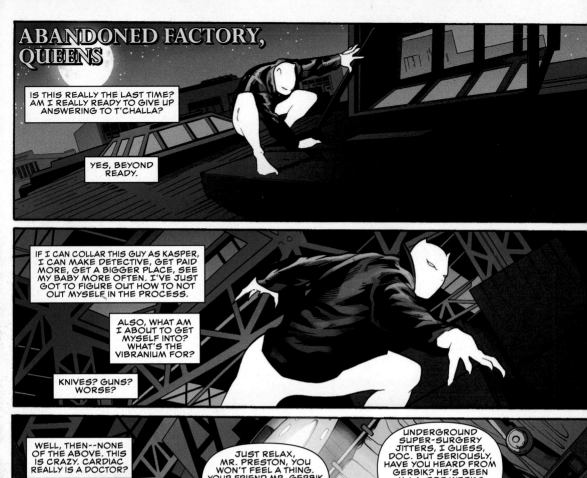

ABANDONED FACTORY,
QUEENS

IS THIS REALLY THE LAST TIME?
AM I REALLY READY TO GIVE UP
ANSWERING TO T'CHALLA?

YES, BEYOND
READY.

IF I CAN COLLAR THIS GUY AS KASPER,
I CAN MAKE DETECTIVE, GET PAID
MORE, GET A BIGGER PLACE, SEE
MY BABY MORE OFTEN. I'VE JUST
GOT TO FIGURE OUT HOW TO NOT
OUT MYSELF IN THE PROCESS.

ALSO, WHAT AM
I ABOUT TO GET
MYSELF INTO?
WHAT'S THE
VIBRANIUM FOR?

KNIVES? GUNS?
WORSE?

WELL, THEN--NONE
OF THE ABOVE. THIS
IS CRAZY. CARDIAC
REALLY IS A DOCTOR?

JUST RELAX,
MR. PRESTON, YOU
WON'T FEEL A THING.
YOUR FRIEND MR. GERBIK
SIMPLY *WENT TO PIECES*
DURING HIS APPOINTMENT
AND I FEAR THE
SAME FOR YOU.

UNDERGROUND
SUPER-SURGERY
JITTERS, I GUESS,
DOC. BUT SERIOUSLY,
HAVE YOU HEARD FROM
GERBIK? HE'S BEEN
M.I.A. FOR WEEKS
NOW AND WE HAVE A
TRIP TO SOKOVIA
COMING UP.

OH, I KNOW
*ALL ABOUT* YOUR
TRIPS TO SOKOVIA,
MR. PRESTON, AND
WHAT YOU AND YOUR
FRIENDS DO
ON THEM.

HM?

TAKE A
DEEP BREATH.
YOU WON'T WANT
TO FEEL WHAT
COMES NEXT.

YOU'RE
GOING TO PAY
FOR YOUR CRIMES,
MR. PRESTON. ALL
OF YOU WILL.

CLK

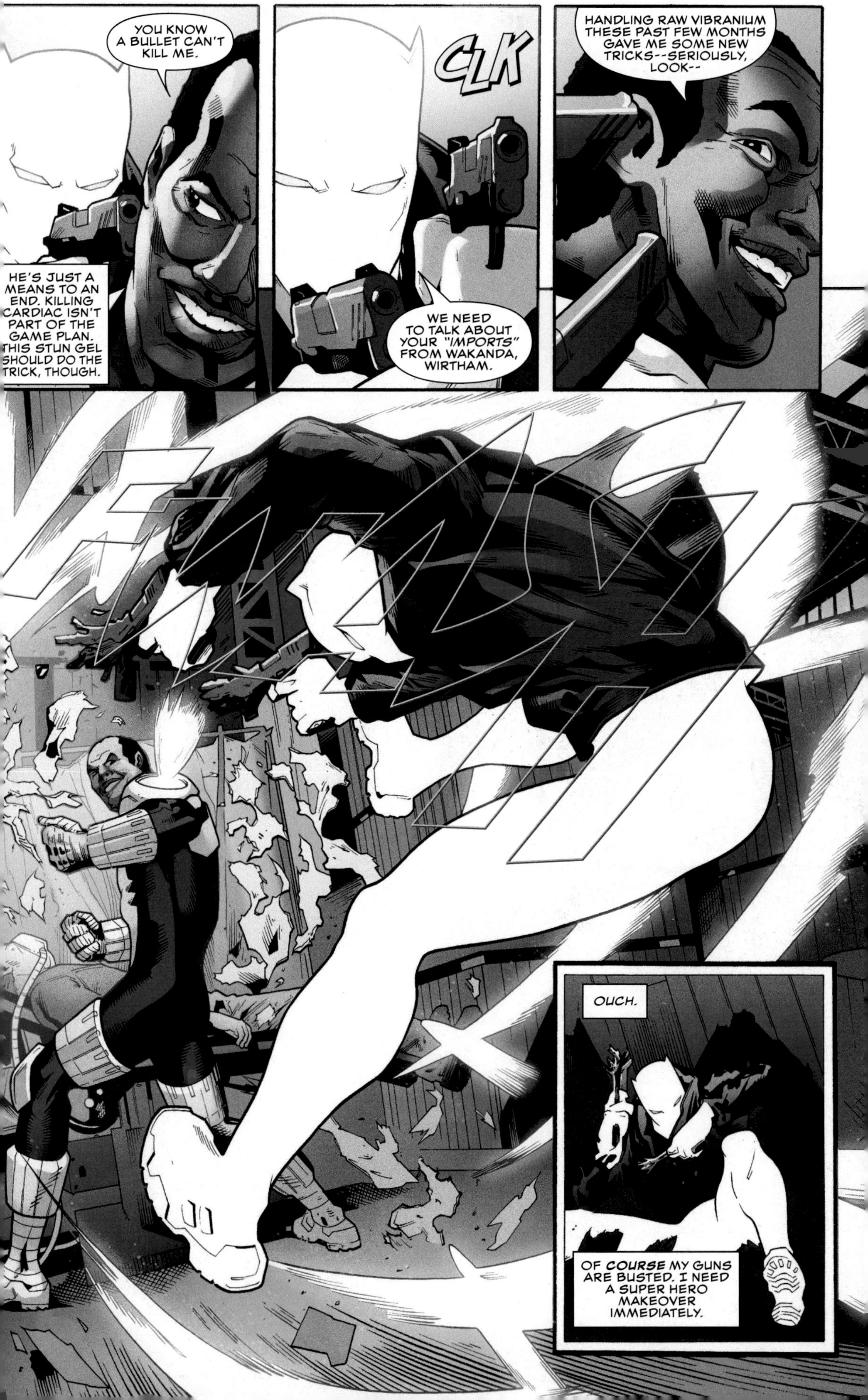
YOU KNOW A BULLET CAN'T KILL ME.
HE'S JUST A MEANS TO AN END. KILLING CARDIAC ISN'T PART OF THE GAME PLAN. THIS STUN GEL SHOULD DO THE TRICK, THOUGH.
CLK
WE NEED TO TALK ABOUT YOUR "IMPORTS" FROM WAKANDA, WIRTHAM.
HANDLING RAW VIBRANIUM THESE PAST FEW MONTHS GAVE ME SOME NEW TRICKS--SERIOUSLY, LOOK--
OUCH.
OF COURSE MY GUNS ARE BUSTED. I NEED A SUPER HERO MAKEOVER IMMEDIATELY.

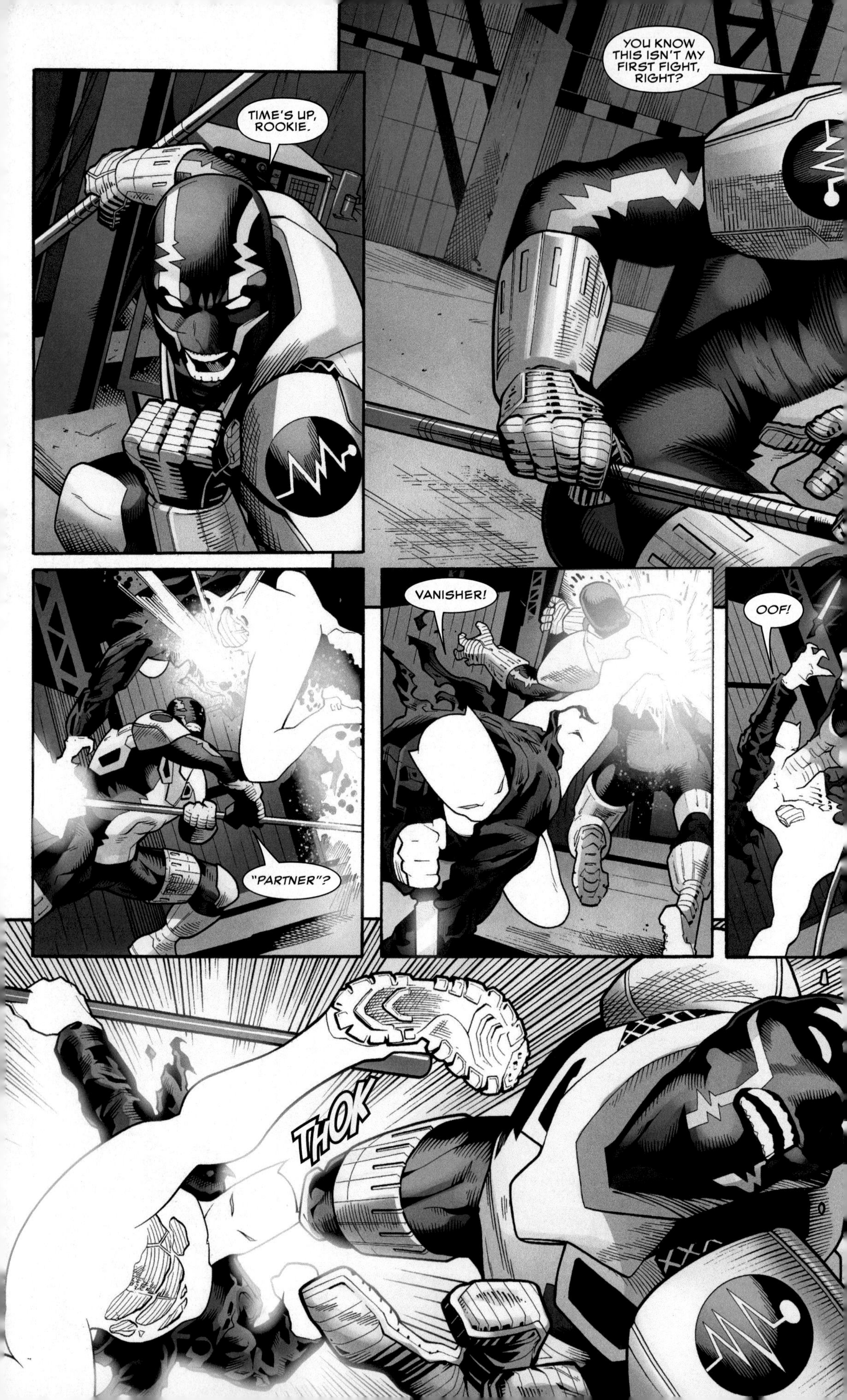
TIME'S UP, ROOKIE.
YOU KNOW THIS ISN'T MY FIRST FIGHT, RIGHT?
"PARTNER"?
VANISHER!
OOF!
THOK

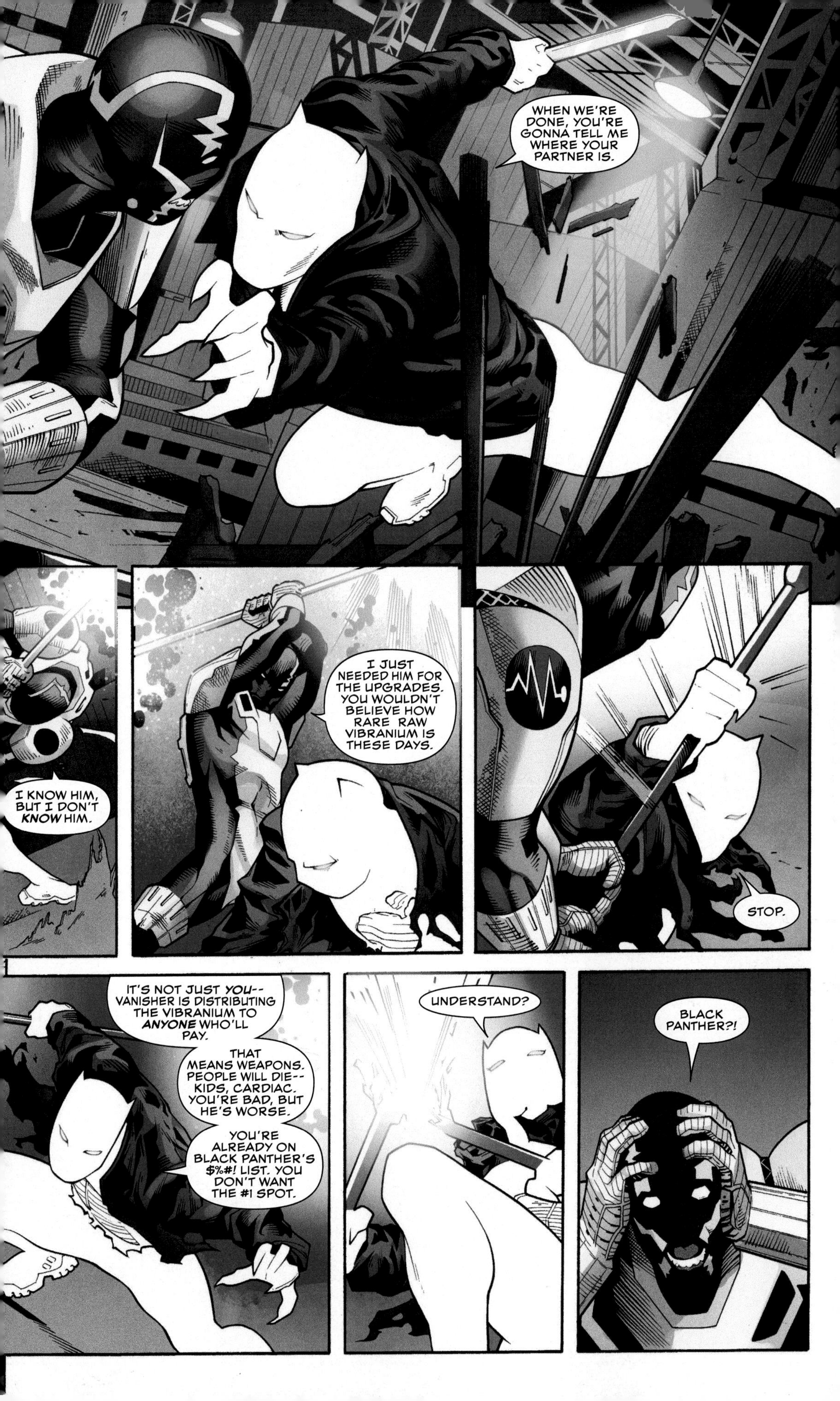
WHEN WE'RE DONE, YOU'RE GONNA TELL ME WHERE YOUR PARTNER IS.
I KNOW HIM, BUT I DON'T *KNOW* HIM.
I JUST NEEDED HIM FOR THE UPGRADES. YOU WOULDN'T BELIEVE HOW RARE RAW VIBRANIUM IS THESE DAYS.
STOP.
IT'S NOT JUST *YOU*--VANISHER IS DISTRIBUTING THE VIBRANIUM TO *ANYONE* WHO'LL PAY.
THAT MEANS WEAPONS. PEOPLE WILL DIE--KIDS, CARDIAC. YOU'RE BAD, BUT HE'S WORSE.
YOU'RE ALREADY ON BLACK PANTHER'S $%#! LIST. YOU DON'T WANT THE #1 SPOT.
UNDERSTAND?
BLACK PANTHER?!

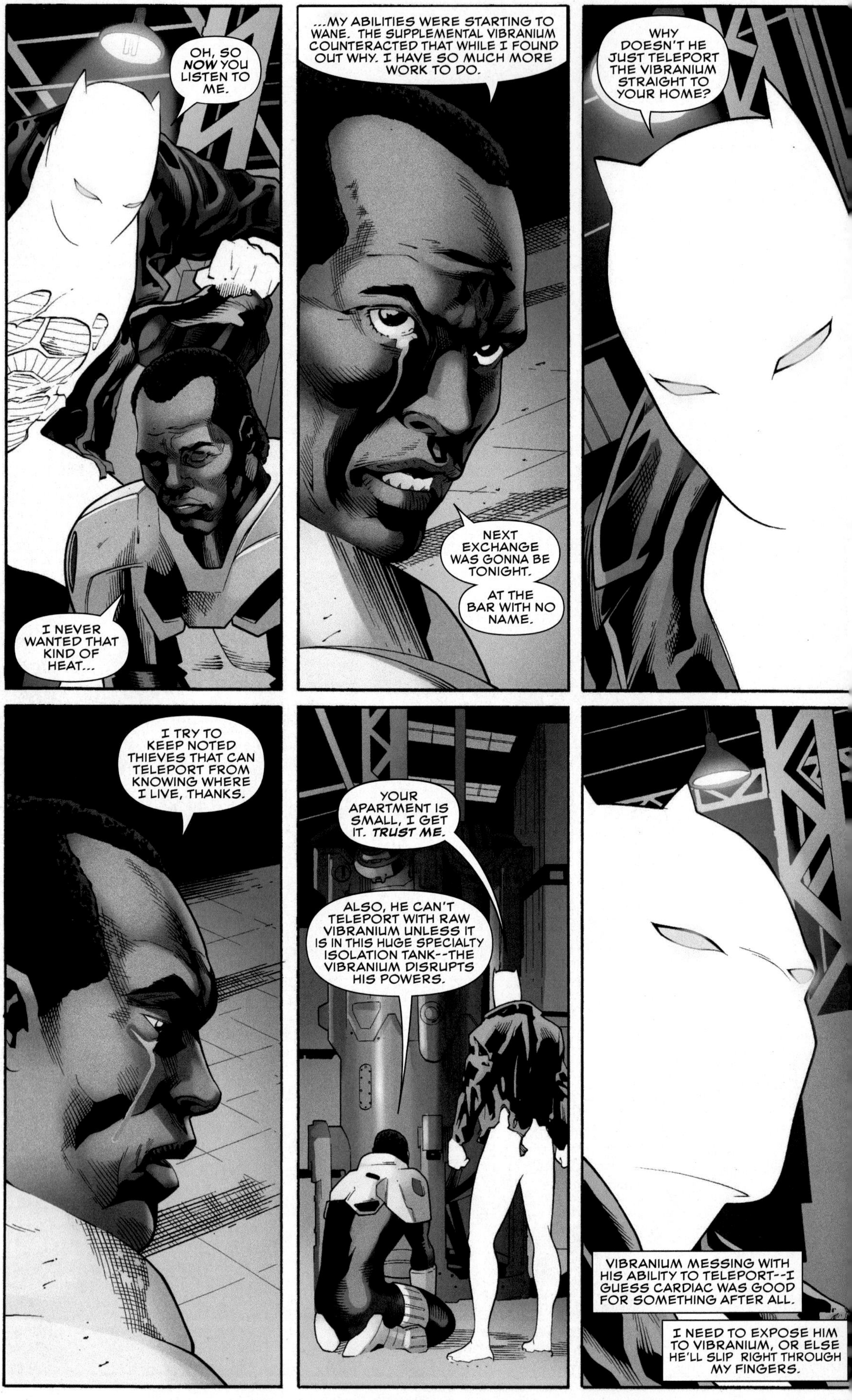
OH, SO NOW YOU LISTEN TO ME.
I NEVER WANTED THAT KIND OF HEAT...
...MY ABILITIES WERE STARTING TO WANE. THE SUPPLEMENTAL VIBRANIUM COUNTERACTED THAT WHILE I FOUND OUT WHY. I HAVE SO MUCH MORE WORK TO DO.
NEXT EXCHANGE WAS GONNA BE TONIGHT.
AT THE BAR WITH NO NAME.
WHY DOESN'T HE JUST TELEPORT THE VIBRANIUM STRAIGHT TO YOUR HOME?
I TRY TO KEEP NOTED THIEVES THAT CAN TELEPORT FROM KNOWING WHERE I LIVE, THANKS.
YOUR APARTMENT IS SMALL, I GET IT. TRUST ME.
ALSO, HE CAN'T TELEPORT WITH RAW VIBRANIUM UNLESS IT IS IN THIS HUGE SPECIALTY ISOLATION TANK--THE VIBRANIUM DISRUPTS HIS POWERS.
VIBRANIUM MESSING WITH HIS ABILITY TO TELEPORT--I GUESS CARDIAC WAS GOOD FOR SOMETHING AFTER ALL.
I NEED TO EXPOSE HIM TO VIBRANIUM, OR ELSE HE'LL SLIP RIGHT THROUGH MY FINGERS.

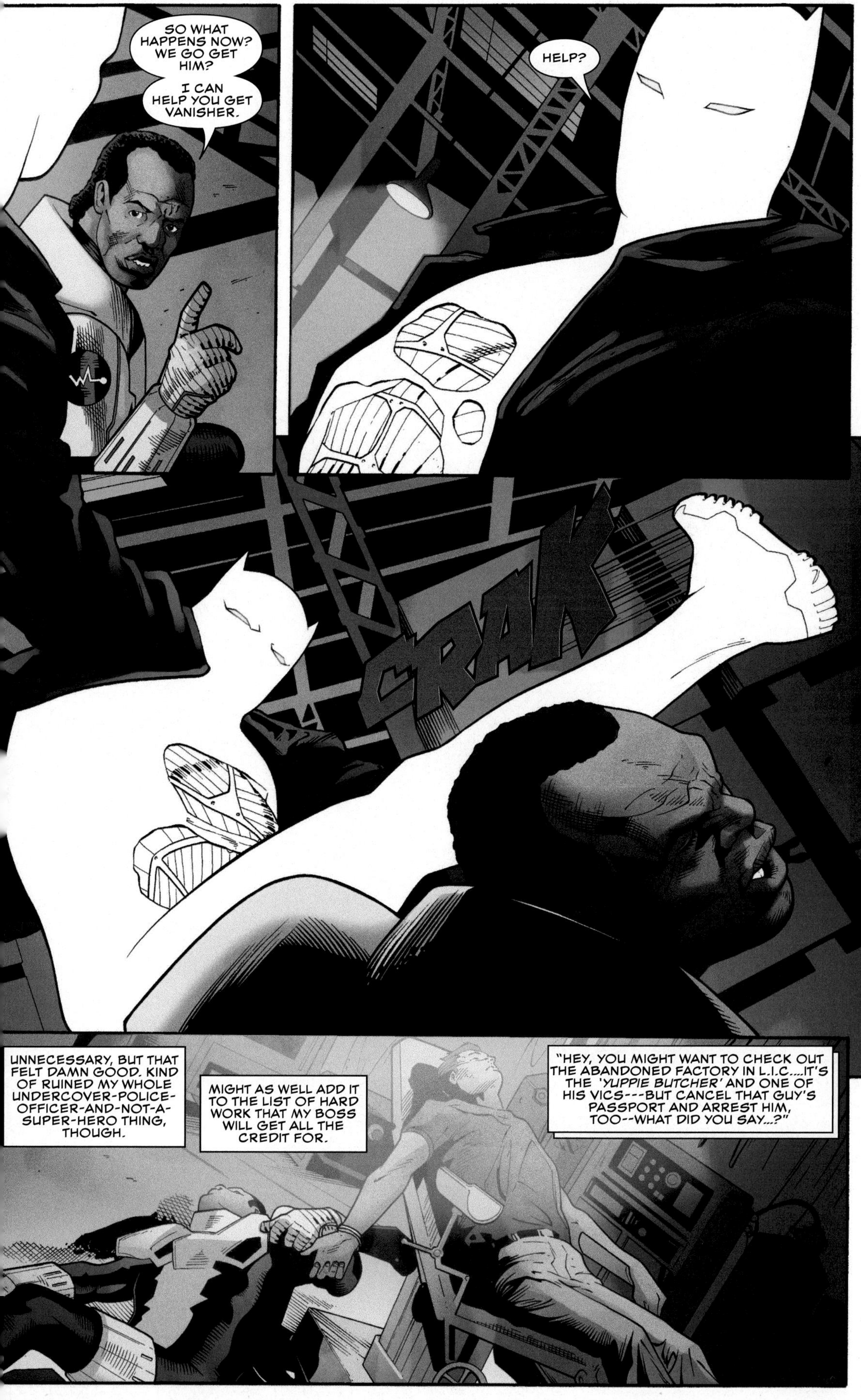
SO WHAT HAPPENS NOW? WE GO GET HIM?
I CAN HELP YOU GET VANISHER.
HELP?
CRAK
UNNECESSARY, BUT THAT FELT DAMN GOOD. KIND OF RUINED MY WHOLE UNDERCOVER-POLICE-OFFICER-AND-NOT-A-SUPER-HERO THING, THOUGH.
MIGHT AS WELL ADD IT TO THE LIST OF HARD WORK THAT MY BOSS WILL GET ALL THE CREDIT FOR.
"HEY, YOU MIGHT WANT TO CHECK OUT THE ABANDONED FACTORY IN L.I.C....IT'S THE *'YUPPIE BUTCHER'* AND ONE OF HIS VICS---BUT CANCEL THAT GUY'S PASSPORT AND ARREST HIM, TOO--WHAT DID YOU SAY...?"

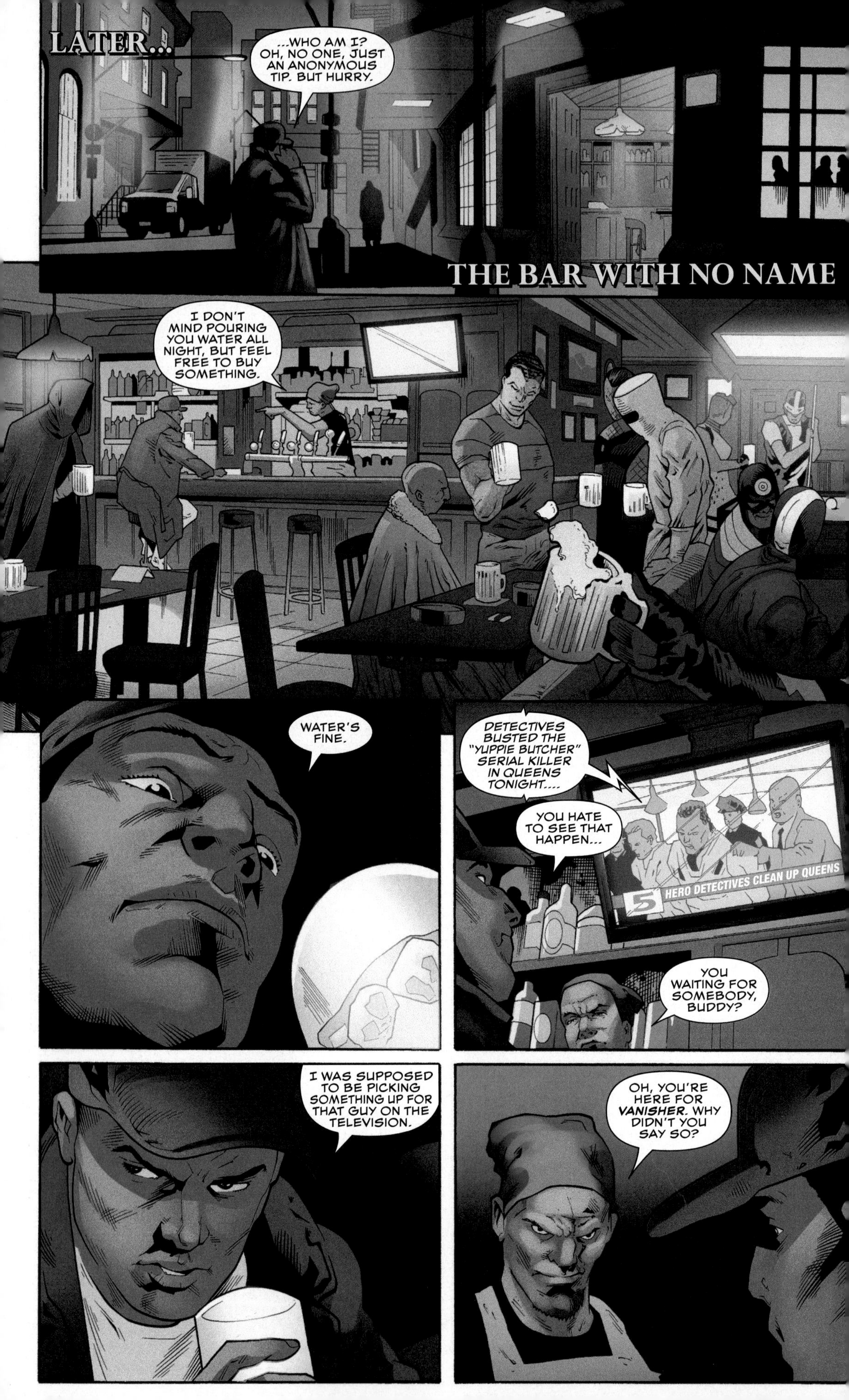
LATER...
...WHO AM I? OH, NO ONE, JUST AN ANONYMOUS TIP. BUT HURRY.
THE BAR WITH NO NAME
I DON'T MIND POURING YOU WATER ALL NIGHT, BUT FEEL FREE TO BUY SOMETHING.
WATER'S FINE.
DETECTIVES BUSTED THE "YUPPIE BUTCHER" SERIAL KILLER IN QUEENS TONIGHT....
YOU HATE TO SEE THAT HAPPEN...
HERO DETECTIVES CLEAN UP QUEENS
5
YOU WAITING FOR SOMEBODY, BUDDY?
I WAS SUPPOSED TO BE PICKING SOMETHING UP FOR THAT GUY ON THE TELEVISION.
OH, YOU'RE HERE FOR VANISHER. WHY DIDN'T YOU SAY SO?

CAN YOU POINT HIM OUT?

FOR A PAYING CUSTOMER, MAYBE.

MONEY? I GOT MONEY.

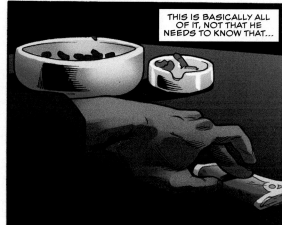

THIS IS BASICALLY ALL OF IT, NOT THAT HE NEEDS TO KNOW THAT...

ARE YOU KIDDING?

ANOTHER TWENTY. THERE GOES THE EXTRA MONEY FOR GWEN AND THE BABY.

NOW WE'RE TALKING.

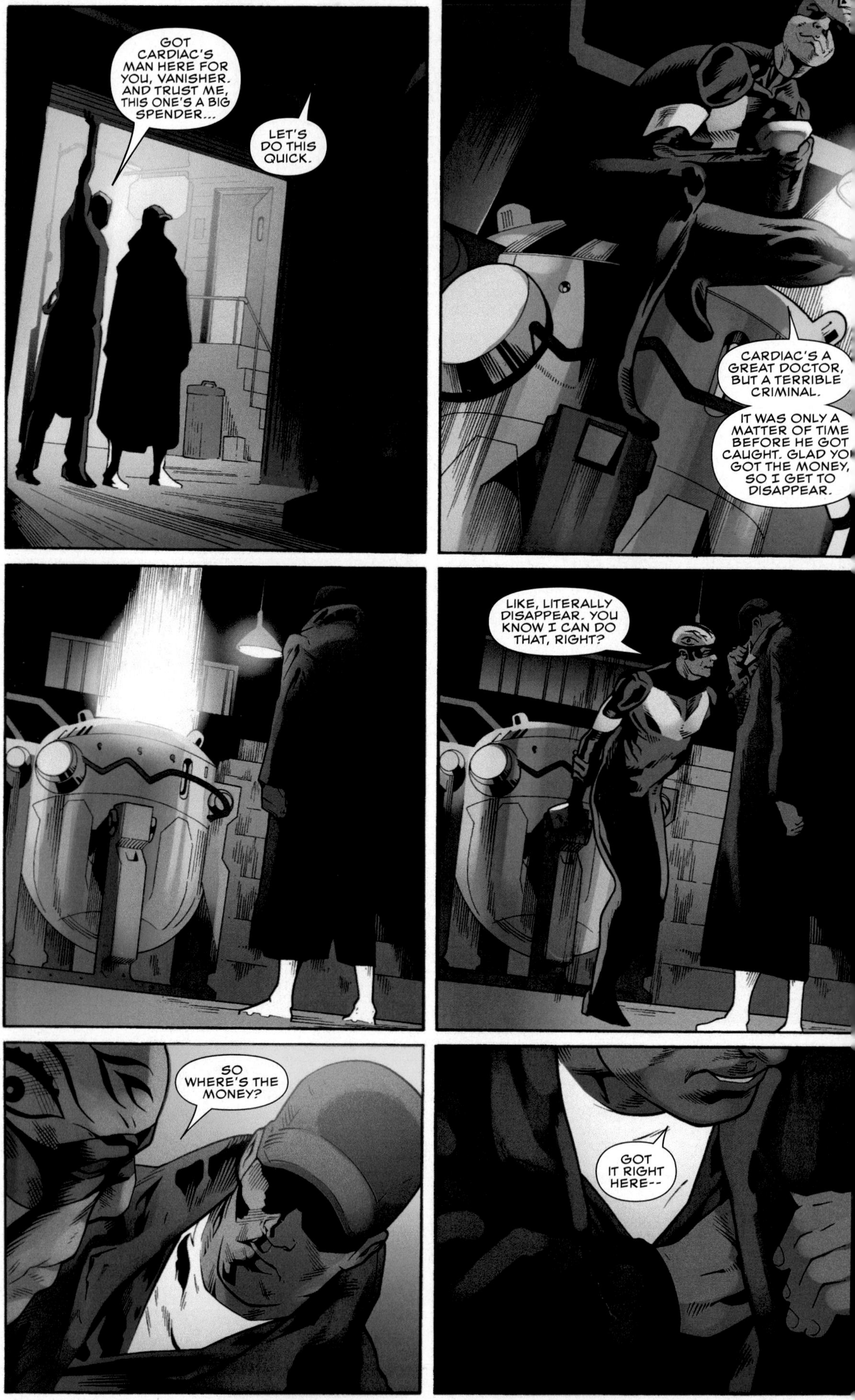
GOT CARDIAC'S MAN HERE FOR YOU, VANISHER. AND TRUST ME, THIS ONE'S A BIG SPENDER...
LET'S DO THIS QUICK.
CARDIAC'S A GREAT DOCTOR, BUT A TERRIBLE CRIMINAL.
IT WAS ONLY A MATTER OF TIME BEFORE HE GOT CAUGHT. GLAD YO GOT THE MONEY, SO I GET TO DISAPPEAR.
LIKE, LITERALLY DISAPPEAR. YOU KNOW I CAN DO THAT, RIGHT?
SO WHERE'S THE MONEY?
GOT IT RIGHT HERE--

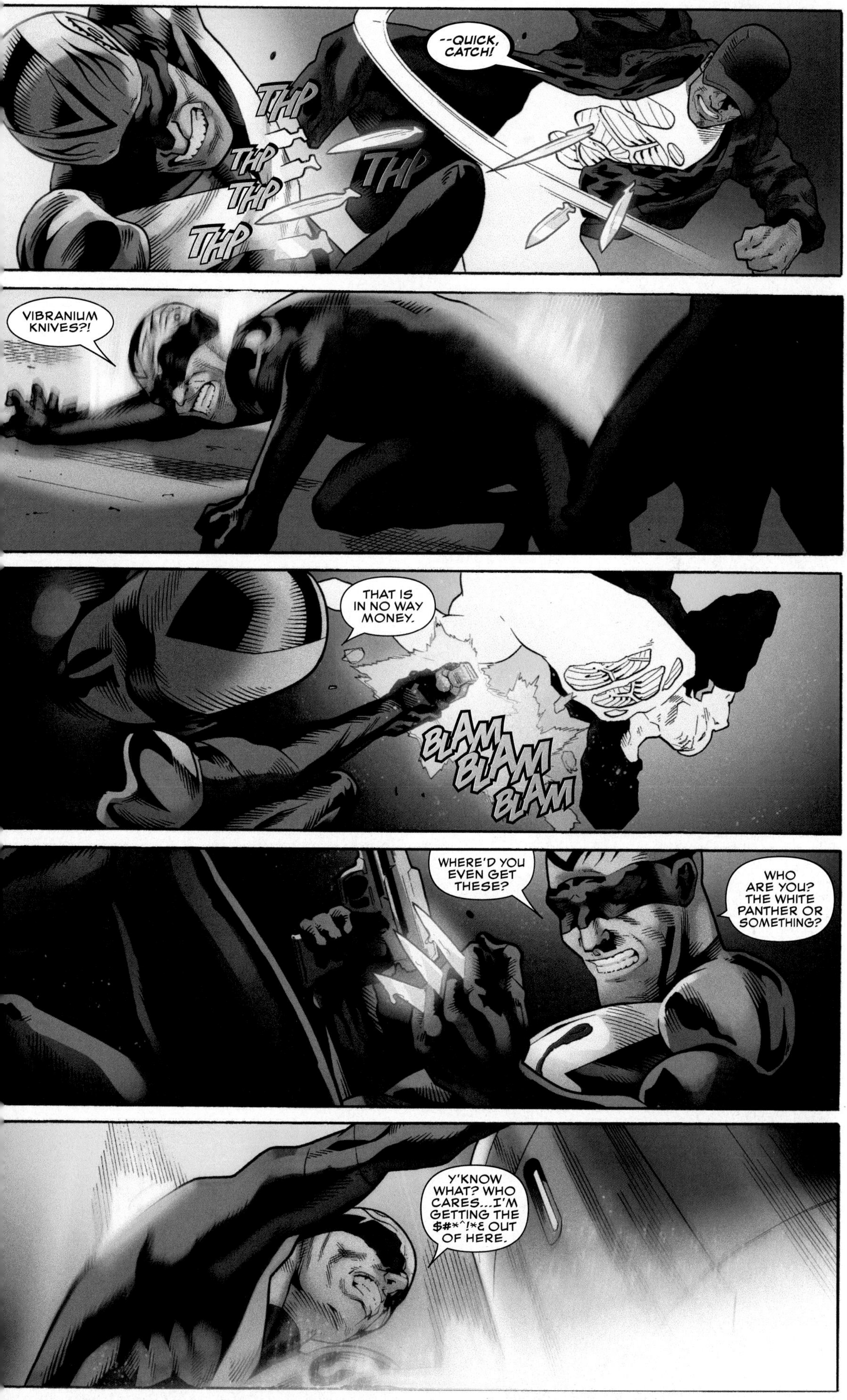
--QUICK, CATCH!
THP
THP
THP
THP
THP
VIBRANIUM KNIVES?!
THAT IS IN NO WAY MONEY.
BLAM
BLAM
BLAM
WHERE'D YOU EVEN GET THESE?
WHO ARE YOU? THE WHITE PANTHER OR SOMETHING?
Y'KNOW WHAT? WHO CARES...I'M GETTING THE $#*^!*& OUT OF HERE.

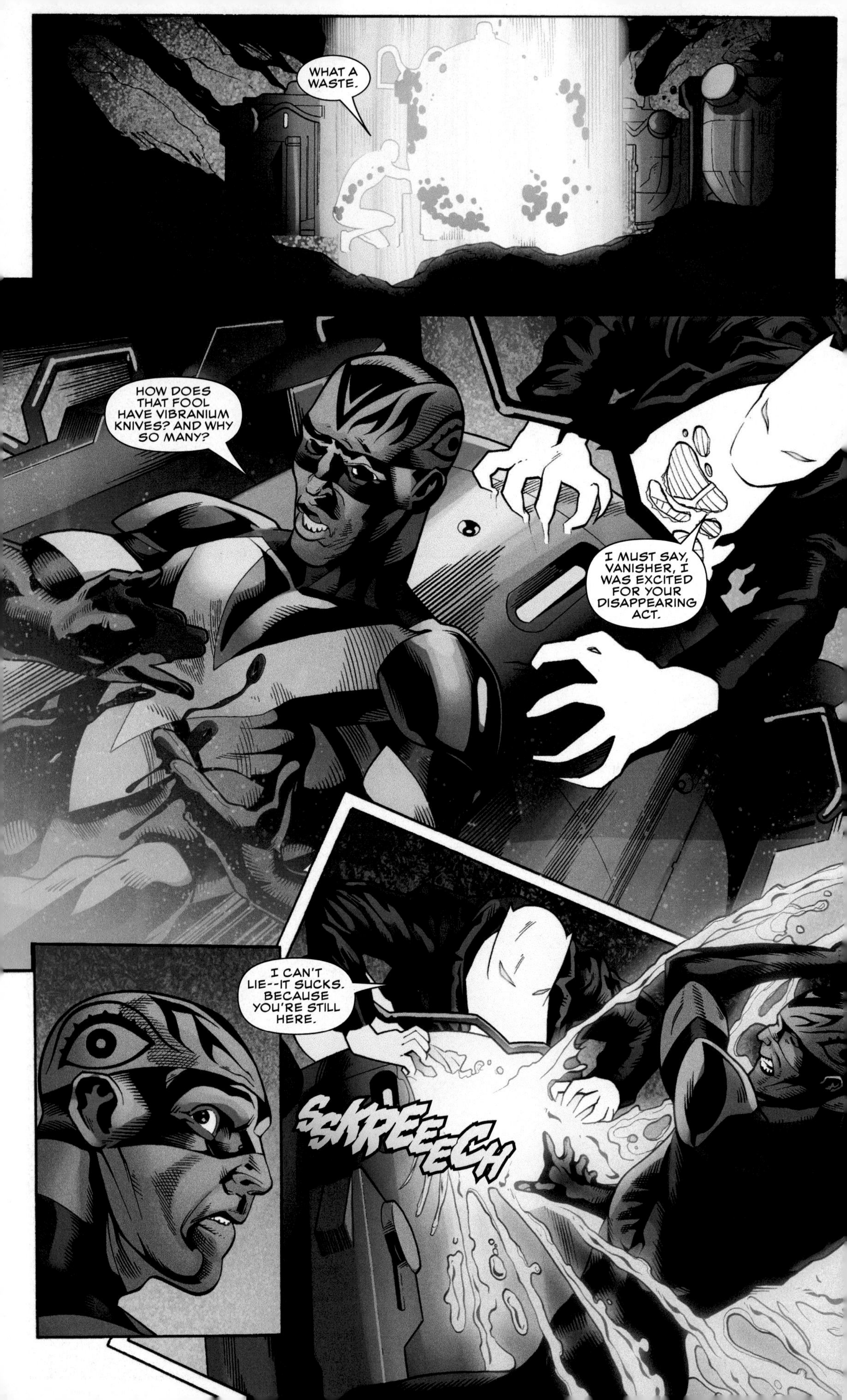
WHAT A WASTE.
HOW DOES THAT FOOL HAVE VIBRANIUM KNIVES? AND WHY SO MANY?
I MUST SAY, VANISHER, I WAS EXCITED FOR YOUR DISAPPEARING ACT.
I CAN'T LIE--IT SUCKS. BECAUSE YOU'RE STILL HERE.
SSKREEEECH

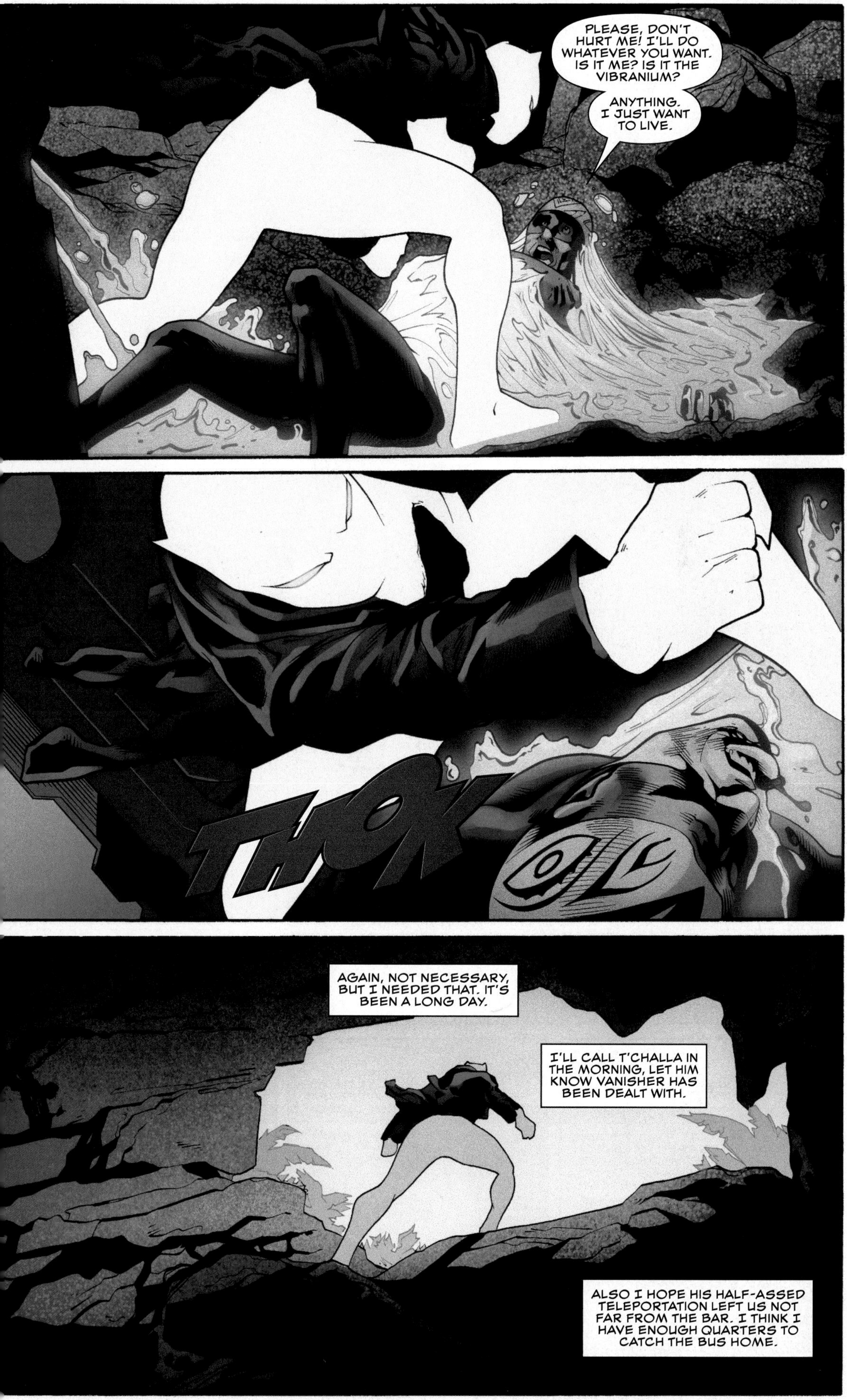
PLEASE, DON'T HURT ME! I'LL DO WHATEVER YOU WANT. IS IT ME? IS IT THE VIBRANIUM?
ANYTHING. I JUST WANT TO LIVE.
THOK
AGAIN, NOT NECESSARY, BUT I NEEDED THAT. IT'S BEEN A LONG DAY.
I'LL CALL T'CHALLA IN THE MORNING, LET HIM KNOW VANISHER HAS BEEN DEALT WITH.
ALSO I HOPE HIS HALF-ASSED TELEPORTATION LEFT US NOT FAR FROM THE BAR. I THINK I HAVE ENOUGH QUARTERS TO CATCH THE BUS HOME.

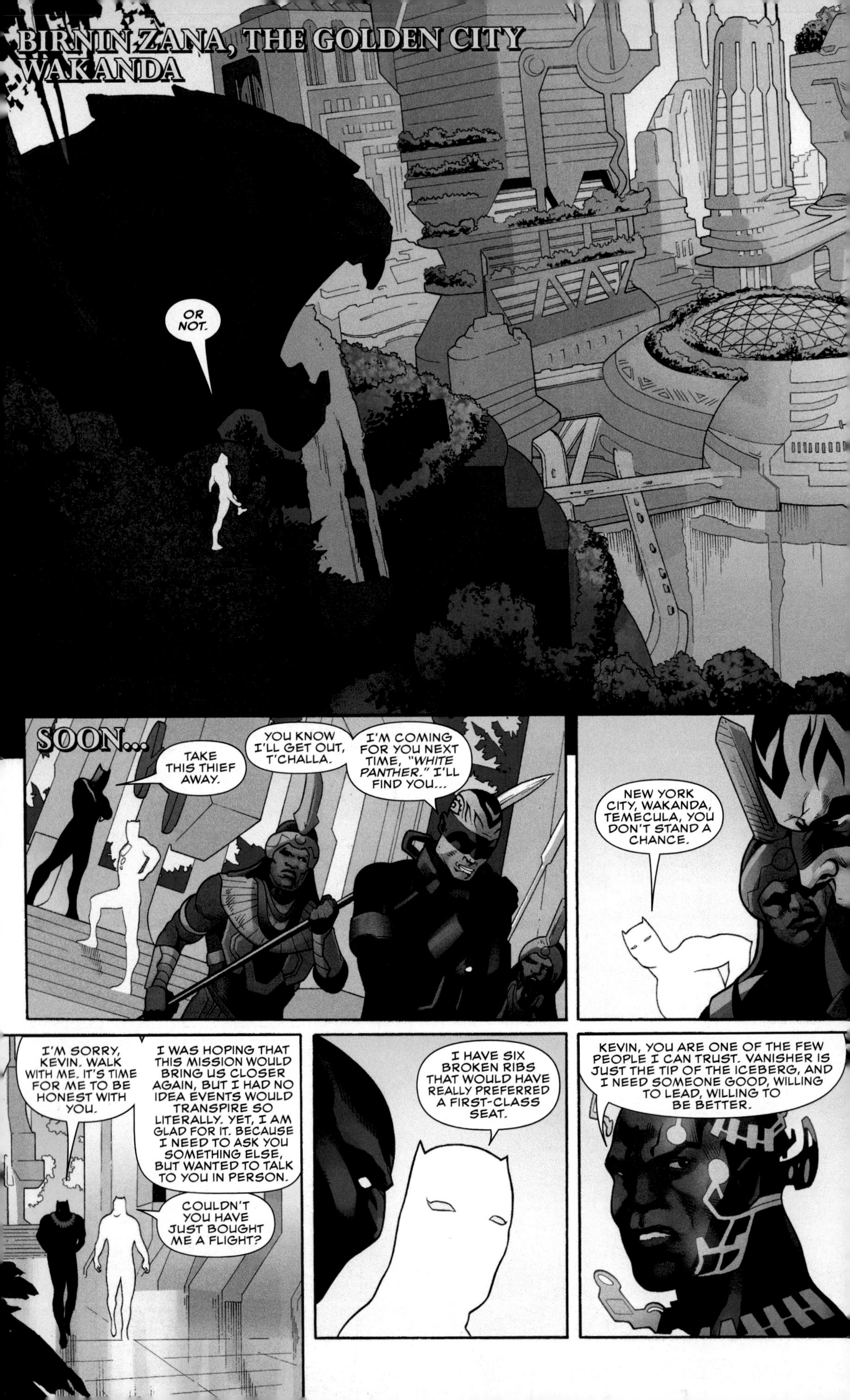
BIRNIN ZANA, THE GOLDEN CITY
WAKANDA
OR NOT.
SOON...
TAKE THIS THIEF AWAY.
YOU KNOW I'LL GET OUT, T'CHALLA.
I'M COMING FOR YOU NEXT TIME, "WHITE PANTHER." I'LL FIND YOU...
NEW YORK CITY, WAKANDA, TEMECULA, YOU DON'T STAND A CHANCE.
I'M SORRY, KEVIN. WALK WITH ME. IT'S TIME FOR ME TO BE HONEST WITH YOU.
I WAS HOPING THAT THIS MISSION WOULD BRING US CLOSER AGAIN, BUT I HAD NO IDEA EVENTS WOULD TRANSPIRE SO LITERALLY. YET, I AM GLAD FOR IT. BECAUSE I NEED TO ASK YOU SOMETHING ELSE, BUT WANTED TO TALK TO YOU IN PERSON.
COULDN'T YOU HAVE JUST BOUGHT ME A FLIGHT?
I HAVE SIX BROKEN RIBS THAT WOULD HAVE REALLY PREFERRED A FIRST-CLASS SEAT.
KEVIN, YOU ARE ONE OF THE FEW PEOPLE I CAN TRUST. VANISHER IS JUST THE TIP OF THE ICEBERG, AND I NEED SOMEONE GOOD, WILLING TO LEAD, WILLING TO BE BETTER.

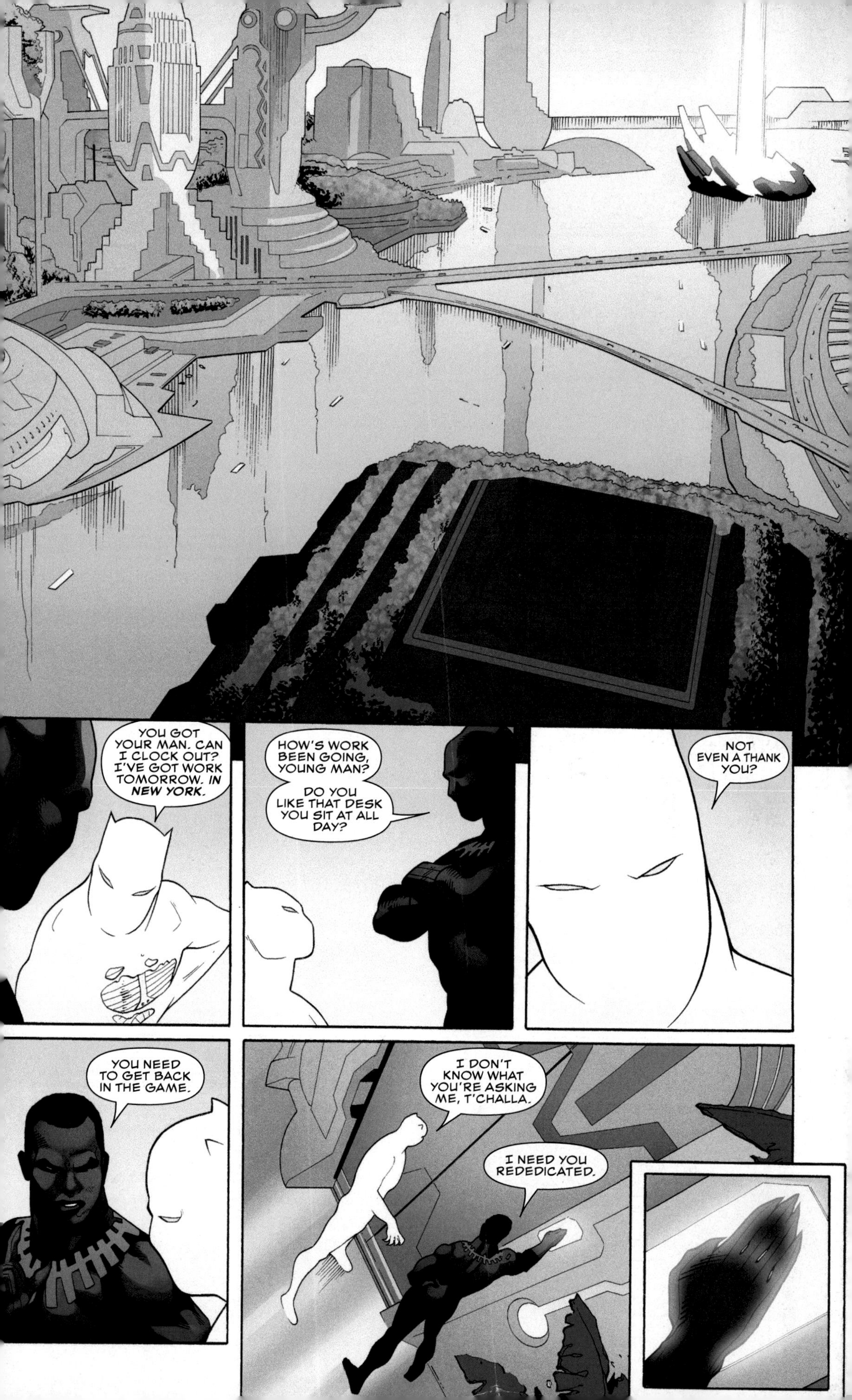
YOU GOT YOUR MAN. CAN I CLOCK OUT? I'VE GOT WORK TOMORROW. *IN NEW YORK.*
HOW'S WORK BEEN GOING, YOUNG MAN?
DO YOU LIKE THAT DESK YOU SIT AT ALL DAY?
NOT EVEN A THANK YOU?
YOU NEED TO GET BACK IN THE GAME.
I DON'T KNOW WHAT YOU'RE ASKING ME, T'CHALLA.
I NEED YOU REDEDICATED.

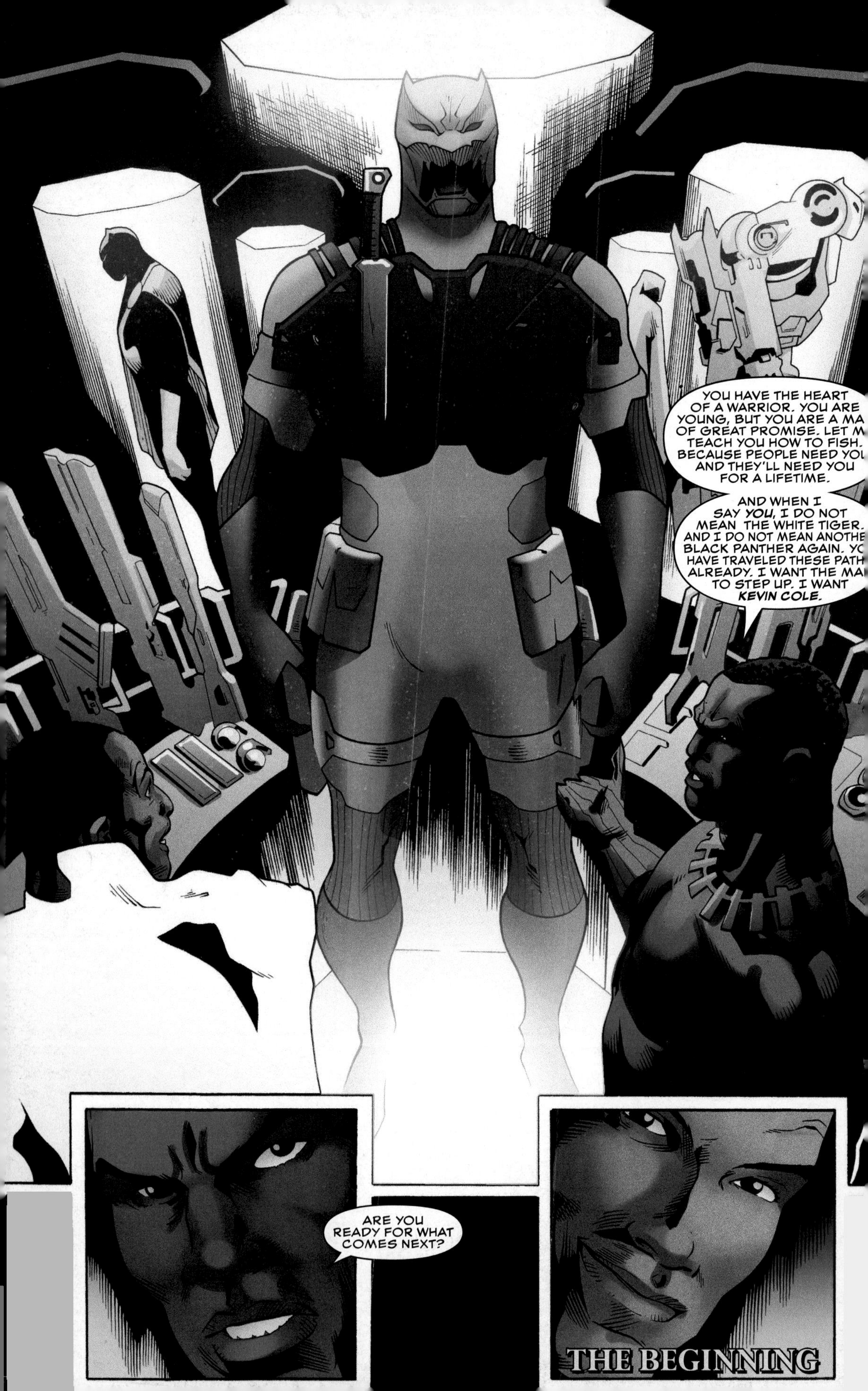
YOU HAVE THE HEART OF A WARRIOR. YOU ARE YOUNG, BUT YOU ARE A MA OF GREAT PROMISE. LET M TEACH YOU HOW TO FISH. BECAUSE PEOPLE NEED YOU AND THEY'LL NEED YOU FOR A LIFETIME.
AND WHEN I SAY *YOU*, I DO NOT MEAN THE WHITE TIGER. AND I DO NOT MEAN ANOTHE BLACK PANTHER AGAIN. YO HAVE TRAVELED THESE PATH ALREADY. I WANT THE MA TO STEP UP. I WANT *KEVIN COLE.*
ARE YOU READY FOR WHAT COMES NEXT?
THE BEGINNING

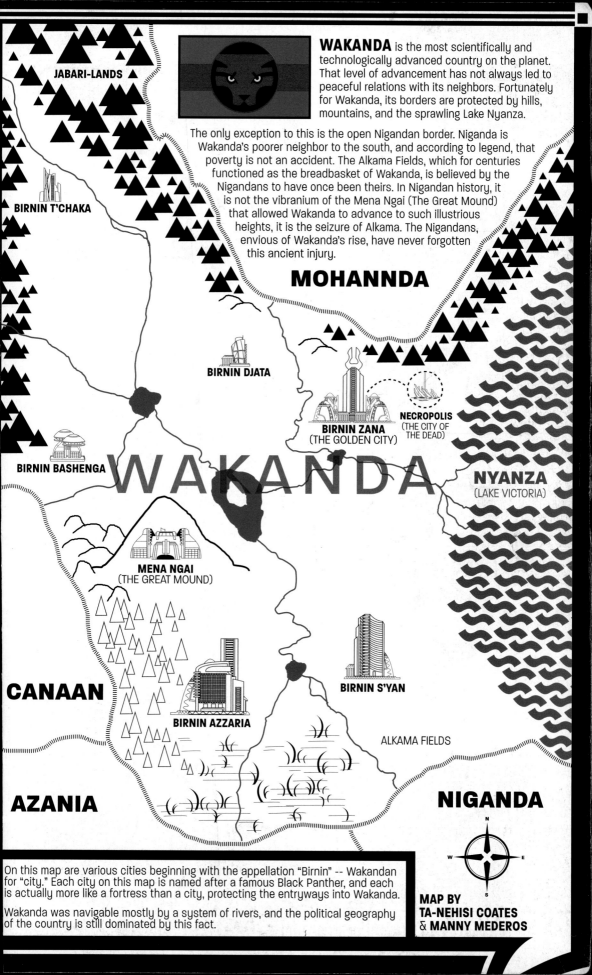

**WAKANDA** is the most scientifically and technologically advanced country on the planet. That level of advancement has not always led to peaceful relations with its neighbors. Fortunately for Wakanda, its borders are protected by hills, mountains, and the sprawling Lake Nyanza.

The only exception to this is the open Nigandan border. Niganda is Wakanda's poorer neighbor to the south, and according to legend, that poverty is not an accident. The Alkama Fields, which for centuries functioned as the breadbasket of Wakanda, is believed by the Nigandans to have once been theirs. In Nigandan history, it is not the vibranium of the Mena Ngai (The Great Mound) that allowed Wakanda to advance to such illustrious heights, it is the seizure of Alkama. The Nigandans, envious of Wakanda's rise, have never forgotten this ancient injury.

JABARI-LANDS

BIRNIN T'CHAKA

MOHANNDA

BIRNIN DJATA

BIRNIN ZANA
(THE GOLDEN CITY)

NECROPOLIS
(THE CITY OF THE DEAD)

BIRNIN BASHENGA

WAKANDA

NYANZA
(LAKE VICTORIA)

MENA NGAI
(THE GREAT MOUND)

CANAAN

BIRNIN S'YAN

BIRNIN AZZARIA

ALKAMA FIELDS

AZANIA

NIGANDA

On this map are various cities beginning with the appellation "Birnin" -- Wakandan for "city." Each city on this map is named after a famous Black Panther, and each is actually more like a fortress than a city, protecting the entryways into Wakanda.

Wakanda was navigable mostly by a system of rivers, and the political geography of the country is still dominated by this fact.

**MAP BY TA-NEHISI COATES & MANNY MEDEROS**

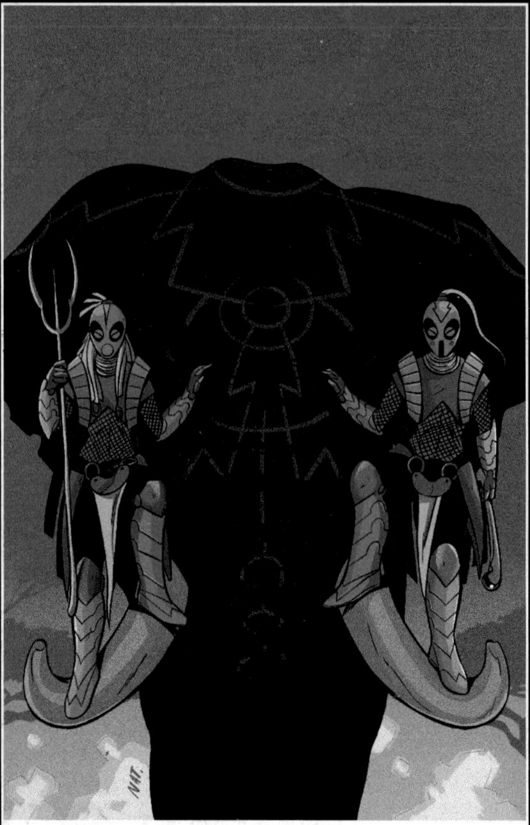

#3 VARIANT BY **NATACHA BUSTOS**

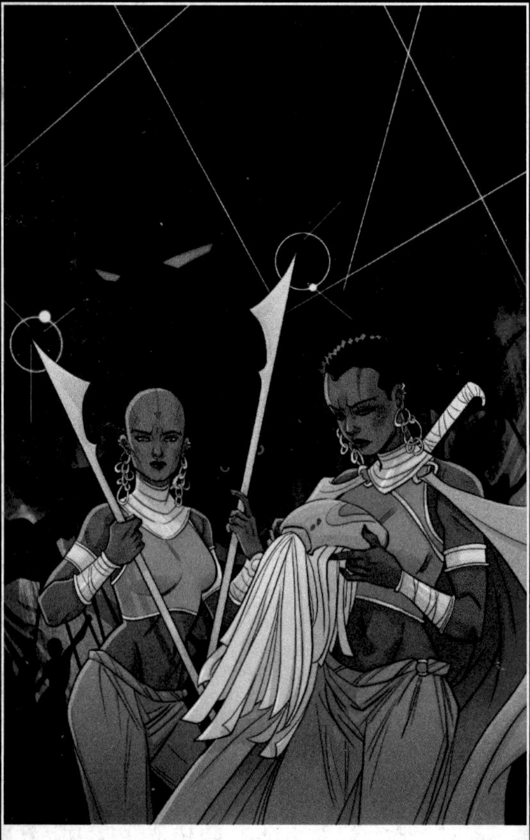

#2 VARIANT BY **MARGUERITE SAUVAGE**

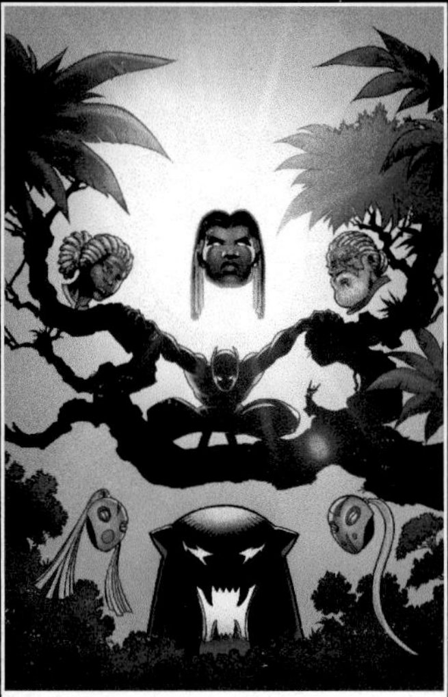

#2 VARIANT BY
**TREVOR VON EEDEN**
**& RACHELLE ROSENBERG**

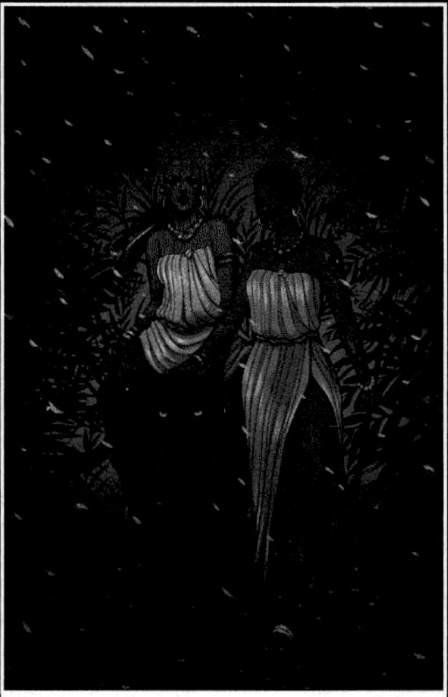

#5 VARIANT BY **JEN BARTEL**

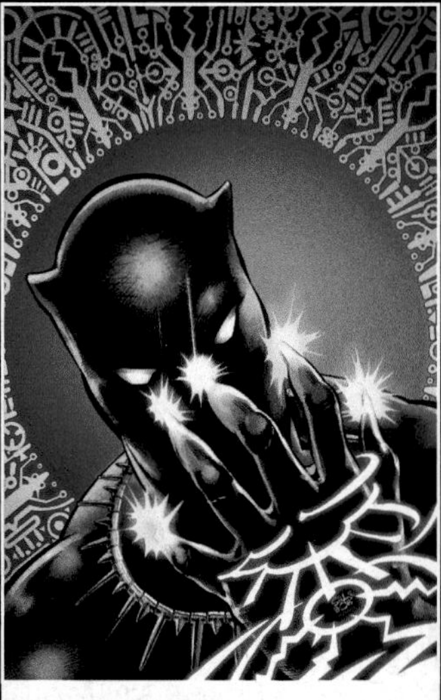

#6 VARIANT BY
**SAL VELLUTO, BOB ALMOND**
**& PAUL MOUNTS**